Radical Assimilation
in the Face of the Holocaust

SUNY series in Contemporary Jewish Thought

Richard A. Cohen, editor

Radical Assimilation in the Face of the Holocaust

Otto Heller (1897–1945)

TOM NAVON

Published by State University of New York Press, Albany

© 2024 State University of New York

All rights reserved

Printed in the United States of America

No part of this book may be used or reproduced in any manner whatsoever without written permission. No part of this book may be stored in a retrieval system or transmitted in any form or by any means including electronic, electrostatic, magnetic tape, mechanical, photocopying, recording, or otherwise without the prior permission in writing of the publisher.

For information, contact State University of New York Press, Albany, NY www.sunypress.edu

Library of Congress Cataloging-in-Publication Data

Name: Navon, Tom, 1982– author.
Title: Radical assimilation in the face of the Holocaust : Otto Heller (1897–1945) / Tom Navon.
Description: Albany : State University of New York Press, [2024] | Series: SUNY series in contemporary Jewish thought | Includes bibliographical references and index.
Identifiers: LCCN 2023015791 | ISBN 9781438495910 (hardcover : alk. paper) | ISBN 9781438495934 (ebook) | ISBN 9781438495927 (pbk. : alk. paper)
Subjects: LCSH: Heller, Otto, 1897–1945. | Jews—Identity. | Auschwitz (Concentration camp) | Heller, Otto, 1897–1945. Untergang des Judentums. | Jewish communists—Austria—Biography. | Journalists—Germany—Biography. | Holocaust victims—Biography. | World War, 1939–1945—Jewish resistance—France.
Classification: LCC DS135.A93 H524 2024 | DDC 940.53/1809436092 [B]—dc23/eng/20230817
LC record available at https://lccn.loc.gov/2023015791

10 9 8 7 6 5 4 3 2 1

*Dedicated to the memory of Otto Heller,
and of my grandfather, Yitzhak Shadmon (Otto Seidner),
prisoners of Auschwitz.*

Contents

Illustrations	ix
Foreword and Acknowledgments	xi
Prologue: A Jewish Question on the Death March	1
Chapter 1. Origins of a Jewish Question (1897–1932)	27
Chapter 2. The Decline of Judaism (1931)	69
Chapter 3. In Flight from Two Dictators (1933–1939)	97
Chapter 4. "The Jew Is to Be Burned" (1939)	123
Chapter 5. In Fight (1940–1945)	155
Epilogue: The Road Not Taken	189
Notes	197
Bibliography	255
Index	283

Illustrations

Figure I.1	Otto Heller.	3
Figure 1.1	Emma Krause.	45
Figure 1.2	Lily Heller.	45
Figure 1.3	Otto Heller.	56
Figure 2.1	Books on the Jewish question from Heller's library.	85
Figure 3.1	Otto Heller's signature.	106
Figure 3.2	Pages from Heller's copy of Alfred Döblin, *Jüdische Erneuerung* (*Jewish Revival*).	107
Figure 3.3	Portrait of Otto Heller.	121
Figure 4.1	Title page of Heller's manuscript "Der Jude wird verbrannt" ("The Jew Is to Be Burned") (Paris, 1939).	124
Figure 4.2	Table of contents from Heller's manuscript "Der Jude wird verbrannt" ("The Jew Is to Be Burned") (Paris, 1939).	145
Figure 4.3	Otto Heller.	149
Figure 5.1	Otto Heller.	157
Figure 5.2	Lily Heller.	166
Figure 5.3	Underground Periodical Report from 1.IX to 20.IX.1944, p. 1.	181

Figure 5.4 Underground Periodical Report from 1.IX
           to 20.IX.1944, p. 2   182

Figure 5.5 Emma and Lily Heller after the liberation.   187

Foreword and Acknowledgments

When I became thirteen, bar mitzvah, my grandfather, Yitzhak Shadmon (Otto Seidner) Z"L, told me for the first time how on the intended day of his bar mitzvah he was deported with his parents from their Hungarian town to Auschwitz. He remembered his mother on the cattle car, delivering him her last will while her tears fell on his hands: "Always remember that you are a Jew and a human being." Thirteen-year-old Yitzhak lost his parents in Auschwitz and kept his mother's will through eight long nightmarish months in the camp and onward along the Death March. He carried her dual imperative with him throughout his entire life, and passed it on to his children and grandchildren, and to thousands of listeners of his testimonies. It took me a few more years to realize the potential tension between the imperative stemming from a particular belonging and the one stemming from universal moral values, as I experienced it in a completely different context growing up in the state of Israel. Ever since, I have been intrigued by the friction between particularism, especially Jewish particularism, and universalism. The story told in this book fascinated me as one of the most explosive manifestations of this tension I have ever encountered.

This book is a biography of the German-speaking intellectual of Jewish descent, Otto Heller (1897–1945). Following his book, *The Decline of Judaism* (1931), Heller became the most prominent communist theoretician of the so-called Jewish question in his time, if not ever. Nevertheless, beyond that, little has been hitherto known about him. Writing his biography entailed two protracted research quests, which began from mere vague clues: one after his lost manuscript and the other after his daughter.

While gathering information about Heller, I found in three scholarly works brief mentions of a manuscript of a second book about the Jewish question, intriguingly titled "The Jew Is to Be Burned," which he wrote in Paris in 1939. In the Viennese archive referred to as the one holding the manuscript, it turned to be mysteriously missing. The thought of the enormous efforts Heller invested in his 271-page-long text, which remained unpublished due to the breakout of war he himself subsequently fell victim to—combined with the fear that it might be lost forever—brought tears to my eyes. I contacted two of the scholars who saw the manuscript in hope to find a copy, but to no avail. Unfortunately, the third scholar was not alive. Maybe she obtained a copy? After some inquiry I found out that her estate was deposited in an archive in Berlin, but alas, not yet cataloged. I had the privilege to receive the help of a dedicated archivist, who searched through the estate for me. To my great amazement and relief, she found therein a full copy of Heller's manuscript, which made this research possible.

From existing documentation, I knew that Heller had one daughter, named Lily. During the war she had been confined with her mother Emma Heller (née Krause) in the women's concentration camp, Ravensbrück, in Germany. I knew that they both survived and after the liberation found their way back to France, but from that point on I lost Lily's trace. How can one find a person bearing such a common first name and surname—someone who in addition was probably carrying an unknown married name? Skeptical of my odds, I sent an inquiry to every person, organization, or forum I could think of as potentially helpful. I encountered many kind people with much willingness to help and discovered information about Heller that I did not even expect to find. But I had not yet found Lily.

After my endeavors have been almost frustrated, I received an email from a scholar, who indirectly came across my message, and somehow attained an incredible finding: a short item from a local newspaper of a small town in the outskirts of Paris, Gif-sur-Yvette, from 2015, announcing that the town resident Lily Heller was granted the Legion of Honor Award for her participation in the French Resistance. It was already 2018. Was she still alive? All attempts to track her through the local municipality and address book were in vain. A turn came thanks to the relentless efforts of one person, Georges Mayer, the founder of the website Convoy 77, commemorating the deportees of one transport from France to Auschwitz, among them Mayer's father and Otto Heller. Assisted by friends in France, Mayer managed to find out Lily's married name, Papineau, and thus to locate her address in Gif-sur-Yvette. But, to my grave disappointment, her residence was now a dental clinic. Lily had just left to a home for elderly. No one could tell where.

It took a while until I received a very exciting email from a woman who presented herself as Lily's daughter, Nicole Papineau. My letter to her mother's former address followed her to Paris. This was a moment of revelation. Nicole informed me that her mother, born in 1924, was still alive, but sadly impossible to communicate with. I also learned that after the war Lily had married a Frenchman, became a nuclear physicist, and continued being active in the Communist Party. About Otto Heller I could not learn much from Nicole, for her mother had barely spoken about her own father. Lily had also not shared with her daughter her own experience of exile, flight, activity in the Resistance, and eventually confinement in Ravensbrück. Nicole remembers Emma very well, who passed away in 1980, as a loving grandmother, but about her previous life as Otto's wife and a communist activist she could not say much.

It was a few months later that the family emptied the attic in Lily's former apartment and discovered a treasure: Otto Heller's private library, or presumably what survived of it through all his hardships, containing some 500 titles; and several boxes of family documents and correspondences, which Lily had never shared with her two daughters. This collection also included two other drafts of "The Jew Is to Be Burned," different from that I had already known, and a lot of Heller's working material. Thanks to the generosity of Nicole and other family members, Heller's book collection was donated to the library of the Leibniz Institute for Jewish History and Culture—Simon Dubnow, in Leipzig, where it is now cataloged and available for researchers. The documents remained in the possession of the family, who kindly allowed me to copy every piece of paper required for this biography.

∽

Every scholarly book is a product not only of its author's endeavor, but of a cooperation of many. The two unique quests I experienced during the writing of this book made it even more so. The following especially long list of acknowledgments reflects the extent of joint efforts that were pulled together in its creation. My greatest gratitude is to Nicole Papineau, who had generously hosted me and my daughter Naomi in her apartment in Paris, donated her grandfather's library, and allowed me access to the family archive. It is also an opportunity to thank Naomi for accompanying me in this visit and helping me by taking photos and packing ten boxes of books for delivery to Leipzig.

It is my pleasure to thank the people, without whose help I would have never found Heller's descendants: Knut Bergbauer from the Technische Universität Braunschweig, who located the newspaper item that led me to Lily; the above-mentioned Georges Mayer; and my dear friend Yanai Ben-Eliyahu, who communicated with French authorities on my behalf. Throughout the search for Lily, I had the privilege to encounter genealogist Evelyn Wilcock, who kindly reconstructed Heller's family tree for this research. Following this family tree, I could contact a member of the London branch of the family, Thomas Heller, the great-grandson of Otto's brother Ernst, who contributed some important hints, too.

Next, I shall thank all the people who contributed their valuable hints that eventually led me to Heller's lost manuscript: The archivists who did not spare any effort in the search after the manuscript at the Dokumentationsarchiv des österreichischen Widerstandes (Documentation Centre of Austrian Resistance [DÖW]) in Vienna, especially Ursula Schwartz; and at the archive of the Akademie der Künste (Academy of Arts [AdK]) in Berlin, especially Petra Uhlmann. Without archivists, we historians are helpless. Therefore, my thanks are sent to the archivists in all the archives listed in the bibliography, whose work facilitated this book, as well as to the staff of the International Institute of Social History in Amsterdam, who provided me with copies of some rare publications from their rich collection. I owe much to the two scholars who mentioned Heller's manuscript, historian John Bunzl and journalist Edgar Schütz, thanks to whom I learned of its very existence, and who also offered much assistance in retracing it. I thank the writer Volker Braun, who led me to the estate of his late friend, the literary scholar Silvia Schlenstedt, in AdK, where a copy of the manuscript was eventually found.

This book was written during my wonderful research fellowship at the Leibniz Institute for Jewish History and Culture—Simon Dubnow. My stay there was kindly funded by the Minerva postdoctoral fellowship program. I could not imagine a better environment for this research than the Dubnow Institute. I am deeply grateful to the entire scientific and administrative staff of the institute, and especially to its director, Yfaat Weiss, and to the head of the Research Unit Politics, in which I took part, Jan Gerber, for their close escort, support, and encouragement. This book would have not been the same without many helpful comments that I received from many colleagues in Dubnow Institute, and especially in the Research Unit Politics and in the institute's Postdoc Circle, who had carefully read drafts of its chapters and discussed them in depth. I must express my special thanks to Annika Padoan for her invaluable help with surveying a huge number of German and Austrian newspapers; to Martin Jost, Momme Schwartz, Judith Siepmann, and John Will, who helped me decipher some of the most challenging German handwritings; to Enrico Lucca, who translated for me French documents, and to Angelique Leszczawski-Schwerk, who translated documents written in Russian for me; to Brett Weinstock, whose assistance in refining my English was indispensable; and to our devoted librarian, Grit Schäfer, who besides providing me with every required book, took Heller's book collection under her professional custody, together with her academic assistant Baptist Gabriel.

This book is based on research that had begun already during my doctoral studies in the University of Haifa. Therefore, I am deeply indebted to my doctoral supervisors, Dani Gutwein and Gur Alroey, as well as to my German teachers Renate Dubert and Nicole McTaggart, thanks to whom I could eventually read the sources for this book. While writing my dissertation I was working at Hashomer Hatzair's Department of History in Givat Haviva, from which I received much support. Shoshana Efrati from Kibbutz Ma'abarot, who was volunteering there, had put in my disposal her native knowledge of German, when I was still a beginner in this language. My dear friend from Hashomer Hatzair department of history, Noam Leibman, kept supplying me with needed materials any time I asked.

Many friends, colleagues, and teachers from around the globe have read drafts of this work or parts of it and contributed important comments and insights: Jan Rybak, Konrad Kwiet, Dan Michman, Jeffrey Herf, Mario Kessler, Jack Jacobs, Malachi Hacohen, Philipp Graf, Tal Elmaliach, Yotam Givoli, Willi Weinert, Jan Burzlaff, Anton Marks, Lindy Grant, Kosta Harlan, Jeffrey A. Bernstein, and other anonymous peer reviewers. Other colleagues have kindly shared with me sources and ideas: Carolina Tischler, Sophie Hochhäusl, Konstantin Baehrens, Anja Jungfer, and Leonard Wilhelm (the latter volunteered for the Convoy 77 project and wrote the biographical entry on Heller for its website). I am grateful to Eva Vadasz for her help with Hungarian documents, and to Tatiana Takczenko for her help with Russian documents. I would like to thank the language editors in Editing Press and Academic Language Experts for their professional services. Working with the editorial staff of State University of New York Press on this book was a great professional and human experience. However, the responsibility for any flaw or shortcoming of this book is of course exclusively mine.

My dear friends in Kibbutz Mish'ol and Merqaz Derekh, both affiliated with the movement Qvuṣot ha-Bḥira shel Ha-Maḥanot ha-Olim in Israel, have listened to my talks about Heller and contributed their remarks and questions, which intrigued and stimulated further thought and research. Last, without the support and partnership of my beloved life companion, Morit Navon, this book would not have come to life.

Note on Transliteration: With the exception of names and words having a common spelling in English, the following characters are being used in transliteration:

From Hebrew: ḥ = ח; k = כ; kh = כ; ṣ = צ; q = ק
From Yiddish: kh = ח, כ; ts = צ

Prologue

A Jewish Question on the Death March

"Rarely a false historical misjudgment is so tragically refuted."[1] This statement is a characteristic evaluation of Otto Heller (1897–1945), the German-speaking intellectual of Jewish descent and prominent communist theoretician of the Jewish question. After he envisioned, in his controversial book *The Decline of Judaism* (1931), the complete disappearance of European Jews through assimilation, it was the irony of history—it is frequently claimed—that he himself fell victim to another, totally different vision of the disappearance of the Jews, as he was murdered in a Nazi concentration camp. According to many of his critics, Heller's horrible end decisively rebutted his own theoretical prognosis. Such a direct line, commonly drawn between the only two known points in Heller's life—his book and his death—leaves many unanswered questions. Through uncovering Heller's story, this biography explores the confrontation of radically assimilated Jews, especially socialists, with the violent collapse of their envisioned integration into a cosmopolitan European society.

Yisra'el Gutman—the Warsaw Ghetto fighter, who later became Heller's fellow resistance member in Auschwitz, and subsequently a prominent Israeli historian of the Holocaust—testified: "I remember that during the evacuation of Auschwitz, in the endless peregrination on the snowy roads of Silesia and Austria, one of our friends [from the socialist-Zionist youth movement, Hashomer Hatzair]—I believe it was Leybek Braun, approached Heller and asked him if he still held onto the conception expressed in his book. I do not remember Heller's reply."[2] Both participants in this reported hallucinatory dialogue,

Heller and Braun, one of the leaders of the Zionist underground in Auschwitz, did not survive to recount Heller's response.[3] As a report on traumatic events written from a retrospective of some dozen years, Gutman's testimony does not necessarily accurately reflect an actual event. Yet, the understandable memory lapse of the witness is in itself emblematic. Whether indeed asked or not, the question ascribed to Braun can be read as a historiographic question asked by Gutman, the historian. The fact that Gutman left the question unanswered is heuristic. His forgetfulness may hint at repressed traumatic content, on both the individual and collective level. It reveals an open wound in Jewish history, a sensitive nerve left exposed: the tragic fate of "assimilated" Jews, as Gutman defined Heller, who were murdered by the same society to which they so eagerly wished to belong. In this case, the encounter "on the snowy roads of Silesia and Austria" symbolizes the apocalyptic intersection of two seemingly antagonistic roads that diverged in modern Jewish history: assimilation and nationalism.

This biography's epistemic point of departure concerns the question allegedly addressed to Heller during the Death March: What was the impact of the Holocaust on him, as a radically assimilated Jew? Heller's entire biography is required to reconstruct or estimate his answer. His late annals, from 1931 to 1945—including his escapes from Nazi Germany and Soviet Russia, participation in the Resistance in occupied France, and deportation to Auschwitz—are obviously necessary to trace the development of Heller's conception of the Jewish question after writing *The Decline of Judaism*. Furthermore, as the common reference point for his entire life, his 1931 book in itself demands reexamination. To what extent did this book actually manifest what was conceived by Gutman as a typical communist attempt "to prove that a Jewish nation does not exist, and has never existed"? How did this alleged position coexist with the fact that Heller praised, in the very same book, the "Birobidzhan-experiment" of Jewish national autonomy in the Soviet Union, as Gutman himself admitted?[4] What brought Heller to write such an apparently paradoxical book in the first place? These questions cannot be tackled without tracing Heller's early life: from his childhood and youth in fin-de-siècle Vienna; through his endorsement of communism in interwar Czechoslovakia, which brought about his banishment from the country in 1926; his resettlement in Berlin as a German communist journalist; and his journeys across the Soviet Union, up until the writing of his book back in Berlin.

Heller's life story epitomizes several core issues in modern Jewish, European, and human history, which are still hotly debated: the meaning of being a Jew in the modern world, ranging across the spectrum from assimilation to nationalism; the tension between the intellectual's adherence to the truth and his commitment to a redemptive political vision; and the conflict between particularistic and universalist interpretations of the Holocaust. Through Heller's life and work, this book complicates seemingly unbridgeable dichotomies.

Contrary to Heller's common image as the utmost advocate of the traditional Marxist denial of Jewish nationalism, this biography

Figure I.1. Otto Heller. Courtesy of the Papineau-Heller family archive (PHFA), Paris.

shows and explains how he came to lay the foundations for a groundbreaking communist acknowledgment of the Jews as a nation. By that, he anticipated an alternative to the communist mainstream, which gained force only when he himself had already gone underground and was occasionally arrested and transferred from one concentration camp to another. This alternative line culminated after Heller's death, but was subsequently defeated and thus sent to oblivion. Beyond his own personal fate, and apart from the path he represented in Jewish history, Heller's biography also tells the history of the rivalry between communism and Jewishness, as well as the rise and fall of an attempt to reconcile them.

The Decline of Judaism, Its Decline, and Its Discontents

The historical departure for this study is Heller's book *The Decline in Judaism: The Jewish Question, Its Critique, Its Solution through Socialism*, which simultaneously made him famous and infamous, and engraved his name in history.[5] Historian Edmund Silberner noted that the vast German-language socialist and communist literary tradition produced only two books dedicated to the Jewish question: Moses Hess's *Rome and Jerusalem* (1862) and Heller's *The Decline of Judaism*.[6] The latter is thus considered a crucial source for the history of socialism, Marxism, and communism vis-à-vis the Jewish question.[7]

The Decline of Judaism is a book consisting of three parts: Marxist interpretation of Jewish history as leading to complete disappearance of the Jews through assimilation, at least in Western countries; presentation of the Soviet policy as the ultimate solution to the Jewish question through reviving the Jewish nation in a socialist framework; and a reportage of Heller's journey to the newly announced region allocated for Jewish autonomic settlement in the Soviet Far East, Birobidzhan. This brief summary is enough to demonstrate the tension, if not contradiction, between the title and the first part of the book, on the one hand, and its two other parts, on the other hand.

When the book came out, in 1931, the provocative title *The Decline of Judaism* was enough to attract much "public attention" and to instigate a fierce public debate, as noted by the Israeli historian and journalist Shmu'el Almog.[8] His attribution of the impact of the book on contemporaries to its title is true also regarding later scholars, who tend to focus their discussion on the book's title. Accordingly, they concentrate on the historical part of the book, which explicates the title, while paying lesser attention to the other sections, which undermine it.[9] But while contemporaries—even Heller's adversaries—tended to take his book seriously, most postwar historians dismissed its intellectual worth. Many of them found it hard to maintain a scientific indifference, asserting harsh moral judgments against the book's title, content, and methodology, and thus joining the historical debate over the book instead of analyzing it. Since Heller is mentioned in scholarship almost exclusively as the author of *The Decline of Judaism*,[10] the interpretation of the book determined his own image in historiography as well.

Many scholars tended to read the title *The Decline of Judaism* retrospectively through the dark lens of the Holocaust, focusing on Heller's own tragic fate, not without a whiff of gloat. "An author who chose to title his book 'The Decline of Judaism' on the eve of the Nazi rise to power," wrote the Israeli historian Shlomo Na'aman, "did not understand his own time: he was annihilated in Auschwitz."[11] Such an a posteriori wisdom was expressed in the claim of another leftist Zionist intellectual, Meir Talmi, who mentioned as a "curiosity" the fact that "in 1931 one could *still* find" an "assimilation prophet," pointing at Heller.[12] Referring to the question addressed to Heller on the Death March, whether he still stood behind his "decline" thesis, Gutman concluded: "the bitter experience has answered by its own manner. Merciless history adjudicated who was right."[13]

These ironic and anachronistic condemnations of *The Decline of Judaism*, based on the cruel death of its author, reflected the traditional clash between Zionism and communism, which was intensified by the anti-Israeli policy of the Soviet Union. But such a reading of the book was not reserved for Israeli scholars. Against the background of the Cold War, and following the subsequent downfall of communism, intellectuals in other Western countries had enough reasons of their own to condemn Heller. The German journalist Eike Geisel, referring to the Jewish-communist-youth armed underground group in Nazi Germany led by Herbert Baum, mentioned that the group took inspiration from Heller's idea that only the triumph of communism can help the Jews. In parentheses he commented as follows: "(One of the most grotesque footnotes of history, that belongs to this context, is that Otto Heller, the author of the widely read book 'The Decline of Judaism' experienced the title of his work in a barbaric manner: he was murdered in Mauthausen concentration camp)."[14]

Much of that retrospective criticism was aimed at Heller's alleged failure to foresee the coming Holocaust. The German-Jewish-American historian, George Mosse, declared: "It soon became evident how tenuous his [Heller's theoretical] construct proved to be."[15] Referring, along with the Holocaust, to the burst of Stalinist antisemitism in the early 1950s, the German literary scholar Silvia Schlenstedt wrote: "Whoever reads the title nowadays, experiences the main word in the title, 'decline,' as nightmarish, and the claim of the subtitle, regarding the 'solution through socialism' as illusionary [. . .]. The road to illusion and narrow-mindedness is undoubtedly characteristic of Heller's conception, but nonetheless, and perhaps also therefore, his impact on the thought of socialists and communists, especially of Jewish origins, was significant."[16] The convention that socialists and communists, Heller first and foremost, were prone to "narrow-mindedness" is another one questioned in this biography.

According to the German-Israeli-American scholar, Walter Laqueur, Heller's argument was "persuasive [. . .] and, if its ideological premises were accepted, logical and consistent despite its shrillness and arrogance."

> But the book had one major flaw: *it ignored the writing on the wall*. When it appeared in the bookshops Hitler's brown shirts were already marching through the cities of Germany. [. . .] A few years later Heller and many other Jewish communists lost their lives in Nazi concentration camps or in one of the Soviet prisons from which there was no return. [. . .] the views he expressed were shared by thousands of young Jewish communists all over Europe [. . . and] a growing number of fellow travelers.[17]

This judgment was lately reiterated by the American Zionist journalist and scholar, Susie Linfield, who criticized Heller for "crippling blindness" concerning the Jewish question, "preserved even as Hitler rose to power." Referring only to his 1931 book, obviously written prior to Hitler's seizure of power, and only through secondhand references, Linfield could not even validate this claim, using only the customary argument that "he was murdered in a Nazi concentration camp."[18]

Leaving aside the question who else could have seen "the writing on the wall" in 1931, retrospective judgments teach us neither about the book itself nor about its author, and do not explain how the perceptions attributed to him and to many of his followers came to be and in what context. Some of these issues were briefly addressed by the less common, though no less denouncing, scholarly criticism aimed at Heller's historical philosophy and methodology. The German-American rabbi and historian Julius Carlebach, apart from the customary labeling of Heller's fate as "the tragic and final refutation" of his arguments, criticized him also for his attempt "to compress three thousand years of Jewish history into a single book," and for taking "considerable liberties with the facts of history and the work of historians" to fit them into his theory.[19] He attacked Heller's historiography for its "staggering superficiality" and "inaccuracy," and as "expressing contempt" for the Jewish religion.[20] Similarly, Silberner criticized Heller's "analysis" for being "rigid and mechanical."[21] As many other scholars mentioned here, both Carlebach and Silberner merely reiterated critical arguments already made by contemporaries regarding Heller's book.[22]

Other scholars questioned Heller's theoretical originality. They too repeated the accusations made by contemporary socialist-Zionists and social-democrats, who accused him of plagiarizing their own theoreticians. The Israeli historian Robert Wistrich, for example, judged Heller's "prophecy, that the assimilation of the Jewish bourgeoisie in Western Europe and of the Jewish proletariat in Eastern Europe, is an inevitable historical process," as an imitation of "Kautsky's thesis in a pious Leninist formulation."[23]

Some more recent German historians, such as Thomas Haury and Olaf Kistenmacher, targeted Heller's thought from yet another direction, interpreting it as a form, though mild, of "antisemitism from the left." According to Haury, "the antisemitic tendency" was revealed, for example, in Heller's descriptions of the transformation of "the junk-dealer [Trödler] and peddler of Podolia" into a farmer in Birobidzhan.[24] Kistenmacher presented Heller's book as exemplar of an antisemitic discourse he identified in the Communist Party of Germany (Kommunistische Partei Deutschlands, KPD).[25] In this case, too, the only example of Heller's alleged antisemitism is his reference to "residues of the Ghetto-scholarliness, the Jewish tendency to spiritual activity, a shadow of the past," as still noticeable in Birobidzhan.[26] It is hard to define such criticism of the Jewish occupational structure as antisemitic, if we remember that it was characteristic also to the Zionist discourse. Aharon David Gordon, for example, one of the most influential thinkers of Labor Zionism, wrote: "Would our Jews not always prefer commerce, peddling, brokerage, and especially, businesses, in which others will work and they will manage the business?"[27] This view was not reserved to Zionists, but shared by many Jewish philanthropists, community activists, and social scientists of various political currents, who, similarly to Heller, advocated "productivization," though in different manners and locations.[28]

On the other hand, there were also historians of Marxist inclination, like John Bunzl and Alfredo Bauer, who incorporated some of Heller's insights into their own research.[29] The German historian Mario Kessler expressed an exceptional evaluation, claiming that Heller's miscalculation of future tendencies should not be understood as "conscious ignorance," but as a genuine "faith in the capability of the workers movement" to win over and turn society upside down.[30] However, besides a minority of more nuanced interpretations,[31] the bulk of scholarship sees Heller's book as representing an allegedly dogmatic and homogenous anti-Jewish communist tradition.

Most scholars agree that *The Decline of Judaism* was expressing the "official party position" of the KPD,[32] the biggest and strongest Communist Party outside of the Soviet Union at the time, to which Heller belonged when he wrote his book. This understanding of the book becomes peculiar when it is examined against the historical context of its publication. From its very inception in the first days of the Weimar Republic, the KPD deliberately avoided addressing the Jewish question. In the early 1930s, in response to growing antisemitism, the Party moved many of its functionaries of Jewish background behind the scenes. Facing a rapid increase in Nazi popularity among unemployed workers during those years, the communists endeavored not to appear as a pro-Jewish party, and, thus, Jewish issues were mostly ignored of.[33] Why would the KPD, while hiding its Jewish activists and virtually avoiding formal statements regarding the Jewish question, be interested in a highly provocative book-length account of this problematic topic, written by a prominent Party intellectual with Jewish origins? In fact, it was harshly criticized in the formal daily of the KPD.[34] Heller's *Decline of Judaism* actually counteracted the Party policy, causing political turmoil. This context illuminates the book as a much more complex and enigmatic text than hitherto assumed.

Adding to the puzzle is the manuscript of a second book on the Jewish question, written by Heller in 1939 during his exile in France, prophetically titled "The Jew Is to Be Burned."[35] This unpublished text, hardly mentioned in scholarship, should also be added to the short list of most important communist works on the Jewish question.[36] Following the publication of *The Decline of Judaism*, Heller declared that "the Jewish question did not interest him from the standpoint of the Jews at all," but only as a communist.[37] Having written a second book on the exact same topic within less than a decade, Heller's preoccupation with his denied Jewish "standpoint" seems almost obsessive. Why did Heller write this second book, and how did his views reflect the vicissitudes of the 1930s? As the most extensive communist account of the Jewish question from the period of the Third Reich, "The Jew Is to Be Burned" sheds a new light not only on Heller's own Jewish belonging, but also on the broader history of Marxist discussion of the Jewish question under Nazism.[38]

While in the first few years after its publication *The Decline of Judaism* sparked an intensive theoretical and political debate, after the end of the Second World War and the death of its author this debate degraded into a series of habitual, superficial, and anachronistic accusations of dogmatism, false prophecy, and antisemitism. This simplified and politicized image of the book left its author on the fringes of scholarly interest. Therefore, hardly anything is known about Heller, nor about the context of the publication of his book and about its reception by contemporaries. Besides the questions stemming from the content of the book itself, Heller's hitherto unknown life story challenges the common view of his book. What is missing in the current one-dimensional scholarly depiction of Heller, based on a straight line drawn between *The Decline of Judaism* and his death? This biography addresses that question too.

On Radical Assimilation and "The Non-Jewish Jew"

Gutman's narration of the question on the Death March exemplifies the tendency of many of Heller's contemporaries, as well as of much of the above-cited scholarship, to pose "assimilation" in dichotomic opposition to "nationalism." Contrastingly, recent scholarship distinguishes between diverse degrees and ways of integration of Jews into their social, national, political, or religious environments: from mild acculturation to "Jewish self-hatred." Demonstrating this approach, historian Todd Endelman has recently coined the term "radical assimilation," addressing the extreme edge of this spectrum. This category includes various manners of alienation from one's Jewishness. Heller's case fits well into the category of radical assimilation, as he practiced all of its manifestations mentioned by Endelman, besides religious conversion. In 1917 Heller "secede[d] from the state-sponsored [Jewish] *Gemeinde* [community]" of Vienna; in the following year he registered to the city's university as *"konfessionslos"* (undenominational); in 1922 he took a "Christian spouse"; and, on top of that, he buried his "Jewishness in the cause of socialism."[39]

Heller belonged to those radically assimilated Jews, who did not convert their Jewish religion to another, but rather rejected religion altogether in favor of a secular faith and belonging, in this case Marxism, and more specifically, communism. Beyond their own individual absorption, Jewish communists aspired to a complete upheaval of their surrounding society. They envisioned a united and equal humanity that would overcome every distinction based on religion, ethnos, or nationality. He was also among those who experienced the cruel trampling of their beliefs, as they were hunted to death for the very Jewish origins they attempted to leave behind. Adding to the tragedy, some of them, Heller included, were persecuted from within the communist movement to which they dedicated their lives.[40] Unlike many who shared similar experiences, Heller devoted years of theoretical contemplation to the topic of Jewish assimilation. For that, his individual life story offers an exceptional prism into the wider historical phenomenon of radical assimilation.

Heller was a representative of a specific prototype of a radically assimilated Jew, known as "the non-Jewish Jew." In his lecture at the World Jewish Congress in 1958, the Polish-British Jewish intellectual and historian Isaac Deutscher (1907–1967) had coined this oxymoron to signify "the Jewish heretic who transcends Jewry," but exactly for that reason "belongs to a Jewish tradition" of dissenters from Judaism, who devoted their lives to universalistic missions.[41] Deutscher identified this typecast with certain giant historical figures like Benedict Spinoza and Sigmund Freud. Yet, the other examples he mentioned—Karl Marx, Heinrich Heine, Leon Trotsky, and Rosa Luxemburg—clarify the specific political orientation to which this neologism is particularly relevant. The category of non-Jewish Jews is applicable to a much wider range of historical figures: socialists of Jewish origins, including Deutscher himself, and many thousands of others. This sociologically broadened and politically specified interpretation of the non-Jewish Jew serves as the conceptual framework for this biography of Otto Heller.

There are, however, other shortcomings in Deutscher's essay that require a further revision of his conceptualization of the non-Jewish Jew. Deutscher focused his discussion on pre–Second World War figures, and thus bypassed the cardinal question: How was the position of non-Jewish Jews affected by the Holocaust? In other words, is "non-Jewish Jewishness" still possible after Auschwitz? His only allusion to this issue was somewhat apologetic.

> We are now looking back on these believers in humanity through the bloody fog of our times. We are looking back at them through the smoke of the gas chambers, the smoke which no wind can really disperse from our eyes. These "non-Jewish Jews" were essentially optimists; and their optimism reached heights which it is not easy to ascend in our times. They did not imagine that it would be possible for "civilized" Europe in the twentieth century to sink to a depth of barbarity.[42]

I accept Deutscher's claim that judging pre-Auschwitz non-Jewish Jews against the scale of the eventual catastrophe, as Heller was frequently judged, is anachronistic. An appropriate topic for historical research would be the reaction of non-Jewish Jews to the Holocaust. This aspect was overlooked by Deutscher, perhaps for the sake of his own "non-Jewish Jewishness." In a later interview, he implied the significance of this issue, first generally: "Auschwitz was the terrible cradle of the new Jewish consciousness," and then regarding his own Jewish consciousness: "I am [. . .] a Jew by force of my unconditional solidarity with the persecuted and the exterminated."[43] But he also confessed that, for him, the "mystery" of the Holocaust "passes the comprehension of a historian."[44] Indeed, the particular confrontation of non-Jewish Jews with the Holocaust is a virtually neglected topic in historiography. Especially in the case of Jewish communists, the antisemitic myth of Judeo-Bolshevism has cast its long shadow over decades of historical research, making any engagement with this linkage almost taboo.[45] Heller's story, in that sense, offers an observation inward—the history of a non-Jewish Jew facing the Holocaust.

The second qualification concerns the term itself. While the "non-Jewish" aspect is self-evident regarding persons who consciously distanced themselves from their Jewish heritage, less obvious is what makes them nonetheless *Jews*. Whereas in his above-mentioned interview Deutscher offered only a "negative" definition of "Jewish consciousness" as "a reflex [. . .] of antisemitic pressures,"[46] in "The non-Jewish Jew," he assumed a positive one: "In some ways they were very Jewish indeed. They had in themselves something of the quintessence of Jewish life and Jewish intellect. They were *a priori* exceptional in that as Jews they dwelt on the borderlines of various civilizations, religions, and national cultures."[47] According to this definition, the universal dimension of the visions of non-Jewish Jews was essentially Jewish. Deutscher's explicit rejection of the notion of "Jewish genius" notwithstanding, proclaiming the existence of "Jewish intellect" is almost as essentialist. Deutscher attempted to anchor it on the social existence of Jews "on the margins or in the nooks and crannies of their respective nations."[48] Yet the so-called Jewish intellect Deutscher notes cannot be assumed as "*a priori* exceptional," since many Jewish intellectuals did not adopt the universalism he ascribed to "Jewish intellect," while many non-Jews did.

In my view, what maintained them as Jews was not the content of their thought, but rather the bare fact that, in modern Europe, it was almost impossible for people to altogether dispose themselves of their identification as Jews by others. In his 1944 essay, *Reflections on the Jewish Question*, Jean-Paul Sartre went as far as to claim that this external perception is exactly what constitutes "the Jew." Relating specifically to the assimilated Jew, he noted: "He wants people to receive him as 'a man,' but even in the circles which he has been able to enter, he is received as a Jew."[49]

His existentialist philosophy notwithstanding, Sartre did not see "being a Jew" as an existentialist position, but as a mere fact of existence, projected on the subject from the outside. His view should be supplement by the internal subjective experience generated through this existence. The Israeli philosopher Avi Sagi pointed to the work of the Hebrew writer Yosef Chayim Brenner (1880–1921) as a foundation for "Jewish existentialism": "Jewish existence is the existence of living people, whose Jewish being is not contingent on anything. Their existence is not part of a set of beliefs and viewpoints but a primary elementary fact that begins with the coerced fact—thrownness into Jewish existence and fate." Having been thrown into existence as a Jew, one can either willingly endorse his Jewish existence or alienate himself from it, but one cannot efface it.[50] Leaving aside the question of the temporal and geographical scope of "Jewish being[ness]," for the purposes of this book, it is sufficient to apply this understanding to modern Europe, into which both Brenner and Heller were "thrown" as Jews.

More than Brenner, who was born to an East European orthodox Jewish family, Heller's life exemplifies a case of "thrownness" into Jewish existence after having assumed it had already been successfully overcome. He shared this fate with Jean Améry (1912–1978), who, in his article "On the Necessity and Impossibility of Being a Jew," saw himself as one of the many "contemporaries, probably numbering into millions, whose being Jewish burst upon them with elemental force." Like Deutscher, Améry defined himself a "Jew without positive determinants," a "catastrophe Jew," a "Non-non-Jew." At the same time, he declared: "I am a Jew." As a Jewish existentialist (in the sense of Sagi's interpretation of Brenner), Améry endorsed his coerced Jewish existence: "I must accept this and affirm it in my daily existence."[51] The non-Jewish Jew is thus seen here as a Jew in an existentialist, rather than an essentialist, manner. Based on this interpretation, this biography follows the constant tension between Heller's refusal to endorse Jewish existence and his inability to escape it.

My last reservation concerns the ahistorical character ascribed by Deutscher to the intellectual achievements of the non-Jewish Jews as rising "above their societies, above their nations, above their times and generations," and as striking out "mentally into wide new horizons and far into the future."[52] Indeed, some of those defined by Deutscher as non-Jewish Jews demonstrated long-lasting and universally acknowledged intellectual breakthroughs. Yet, it should be contested to what extent they rise "above" their respective times and places. Marx, for example, could not be understood outside the context of the industrial revolution in Western Europe. The spread of Marxism in other technological and cultural circumstances should be explained through those circumstances themselves. Even more, when applying the term *non-Jewish Jews* to a much larger group of Jewish Marxists, who did not all rise to the same intellectual brilliance of Marx, historical contextualization is crucial. The abundance of (non-Jewish) Jews in socialist movements in the first half of the twentieth century requires its own explication. Otherwise, the understanding of Heller and the social phenomenon he stands for would be deficient.

On Socialism, Marxism, Communism, Jewish Nationalism, and the Jewish Question

As a salient socialist of Jewish descent, Otto Heller represented another broader historical phenomenon: the discernible presence of Jews among socialists and of socialists among Jews. Though in both cases it was hardly ever a majority, the conspicuous role of Jews in socialist movements often raised the question: What kind of Gordian knot connected Jews with socialism? One explanation attributed this connection to an alleged inherent moral proximity between socialism and traditional Jewish concepts of social justice and prophetic or messianic visions.[53] This sort of essentialist explanation was refuted through several convincing arguments. Most Jews who turned to socialism did so not as a continuation of Jewish tradition, but as a rejection of it.[54] At the same time, other Jews found the Jewish tradition coherent with rightist or liberal social values, while socialism could be also linked to Christian concepts of justice and redemption.[55] While the influence of the Jewish cultural heritage should not be altogether dismissed, it must be a complimented by the social predicaments behind the appeal of socialism for Jews.[56]

The strongest argument against an essentialist interpretation, and in favor of a historical circumstantial one is that the bold connection of Jews to socialism was limited in time and space. Starting from the mid-nineteenth century in Central Europe, it culminated in the first half of the twentieth century among the emerging Jewish working-class in Eastern Europe. Along their emigration routes, East European Jewish workers carried their socialism to their destinations in Western Europe, America, and Palestine-Israel.[57] During the second half of the twentieth century, that bond declined, following the extermination of the Jewish working masses of Eastern Europe, the oppression of Jewish culture in the Soviet Union, and processes of de-proletarianization in the United States and Israel.[58] At the same time, Jewish leftist traditions found some continuity in the form of the "new left," though this trend was more marginal within Jewish society and less affiliated to socialism and labor movements.[59]

Considering the distinct scope of the historical affinity of Jews and leftist politics, a predominant external factor was suggested as an explanation. The twofold oppression, both ethnic and social, inflicted on Jewish minorities, especially in Central and Eastern Europe, explicates their interest in the overarching emancipatory vision of socialism, offering both political and economic equality.[60] For that reason, the alliance of Jews with socialism was especially strengthened facing the rise of Nazism, while the alienation from Jewish belonging and nationalism, characteristic of certain socialist circles, was softened, to an extent, during that period.[61] These dynamics unfold in Heller's story.

The subtitle of Heller's book, *The Decline of Judaism: The Jewish Question, Its Critique, Its Solution through Socialism*, implies that the Jewish question is an integral part of the general "social question" prompted by modernization. Accordingly, the encompassing solution offered by socialism was supposed to automatically solve the Jewish question as well, by abolishing the economic relations that were understood as preserving Judaism.[62] The subtitle of Heller's unpublished manuscript, "The Jew Is to Be Burned: Studies on the Jewish and Racial Question," also explicitly refer to the Jewish question, though this time without an attached solution. Both titles, however, link the Jewish question to other major questions. Bundled together with "the social question," "the racial question," "the national question," and other such questions, the Jewish question was part and parcel of what Holly Case referred to as *The Age of Questions*, in her book bearing this title. Like other modern questions, the Jewish question was not a mere theoretical "question" demanding an "answer," but primarily a "problem" demanding a "solution."[63]

Although the Jewish question was first posed by antisemites, as Case argued, it was nonetheless actively asked by Jews as well. Many of the various formulations of the Jewish question, reflecting different proposed solutions, were formulated by Jews. In that sense, the original German term, *Judenfrage*, correctly translated as "the question of the Jews," is more accurate than the more common and compact English equivalent, "the Jewish question," which has become idiomatic. The question itself was not Jewish, it was asked by Jews and non-Jews alike, regarding the relations between them. To avoid confusion and complication, here I use the widely accepted English form, yet the reader should bear its shortcomings in mind.[64]

By "the Jewish question" I refer to the question raised regarding the possibility and nature of Jewish existence in modernity. What is the meaning of being Jewish in modern society? Is it a mere religious confession? Is it a nation? Perhaps a class? A race? Or is it doomed to vanish altogether? This theoretical question reflected a very practical political problem: How should the modern state relate to the Jewishness of its Jewish citizens? Is it only a private matter, or should it be defined as a formal status, and if so, what kind (i.e., religion, nationality, race)? Should the Jews be emancipated, namely, bestowed equal civil rights, and, if so, under which conditions? Moreover, how should the state treat emerging antisemitism and the socioeconomic and political frictions, frequently violent, between non-Jews and Jews? All these complications, and more, preoccupied European politics and were addressed by all political parties, Jewish or not. Starting even before Marx's famous polemic, *On the Jewish Question* (1844), through to Theodor Herzl's *The Jewish State: An Attempt at a Modern Solution of the Jewish Question* (1896), and all the way to Abram Leon's *Materialist Conception of the Jewish Question* (1946), written during the implementation of Hitler's so-called Final Solution, the Jewish question constituted a major controversy in modern Europe.[65]

Before focusing on the socialist solutions to the Jewish question, I shall discuss one other answer, Jewish nationalism, which Heller explicitly rejected and implicitly endorsed at the same time. This seemingly contradication was possible due to the diverse character of Jewish nationalism, which consisted of a variety of different, and frequently opposed currents, and thus should be more accurately referred to in plural as Jewish nationalisms. Despite having some roots in Central Europe, the main hotbed of modern Jewish national consciousness was Eastern Europe. From the late nineteenth century, Jews in Eastern Europe started demanding to be recognized as a nation, entitled to collective political rights. However, various groups among them emphasized different rights. Autonomists defined the Jewish nation as a nation without a territory and, respectively, demanded personal cultural autonomy. Other national streams aspired to a Jewish national territory. Those who envisioned it in the Land of Israel, or Palestine, came to be known as Zionists. Others, who searched for other national territories for the Jewish people around the globe, were called territorialists. The Birobidzhan project in the Soviet Union, advocated by Heller, can be seen as a case of Jewish national territorialism. Each of those main currents—autonomism, Zionism, and territorialism—contained many subcurrents, combining its basic national conception with socialism or liberalism, Jewish religion or secularism, Yiddishism or Hebraism.[66]

Like the different Jewish nationalisms, and like almost every other Jewish or non-Jewish political stream, socialists offered their own solutions to the Jewish question. What was the socialist stance on the Jewish question? This is a highly controversial topic in historical scholarship. Scholars from the Cold War period tended to portray a monolithic image of socialism as being hostile toward Jews, even—or rather, especially—among socialists of Jewish descent, such as Marx.[67] As suggested here, Heller's image tended to be incorporated into this historiographic framework. This essentialist representation of socialism did not correspond with the fragmented and shifting history of socialist politics. Since the 1990s, a new generation of scholars has demonstrated a divergent spectrum of approaches to the Jewish question among socialists: from assimilationism to Jewish nationalism, including neutral stances in between these two poles. They have also displayed a diversity of socialist attitudes toward antisemitism: from anti-Jewish insinuations, through overt neutrality between antisemitism and philosemitism, to a fervent anti-anti-semitism.[68] Nowadays, vis-à-vis growing criticism against the Israeli stance in the Middle East conflict among leftist circles, which in some cases intersect with antisemitic discourse, we might be witnessing a return to Cold War trends. While maintaining the conception of diverse leftist positions toward the Jewish question, recent scholarly attempts to reframe the history of Jews and the left tend toward antagonistic interpretations of this relation.[69]

The conceptual framework referred to in this book is that of a diversity of socialist stances on the Jewish question. In this respect, Heller expressed one among them, and even his own position underwent changes during his life. It is through his constant debate with socialists of many other streams, mostly of Jewish background, that his biography displays the wide spectrum of socialist discourse on the Jewish question. Moreover, even within his own stream of communist Marxism there was no one monolithic view, as reflected in Heller's frequent disputes with fellow communists.[70]

As Heller was a Marxist and a communist, I shall now focus on the history of the attitude of these specific currents in socialism to the Jewish question up until his appearance on that scene. Marx himself did not bequeath to his disciples an unequivocal conception on this matter. His early essay "On the Jewish Question" (*Zur Judenfrage*, 1844) became highly controversial among Marxists, due to the antisemitic whiff equating the Jews with the bourgeoisie, and identifying them with trade and profit.[71] Moreover, some of his later scattered statements on the subject paved the way for an opposite interpretation, identifying a contrast between the Jews and modern capitalism.[72] After Marx's death, during the Second Socialist International (1889–1914), Marxist discussion on the Jewish question intensified against the background of the emergence of modern antisemitism since the 1870s, both in the German-speaking sphere and in Tsarist Russia, with its large Jewish population.

Following the Bolshevik revolution in Russia in October 1917, socialist movements around the globe split into Communist Parties, who adhered to the Soviet model of revolutionary coup d'état, and Socialist or Social-Democratic parties, who also strived for a socialist regime, albeit through evolutionary democratic reforms. While both sides continued to sustain Marx's heritage, the communist branch of Marxism became increasingly centralized and homogeneous regarding the Jewish question, as in every other field. A select set of statements by certain canonized Marxist theoreticians and leaders had been solidified and acknowledged as the "orthodox" Marxist view, in general, and of the Jewish question and antisemitism, in particular.

Although not a communist, the German social-democrat Karl Kautsky played a pivotal role in shaping orthodox Marxism, especially regarding the Jewish question. He characterized historical Jewry as a merchant "caste," predicting its complete assimilation into capitalist societies.[73] Continuing this line, the Bolshevik leader Joseph Stalin maintained that the Jews could not be considered a nation since they did not fit his theoretical definition of a nation as a social group sharing common history, language, territory, economy, and culture.[74]

Friedrich Engels, the initiator of the orthodox approach to the legacy of his close friend and partner Marx, had a crucial role in shaping the Marxist understanding of antisemitism. Engels saw antisemitism as a mere "reaction of declining medieval social strata against a modern society."[75] Vladimir Lenin, the dominant thinker of Bolshevist Marxism, added that reactionary regimes merely used hatred against the Jews as an instrument "to incite ignorant workers and peasants."[76] Lenin's view conformed with the earlier optimistic prediction of August Bebel, one of the founders of the German Social-Democratic Party, that antisemitism "will end immediately with the decline of bourgeois society."[77] All of these orthodox Marxist references to Jews and antisemitism were cited by Heller in *The Decline of Judaism*, which was thus rightly conceived as representing the "traditional Marxist conception" of the Jewish question.[78]

These conventions, denying Jewish nationalism and underestimating the potential threat posed by antisemitism, prevailed at the Third International (or Communist International [Comintern], 1919–1943). They became especially bold during the extremely revolutionary and antinationalist policy of the Comintern—known as the "Third Period"—introduced at its sixth world congress in 1928 and intact until 1935.[79] Although not referring directly to the Jewish question, the propositions of this policy implied that, just like communists of all nations, Jewish communists should neglect their particular interests. Communists were called to focus their efforts on what was seen as an imminent international revolution that, among all other manifestations of the old order, would eliminate antisemitism, which was dramatically rising during the economic crisis that broke out in 1929. It was against this background that Heller wrote *The Decline of Judaism*.

During the interwar period, the intensifying struggle between Stalin and Leon Trotsky over the leadership of the Soviet Union, and Trotsky's eventual defeat and exile, created a rival subcurrent within Marxist communism known as "Trotskyism." As part of their overall critique of Stalin's regime, Trotsky and his followers gradually deviated from Soviet conventions, including those concerning the Jewish question. This difference played a role in debates over Heller's conception and political orientation within the communist movement, as he was frequently suspected as a deviant or Trotskyite. If the Stalinist propaganda against Trotsky insinuated that his alleged treason stemmed from his Jewish descent, in Heller's case, too, his origin was also implied in the accusations against him.

In 1931, with the publication of *The Decline of Judaism*, Heller introduced himself as a main figure in the Marxist discourse on the

Jewish question. From then on, the history of the relation of Marxists and communists to Jewish issues could not be told without considering Heller's contribution and impact, and, therefore, it will be integrated into his life story throughout the chapters of this biography.

Structure, Sources, and Methods

"Under Hitler's occupation Heller was arrested, burdened with a dual sin: being communist and Jewish," wrote Gutman.[80] This biography of Otto Heller accordingly has a double nature. On the one hand, it is a communist biography, a rather novel genre that offers a new outlook on the "Communist movement whose proverbial conformism, intrusiveness and monolithicity were backed up by the strict codes of Party discipline." Unlike the traditional political and organizational historiography, which studied communist movements as collectives, the communist biography examines this history through the eyes of the individual. It "also addresses the particular complexity of Communist lives, at once complicit, however remotely, in some of the greatest crimes of the century, and yet displaying a commitment to social justice which in many cases was disinterested to the point of death."[81] In this context, the present biography asks how Heller withheld his loyalty to communism vis-à-vis the crimes perpetrated on behalf of the red flag, particularly against devoted communists, including himself, among millions of other victims. On the other hand, this is a Jewish biography, as it focuses on the Jewish aspect of Heller's experience, namely, on his continuous oscillation between his Jewish origins and his universalist political conviction.

At the heart of this book lies the confrontation of a communist and a Jewish biography. The editors of a collection of "Jewish life trajectories in the twentieth century" have asked: "What meaning could be ascribed to the Jewish origins, when these are not considered by the protagonists as biographically relevant, as it is in socialist, communist or even leftist liberal contexts, often a priori?" Socialist and communist Jews tended to "dissolve their Jewish origins into the egalitarian belonging to the working class." "And yet," as exemplified in the discussed collection, in Heller's case, too, "the theme of belonging [. . .] is not absent."[82]

The Decline of Judaism was the point in Heller's life when the diverged roads of communism and Jewishness reconverged. Reading this book constituted for me the starting point of my research journey after its forgotten author. The discovery of the unpublished "The Jew Is to Be Burned" constituted the next station. The enigmatic aspects of both works encouraged me to continue the investigation by filling in the biographical gaps prior, in-between, and after Heller's two major "Jewish" works. This research appeared as instrumental to understanding not only Heller's own writings, but the entire communist discourse on the Jewish question. Moreover, his life course itself appeared as highly turbulent and intriguing, as it crossed through the tense nerve centers of Europe in the first half of the twentieth century, making his biography a transnational study. The structure of this book reflects my mode of inquiry. Two of the five chapters (chapters 2 and 4) focus on Heller's two main works on the Jewish question, while the other three (chapters 1, 3, and 5) discuss the events of his life.

The first chapter traces the path Heller was on until writing *The Decline of Judaism*, by reconstructing his life story up until that moment: from Vienna, through the new Czechoslovakian republic and Berlin of the Weimar period, all the way to Birobidzhan in the Soviet Far East. The second chapter delves into this book and the agitated debates it aroused among every conceivable Jewish or socialist political stream. The common understanding of this book is contested by exposing unresearched areas in the history of its reception.

After problematizing Heller's major publication, the third chapter follows and the blustery upheavals in his life and in European history during the years between *The Decline of Judaism* and "The Jew Is to Be Burned": his flight from Nazi Germany and, subsequently, from Stalin's Moscow; his participation in the Spanish Civil War; and his exile in Paris. The fourth chapter then examines "The Jew Is to Be Burned" and reveals the tensions and contradictions concealed in this unpublished and virtually unknown manuscript, which originated in a mixture of continuities and sharp turns that characterize this text in comparison to Heller's former book.

From the time of the Second World War, only a few writings of Heller's are known, and most of them do not explicitly discuss the Jewish question. Hence, the fifth and last chapter follows his actions and scant textual footprints dating to the last years of his life, between

1939 and 1945, including his activity in the French Resistance and the underground in Auschwitz. Last, the Epilogue contemplates Heller's possible answer to the question addressed to him (or to his historiographic representation) amid the Death March, by integrating the development of his conceptions of the Jewish question throughout his life. At this point, Heller is placed back into the wider communist discourse on the Jewish question, examining his ideas in the context of the innovative trends that emerged in this area in the 1940s, and estimating his role in bringing them about. In that manner, Heller's story offers a window into the wider history of radically assimilated Jews, and especially of non-Jewish Jews facing the Holocaust.

The structure of this book allows readers who are more interested in the story of Heller's life a reading of chapters 1, 3, and 5 alone as a coherent biographical narrative. Readers who wish to focus on Heller's theoretical writings on the Jewish question can similarly suffice with chapters 2 and 4 as self-containing text analyses. However, only in its entirety does this book offer a holistic view of the two most outstanding communist works on the Jewish question embedded in the biographical, historical, intellectual, and political contexts of their creation.

Beyond his published writings and important unpublished manuscript, the documentation of Heller's life is rather fragmented. As a relatively low-ranking Party activist, his conduct is naturally less documented in Party archives than that of high-ranking leaders and politicians. Moreover, as a wandering refugee in his last twelve years and, eventually, a victim of the Holocaust, much of his private documents did not survive. Such a state of documentation, characteristic of the "ruptured life trajectory" of many European Jews in the mid-twentieth century, confronts the biographer with a "methodical challenge, to put these breaches [. . .] into a narrative."[83] I approached this challenge both through a thorough search for every possible source that could provide any hint on my protagonist's life, as well as through interpretive methods.

A few documents, preserved in the Documentation Centre of Austrian Resistance (DÖW) in Vienna, have hitherto constituted the main sources about Heller used by scholars. The most useful among these materials, for biographical purposes—a five-page account of Heller's life, written in 1967 by his widow Emma—is quite a problematic document.[84] First, it relates to events that occurred from two to seven decades previously, some even before Emma had met her husband. Second, though written in a very informative and impersonal style, Emma's reconstruction still represents the point of view of a loving wife and a mourning widow, who was herself a communist activist like her husband and, thus, also politically biased.

To facilitate the present research additional documentation was required. Several new documents, collected from over a dozen archives in various countries, including a private collection recently discovered in the apartment of Heller's daughter in France, were revealing, but not sufficient. The main corpus on which this research is based comes from Heller's Comintern file, found in the Russian State Archive of Socio-Political History (RGASPI) in Moscow. Its contents of more than eighty pages make this dossier the richest known resource on Heller, and it is examined here for the first time. Apart from correspondences and reports written on Heller by others, it contains several autobiographical accounts, consisting of six pages.[85]

Heller's autobiographical documents, in total only slightly longer than Emma's posthumous biography, are by no means less problematic. While providing the most detailed existing information on his life, they probably cover more than they uncover. Written for the very practical purpose of applying for a job or for Party membership, these documents could not be treated as other ego-documents or autobiographical testimonies, such as memoirs, diaries, or private letters, which reveal the author's subjective experience and interpretation of the events of his life. Against the background of the extremely suspicious political atmosphere that prevailed within the Comintern in the 1930s, Heller's accounts should be viewed as highly apologetic texts, which might contain not only significant distortions but also straightforward lies. In addition, they do not cover the last decade of Heller's life.

Juxtaposing Heller's accounts with Emma's was one method to overcome some of the disadvantages of both versions. On a chronological level, while Heller could report on the first two decades of his life, Emma could report on his last decade. But the two versions are especially complementary regarding the period they both covered. Even if Emma had read Otto's applications at the time, they were surely not at her disposal while writing about him thirty years later. Hence, every similarity in both sources acquires stronger credibility. Moreover, while Emma's account omitted her husband's frictions with the Party, Otto focused on them, which he had to justify. Nevertheless, in the end, these are two apologetic sources, which should be treated accordingly.

Those eleven pages of dubious biographical information are obviously not enough to reconstruct a forty-eight-year life story, spread over at least seven countries in the core region of one of the most unstable periods in human history. Another method I found useful, as well as captivating, to overcome this obstacle was filling the voids in Heller's biography by reconstructing his various social milieus, based on rich secondary literature. In the words of historian Volker Berghahn, this is an attempt to view "the chosen individual firmly in its interactions with other human beings, groups, institutions, and larger communities."[86] Apart from the various geographical and social contexts where Heller was active, the intellectual and political discourses that he was exposed to are addressed as well: Marxist thought, especially regarding the Jewish question and Jewish history; German sociological discourse on the relation between Jews and capitalism; theoretical and political controversies over the nature and prospect of antisemitism; and the mentality of the communist international movement.

One corpus of documents posed a special methodological challenge: a handful of reports smuggled out of Auschwitz to inform the world of the atrocities perpetrated behind the camp's fences.[87] Written with Heller's participation, these reports are his last textual footprints and perhaps the only potential clue for his attitude to the Jewish question facing the "Final Solution." The fact that the reports were composed collectively by four or five resistance members, reedited once outside of the camp, and survived only in their Polish translation, makes it extremely difficult to reconstruct Heller's role. Nevertheless, a thorough analysis of the reports and the identification of their other authors allowed me to cautiously estimate his possible contribution.

Another methodology employed here is inspired by the field of prosopography, or collective biography. Although this work is an individual biography, the fragmented information on Heller can be complemented through the biographies of persons whose life trajectories parallel his, at least partially, some of whom left rich autobiographical literature, while others left theoretical and political writings. Most of them, like Heller, were non-Jewish Jews of Central European origins, with leftist political inclinations, and intellectual vocations.

Some of them were acquaintances, comrades, or friends of Heller's, such as Bruno Frei, Siegfried (Friedel) Fürnberg, Egon Erwin Kisch, Anna Seghers, Willi Münzenberg, Árpád Haász (Albert Haas), and Bruno Baum. Others he did not necessarily know personally, though their lives shared certain resemblances: Stephan Zweig, Joseph Roth, Arthur Koestler, and Paul Merker. Additional figures such as Albert Norden, Ignazio Silone, Alfred Döblin, Lion Feuchtwanger, Raphael Mahler, Moyshe Kats, and Abram Leon confronted Heller as intellectual, political, or theoretical rivals. Together, pieces of their stories and writings not only fill in gaps in Heller's biographical mosaic, but also broaden its scope into a collective story of the non-Jewish Jew.

Most of the figures mentioned above are men. Further, most of the archival documents about Heller were written by men. As Party politics and political literature were dominated by men, documents written by the men around Heller, and by him, focus either on political or theoretical issues (sometimes hiding political intrigues). For that reason, the handful of reports written by women who knew Heller are indispensable. Besides the accounts of Heller's wife Emma and his daughter Lily, who as family members obviously knew him more intimately, a few other women left invaluable testimonies about him: Babette Gross, Münzenberg's life companion; Lily Jergitsch, a German translator who worked with Heller in Moscow; Elisabeth Freundlich, the Austrian writer and his close friend; and Gerty Schindel, his comrade from the Resistance.[88] All these women were politically active, and they too addressed political issues in their accounts. However, whether due to their entitlement to less-prominent political roles, or thanks to a higher level of sensibility and frankness, they provide rare glimpses into Heller's emotional world and human relationships. While reflecting traditional stereotypes, those distinct gendered viewpoints provide the biographer with a fuller image of the protagonist. Although these scant accounts do not allow reconstructing the family life of the Hellers or the role of Otto's politically active wife and daughter in his life, they reveal aspects of his political behavior that would have not been evidenced otherwise: oral utterances that he did not dare writing, physical gestures, and emotional outbursts. In doing so, they contribute crucial elements to this political-intellectual biography.

Interestingly, it was another woman—Erna Stahlmann, the German communist activist and Heller's acquaintance from Paris—who, in the late 1960s, started working on his biography (or at least, a "memorial book"), while working at the Institute for Marxism-Leninism in East Berlin.[89] Unfortunately, she died in 1967, leaving this project unfinished.[90] Considering the unique qualities of the handful of existing feminine perspectives on Heller, it would have been exciting to read his life story through the eyes of a female writer.

Alongside the objective limitations of fractured evidence, it is also my subjective viewpoint as a man, a Jew, an Israeli, and more, that set the boundaries of this biography, in which many questions from Heller's life and times are left open for further findings and interpretations.

Chapter 1

Origins of a Jewish Question (1897–1932)

> The time was on the move . . . But in those days, no one knew what was it moving towards. Nor could anyone quite distinguish between what was above and what was below, between what was moving forward and what backward.
>
> —Robert Musil, *The Man without Qualities*

Otto Heller was born into a time that was undeniably "on the move," as the Austrian writer Robert Musil wrote of Vienna of the early twentieth century. The question was what was moving where, what was declining, and what was ascending. The title Heller chose for his 1931 book, *The Decline of Judaism: The Jewish Question, Its Critique, Its Solution through Socialism,* implies a conclusive answer to this question: Judaism is declining, socialism ascending. But, as it will be shown in the next chapter, Heller's book is not as unambiguous as it might seem. The sources of ambiguity in *The Decline of Judaism* must be sought in Heller's life.

On the one hand, Heller became an exemplary communist of Jewish origins, a "non-Jewish Jew." In this respect, Arthur Koestler's description of his own autobiography also applies to Heller's biography: a "typical case-history of a Central-European member of the educated middle classes," born around the turn of the twentieth century.[1] On the other hand, as a communist who became an expert on the Jewish question, Heller was unique among the "non-Jewish Jews." By following Heller's biography until the writing of *The Decline of Judaism*, this chapter aims to explain both his typicality and his uniqueness, as well as the tension between them, in a search for the origins of Heller's own personal Jewish question as a reflection of *the* Jewish question.

Fin-de-siècle Vienna

Otto Heller was born in Vienna on December 14, 1897.[1] Living in the First District of city, the family must have had considerable wealth.[2] Otto's father, Franz, was a businessman (*Kaufmann*), who worked for many years for a Swiss-Austrian textile company as an authorized commercial agent (*Procurist*) in Vienna.[3] In 1908, he and a partner established a cotton trade business, "Heller & Grundmann." Their office was located in the same district, 100 meters from Heller's home.[4] Like nearly half of Vienna's Jews, Franz Heller's livelihood came from trade.[5] This might have stood in the background of Otto's later insistence on identifying Jews with commerce. However, unlike many of them, Franz Heller belonged to the higher stratum of Jewish merchants.

Otto's mother, Maria Heller, née Löwy, was born in the Bohemian town of Jungbunzlau (Mladá Boleslav).[6] Typically, she arrived at the capital as part of the Jewish and general mass migration from the provinces during the second half of the nineteenth century. If, in 1869, 40,000 Jews constituted almost 7 percent of Vienna's inhabitants, by 1900 they were more than tripled to 147,000, bringing them close to 9 percent of the city's rapidly growing population.[7] Semi-proletarianized Jewish immigrants, many from Galicia, constituted a third of the residents of the poor Second District, known as "Leopoldstadt ghetto."[8] Across the Danube canal, in the neighboring haute bourgeois First District, Otto Heller's childhood home, every fifth inhabitant was Jewish.[9]

The Hellers were not an observant Jewish family, as far as the scant evidence reveals. The fact that two of Otto's older siblings, Emma and Ernst, formally exited the Jewish community—the latter marrying a non-Jewish woman—hints at the family's high level of acculturation and integration. Yet Franz and Maria maintained their community membership.[10] Their socioeconomic profile fitted the well-developed network of "religious, charitable, and social organizations" of the wealthy liberal Viennese Jews.[11] Thus, the house in which Heller was raised was not detached from Jewish belonging.

Otto was the youngest of five siblings. In their adulthood, Emma, Joanna Hanni, Ernst, and Karl were all "earning well."[12] The latter is known to have obtained a doctoral degree in law (*Dr. Jur*).[13] Ten-year-old Otto had followed the educational footprints of his brothers (there is no information regarding his sisters' education) by entering a *Realgymnasium*.[14] The elitist and exclusive middle-school system was an obvious path for the upper echelon of Viennese Jewish bourgeoisie. The gymnasium not only offered access to university, and thus to prestigious careers, but it was also a powerful vehicle of acculturation and integration. Nevertheless, assimilation was tempered by the high proportion of Jews in these institutions. Approximately four out of ten of Heller's classmates came from the same milieu of wealthy Jewish families. Socialization with non-Jewish students was hindered through increasing antisemitism, too.[15] But Heller left no written memory from his schooltime relating to this aspect.

Retrospectively, Heller wished to leave the impression of being a not-too-disciplined pupil. At fifteen he joined the youth movement "'Free Wandering Bird,' Oppositional Free-German Organization ['Freier Wandervogel,' oppositionelle, freideutsche Organization]."[16] Having no information on that specific local organization and considering the strong antisemitic tendency of the mainstream Wandervogel movement, it could be assumed that Heller entered some kind of alternative youth association.[17] Though a "bourgeois" movement, as Heller apologetically admitted, he did claim that his membership brought him "in conflict with the school management."[18] It can be imagined that Heller's school experience did not differ much from that portrayed by Stefan Zweig, who attended a Viennese gymnasium a few years earlier, as "a constant and wearisome boredom, accompanied year after year by an increased impatience to escape from this treadmill."[19]

As an emblem of pre–World War I Europe, Zweig referred to Vienna as the "world of security."[20] But, already when Heller was born, the foundations of this world began to tremble. In the same year of Heller's birth, 1897, Vienna was shaken by a row of substantial turbulences in almost every sphere of public life. The Social-Christian leader Karl Lueger, an outspoken antisemite, was nominated as mayor of the Habsburgian capital. Leuger's growing popularity, especially among the petite bourgeoisie, coerced the reluctant Kaiser, Franz Josef, to ultimately approve his election. Simultaneously, the question of nationalities reached a breaking point, predominantly in the Austrian half of the empire. In Moravia and Bohemia, where the Hellers had roots and probably relatives, the conflict between Czech and German nationalists collided, making the Jews targets for antisemitic attacks from both sides.[21]

Following those developments, the Social-Democratic Workers' Party (Sozialdemokratische Arbeiterpartei [SDAP]) of Austria-Hungary discussed the Jewish question for the first time at its 1897 congress in Vienna, attempting to confront the success of antisemitism without slipping into so-called philosemitism.[22] A more central issue in that congress was the national question, which brought the SDAP to conclude that "there is no longer a single Austrian social-democracy, but a united party composed of different nationalities."[23] This congress saw the birth of Austro-Marxism, which provided the nationally divided working-class of the Austro-Hungarian empire with a materialistic foundation for the concept of nation, and a socialist legitimization for a federalistic vision of national autonomies.[24]

In the very same year, a Viennese Jewish journalist, formerly an exemplar of Jewish assimilation, Theodor Herzl, established the Zionist movement in Basel; and a Viennese Jewish doctor, Sigmund Freud, introduced the Oedipus complex.[25] Antisemitism and the Jewish question, social-Catholicism and socialism, nationalism in general, and particularly Zionism, as well as psychoanalysis, were only some of the symptoms that brought historian Carl Schorske to diagnose 1897 as the "formal close" of "the era of classical liberal ascendency in Austria."[26] Those entangled phenomena will accompany the life trajectory of the 1897-born Heller as leitmotifs.

Heller's childhood coincided with the downfall of liberalism, the decay of which worsened during the course of his youth. Industrialization, urbanization, and laissez faire, while liberating from the fetters of the past, called forth the revolutions of the future.[27] Herzl feared that, "pressed against the wall" by antisemitism, Jews "will have no other alternative than Socialism."[28] Many examples proved him right. Some even tried to forsake their Jewish origins altogether through baptism, including the founding leader of Austrian social-democracy, Victor Adler.[29] Herzl himself contemplated complete assimilation through a collective mass conversion as a solution to the Jewish question.³⁰ Some Austrian Jews followed Herzl's later and preferred solution, Zionism. And yet most Jews, especially the wealthier, found neither socialism, baptism, nor Zionism desired solutions. Instead, they maintained their faith in dying liberalism that had paved their way to emancipation and prosperity—its last devoted champions.³¹ This was the case for Heller's parents.

Years later, in several apologetic curricula vitae submitted to Comintern authorities, Heller had to admit his bourgeois origins, trying to temper them with some liberal-democrat revolutionary traditions: "My parents are bourgeois, of German-Jewish descent, democratic family, with political traditions (1848)."³² And elsewhere: "My father was a merchant, [. . .] politically affiliated with German-Jewish-Liberal bourgeoisie, friended with Pernerstrofer and Ofner."³³ Engelbert Pernerstorfer and Julius Ofner were both Austrian politicians. Ofner was a left-wing liberal, who was supported by the Social-Democratic Party, although he was not affiliated with it. He enjoyed great popularity among the impoverished *Galizianer* (Galician Jews) of Leopoldstadt, who elected him as their representative to the Reichstag.³⁴ How likely was a rich merchant like Heller's father to befriend such a radical democrat and a working-class hero? Though unlikely, it was not impossible. Even if true, why did Heller, as a communist, specifically choose to mention this contact with a nonsocialist?

Franz Heller's other alleged friend, Pernerstorfer, raises even more questions. In both of his books on the Jewish question, without disclosing any personal connection to him, Heller attributed to Pernerstorfer the coining of the famous socialist slogan, which defined antisemitism as "socialism of the fools."³⁵ This was a popularization of the classical Marxist interpretation, which characterized antisemites as confusing the true cause for their suffering—capitalism—with a false one—the Jews. This confusion was, in turn, used by conservative politicians to distract the pauperized masses from their real exploiters and to channel their fury against the Jews. Though traditionally attributed to the German social-democrat August Bebel, who used it in an interview in 1894, nowadays, most scholars agree that it was expressed earlier, in 1890, by the Viennese democrat politician Ferdinand Kronawetter.³⁶ He himself might have adopted it from anonymous Vienna coffeehouse witticisms circulating during the 1880s or even 1870s, against the backdrop of growing popularity of antisemitic leaders such as Lueger and the pan-Germanist Georg von Schönerer.³⁷

Indeed, in the 1897 social-democratic congress, Pernerstorfer spoke in that spirit on "these stupid masses," who were suddenly "made Catholic" and voted for Lueger instead of voting for social-democracy. But so did Adler and many others.[38] No one besides Heller has ever attributed "socialism of the fools" to Pernerstorfer. Heller's claim is very unlikely, since Pernerstorfer became a social-democrat only in 1896, and, before that, was himself a close political associate of the provocative antisemitic demagogue von Schönerer. Why did Heller repeatedly affiliate himself with a former reactionary? It should be doubted whether mentioning Pernerstorfer, as a friend of the family or even as a socialist thinker, would have helped Heller's reputation in communist circles.

Pernerstorfer was a peculiar social-democrat. He was not a Marxist, but rather an "aesthetic socialist," who rejected the Marxist view of nationalism as a bourgeois ideology. He even rejected mainstream Austro-Marxism, because, though more receptible for nationalism, it denied Jewish nationality. Unlike leading Austro-Marxists, such as Otto Bauer and Adler, both of Jewish background, the non-Jewish Pernerstorfer had been Zionist sympathizer ever since Nachman Syrkin's first socialist-Zionist manifesto of 1898.[39] In 1916, Pernerstorfer published an unequivocal statement in favor of Zionism in Martin Buber's Zionist periodical *Der Jude*. He explicitly negated the hope for a decline of Judaism through assimilation: "With the extinction of the Jewish people important cultural elements of a special kind would disappear. Admittedly, they would not be wholly lost through absorption by other nations, but they would be diluted and in Western Europe at any rate, they would probably disappear altogether. The enhancement of mankind cannot be achieved through external mingling but only by inner differentiation."[40]

Why, then, did Heller insist on relying on an antisemite, who became a non-Marxist socialist and, eventually, a Zionism advocate, thus undermining all of Heller's own beliefs? Since this name clearly had no apologetic value for Heller, it can be inferred that his father truly was friends with Pernerstorfer. In that case, the attribution of such a consensual socialist catchword to him might have been Heller's desperate attempt to improve the reputation of one of his family's only possible connections to socialism. This says less about Heller's actual family history than about the meaning that "social origin" acquired in Communist Parties in the 1930s. In Koestler's words, under communism, "social origin" was "as decisive [. . .] as racial origin was under the Nazi regime."[41]

Vienna of the early twentieth century served as a hub not only to Central European socialist and Jewish politicians, but also to leading figures of various East European political streams—such as the two main fractions of Russian social-democracy: the Bolsheviks and the Mensheviks, as well as the General Bund of Jewish Workers in Lithuania, Poland, and Russia. The latter, also known as the Jewish Labor Bund, was established in the same decisive year, 1897, not in Vienna, but rather in Vilna. A year later, the Bund played a key role in the foundation of the Russian Social-Democratic Party. In the years to come, the main principle advocated by the Bund, national autonomy for the Jewish workers—namely, autonomy within Russian social-democracy and in the future socialist state—became a constant controversy, in which Vienna also played a role.

In 1912, while Heller was a gymnasium student, representatives of the Bund convened in Vienna with Trotsky and other Russian social-democrats, to announce the Menshevik fraction as an independent party that acknowledged the Bund as its autonomous Jewish section.[42] As a Bolshevik response against this Russian far-reaching version of Austro-Marxism, in 1913, Lenin sent Stalin to Vienna to study the question of nationalities in the Habsburg monarchy.[43] The result was Stalin's *Marxism and the National Question*, which fiercely debated both the Bund and Austro-Marxism and which will be extensively used by Heller.[44] Despite all of their differences, both Austro-Marxists and Bolsheviks denied the Jews the title of a nation.[45] Vienna, where Heller grew up, epitomized the intersection of two main roads in both Jewish and socialist history, between which Heller continuously oscillated: nationalism and internationalism.

Not only did the future bitter rivals, Stalin and Trotsky, reside in Vienna at this time, but so did the young Adolf Hitler. Although it is doubtful that the future German Führer was already an antisemite during his Vienna years (1908–1913), the city's antisemitic political currents must have impacted his later lethal form of antisemitism.[46] As an admirer of Schönerer and Lueger, Hitler "studied" antisemitism in Vienna, even if he was not yet practicing it.[47] Antisemitism was another aspect of Heller's hometown that preoccupied him throughout his life.

The year 1914 was also decisive both for the Empire ruled from Vienna and for the Heller family. In the summer, Austria-Hungary embarked on what was to become the First World War. In the Fall, Franz Heller died at the age of sixty-two.[48] The death of his father can be seen as a departure point for Heller's subsequent revolt against his family's heritage. It was following the loss of his own father that Freud introduced the Oedipus complex. As this is not a psychoanalytical biography, I mention this context following Schorske's precedent, who pointed out the political dimension of Freud's theoretical breakthrough, which is also relevant in Heller's case. The revolt against liberalism was a collective generational rebellion against liberal fathers. Only in the absence of his father could Freud give his generation "an a-historical theory [. . .] that could make bearable a political world spun out of orbit and beyond control."[49] In 1914, this world completely lost control.

Paradoxically, in Heller's case, the war might have only postponed his own "oedipal revolt." In March 1915, the gymnasium student who had three years earlier confronted his school management over his membership in a "free" youth movement, left school amid his last year to volunteer in the Imperial Army.[50] On the one hand, it was the least rebellious deed, as it reflected not only mainstream patriotic enthusiasm, but also the distinguished loyalty to the supranational empire prevalent among Jews, who perceived the crown as their protector from nationalist and antisemitic threats and as allowing for their prosperity.[51] Volunteering prior to the obligatory recruitment age became so ubiquitous (at least among bourgeois gymnasium students) that only three pupils remained in eighth grade at Heller's school that year. The rest, including Heller, quit in order to serve their homeland and kaiser. This sweeping voluntary mobilization became known as *"Kriegsabitur"* (war graduation).[52] On the other hand, it could be seen as a latent revolt, expressing the "increased impatience to escape from this treadmill" of the gymnasium, in Zweig's words.[53]

Heller's more explicit revolt occurred only on the front lines, where he became increasingly critical of the war and the society from which it emerged. In the fall of 1915, Heller was placed in an artillery battery based in Southern Tyrol and sent to the Isonzo front against Italy. There, he attended illegal antimilitarist lectures by the socialist poet and educator of Jewish origins Josef Luitpold Stern, who invoked in Heller a "strong pacifist and anti-Austrian mood."[54] A friend from his unit remembered Heller, later a deputy-battery-commander, as "full of self-irony" and "mockery" toward the military formalities. And yet, he was an "exemplary soldier and excellent comrade," affectionately called by his fellow soldiers "*der kleine* [little] *Heller.*"[55] Again, a mixture of discipline and subversion appears in Heller's personality.

Another revolutionary year was 1917, in both the histories of socialism and Zionism, and in the life of twenty-year-old Heller. Russia saw two revolutions in that year: in February, a liberal one (with strong socialist support) and, in October, the Bolshevik communist revolution. In the same week (in November, according to the Gregorian calendar), the British government published the Balfour Declaration, acknowledging the right of the Jewish people to have "a national home" in Palestine. Interestingly, in that same year, Heller was also attracted by these two different, though at that time still frequently overlapping, political paths: socialism and nationalism. His early interest in nationalism, though not particularly of a Jewish kind, is quite peculiar, as it was never mentioned by Heller himself, only by his wife. Emma Heller's posthumous biographical memoir begins with Otto's acquaintance on the front line with Yugoslav and Czech officers, who introduced him to their irredentist "ideas of independence of their countries." She described this "environment" as "decisive for his political development."[56] As a communist, an older Otto might have tried to obscure such nationalist inclinations, but years after her husband's death, Emma had no reason to conceal them. However, since she was not a nationalist, she also had no reason to overstate them.

Heller's other 1917 revolution, the socialist one, is more comprehensible in light of his future political trajectory. He recalled that his interest in socialism was sparked by the assassination of the Austrian minister-president Graf Stürgkh by the socialist Friedrich (Fritz) Adler, the son of Victor Adler, in October 1916.[57] During the next year, Heller delved into the writings of Karl Marx, an experience that he retrospectively described as a rebirth: "I began to live for the second time, truthfully for the first time, because I began for the first time to understand life altogether."[58] In October 1917, still a soldier, Heller illegally joined the Socialist Workers' Youth of Austria.[59] In November, during a vacation from the front line, he participated in a large illegal peace demonstration. Simultaneously, he joined the Social-Democratic

Party, probably under the influence of Stern.⁶⁰ Heller's social rebellion coincided with his revolt against his Jewish origin. Around the same time, he officially abandoned the Jewish religion.⁶¹ Unlike his older siblings who left the Jewish community but maintained their bourgeois liberal legacy, Heller's postponed oedipal revolt was directed both against his Jewish and "social" origins.

In 1918, the "January-strike-movement" against the war broke out in Austria-Hungary. In these tumultuous days, Heller was still a soldier. One evening, he was supposed to give a "class" in his battery. Instead, according to his own account, he dared to deliver an anti-militarist speech.⁶² For that, he was reprimanded and subsequently dismissed from his unit. He was later placed at the Verdun front in France, where, in October, he was severely poisoned in a gas attack.⁶³ The injured Heller returned home in late November, namely, after the capitulation of the Central Powers. He described early 1919 as the time of his recovery.⁶⁴ However, recurring lung illnesses throughout his life, especially in stressful times, might have resulted from the Verdun injury.

Heller entered the University of Vienna in the summer semester of 1918, probably between the time of his dismissal from Tyrol and his new military post in France. After the war, he continued his studies in the faculty of philosophy, focused on German and French literature, for three more semesters. One course worth mentioning that he took was "the materialistic concept of history," taught by the Marxist philosopher Max Adler.⁶⁵ There, Heller might have encountered his future critic, Raphael Mahler, who also studied history and philosophy in Vienna between 1919 and 1922, and cited Adler in an article a few years later.⁶⁶ It is unsurprising that Mahler, who was from Galicia, a region densely populated with Yiddish-speakers, would become a Zionist socialist, while the Viennese Heller would become an assimilated socialist.⁶⁷

Retrospectively, Heller wished to present his professional track as part of his revolt against his origins: "Following father's death, [despite] no resources, [I] rejected trading profession."⁶⁸ His registration at university as *"konfessionslos"* signified his rejection of his father's religion. Heller's choice of humanistic studies instead of law, the usual path to a business career, revealed his rejection of his father's vocation. Nevertheless, his university studies themselves show that he did not completely rebuff every expectation of him as a bourgeois

Viennese Jew. As a student, Heller lived with his mother, now in the also-respectable Ninth District of Vienna.[69] A friend from the army remembered from his visits how worried Otto's mother was that her youngest son did not follow his brothers' path, but rather became "a journalist to the bone [*mit Haar und Haut*]." Yet, she was "even more worried of his political tendencies."[70]

As a student, Heller must have infrequently attended his classes. Alongside his military duties and injury, his political activism must have been a distraction. The "January [1918]-strike-movement" was an overture to the Austrian workers-councils movement. Strike committees, assembled in different parts of the country, continued functioning beyond the strike as revolutionary organs, not only protesting, but also providing workers' daily needs, such as food and accommodation.[71] In early 1919, Heller was elected to the "Workers-Council of Vienna [District] 1," as a representative of the university.[72] Simultaneously, he joined the newly founded Social-Democratic Party of Austria (Sozialdemokratische Arbeiterpartei Deutschösterreichs [SDAP; sometimes mentioned in the sources as SPÖ]) and was involved in the socialist association for children, "children-friends" (Kinderfreunden).[73] In the new Austrian Republic, under a government led by the social-democrat Karl Renner, the workers' councils still fulfilled an important role. After the end of the war, they were joined by soldiers' councils. Unlike in Russia, the Austrian council movement was dominated by the social-democrats, which caused increasing frictions between radical forces within the councils and the Party leadership.[74]

In the second government of Renner, formed in March 1919, the social-democrat Julius Deutsch was nominated as state secretary for Army Affairs (Staatssekretariat für Heerwesen). In order to strengthen the social-democratic influence on the soldiers' councils and on the Austrian People Army (Volkswehr) as a whole, Deutsch established a military Education Office (Reichsbildungsamt). The office organized lectures, exhibitions, libraries, and sport activities, all directed toward a "revolutionary" and "Marxist" education, to develop "class consciousness" among the soldiers. The head of this office was Joseph Stern, known to Heller from the Italian front.[75] Heller worked as Stern's secretary from March 1919, until Heller left the country in January of 1920.[76]

Heller's year in the Education Office was characterized by constant tension within the army, which reflected the situation in the state.

The revolutionary "left wing" of the Viennese soldiers' council, led by Josef Frey, tended to communism and aspired to shape a proletarian army, following the model of the Red Army. Against him stood Julius Braunthal, who represented the formal Party line, in favor of a general popular army, recruited from all classes. Braunthal maintained that Frey's direction would throw the country into the chaos of civil war.[77] Which side did Heller support? In a later autobiographical report, he claimed to be a member of the "left block." Yet he stressed that his work with Stern was "under Julius Braunthal." Heller tried to take a middle position: "Always on the left wing [missing word] but definitely against KPÖ [Kommunistische Partei Österreichs, Communist Party of Austria]." It was probably for his leftist tendency that Heller was eventually "denied access to active state-service" and thus had to leave the army and "worked briefly in the SPÖ Party archive."[78]

Heller's loyalty to social-democracy was also reflected in his first journalist publication from that time. In a public speech celebrating "One Year for the Republic," published on the front page of the social-democratic journal for education, Heller sounded like an enthusiastic social-democratic reformist: "We [the SDAP] could not storm forwards . . . [to achieve] a social republic. But we could achieve work that would set the stage for the time to come. During this year we turned our state into a commonwealth . . . [and] by means of social policy, we have significantly exceeded political democracy [so] that it can become the base of the [future's] social-democracy." He concluded his speech by combining national and proletarian patriotism: "November 12, 1918 [the formation date of the Austrian Republic] had awakened the workers to new life."[79]

It was only much later, after he had already switched to communism, that Heller retrospectively recalled an experience from the same time, November 1919, as one that invoked his doubts and critique toward Party leadership. According to his story, as a representative of the Education Office, Heller went to meet the Party leader, Chancellor Renner. From the very beginning, Heller's description of the socialist chancellor's office was negative: "a servant in a tailcoat, secretaries, that were still there from Stürgkh times." In the meeting itself, as Heller reported, Renner handed him an envelope containing a substantial sum of money, "for the fight against the Bolsheviks in the *Volkswehr*."[80] Heller depicted this incident as a milestone on the road that eventually led him to communism.

Heller's revolt against his deceased father and everything he stood for took a political shape, in accordance with Schorske's distinction. In his later apologetic pleas to the Comintern, Heller attempted to minimize this revolt by presenting his path to socialism as a continuation of his family roots: "[I] joined the social-democrats [. . .] known to me through a brother and the father, a friend of Pernerstorfer."[81] Even if one of Heller's brothers once leaned toward socialism, eventually, as Heller himself disclosed in another such curriculum vita, his "siblings (two brothers, two sisters) *belong without exception to the bourgeoisie, they live in Vienna, Warsaw and Zürich*."[82] Emma unequivocally asserted that his family "did not accept" his political position.[83] Why was it only Otto, of all his siblings, who became a socialist? Perhaps as the youngest, who came to maturity after their father's death, it was easier for him to sever his legacy. Heller's older siblings had more of an opportunity to experience the still-flourishing liberalism and could thus cling onto it. For 1897-born Otto, the fin-de-siècle decay of Viennese liberalism became an obvious reality. He belonged to the generation that experienced the horrors of the Great War as the final collapse of "the world of security," and returned to a different, revolutionary, red Vienna.

Czechoslovakian Bohemia

When Heller left Vienna, in January 1920, he was still a social-democrat. It is unclear exactly why he moved to Czechoslovakia. Heller once mentioned that it was "suggested by [Ferdinand] Skaret, the secretary of SPÖ," to send him as an education activist to the German Socialist Workers Party of Czechoslovakia (Deutsche sozialdemokratische Arbeiterpartei der Tschechoslowakei), which, until recently, had been a part of the Austrian Party.[84] According to Emma, "under strong pressure of his family, who did not accept this political position, he left the university of Vienna to continue his studies in Prague (Faculty of Law)."[85] Heller, indeed, did not graduate from his studies in Vienna, but the reasons are unclear. Did he choose to leave Vienna in order to escape his family pressure? Or did his family pressure him to relocate his studies to Prague to distance him from socialist activity and, at the same time, to put him on track to a business career through studying law? If the latter was the case, this plan clearly failed, as Heller does not appear in the University of Prague's student register. However, removed from his family's supervision, Heller's political activity only intensified, soon to become extremely radicalized.

The Austro-Marxist ideal of a socialist federation of national autonomies that would replace the Habsburgian monarchy collapsed with the division of the East-Central European empires into a mosaic of nation-states: Austria, Hungary, Czechoslovakia, Yugoslavia, Poland, and others. Already in early 1918, the SDAP was preparing itself for such a scenario, deciding that each national section will continue fighting within the framework of its own nation-state against its respective national bourgeoisie.[86] After the dismantling of the Austro-Hungarian empire, a certain fluidity of activists existed between the Socialist Parties in its successive states. It is against this context that Heller's move to Bohemia should be understood.

The question of nationalities was far from settled by the formation of the new nation-states, which themselves encompassed substantial national minorities, whose rights were acknowledged in a row of international minority treaties. In the northwestern regions of Czechoslovakia lived a large German-speaking minority, later to be renowned as the Sudeten Germans, who stood at the center of an acute international crisis in the late 1930s. In the young Czechoslovakian state, social-democracy was not consolidated in one unified party, but was rather split into several national parties: Czech, Slovakian, German, and others. As a German-speaker, ignorant of the Czech language, Heller was integrated into the German Socialist Workers Party of Czechoslovakia, centered in northern Bohemia.[87] In early 1920s, he settled in Teplitz-Schönau (Teplice-Šanov), as head of the Party's educational activity, editor of its youth journal, and secretary of the Party's leader Josef Selinger.[88] Like the Austrian Social-Democratic Party, its German-speaking counterpart in Czechoslovakia was also experiencing a bitter internal conflict between the reformist right and the revolutionary left. In the beginning, Heller took "a centralist position," following his patron Selinger.[89]

In a public speech toward the elections to the Czechoslovakian national assembly, Heller's centralist position took the shape of revolutionary rhetoric, serving reformist ends.

> The German social-democracy in the Czechoslovakian Republic [. . .] does not deny any instrument of revolution-

ary class struggle. The elections for the national assembly push one of these instruments into our hand. The German class-conscious workers can take the legislation and administration of this state in a socialist direction; [to that end] they must strive to elect as many as possible of their candidates to the Nationalities-Parliament in Prague [and] to work also from there for the liberation of the proletariat.

If earlier in Vienna he expressed mild patriotic admiration for the German-Austrian state, in the Czechoslovakian context his nationalist tone became even bolder: "The Germans as a defeated people are ruled and administered by the dictatorship of the victor." Soon enough, Heller will replace this negative nationalist connotation of "dictatorship" with a positive internationalist one, "the dictatorship of the proletariat." Meanwhile, his German nationalism was tempered only to some extent with proletarian internationalism: "The German workers know that the struggle between the Germans and Czechs is the struggle between German and Czech entrepreneurs; the Czech worker is not the enemy of the German worker. He can be indeed used as a tool [for dividing the working-class through nationalist propaganda], but above all he is a *worker*!" And yet, "the victory must be obtained first by the workers of the individual nation; then the International will have won." Hence, the conclusion was: "vote for the German Socialist Workers Party."

Still a social-democrat, in his speech Heller praised the role of intellect in socialism: "For the proletariat knowledge is not only a means but also an end. [. . .] The way to a socialist culture goes through workers' libraries, schools, lectures. [. . .] We must create libraries."[90] This raises doubts regarding his retrospective, communist-styled, apologetic anti-intellectual self-depiction: "I was lucky to live among industrial workers for many years. I learned what a powerful force Marx, Engels, and Lenin have triggered. I have seen how Marx was understood by workers, indeed more difficultly, but always more deeply and truly than by easy reading intellectuals."[91] In Bohemia, Heller had indeed "lived among industrial workers," as this region, rich with coal and iron mines, was an important industrial center. Besides Teplitz, Heller worked in Aussig (Ústí nad Labem), a town of chemical industry, and primarily in Reichenberg (Liberec), an important textile center.[92] Already before the war, Reichenberg's socialist workers inclined toward the radical left.[93] Bohemian Jews stood out in both the bourgeois and proletarian camps. Jewish entrepreneurs were salient among the Bohemian industrialists. A local newspaper in Austria once denounced many of "the leaders of the German-Bohemian social-democracy" as coming from Jewish bourgeois families. Heller's "parents" (though his father was no longer alive) were mentioned in that list as "heavy shareholders of sugar mills."[94] Although the journalist was wrong to count Heller, by then already a communist, as a social-democrat, the information regarding his family seems reasonable, since Jews had a prominent role in developing the sugar refineries of Bohemia, and Heller's mother had family roots in that region.[95]

Heller's election speech well-reflected the atmosphere among German socialist circles in the new state of Czechoslovakia—vacillating between social-democracy and communism, nationalism and internationalism. The radicalization of German-speaking socialists in Czechoslovakia was inseparable from their new minority position. The "Reichenberg left," which had responded enthusiastically to the October Revolution, was to become the nucleus of the future German section of the Communist Party of Czechoslovakia (Komunistická Strana Československa [KSČ]). The same group took a German nationalist stance, demanding self-determination and accusing the rightist socialists of succumbing to the "Czech bourgeois chauvinists."[96] As in other East-Central European emerging nation-states, a major source of recruitment for the communist cause was disaffected minorities, who wished to overcome the disadvantages imposed on them as minorities through affiliation with an international egalitarian movement.[97] Belonging to the German and, at least by default, also to the Jewish minority, Heller's turn to the left was typical.

The minority complex in Czechoslovakia aroused a distinct "Czechoslovakian problem" in the Comintern. The establishment of a unified Communist Party took longer here than in other countries and was accomplished as late as mid-1921. The German-speaking leftist socialists were the first to form a Communist Party in the country in March. When the KSČ was founded in May, the German faction did not immediately join it. The split between German and Czech communists in Czechoslovakia became a key issue in the third world congress of the Comintern, which took place in Moscow during June and July of 1921. The congress saw a bitter conflict between the

Czech Party leader Bohumír Šmeral, who also represented the right, and the spokesman of the German communists in Czechoslovakia, Karl Kreibich, who led the left. The latter, blaming the former of "social-democratic opportunism," was backed by senior members of the Comintern department for nationalities: Béla Kun, Mátyás Rákosi, and Gyula (Julius) Alpári—all former leaders of the short-lived 1919 Hungarian Soviet Republic (the first two were of Jewish origins). The matter was settled only with the intervention of Lenin, who required the unification of all ethnic sections in Czechoslovakia into one party as a condition for membership in the Comintern.[98]

Heller integrated himself into the "Reichenberg left." As early as May 1920, he was among those social-democrats who "flitted" to the Comintern, and in March 1921, he was one of the twenty-five founders of the German communist faction, alongside his friend Siegfried (Friedel) Fürnberg, who also came from a Jewish background.[99] Heller attributed this track to the influence of Kreibich and his Hungarian supporters in the Comintern. Besides working closely with Kreibich himself, Heller mentioned "the impression" that Alpári and Rákosi made on him.[100]

In the Communist Party, Heller continued with his former focus on education, organizing a Party-affiliated school. Already in 1920, he published a booklet calling on the socialist youth to join the world of the revolution: "What differentiates us from the social-democrat youth leaders is the acknowledgement that the proletarian youth today can no longer be educated in preparation for struggle, but—following the social revolution, which is constituting with full power—[should be educated] only for the struggle itself."[101] This was a clear break from social-democratic mild evolutionism. Heller joined the Communist Youth International, where he became acquainted with his future patron, the German communist Willi Münzenberg (1889–1940), the organization's first president.[102] The youth circles in Bohemia, in which Heller took a leading part, contributed to the establishment of the communist movement in Czechoslovakia as they created, already in January 1921, the Communist Youth Union.[103] Heller was remembered from that period, at least by two of his disciples, his future wife and her sister-in-law, as a "distinguished orator," to whom "all the young comrades listened with full attention."[104]

In June 1921, soon after the establishment of the united Communist Party, Heller moved to Reichenberg, where he was officially registered as working in a bookstore.[105] That must have been a legal cover for receiving a residence permit. Heller's political activity would have not left time for another permanent job. From mid-1921 until early 1926, he filled various leading functions in the Communist Party there: trade union representative, region secretary, member of the Party's central committee, and editor of its newspaper *Vorwärts* (Forward), the well-known mouthpiece of the Reichenberg left ever since 1914.[106]

In August 1922, Heller married Emma Krause (see figure 1.1), who was born in 1903 in Friedland (Frýdlant), not far from Reichenberg. Emma came from a non-Jewish German family of handworkers. On their marriage certificate, they both announced themselves as confessionless. Otto and Emma had met within the communist circles in Reichenberg. According to all existing evidence, their marriage was founded on mutual love and shared beliefs. And yet, those would not be undermined by the assumption that, through his choice of a life companion, at least unconsciously, Heller had also concluded his revolt against his ethnic and class origins. By marrying Emma, he assimilated out of Judaism and into the proletariat. In April 1924, the couple's only daughter, Lily, was born (see figure 1.2). A few months later, the family moved to Ruppersdorf (Ruprechtice), a suburb in the northern outskirts of Reichenberg.[107]

Heller's years in Czechoslovakia were accompanied by a series of rivalries between constantly varying fractions within the Communist Party, which would later haunt him. One main controversy was over the question of trade unions. In 1921, the trade union leader Josef Hais led some communist-dominated unions to spilt from the national trade unions organization, which was ruled by the social-democrats.[108] That was considered an "ultra-leftist" deviation from the Comintern's policy, which at the time stood for a unified unions' movement.[109] Regarding that dispute, Heller later claimed, he "opposed the Syndicalist-opportunist politics of the men around the later traitor Hais."[110]

The trade union question was followed by the national question, which erupted in 1924. This time, under leftist pressure from the Comintern, the left wing of the party called for the "separation of the oppressed peoples" from Czechoslovakia, while the rightist leadership was accused of supporting the "new small imperialist state."[111] Against this background came the "Bubnik affair," named after the old-guard "rightist" secretary of Prague, who was expelled from the Party by a group of young leftists, appointed to the central committee

Figure 1.1. Emma Krause. Courtesy of the Papineau-Heller Family Archive (PHFA), Paris.

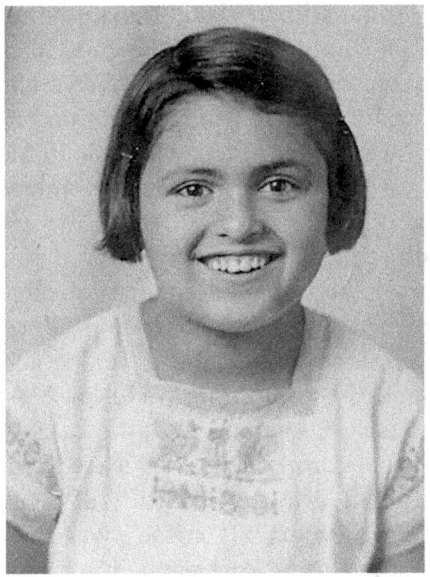

Figure 1.2. Lily Heller. Courtesy of the Papineau-Heller Family Archive (PHFA), Paris.

under pressure by the Comintern. Kreibich, who meanwhile turned rightward, joined with Šmeral in an attempt to hinder a leftist takeover of the Party. As a result, they were both dismissed from the central committee and distanced to remote positions by the Comintern.[112] In this regard, Heller maintained: "I conducted in *Vorwärts* the sharpest campaign against Šmeral and Kreibich."[113] Generally, he claimed to stand "in the left wing," which eventually prevailed.[114] And thus, as one historian from the German Democratic Republic (GDR or East Germany, 1949–1990) portrayed him, "as journalist and functionary [Heller] disputed from the beginning against any opportunist rejections of the party-line," namely, of the emerging Stalinist line.[115] At that point, it was also a nationalist line.

In early 1926, Heller traveled for the first time to the Soviet Union, as a member of the Czechoslovakian delegation to the plenum of the wider Executive Committee of the Communist International (ECCI).[116] In Moscow, he fell badly ill with pneumonia, possibly aggravated by his past gas poisoning, and could not participate the plenum. As the illness delayed his return trip, his Czechoslovakian travel pass expired, and he could not return home. As an Austrian citizen, Heller lived in Czechoslovakia with a temporary residence permit. As he interpreted it: "The Czech police used this occasion to suspend my entrance pass."[117] Emma added: "Due to his political activity [. . .] he was expelled."[118] The communist press claimed to cite the Czechoslovakian authorities' reasoning: "We already have enough communists of our own."[119] *Vorwärts* declared the prevention of Heller's return to the country as an "act of terror," characteristic to the "terror method" employed by the government against many communist activists who were banished from the country.[120]

Heller himself sarcastically criticized the decision by connecting it to a police interrogation opened against him five years earlier. In 1921, according to his own report, Heller was accused of assisting the robbery and murder of a social-democratic activist, allegedly in an attempt to blame the communists. He has been never charged, presumably due to lack of evidence, but the case was never formally closed. Against this backdrop, Heller never received a permanent residence permit. He pointed to the absurdity of banishing a suspected "robber-murderer," whose actual "crime" was being a "communist, who got pneumonia in Russia."[121] Despite his expulsion, Heller eventually returned to Reichenberg and stayed there illegally for several weeks, during which time he continued working in *Vorwärts*'s editorial office, before moving to Berlin in June.[122]

Weimar Berlin

Having been expelled from Czechoslovakia, why did Heller not return to his hometown, Vienna? Emma attributed this to his tense relationship with his family.[123] It can also be explained through the phenomenon of "venturing to Berlin," which was typical of interwar communist intellectuals of Jewish-Habsburgian origins, such as Heller's friend and colleague, the reporter Egon Erwin Kisch. As a metropolis in which the category of "nationality" played a much lesser role than that of "class," Berlin "promised the option of a final goodbye to one's origin."[124] Heller himself mentioned a professional reason to go—an invitation from Willi Münzenberg to serve as the "political editor" of the newspaper *Die Welt am Abend* (The World in the Evening).[125] Heller had known Münzenberg since 1920, from the Communist Youth International, before the latter became known as "The Red Millionaire." In the early 1920s, when the Bolshevik Revolution was struggling to survive and the Russian population suffered from hunger, Münzenberg established the International Workers Aid (Internationale Arbeiterhilfe [IAH]), to collect donations from Western workers and sympathizers for the starving Soviet population. In this way, he initiated what would become the communist Western propaganda mechanism known as the "Münzenberg trust," a transformation of the IAH from a charity into a mass media organization.[126]

Die Welt am Abend was a marginal Berlin newspaper. Like other leftist periodicals, it had a small readership. Münzenberg's vision was to create communist newspapers that would compete the more popular bourgeois press that opposed the workers' movements. In 1926, he bought *Die Welt am Abend* from its nonaffiliated leftist editor, Emil Rabold.[127] The renewed newspaper was meant to be communist in content and bourgeois in form. Münzenberg hired Heller, who had earned his reputation as editor of the Reichenberg *Vorwärts*, to "politically stabilize and shape the content" of the newspaper.[128] Heller the joined a "three-headed" editorial team as the politically reliable party-member, alongside former editor Rabold and another unaffiliated partner, Kurt Kersten.[129] Under their leadership, the newspaper became "sensationalist," and thus succeeded in fulfilling Münzenberg's goal. Circulation "grew geometrically," from 67,000 copies in 1926 to 174,000 in 1928, in Berlin alone.[130] At the same time, Emma was employed as a typist in another Münzenberg media enterprise, the *Internationale Pressekorrespondenz* (International Press Correspondence, *Inprekor*), the Comintern's German language weekly.[131]

The Hellers arrived in the German capital during the short time when the Weimar Republic enjoyed a relatively economically and politically stable period (1924–1929). Immediately after his arrival in Berlin, Heller joined the KPD and, after a while, was "co-opted with advisory vote in the district committee of Berlin-Brandenburg."[132] In the mid-1920s, though not abundant among the members of the KPD (0.7 percent), many functionaries of Jewish origins were to be found in the party apparatus (about 10 percent), including as some of its senior leaders.[133] Heller's integration into the Party's establishment seemed almost natural.

At the same time, a process of "Stalinization," namely, centralization and subordination to Moscow, had begun in the KPD.[134] According to the formal ideology, the Party was going through a "concentration of forces," becoming an organization of "Bolshevist professional revolutionaries," following the Leninist model. Practically speaking, internal Party democracy and open exchange of opinions between different fractions were extinguished. The fractions were not formal associations, but more or less temporal alliances between Party members who shared a common concept or strategy. The exercise of "fractions politics (*Fraktionspolitik*)" meant the use of various maneuvers to denounce, demote, and expel the members of a rival fraction up to its total liquidation. This method caused functionaries to distrust and work against one another.[135] Since the fractions had no formal membership cards, every Party member was potentially a suspected supporter of this fraction or the other.

In the process of Stalinization, groups and individuals who did not succumb to Stalin's authority were expelled from the Party. The first to be "purged" in 1926 was the "ultraleftist" fraction, headed by Ruth Fischer and Werner Scholem (both Jews, the latter was the brother of the renowned Zionist scholar, Gershom Scholem). Ernst Thälmann, Stalin's most faithful German proxy, took over the Party's leadership together with other pro-Comintern leftists, who later implemented themselves an ultraleftist course.[136] Two main opposition groups remained, the "rightists" (led by Heinrich Brandler and August Thalheimer, the latter Jewish), and a "center group," the so-called conciliators (*Versöhnler*). The conciliators—led by Ernst Meyer, Arthur Ewert, and Gerhart Eisler (Ruth Fisher's brother)—took a middle stance, between the right opposition and the prevailing left. In later years, Heller would constantly be haunted by his denunciation as a conciliator.

Both the right and the conciliators supported a united front with the Social-Democratic Party of Germany (Sozialdemokratische Partei Deutschlands [SPD]). They opposed the radical ultraleftist line, which was enforced from 1928 by the Comintern's "Third Period" policy, and directed its poisoned propaganda arrows against social-democracy as the "main enemy" of communism, condemning it as "social fascism." This controversy's magnitude cannot be overstated. A few years later, the refusal of the KPD leadership to form a joint front with the SPD, as offered by the rightists and conciliators, helped pave Hitler's way to power.

The difference between the rightists and the conciliators was that the latter group endeavored to prevent a split in the Party and, hence, avoided publicly criticizing the Comintern or the Soviet Union.[137] Due to their wish to reconcile the dominant leftist Party line with the rightist opposition, they were defamatorily called "conciliators" after the Bolshevik group, which in 1904 desired a reunion with the Mensheviks.[138] One of the main issues in dispute was the trade unions policy. In the fourth congress of the Red (communist) Trade-unions International (Rote Gewerkschafts-Internationale [RGI]), in 1928, the previous tactic of united trade unions (whose collapse in Czechoslovakia was described above) was neglected. Following that resolution, the communists in Germany formed the Revolutionary Trade-unions Opposition (Revolutionäre Gewerkschafts-Opposition [RGO]) and, thus, brought about a split of the trade unions movement.[139]

Against the background of those fraction struggles, the Party was shaken by the "Wittorf affair." John Wittorf, the Wasserkante region secretary and Thälmann's brother-in-law, had embezzled the Party's election campaign fund. Thälmann's attempts to cover up his relative's scandal failed, and it was exposed. The rightists and conciliators tried to use the opportunity to remove Thälmann from office. Facing the danger of losing his German protégé, Stalin personally intervened in Thälmann's favor, forcing his rehabilitation on the German Party. Now the rightists and conciliators were accused of conspiring against Thälmann, and their leaders were deposed from the central committee. In accordance with Stalin's emerging personality cult, a German parallel was inaugurated around Thälmann as the *"Führer des Proletariats,"* challenging another ascending Führer.[140]

Following the "Wittorf affair," by the end of 1928, the rightists were completely defeated.[141] The conciliators' turn came in the following year, as many of them were "purged" from most Party institutions, while others remained as a minority, lacking actual influence. Since the Twelfth Party Congress in 1929, attacks against the conciliators became an informal rhetorical obligation. In 1930, those who stayed in the Party officially surrendered to Party discipline, and any internal conciliator group was dismantled. In that way, the last opposition fraction formally disappeared, and "Stalinization" was complete. And yet, some conciliators, especially younger members, remained active in secret groups inside and outside the Party.[142]

In February 1929, amid that turmoil, Heller was dismissed from the editorial of *Die Welt am Abend*.[143] According to Heller, "that led to the rumor that I myself was a conciliator and that it was the main reason for distancing me from *Die Welt am Abend*."[144] In the following years, Heller would repeatedly need to deny this rumor, trying to defend himself from its deadly implications. To what extent was Heller actually connected to the fraction of conciliators? It is hard to tell. The accusations against him, based on the fact that a few conciliators worked in *Die Welt am Abend*, remained "unverified."[145] However, Heller himself endeavored to remain in the Party and, thus, rejected those accusations.

Nevertheless, Heller did admit committing "a severe political mistake regarding the trade-union question [. . .], which brought me close to the conciliators on *this* question; while on all other questions I stood in a grave conflict with the conciliators." His "mistake" was opposing the split of the trade-unions in 1928: "I did not understand the meaning of RGO, and I was still influenced by the ultra-left flaw regarding the union question, made by the KPČ in 1921–22.[146] As a result, in BL [*Bezirkleitung*, district committee] B-Brdbg. [Berlin-Brandenburg] [I stood against] the dismissal of the conciliator union leader Max Frenzel."[147] To Heller's misfortune, Frenzel became an important figure in the secret conciliator "underground" within the Party.[148] And so, Heller forever became a suspect of *"Versöhnlertum"* ("conciliatorism"). No matter how fiercely he claimed that he opposed "Ruth Fischer and her people" (the ultraleft), the "Brandlerians" (the right) and "the so-called middle-group" (conciliators); and stood in the Wittorf-affair "from the first moment on by comrade Thälmann"—all of his arguments did not help Heller to clear his name from suspicion until the very end, as will later be told.[149]

If not for political reasons, how did Heller explain his dismissal from the newspaper editorial? He attributed it to human relations problems with his two coeditors, who "made every conceivable difficulty out of individualist reasons," until "the situation in the editorial became unbearable. [Therefore,] I demanded from Münzenberg to dismiss the troublemaker Rabold," who later became a Gestapo agent, according to Heller.[150] "But instead," Heller continued, "I was dismissed myself." His simultaneous "political dispute with the ZK [*Zentralkomitee*, Central Committee]" over the trade union question, he claimed, brought Münzenberg to "shove all the blame" for the difficulties in the editorial on him. In his defense, Heller maintained that "comrade Thälmann offered me another editorial position in the province, but I suggested that I would take a temporal vacation." And moreover, "after I had left, Münzenberg offered to let me continue working in his newspapers. All that mattered to him was to get some air in *Die Welt am Abend*."[151] A tragic coincidence, maintained Heller, "made the impression, that my sudden dismissal had political reasons. From that time onwards, rumors kept circulating that I was a conciliator."[152]

A different angle to these events was offered by Münzenberg's life companion, Babette Gross. In her late memoir, she recalled that it was Thälmann who demanded Heller's discharge, which might support the political explanation.[153] The fact that, since 1929, *Die Welt am Abend* had hardened its line against "social fascism," in agreement with the Comintern's new strategy, might explain Thälmann's and Münzenberg's fear of the slightest deviation by someone holding such a politically sensitive position as a newspaper editor.[154] Heller was indeed replaced by a comrade with a highly reliable résumé, Paul Friedländer, one of the founders of the Viennese communist daily, *Die rote Fahne* (The Red Flags).[155] Gross also outlined the implications of Heller's deposition on his subsequent actions: "Münzenberg, who had personally appreciated Heller, did not stand behind him, but rather let him fall, as Heller tearfully told his colleagues. But as always, whenever Münzenberg had to act against his conviction under pressure from the party, he tried to atone whatever was atonable. He arranged for Heller to go on a journey through Russia and Siberia." The formal excuse for Heller's departure was for him to write a book about Soviet Siberia for one of Münzenberg's publishing enterprises.[156] Informally, it was a pretext to distance Heller from political activity in Berlin.

In the summer of 1929, Heller started his journey to Siberia on the deck of the icebreaker *Krassin*.[157] Overall, his subsequent book on Siberia is quite a standard communist journey reportage, glorifying the Soviet subjugation of the wilderness.[158] Nevertheless, a few of his encounters are remarkable, as is the way he reported them. One incidence begins as simply as: "'Down with the Soviet government! Down with the GPU [Soviet secret police] criminals!!' I heard correctly; it was not a mistake." This unbelievable protest came from the mouth of a young anarchist, banned to exile in Siberia. A doctor working nearby explained the situation to a perplexed Heller: "What could be done with such people? It is very good for them here. Here they can shout as much as they want."[159] Heller's straightforward account of this outspoken protest depicted an alleged benevolent grace of the regime toward its opponents.

In one of his sailings in Siberia, he met a German dentist, who, to Heller's rather bourgeois surprise, had traveled in the fourth class. To Heller's inquiry, the doctor replied a bit sarcastically: "I am an ideal communist, should I travel in the first class and these poor people in the fourth?" Heller was not convinced: "What does it have to do with communism? In a few years we shall all equally travel easily and cleanly!"[160]

In a remote town, "three days far from the main road of Siberia, on the edge of culture," Heller was shocked to find "a very beautiful synagogue with a big dome." The place was almost entirely empty of Jews. One of the few Jews he met there, with whom Heller could somehow communicate in broken Germanized Yiddish, was banished from Kiev for speculative trade in foreign currency. Another one, the local *Shames* (synagogue attendant), Moyshe, depicted as a backward traditional Jew, according to the stereotype of the so-called *Ostjuden* (German pejorative for Jews from Eastern Europe), informed the suspicious stranger that only fifteen Jews were left in the place, while the rest had emigrated. The synagogue was then destined to become a club for the railroad workers. Heller expressed his empathy toward Moyshe's sorrow, but with his readers he shared his joy: "Next year the red flag will flutter over the last synagogue in northern Siberia."[161]

Later in his travels, Heller met a certain Abramowicz, obviously a Jew, who offered him some of his alcoholic goods. The communist idealist was again puzzled: "Are there still private breweries here? [. . .] Owning private breweries and houses, how do you actually imagine the dictatorship of the proletariat?"[162]

Heller's confusion from certain unexpected realities that he experienced in the Soviet Union can be well understood though the words of another German-speaking Jewish communist, Arthur Koestler, who traveled as a journalist through the land of "Utopia" a few years after Heller. Retrospectively, after he had already broken with communism, Koestler reflected on this experience.

> I learnt to classify automatically everything that shocked me as the "heritage of the past" and everything I liked as the "seeds of the future." By setting up this automatic sorting machine in his mind, it was still possible in 1932 for a European to live in Russia and yet to remain a communist. [. . .] The communist mind has perfected the techniques of self-deception in the same manner as its techniques of mass propaganda. The "inner censor" in the mind of the true believer completes the work of the public censor; his self-discipline is as tyrannical as the obedience imposed by the regime; he terrorizes his own conscience into submission.[163]

The fact that Heller, just like Koestler, spoke only "some Russian," probably made the work of the "sorting machine" even easier.[164] Besides his surprise from the gap between the communist ideal and the Soviet reality, Heller's reports also reflect his stereotypical impressions from his first encounters with Jews in Russia. In his eyes, they appeared as either backward traditional people or as illegal small traders. In any case, they have not yet integrated into the new socialist society, which supposedly offered them full emancipation for the first time in history. Was it there, in Siberia, that the idea to write a book on the Jewish question in the Soviet Union was born?

Following his return to Berlin, by the latest in January 1930, Heller's book *Sibirien* indeed was published in Münzenberg's

"Communist book of the month club," named *"Universum-Bucherei für Alle"* (Universe-Library for all), which, similarly to *Die Welt am Abend*, addressed as wide a readership as possible.[165] Nevertheless, Heller did not return to fill any significant function in the Party or in its press, only occasionally contributing to *Inprekor* or to *Berlin am Morgen* (Berlin in the Morning), the new morning edition of *Die Welt am Abend*, edited by Heller's Austrian (and Jewish) colleague, Bruno Frei.[166] Heller mainly traveled around Europe, lecturing about Siberia, funded by Münzenberg's gigantic propaganda mechanism.[167] One of the stops on his lecture tour was Vienna.[168] One can only wonder if he met his mother and siblings on this occasion, and, if so, how they received his political activity.

Besides the possible personal and political reasons for Heller's dismissal, it should also be considered in a Jewish context. Parallel to its "Stalinization," the German Communist Party went through a less discernible but determined process that could be called de-Judaization. Under Thälmann's leadership, since 1925, fewer Jews appeared in representative functions on behalf of the Party. In 1924, six of the sixty-two communist Reichstag members were of Jewish origins. In the late 1920s, the number fluctuated between one and three, and in 1932, among hundred communist representatives none were Jews.[169] Fischer, Scholem, Eisler, Thalheimer, and many other high-ranking communists of Jewish descent were "purged." Despite some exceptions within the lower ranks, such as the above-mentioned nomination of Frei, Heller's Jewish origins must have also added to the political and personal background behind his dismissal.

The de-Judaization of the Communist Party accelerated from 1930 onward. By late 1929, the economic crisis that had begun on Wall Street had thrown Europe, particularly Germany as the most industrialized country in the continent, into a severe and prolonged period of recession and unemployment. Against this backdrop, nationalistic and antisemitic propaganda, especially of the National-Socialist German Workers Party (Nationalsozialistische Deutsche Arbeiterpartei [NSDAP]), gained growing successes. In 1931, the KPD, by Stalin's command, adopted a "national-communist" propaganda line to compete the one propagated by the Nazis.[170] Though the KPD could not be considered an antisemitic party, it had occasional anti-Jewish "lapses" in its history; the most salient of which occurred during its nationalistic campaign of the early 1930s.[171] More than antisemitic views, it was the tactic of avoiding being publicly conceived as a pro-Jewish party that directed KPD propaganda. This was particularly important, since antisemitism was rapidly spreading among the growing public of unemployed workers, who increasingly tended toward Nazism. Many members and voters left the Communist Party in favor of Nazism.[172] To some extent, this process was also used as a pretext to expel many of Thälmann's rivals, who happened to be of Jewish descent.

Alongside with Stalinization and de-Judaization, an anti-intellectual atmosphere was unfolding in the Communist Party, following the admiration of leaders of proletarian origins, especially the praised Thälmann, who were conceived as gifted with "a kind of instinct rooted in class-consciousness." There was here, as Koestler remarked, "a distinct parallel [. . .] with the Nazis' contempt for 'destructive Jewish cleverness' as opposed to the 'healthy and natural instinct of the race.'"[173] Since most of the Jewish functionaries, whose presence was diluted, were also intellectuals, it was more than a mere "parallel." KPD anti-intellectualism was practically, to a great extent, directed against its Jewish members as a pretext to distance them. In his apologetics regarding both his bourgeois origins and his intellectualism, Heller was implicitly apologizing for his Jewishness, too.

What impact did the Communist party's anti-Jewish inclination have on Heller's decision to write *The Decline of Judaism*? Was this the origin of his interest in the Jewish question, or did it already exist in a latent form, awakened by the events? As crucial as these questions are for the present research, they have no definite answers. In March 1929, shortly after he lost his job in the newspaper, Heller wrote a letter to the Austrian-Jewish writer Robert Neumann, telling him that now, as he was unemployed, he has "time to read novels." Harshly criticizing Neumann's latest novel, Heller admitted his envy of his addressee's writing skills: "I say [it] with envy. Because for two years I have been carrying a book and I cannot write it. You are better off."[174] Did Heller attempt to write a novel, or was it *The Decline of Judaism* that he was struggling with? It is not even known if in June 1930, when Heller left for Birobidzhan, he viewed it as merely another journey reportage, or as a comprehensive book on Jewish history and the Jewish question.

56 | Radical Assimilation in the Face of the Holocaust

Figure 1.3. Otto Heller. Courtesy of the Papineau-Heller Family Archive (PHFA), Paris.

Off to Birobidzhan

It is unknown whether Heller took this journey to Birobidzhan, through many other Jewish colonies and communities in the Soviet Union, of his own accord or if he was ordered by some communist institution. Considering the KDP's lack of interest in the Jewish question, it is unlikely to have been a German initiative. Indeed, *The Decline of Judaism* was not published by the KPD, but rather by a Comintern-affiliated publishing house.[175] Moreover, for his travel in the Soviet Union, Heller received a letter from the Executive Committee of the Comintern (ECCI), signed by a prominent German representative, approving that Heller was "known to us as a reliable comrade," notwithstanding the previous suspicions against him.[176] Maybe his reputation in the Party had somewhat recovered after the publication of

Sibirien. Such "to whom it may concern" letters, explained by Koestler from his own experience, "serve as a kind of passport in the Soviet Union. It is on their strength that the citizen [or visitor] obtains his permits, his accommodation, ration card, and so on."[177] Heller's certificate, from the ECCI, was considered "strong." However, it disclosed nothing about the journey's destination or its anticipated product.

Regardless of whoever initiated the journey and the wished-for outcome, the motivation behind it must be understood against the background of the developments in the Soviet policy concerning the Jewish question. Different from the "paradigm of assimilation" that prevailed among Marxist Jews in Western Europe, in the Soviet Union, Jewish national consciousness was practically enhanced by the regime, starting from the revolution in 1917 up until the early 1930s.[178] This policy was not reserved for Jews. As the historian of Soviet nationalities policy Terry Martin showed, the Soviet Union was systematically promoting the national consciousness of its ethnic minorities, as part of what the Bolsheviks saw as a decolonization process. Martin defined the early Soviet Union as *The Affirmative Action Empire* for its support of national territories, languages, elites, and identities, which made it a multiethnic state. This affirmative action was, nevertheless, instrumentally designed to recruit ethnic support for the revolution, while at the same time disarming nationalism by granting minorities some "forms" of nationhood. The Bolsheviks saw nationalism as an unavoidable historical phase on the way to internationalism that would persist under socialism and, initially, even increase. Only in the long run, after all of the oppressed nations obtained complete freedom, would an inevitable fusion of nations peacefully occur. As the Bolsheviks adhered to a territorial form of nationhood, territorially dispersed national minorities formed a unique problem for the regime. This challenge was approached by establishing national territorial soviets (councils, or administrative units), based on the demographic majority in every republic, district, or municipality, down to the level of the village, until this system paradoxically "merged seamlessly with the [principle of] personal nationality," which was theoretically rejected.[179]

The Jewish question posed an even greater dilemma for the Bolsheviks, who, on the one hand, opposed antisemitism, while, on the other hand, were hostile to what they saw as Jewish commerce. The compact resettlement of Jews in agricultural colonies was suggested as a solution to both the territorial as well as the economic aspects of the problem. By 1931, 127 Jewish national village soviets and four national districts were formed in south Ukraine and Crimea, to allow the Jews "to better develop their national culture."[180] The Soviet nationalities policy, in general, and in the Jewish case, particularly, stood in contrast to the Western Marxist paradigm of assimilation, as it actively "opposed assimilation and supported the preservation of nationality."[181]

While ideological support for Jewish nationalism within the Soviet Union persisted throughout that period, the actual policy toward the Jews shifted. In the early years, under Lenin, the Jews were acknowledged as one among the various nationalities of the Soviet Union, whose formal national language was Yiddish. The *Evsektsiia* (the Jewish Section of the Communist Party) supported Yiddish cultural, educational, and administrative institutions. The *Evsektsiia* oversaw the establishment of Jewish agricultural settlements, which enjoyed various degrees of autonomy. Besides the ideal of "productivization," the resettlement served the acute need of hundreds of thousands of Jews, damaged and impoverished by pogroms, civil war, and the exclusion from their former livelihoods as small traders and artisans.[182]

Like many other policies under Stalin, the nationalities policy changed as well, as national oppression gradually emerged during the 1930s. While in the eastern parts of the Soviet Union the cultivation of so-called backward nationalities increased, oppressive measures started targeting "advanced" nationalities that inhabited the western regions, with special emphasis on diasporic nationalities.[183] This shift critically impacted Soviet Jewry, though in a perplexing way, because, in the beginning, their national oppression was disguised as a far-reaching acknowledgment of their national rights. In 1928, the Soviet government allocated a territory in the Soviet Far East, between the Bira and Bidzhan Rivers, "for the purpose of the dense settlement of free land by working Jews," with the possibility of forming a "Jewish, national, administrative-territorial entity."[184]

Why settle Jews in this remote wasteland on the Chinese border, 4,000 miles from the centers of Jewish life in the western Soviet republics and undermine the prospect of the already started settlement movement? Scholarship has established that, notwithstanding its rhetorical legitimization of Jewish nationalism, the Stalinist regime tried to manipulate Jews to Birobidzhan to serve its own goals. Some of these goals particularly concerned the Jews, such as channeling the remnants of Jewish nationalist ideologies, mainly Zionism and Bundism, as far as possible from the political centers of the state; easing the protest of non-Jewish farmers, especially Tatars in Crimea, against Jewish settlement in their surrounding; and diluting the salient presence of Jews among white-collar professions in the cities. Other, more important goals were entirely unrelated to the Jews, such as populating the Far East as a bulwark against Japanese imperialist aspirations and Chinese infiltration; utilizing the natural resources of the region; and generally diluting the overcrowded urban centers in the west of the country. The Jews were viewed as a convenient instrument for these and other goals, due to their ability to raise financial and political support from their brethren in Western countries, on behalf of the traditional philanthropic cause of settling Jews on the ground in the East (be it in Tsarist Russia or in Palestine), and thus decreasing their immigration to the West.[185]

If any of these undeclared goals were known to Heller as he set off on his long journey to Birobidzhan in June 1930, it did not affect his enthusiasm, expressed in his paraphrase on the Jewish traditional liturgic yearning for Jerusalem: "Next year in Birobidzhan!"[186] Like many other sympathizers, whether communist or not or Jewish or not, Heller was enchanted by the bold pioneering plan of Jewish settlement, serving both Jewish productivization, as well as Soviet conquest and the cultivation of the wilderness. Moreover, for opponents of Zionism, Birobidzhan provided a heroic alternative to the Zionist ethos of "a new Jewish man," the farmer-settler pioneer (ḥaluṣ). In Heller's words, it was a "completely different Palestine, the red counter-Palestine."[187]

Later, in *The Decline of Judaism*, Heller attempted to interpret the Soviet form of Jewish national ideology in an intelligible way for his German-reading audience. This intermediation was challenged by inner contradictions and struggles, which characterized the development of the Soviet nationalities policy. The different lines implemented under Lenin and Stalin were both represented within the *Evsektsiia*, creating conflict between the supporters of Crimea and Birobidzhan.[188] Whether he was aware of this rivalry or not, Heller considered both projects as two harmoniously coexisting Soviet models to solving the Jewish question. In fact, behind the scenes, the later policy line was subjecting the former. The realization of the Birobidzhan plan coincided with the dissolution of the *Evsektsiia,* in early 1930, as part of the liquidation of all the Party sections of national minorities in the Soviet Union.[189] While the very existence of *Evsektsiia* expressed the national pluralism from Lenin's time, Birobidzhan, though decorated with nationalist rhetoric, was an instrument of the national oppression of Stalin's time. Heller, however, overlooked this tension. For him, Birobidzhan was to be the jewel in the crown of Jewish settlement and thus the climax of his journey through other settlements in Ukraine and Crimea, as well as Jewish traditional communities in the Soviet Caucasus and Central Asia.

Heller reported on this journey in the third part of *The Decline of Judaism*. Like his previous accounts of former journeys, it was written in the reportage genre, inspired by a new style modeled after E. E. Kisch's reports from his journeys to the Soviet Union in the mid-1920s that combined "factography," history, and political enthusiasm, in a very dynamic form.[190] From the very beginning of his description of the Jewish settlements in Ukraine, Heller employed formal Soviet nationalist terminology regarding Jewish settlers, as, for example, in "the Jewish *National* rayon Stalindorf [Yiddish for Stalin-village]."[191] But more than that, he also enhanced a nationalist emotional language: "Even though *this soil is soaked with Jewish blood*—bloody pogroms occurred in those very same districts, not merely three-hundred years ago, in Chmelnicky's time, but also in the times of Petliura and Denikin—the mutual life of Jews and Ukrainians is distinguished."[192] Here, Heller tried to reconcile a Jewish national martyrologic narrative with an idyllic image of fraternity among the Soviet Union's nations. He could not have known that twelve years later, in the very same district, many of the local Ukrainians would participate in another slaughter of their Jewish neighbors, whom they saw as collaborators of the despised Soviet regime.[193]

In Crimea too, Heller presented the relationship between Tatars and Jews as a proof of the "abyss [. . .] between that kind of [Jewish] colonization and the adventure in Palestine [. . .]. Why should the Jews not farm the empty land [in Crimea]?"[194] But just like Palestine, Crimea appeared not to be empty. Many of the Tatars, who, already in the 1920s objected to Jewish settlement, emerged in the 1940s as the most reliable pro-German group in the peninsula, who enthusiastically took part in the liquidation of Crimean Jewry.[195] Obviously, it is easier for the historian to note these trends retrospectively than for Heller in 1930, and yet, as the tensions between Jewish settlers and local farmers were known, Heller probably consciously idealized a reality of latent conflicts as a harmonious coexistence.

As in his travels in Siberia, Heller again employed what Koestler called the "sorting machine."[196] In the "international" village of Choritza, inhabited by Germans, Jews, and Ukrainians, a synagogue still existed. As Heller entered, he saw only one old man reading the Talmud, a "gloomy" residue of the past. Contrarily, pig breeding by Jewish farmers was "a quiet, humoristic and symbolic protest *against* the past."[197] In the Jewish colony Kalinindorf, named after the contemporary president of the Soviet Union and the ideological champion of the new Jewish nationalistic rhetoric, Heller discovered that young settlers were emigrating "back in the city." His "sorting machine" classified them as "anti-collective, petit-bourgeois elements." Reassuring the reader and himself, Heller disregarded this as a mere "historically conditioned fluctuation," a side-effect of rapid industrialization, which created new opportunities in trained professions, like engineering, management, and so on. This would not change, so he claimed, the general tendency toward an occupational shift (*Umschichtungsprozess*) to productive labor among Jews.[198]

In Crimea, Heller was most excited by the settlement of Nova Vojo (Esperanto for New Way): "It is a commune that was founded in 1928 by returnees from the Zionist commune '*Gdud ha-Avoda*' [Hebrew for Labor Battalion] in Palestine [. . .] under the impression of the *forlornness* of organizing socialist life in Palestine."[199] For Heller, it was the best evidence for the victory of the Soviet way over the Zionist one. In reality, Nova Vojo experienced latent but forceful tensions from its beginning, between pioneers from Palestine and newcomers, among the former themselves, and between the settlers and the authorities. These tensions brought about a grave crisis in the settlement, which broke out in the autumn of 1930, shortly after Heller's visit.[200]

Before traveling to the next center of Jewish communes, Heller had an interlude, visiting some traditional Jewish communities. In Georgia, he met Jews who were so observant that, after a fire in the Jewish quarter had ruined their houses, they refused to receive new ones on the other side of the river, so that, on their way to the synagogue, they would not have to violate the Jewish prohibition of crossing a river on the Sabbath. This was the "heritage of the past," but there were also "seeds of the future." Although the socialization of labor in Georgia was admittedly slow, Heller reported that a collectivization of the crafts was progressing without any serious opposition. He saw the relation of the Jews to the local Soviet authorities as very good. After the Tsarist repression, the Soviet regime was perceived as a "safe roof."[201]

But not everything was idyllic, even to Heller. The Soviet constitution had denied suffrage to "non-working elements." Heller saw the broad implementation of that regulation imposed on Jews as problematic, due to their existence as a "special social stratum": "This constitutional rule has often been applied to Jews in an *oppressive* [*drückenden*] way. [. . .] Moreover, for Jews, the terms trader and entrepreneur were often not clearly determined [*eindeutig bestimmt*]. A trader, merchant, or artisan, who also possibly used the labor of others, even if it was only the labor of his wife, son, or daughter, fell under those whose suffrage was denied, although he is nothing other than a proletarian." In the theoretical part of his work, Heller denied the existence of antisemitism in the Soviet Union, giving rise to the claim that he deliberately covered up the fact that antisemitism was still very common under communism.[202] Nevertheless, here, in his journey reportage, he explained the discussed case not as a mere bureaucratic fault, but rather as stemming from "national hate," existing among "inferior authorities." Heller hurried to reassure his readers that, in Georgia, this problem was solved by bestowing suffrage to each person who had been working for six months and who showed a positive attitude toward the Soviet system.[203] This contradiction between the theoretical denial of antisemitism in the Soviet Union and its empiric depiction exemplifies of the complex nature of *The Decline of Judaism*.

In Central Asia, the Bucharian Jews served as the ultimate proof of Heller's caste theory. Despite their long-standing isolation from other Jewish communities, they filled "exactly that same social function" as the rest of the Jews: "bearers of commodity circulation, traders, intermediaries, and eventually also small artisans. [. . .] There is no other explanation but their common national origins, that restore the same starting point in the sphere of production."[204]

Heller's metaphorical portrayal of his encounter with Buchara's chief rabbi is instructive. "We [Heller and his local escort] entered, blinded, into the dark shades of the gate."[205] The rabbi, emblematic of the darkness of backwardness, expressed his fear of progress: "In twenty years, who will still visit the synagogue?" But when leaving the rabbi's court, if the reader expected the relief of returning into the lights of enlightenment, this was not exactly so: "The door sprang open. We entered the adventurous [*abenteuerliche*] noon-glow."[206] Why was the daylight neither redemptive nor liberating, but "adventurous," an adjective that could be also translated as quixotic or hazardous? Was it merely the strong southern sunshine that Heller's eyes were not accustomed to or the exotic atmosphere of an oriental bazaar?[207] Did the "adventurous noon-glow" symbolize the extremely slow progress of the revolution in Uzbekistan, especially in the Jewish sphere?[208] Or was Heller revealing doubts regarding the Soviet venture?

Headed northward to Novosibirsk, he notes that "the rough Siberian winds had let me forget the Central Asian heat very quickly," perhaps also calming his doubts.[209] Only later will Heller reveal that he was compelled to shorten his tour in Birobidzhan due to a "malicious fever, that I have picked up in Central Asia."[210] Was his old ailment invoked by bad conditions and mental stress? From Novosibirsk, it took Heller five days by train to reach Birobidzhan.[211] At that time, the place was still known as Tikhonkaya, meaning "Little Quiet One," or "someone's polite way of saying 'godforsaken,'" as Masha Gessen suggested.[212] Directly from Moscow, it would have taken no less than ten days.[213]

In the summer of 1930, the Jewish settlement in Birobizhan was still in its very inception, extremely poor: "In the background forest and hills and semi-marsh [. . .] some Cossack huts and barracks." But it was also highly promising: "On the left a cooperative with a Yiddish inscription and [. . .] the first telephone! [. . .] Agrarian plans. Woodland cleaning plans, railroad plans, building plans: the plan is everything."[214] Heller's "sorting machine" was immediately activated. The "heritage of the past" was definitely present, which was appalling for Heller. In the only restaurant, "the host and personnel: Jews, the guests: Jews, the noise: Jewish and unfortunately the dirt too is all too much reminding of the ghetto, which was only just escaped."[215] However, there were also "seeds of the future," though only seeds: "In Birobidzhan, the Jews are not speaking less than anywhere else— though they are less loud, [as] they are preoccupied by the problem of conquering a land. They gesticulate indeed, but their hands are heavy of hard work. The Jews are a nervous people. There is nothing better for their disposition than fresh air. The people in Birobidzhan are loaded with energies and desire, they are tense, explosive—but they are not nervous."[216] Heller's stereotypical image of the *Ostjude*, which was already expressed in *Sibirien*, recurs, emphasizing that the longed-for change has only begun.

Perhaps the most symbolic visual image of the contrast between past and future was the half-paved road to the Jewish colony of Valdheym (Yiddish for Forest-Home).[217] Likewise, in the commune of Birefeld (Bira-Field), "the houses of the colonists are quite poor, the school and kindergarten almost squalid. This is partly due to the colony's poverty and partly due to the unskillfulness of the people in leading and directing these institutions." Yet "Birefeld has great possibilities, [. . .] great future. Though the main condition for that (besides better organization) is the road."[218]

Not to dissuade the reader from communal life, Heller confronted it with the American ethos of the individualist pioneer through his story of "a maverick [*Ein Eigenbrötler*]."

> He was a former lawyer from a medium-sized Ukrainian town. Many of his relatives had fallen victims to pogroms [and] he himself left Ukraine [. . .], sold his library, left the entire Western European culture behind him, and moved to Birobidzhan [. . .]. He broke off with the past, took off the old Adam and took on a new one. No one who met him in Birobidzhan could have had any idea that an intellectual stood before them, an eminent lawyer, who besides Russian and Yiddish, spoke French and German fluently.[219]

But he was "bitter and lonely," because he would not join the collective.[220] Was that Heller's own dream and nightmare at once? Did he see himself abandoning his convenient intellectual life, settling in the wilderness, living in a collective, and materializing a Jewish national community? In that sense, Heller resembled some Western assimilated bourgeois Jews who supported Zionism or Diaspora nationalism as a worthwhile project for the "Eastern Jews," but not for themselves.

Theoretically, however, Heller found in Birobidzhan an antithesis both to Western colonialism and to what he saw as its Zionist variant: "Birobidzhan is not a colonial land with brown, yellow, or black people, who cheaply cultivate the land [. . .] with their bare hands [. . .] but] a collective of people allied by machines."[221] The closing lines of his report are full of pathos: "The Palestine-dream will have been a distant history, when in Birobidzhan cars, trains, and steamers will run, chimneys of huge factories will smoke, and the children of free Jewish workers and farmers will bop around blooming gardens."[222]

Back in Berlin, Heller established the local branch of Geserd (Gesellschaft zur Förderung des jüdischen Siedlungswerkes in der UdSSR, Association for Supporting the Jewish Settlements in the Soviet Union), the German-Yiddish counterpart of the Russian Ozet, a public association initiated by the Soviet state to mobilize support for the enterprises of Jewish settlement.[223] He was likely recruited for this task by Münzenberg.[224] Did Heller take it on because he "returned excited" from Birobidzhan, or because "it must have been very attractive for Heller who was himself Jewish"?[225] Or, was it Münzenberg's way of compensating a cherished comrade, whom he was compelled to cut off from a livelihood in the communist press?[226] Or, maybe, assigning a Jewish activist to a "Jewish" job was another expression of de-Judaization of the Party.

As the secretary of Geserd, in addition to writing for its journal and also composing *The Decline of Judaism*, Heller extensively toured Europe, conducted support assemblies for the organization, and lectured about the Jewish question and its Soviet solution (among other places, in Vienna).[227] He protested against the contribution of Matzot to Soviet Jews as an "anti-Soviet measure," and regularly debated rabbis and Zionists.[228] He provocatively titled one of his fiercest attacks against Zionism "Jüdische Nationalsozialisten" ("Jewish National-Socialists"), implying a common cause to the "*Hakenkreuz*" (swastika) and "*Hakenstren*" (a portmanteau of swastika and Star of David), namely, to National Socialists and Zionists.[229]

At that period, Heller was barely active in the Communist Party. His only "non-Jewish" activity was teaching at the "Marxist workers-school" in Berlin.[230] A handwritten letter from June 1932, from which only the last page has been preserved in the Comintern archives, reveals some of the suspicions that still loomed over Heller's head. The letter denounced him for having a "strong inclination to bourgeois dealings [*Umgang*]," especially lately, as he "was entirely cut off from the party."[231] This explains his restriction to Jewish issues and his exclusion from general party politics.

In mid-1932, Heller took a few months off of his new focus on Jewish issues to go on a journalistic journey to Vladivostok, to report on the Soviet "campaign for the Far East," "the socialist building of

East Siberia," and "the secret of [Japanese expansion in] Manchuria," then triumphantly concluding with "red flags on the Pacific."[232] His reports from that journey also paid some attention to the national question in these remote areas of the Soviet Union. From Irkutsk, he reported the beginning of "the work of editing learning books for each of the individual northern peoples, which live in the district and all of which have obtained their autonomy."[233] In this way, Heller integrated Birobidzhan into a wider context of the Soviet policy of national autonomies that was still flourishing in the East, while in the West its demise had begun.

During this journey, Heller returned to Birobidzhan, two years after his last visit, and he could not hide his disappointment: "Maybe more could have been done in Tikhonkaya-Birobidzhan in those two years. [. . .] There were re-migrants, there were too many of them."[234] Indeed, between 1928 and 1933, 60 percent of the approximately 20,000 Jewish immigrants to Birobidzhan had left.[235] On his first visit, Heller reported that "the Jews constituted eight percent of the population in Birobidzhan," and predicted that, "this percentage will increase to 25–30 until 1933."[236] At its apogee, in 1935, this rate did not exceed 16 percent, meaning 8,000 Jewish inhabitants.[237] The main explanations for the downfall, in this initial stage, were the extremely harsh weather and land conditions, organization difficulties, and a lack of motivation among Soviet Jews to undertake the enormous challenge.[238] These obstacles would pale in comparison with later events that would undermine "Otto Heller's glorious prophecy" for Birobidzhan.[239]

∽

From his childhood in Vienna at the fin-de-siècle, the social, national, and Jewish questions challenged the Jewish bourgeois liberalism into which Heller was born. Only after the death of his father, during the First World War, did Heller begin his oedipal rebellion against his heritage, turning to socialism. Only once he was away from his family in Czechoslovakia did Heller complete his revolt by radicalizing into his unique Bohemian version of communism, with German nationalistic excess. In Germany, that nationalistic twist disappeared, making Heller a typical communist universalist of Weimar Berlin, though leaving in him a special sensitivity to the national question.

Never before had Heller shown the slightest attention to Jewish concerns, until he was struck by the simultaneous Stalinization, de-Judaization, and anti-intellectualism of the KPD. The fact that Heller started showing interest in the Jewish question at the same time he was severely accused in deviating the Party line questions the common understanding of him as an ideal representative of this line. As an unemployed and politically suspicious communist journalist of Jewish origins, Heller found both intellectual refuge and livelihood in the Jewish question. Pushed away from Berlin's Party politics, it was eventually his journey to Birobidzhan that sparked his interest in Jewishness, while he still actively denied his own Jewish belonging. The return of his repressed Jewishness was only beginning.

According to Schorske, each of the great Viennese political rebels against liberalism at the fin-de-siècle had his own domestic foe. For Schönerer, it was German liberalism; for Lueger, Catholic liberalism; and for Herzl, Jewish liberalism.[240] Heller continued this by making Zionism his arch enemy. In this way, he posed himself within a Jewish discourse. Wistrich maintained that "the tensions induced by cultural assimilation in the Austrian context, undoubtedly produced many cases of torn identity and divided selves among the Jewish intelligentsia."[241] This was characteristic of many Viennese Jewish intellectuals and artists who were active around fin-de-siècle, and less common in Heller's later generation, only born around the turn of the century. Many of his contemporary fellow communists of Jewish origins seemed to be freed from such complexes. None of them demonstrated such a "torn identity" and "divided self" as Heller did when he became an expert on the Jewish question through writing *The Decline of Judaism*.

Chapter 2

The Decline of Judaism (1931)

Q.: "In Slovakia, as far as I understand, lectures by Otto Heller were forbidden."

A.: "Indeed. But we arranged lectures *against* him."

—From an interview with Yeḥi'el Harari,
Kibbutz Eyn-Shemer, Israel, 1964

From a retrospective of three decades, a graduate the socialist-Zionist youth movement Hashomer Hatzair (The Young Guard) in Bratislava, Yeḥi'el Harari, was interviewed about his experience in the movement's branch. When he was asked about "personalities, books and world events, which left their impression on the movement" during the interwar period, the first thing that came to his mind was Otto Heller's book, *The Decline of Judaism*.[1] As the movement was facing growing inclination toward communism among its membership, a popular communist book on the Jewish question posed a real threat, and thus was fiercely criticized.[2] This anecdote provides a glimpse into the agitated controversy ignited by that book. While in Germany Heller took part in evenings of public debate over his book, at the same time even in Czechoslovakia, from which he had been expelled in 1926, debates were held in his absence.[3]

The Decline of Judaism fell like a spark into the powder keg known as "the Jewish question" in Europe of the early 1930s. Within less than three years of its publication in October 1931, the book was translated into French and Polish, and a second German edition, "revised and extended," came out.[4] Excerpts were printed in periodicals, not only in German, but also in translations to Yiddish and Hungarian.[5] Reviews appeared in almost every Jewish newspaper and journal in the German language, published by liberal and religious circles, and by Zionists of center, left- or right-wing orientation.[6] Some Zionists even published entire books against Heller.[7] At the same time, it invoked a discussion among opposed Marxist streams: communists, social-democrats, Marxist-Zionists, and unaffiliated Marxist thinkers.[8] Dozens of lectures were held all across Europe, by Heller himself, and by his criticizers.[9] He became a popular speaker, not only in communist youth organizations but also in Zionist ones, who were eager to confront him.[10] In some cases, a lecture given by Heller was answered by a counterlecture, organized in the same city.[11] In some Jewish youth groups that oscillated between Zionism and communism, Heller's book and lectures were received with mixed feelings and initiated internal debates.[12]

The discussion over Heller's book holds the quintessence of the tense, diverse, and contradictory discourse on the Jewish question in the twentieth century. Even many years later, after it had already almost disappeared from the Jewish public discourse, the book kept serving anti-Zionist circles in the Middle East and Europe as a propaganda weapon in their struggle against Israel. As such, the German original was reprinted by the "Palestine Committee" in Bonn in 1975, and was translated to Turkish in 1992.[13]

Why was *The Decline of Judaism* so provocative? This chapter will address this question through the contemporary reception history of the book. The aim of this chapter is neither to reiterate the debate over Heller's book nor to join it, but to exceed it through a critical observation of the discussion itself. So far, the reception of Heller's book was examined through on a handful of reviews, published in journals in the German language.[14] Turning to other spheres of reception—written in Yiddish, in Hebrew, in the German daily press, or even in private letters—reveals two acute aspects that have been overlooked: an intra-communist debate over the notion of a Jewish proletariat, and an intra-Marxist debate over the notion of a Jewish nation.[15] Those new viewpoints shake the widespread notion of *The Decline of Judaism* among scholars as a mere schematic orthodox Marxist book, dogmatically dismissing Jewish nationalism.[16] Few of the more sensitive contemporary readers (and even fewer later scholars), who approached the book from different social and political angles, pointed to many details and inner contradictions that distort this general view. This chapter follows their observations.

Before turning to its reception history, a summary of the book itself is indispensable. *The Decline of Judaism: The Jewish Question, Its Critique, Its Solution through Socialism* is a book combining historical and theoretical inquiry with the assertion of a political stance, shaped according to the Marxist tradition of writing. The quintessence of the book is condensed in one of its opening sentences: "Like all other problems, originated in the contradictions of the former social systems [. . .], the Jewish question comes forward again in the period of extreme intensification of the class-struggles, at the time of the beginning of the proletarian revolution."[17] The language is typically Marxist as well as the method of explaining political and cultural phenomena through socioeconomic relations, and especially class struggles. The Jewish question is viewed here as one of many manifestations of the general social question, which emerged from the rule of private property. Accordingly, it was to be solved as part of the universal solution to the social question, namely, through socialism.

The Decline of Judaism consists of three sections, presenting Jewish history, Soviet policy, and a reportage of Heller's own journey to the Soviet Union. The first, historical part—titled "Beginning and End"—offers a Marxist synthesis of Jewish history.[18] It was the first attempt up until then to bring the entirety of Jewish history under the scrutiny of the materialist method.[19] The chronological narrative was supplemented by discussion of three overarching themes: Jewish religion,[20] antisemitism,[21] and Jewish nationalism.[22] Heller's main historical argument was that throughout their history, the Jews have been a "caste" of traders, existing as a distinct group due to their economic function as facilitating the circulation of commodities and money. Judaism was defined by Heller as a religious super-structure reflecting the economic position of the Jews, while also serving to preserve this position by isolating them from their social environment. The term *caste*, borrowed from the rigid hierarchical structure of traditional society in India and already applied to Jews by Kautsky, Max Weber, and others, characterized the social role of the Jews as precapitalist.[23] In opposition to the division of capitalist society into classes according to their relation to the means of production, castes imply a much more complex social division, in which ethnicity, religion, and social function overlap. In capitalist societies, which were altogether commercialized, where commerce no longer formed a separate segment of the economy, the Jews were to lose their special role, maintained Heller. In the most developed capitalist countries of Western Europe, Judaism was thus doomed to disappear, with the Jews being assimilated into the bourgeoisie.[24]

The second, political part—titled "The Great Work"—presents the policy of the Soviet Union regarding its Jewish population as the ultimate solution to the Jewish question.[25] Here Heller had to reconcile Stalin's former theoretical denial of Jewish nationhood with the leader's new policy, granting Soviet Jewry a national autonomous region.[26] Already in the historical part of his book, Heller claimed that in still "half feudal" and only partly capitalized Eastern Europe, where Jews were still concentrated in densely populated centers, their mainly commercial economic role was to some extent still intact.[27] Thus, they were significantly less assimilated than in Western Europe. For this reason, it was enough for the Soviet government to bestow the Jews with the most important criterion that their nationality lacked, according to Stalin's definition—a territory, to solve the Jewish question in the Soviet Union.[28]

The third part of the book is a "Protocol of a Journey" made by Heller through various Jewish communities and agricultural settlements in the Soviet Union, all the way to Birobidzhan, the newly announced autonomous Jewish district in the Soviet Far East.[29] His glorification of the Soviet solution of the Jewish question stands in bold contrast with his depiction of Zionism as an illusionary attempt, doomed to failure, as it was ensconced within the framework of capitalist society, as a proxy of British imperialism.[30]

Sunset or Sunrise?

The title *The Decline of Judaism* implies a book advocating the disappearance of Judaism, according to an extreme communist version of the assimilationist vision. And indeed, Heller's main argument in the historical part of the book explicates its title, by analyzing the process of assimilation in Western countries as deterministically leading to the total vanishing of the Jewish population. Most contemporary readers and moreover later scholars focused their reactions on the title and the first part.³¹ If Heller aimed not only at attracting attention to his book, but also at putting forward his claim that under socialism Jewish existence would revive—not decline—then the title might have only distracted the readers' mind from this message.

Erich Fromm, the Frankfurt school thinker and psychoanalyst, was one of the few to note that the title was "unintelligible," as it was incompatible with two-thirds of the book, which advocated a Jewish national revival in the Soviet Union.³² Another reviewer suggested, for similar reasons, an alternative title: "the transformation of Judaism."³³ The German word translated here as "decline," *Untergang*, is used also in the context of sunset, *Sonnenuntergang* (literally: decline of the sun). Considering this metaphor, the book's title could be read completely differently: the sun indeed sets in the West—just like Judaism, according to Heller—but it always rises anew in the East, in this case—in the Soviet Far East, in Birobidzhan. Over there, the Jewish nation is not declining, but rather rising.

Further investigation into possible sources that might have inspired Heller in choosing his title raises another question regarding its standard reading. As mentioned by an early insightful Zionist commentator, "the title paraphrases the formulation first coined many years ago by our friend, Dr. Felix Theilhaber, [. . .] but Theilhaber pronounced this word as a *warning*, while Heller impinged it on the world *triumphantly*."³⁴ In 1911 the German physician and Zionist activist, Theilhaber, had published research titled *The Decline of German Jews* (*Der Untergang der deutschen Juden*), where he raised an alarm against the rapid demographic decrease of German Jewry, resulting from assimilation, emigration, intermarriage, and low birth rate.³⁵

Though Heller did not admit it, it is reasonable to assume that he borrowed his title from Theilhaber's book, which he had in his possession.³⁶ This hypothesis can be strengthened by the fact that Heller, notwithstanding his harsh polemic against Zionism, leaned much of his argument on Zionist scholars, such as Arthur Ruppin and Jakob Klatzkin, whose warnings resembled Theilhaber's.³⁷ To indicate that the concept of a "decline" of Judaism was prevalent in German Zionist circles is not to suggest that Heller was a hidden Zionist. However, facing the very same social reality and advocating a parallel, though competing, vision of national revival, he turned to the same conceptual framework: revealing the "decline," the sunset, in order to mobilize for the revival, the sunrise, though in a different East.

Obviously, contemporary readers were not in the mind-set of looking for common argumentative structures, as they were themselves embedded in the struggling political-ideological arguments. *The Decline of Judaism* enticed frantic responses from three main groups: Zionists, liberal German Jews, and Marxists, mostly of Jewish origin, too. Previous scholarly surveys have emphasized how each of these streams reacted as expected.[38] In most cases, with several remarkable exceptions that will be discussed later on, it was true. The harshest criticism came from Zionists, some of whom focused on Heller's materialist argumentation, which in their view undermined the resilience of the Jewish national conciseness along history. The young Viennese Zionist, Eli Strauss (later to be known as the Israeli Orientalist Eliyahu Ashtor), criticized Heller for overlooking the role of Jewish "aspiration for self-preservation" in explaining the long historical continuity of Judaism (see figure 2.1).[39] Others attacked him for the timing of the publication of his book, as he turned "to the Jewish youth in the German lands ruled by Hitler and Goebbels making an appeal for national self-destruction."[40] Knowing that some of his readers might be attracted to Marxism, Felix Weltsch wrote in the central Zionist newspaper in Germany that Heller brought the Marxist methodology "ad absurdum."[41]

Socialist Zionists claimed copyright over Marxist Jewish historiography on behalf of Jewish nationalist leftist thinkers and historians: "Long before him [Heller,] Borokhov, Schipper, Zhitlovsky, and others studied various periods of Jewish history using the materialist concept of history in a much more profound manner than Heller did."[42] Heller was presented as "fighting against the windmills" of the ongoing creation of a Jewish "strategic basis"—following the Borokhovist term—in Palestine.[43] The senior Ukrainian economist and Zionist socialist activist, Shalom Goldelman, focused his critique on the Birobidzhan project, which he detested as a "human wall," built by the Soviets against a potential Japanese attack, cynically using the Jews as a "human material" and as a "sacrificial lamb."[44]

The reception of *The Decline of Judaism* among German-Jewish liberals, concentrated around the Central Association of German Citizens of Jewish Faith (Centralverein deutscher Staatsbürger jüdischen Glaubens [CV]), was milder than that of the Zionists, as they shared with Heller his opposition to Zionism.[45] If Zionists could agree with the book's title, while rejecting much of its content, the liberals announced that "the book is not as bad as its title."[46] Acknowledging the ever-worsening "proletarianization process" of German Jews during the economic crisis of the early 1930s, representatives of the Centralverein tried to compete with Heller over the support of impoverished Jews by confronting him in his own field: Marxist thought. In that manner they tried to face the danger of "red assimilation" among this stratum, for whom communism became more and more appealing. Fritz Aronstein wrote in the Centralverein's newspaper against Heller's alleged

> conception, which sees Judaism and proletarian life as irreconcilably opposed, but sees a complete assimilation into forms and contents of proletarian life together with the dissolution of Judaism as the solution of the Jewish question. The temptation of such a solution is understandable. Antisemitism bars the access to many occupational branches, and also has a strong spiritual effect. The struggle for a solution that will promise the German Jews a somewhat different future is enormous, and a way is required to bring the [various] Jewish layers in Germany to an appropriate situation.[47]

But Heller did not reject a synthesis of Jewishness and "proletarian life" whatsoever. He even advocated such a synthesis, though not in Germany, but rather in the Soviet Union. Maintaining that "our future is in Germany," Aronstein agreed with Heller on the irrelevance of the Zionist solution, but for the same reason he declared the "alleged paradise Birobidzhan" as irrelevant too. He attempted to downplay Heller's argumentation through undermining its Marxist foundations. For that purpose, he cited several Marxist thinkers, among them the Austrian Max Adler, who wrote: "The ideal without the material has no impact, the material without the ideal has no direction. [. . .] That is overlooked by Heller!"[48] A similar tactic was employed by sociologist Eva Reichmann-Jungmann, who presented Heller's thesis as contradicting that of Marx and Engels. The founders of Marxism, maintained Reichmann-Jungmann, did not merely assume a "dependence of the ideological super-structure upon the material basis," but rather an "interrelationship between the two spheres."[49]

As opposed to most later scholars, who tended to disparage *The Decline of Judaism*, Heller's contemporaries, even his fervent rivals, took the book seriously. One Zionist criticizer stressed that Heller's book "should not be a priori disregarded with the wave of hand."[50] In the journal of the prestigious liberal Jewish fraternity in Germany, B'nai B'rith, Sigmund Reis expressed his full appreciation of "the first and only work in the German language that offers a most comprehensive enlightenment, all factual, statistical, theoretical, official information" about the situation of Jews in the Soviet Union. He even considered the book as "relevant to every sober Jew."[51]

In many leftist circles *The Decline of Judaism* was accepted enthusiastically. As expected, most reviews in communist newspapers and journals (though not all of them, as detailed below) were highly supportive: "Extremely worth reading and fills a gap in the Marxist literature";[52] "Now, when National-socialism is presenting an egregious demagogy with antisemitic phrases, it is important for revolutionary workers *to grapple with the Jewish question*";[53] "Many non-Jewish workers, especially young, followed the lecture [given by Heller in Vienna] with much interest."[54] Support exceeded the borders of Germany and Austria. In an introduction to a collection of Lenin's references to the Jewish question, published in the Soviet Union in German translation, the publisher referred the reader to further information on the topic in Heller's book.[55] In Chernivtsi, Romania, it was reported that after a discussion on Heller's book, a group of Jewish youngsters repeatedly yelled: "Down with Palestine! Down with Judaism!"[56] In the same city, a local unaffiliated Yiddish weekly published a very sympathetic review.[57]

During the 1930s and 1940s, the book became an informal guide on the Jewish question for communists, mostly in the German-speaking sphere, but also beyond it.[58] It provided a theoretical basis to combat Nazi antisemitism, not only for communists, but also for other leftist opposition groups. The analysis of antisemitism as an expression of class struggle, put forward in 1939 by the leading Frankfurt School intellectual Max Horkheimer, was probably inspired by *The Decline of Judaism*.[59] Even social-democrats were still citing Heller's book after the war.[60]

The main social-democratic critique of the book did not address Heller's thesis, but rather claimed that it was plagiarized from the social-democrat theoreticians and leaders, Karl Kautsky in Germany and Otto Bauer in Austria.[61] Indeed, in the historical part of his book Heller adopted Kautsky's term *caste*, as well as the "paradigm of assimilation," shared by Kautsky and Bauer.[62] But, as Bruno Frei noted, Heller's concept of Jewish national revival in the Soviet Union stood in complete opposition to the paradigm of both thinkers.⁶³

Nevertheless, not all responses to Heller's book followed the obvious political line expected from their authors. Some of them raise doubts regarding the typical receptions of the book. Those few unusual appreciations—although articulated by esteemed thinkers who were particularly qualified to interpret both Marxism and the Jewish question, such as the above-cited review by Fromm—remained almost unknown for different reasons. Another particularly interesting reception from the left was an unpublished one, whose importance stems from the standing of its author, Walter Benjamin. This exceptionally original and creative Marxist intellectual was highly sensitive to the nuances of language and extremely allergic to dogmatism. His close friend, the Zionist scholar Gershom Scholem, told how, having been asked by Benjamin what he thought of the new book, he replied: "A totally worthless book [. . .] meretricious, ignorant twaddle."⁶⁴ Scholem did not report of his correspondent's opinion, which was quite different. Although Benjamin was repelled by the "absurdity and abstruseness of its materialistic analysis of Jewish religion," he felt "compensated [. . .] by the way the book illuminates the latest development of Jewish politics in Soviet Russia."

One sentence in Benjamin's letter is especially peculiar: "Although the book is impeccably orthodox in terms of party ideology, the official authorities must be making every conceivable difficulty for the author."⁶⁵ Benjamin did not explain what he meant. Why should the Party authorities have made difficulties for Heller, if his book was "impeccably orthodox"? Since Benjamin must not have had knowledge of any internal intrigues in the Communist Party, one can only assume that he was reading between the lines. Deciphering the sources of Benjamin's intuitive feeling requires an analysis of the critical reaction to *The Decline of Judaism* within the Communist Party of Germany.

"Exploited Masses of Jewish Nationality": Is There a Jewish Proletariat?

As mentioned, most of the communist reviews of *The Decline of Judaism* were highly positive, and only at their margins expressed some minor criticism. It is almost impossible to find a completely positive book review. Even close friends and associates, who usually review books written by their colleagues, tend to point to at least one drawback in a book or else they would be suspected as unreliably too supportive. In that manner, Heller's friend and comrade from the German and Austrian Communist Parties, Bruno Frei,[66] wrote in his very enthusiastic review article on *The Decline of Judaism*: "One can leave the question open, whether he [Heller] did not go too far," viewing the Jews as merchants from their earliest history.[67] Similarly, another communist commentator noted: "the historical part is much too simple, too schematic. The role of the Jews in trade is sometimes over-estimated by Heller."[68] Heller's close partner in the Association for Supporting the Jewish Settlements in the Soviet Union (Geserd), Georg Wegener (pseudonym of Arnold Metzger), mentioned another "flaw": "class structure among the Jews," "Jewish proletariat," and "working Jews" are "too briefly depicted."[69]

Due to the wide positive consensus among communists regarding Heller's book, scholars tended to depict it as expressing the "official party-position,"[70] or "the dominant concepts in the KPD regarding the Jewish question."[71] These evaluations overlooked one communist review, the most important of all. While the above-cited communist reviews were published in unaffiliated, international, Jewish-oriented, or Austrian periodicals, this one was published in the leading German communist daily, controlled directly by the Central Committee of the KPD in Berlin, *Die rote Fahne* (The Red Flags).[72] The article was written by the former editor, and current deputy chief editor, the senior communist journalist of Jewish origins, Albert Norden.[73]

Norden's reception of *The Decline of Judaism* was fatal, and articulated in harsh words, attributing to Heller "a row of severe flaws, which already appear in his definition of the term 'Decline of Judaism.' It is not Judaism as such [*schlechthin*] which is declining, but [. . .] what is generally disappearing is what was generated through hundreds of years of oppression of Judaism in all countries, the specific social type of the Jewish trader."[74] No less surprising than the fact that such a grave criticism came from a fellow Party journalist is that the content of this critique came from a communist. What Heller saw as the problematic inherent character of Jewish economy, commerce, was empathically explained by Norden as a historical consequence of "hundreds of years of oppression." Heller's generalizations regarding the Jews seemed almost antisemitic in his comrade's eyes.

The most severe blame was that of deviation from Marxist-Leninist theory. Norden started by quoting Lenin's general postulate: "In every national culture there are, even if not developed, democratic and socialist elements, since every nation has working and exploited masses." Then he vehemently stormed on Heller: "But for Heller, who wanted to write a Leninist essay on the Jewish question, the 'working and exploited masses' *of Jewish nationality* do not exist. He is dealing with the Jews essentially as a homogenous mass of traders. While according to Marx and Engels the history of all peoples is the history of class struggles—in Heller's historical chapters none of that is to be found. [...] He simply ignores the class struggle within Judaism."[75] If Wegener gently suggested that "working Jews" were "too briefly depicted,"[76] Norden fervently accused Heller of overlooking them whatsoever. Interestingly, the emphasis on the social differentiation among Jews, employed by Norden, was characteristic to socialist-Zionist thought.

As I will show below, it was Heller who qualified in his book the definition of the Jews as a "nationality" within the German Marxist terminology. But Norden went even further than Heller in his acknowledgment of a normally structured "Jewish nationality," not only in the Soviet Union, but even in Germany. Nevertheless, his accusations seem exaggerated. In *The Decline of Judaism* Heller did mention a "rapid class-differentiation" into "haute bourgeoisie," "petit bourgeoisie," and "proletariat."[77] It was indeed not as central as in Norden's review, but the latter's complete omission of such references implies that his motivation to attack Heller was not only theoretical, but also political.

And indeed, Norden convicted Heller not only for historical mistakes, but also for his misinterpretation of the "Leninist nationalities-policy, whose still-living representative is comrade Stalin." According to the reviewer, Heller overestimated "the stripping [*Abstreifung*] of the last remnants of nationality" in Eastern Europe, and in this manner contradicted Stalin himself. This was another exaggerated criticism, used by Norden to denounce Heller.

Heller was regarded as off the Party line not only in the sphere of Marxism, but also concerning Zionism. The Zionist newspaper, *Jüdische Rundschau* (Jewish Review), sarcastically reported that "for the reviewer of *Die rote Fahne* [Norden], a known Zionist renegade, Heller's view is not anti-Zionist enough."[78] According to Norden, Heller "came to a false assessment of the Arab uprising of Autumn 1929 [in Palestine], which he qualified as the '*großen Judenpogrom*' [great pogrom against Jews], while in reality it was a revolt of the *Fellachs* [Arab peasants], that were expelled from land and cut off from livelihood by the Zionists." In addition, Heller was criticized for not pointing out the anti-Soviet position of the Zionists.

The final verdict was devastating: "Heller's book lacks too much in the observation of the social aspects of the Jewish problem," which was its main purpose.[79] Norden's review was actually a recommendation to his communist readers not to read Heller's book. As Norden and his newspaper were highly authoritative, this review meant a condemnation of the book and its author alike by no less than the leadership of the KPD. Norden's article had concluded the discussion. Afterward, no more supportive reviews were published by German communists. *The Decline of Judaism* thus did not represent any "official party-position." On the contrary, the "official party-position" stood up against it. If the book became popular among communists, it was not thanks to the support of the Party authorities, but despite their rejection.

Norden's critique can also retrospectively explain why, although Heller was working for the German communist press, *The Decline of Judaism* was not published by a KPD-affiliated publisher. It came out in the *Verlag für Literatur und Politik* (Press for Literature and Politics), which was based in both Vienna and Berlin, affiliated with the Comintern, and thus not subjected to the oversight of the German Party.[80] Unlike the KPD, which experienced its first Stalinist purge already in 1928–1929, prior to 1933 the political purges of the apparatus of the Comintern's Executive Committee (ECCI) involved only members of the Russian Party.[81] Thus, when Heller's book came out in 1931, the Comintern authorities were still less oppressively single-minded than the German Party.

It is unknown whether Heller first tried to offer the book to German communist publishers, but it is reasonable to assume that he discussed this option with his personal acquaintance, the patron of German communist press, Willi Münzenberg.[82] Another writer who was close to Münzenberg at the time told how, when the latter could not convince the KPD leadership to publish a book, he would say that the Party had "raised some political difficulties."[83] It was probably due to such difficulties that *The Decline of Judaism* was not published by the German Party and even decades later has been never "resurrected" or reprinted in the GDR, although much of its conceptions still prevailed in that state.[84]

Norden's review demonstrated the political problematics raised by Heller's book from the point of view of the party leadership. Heller was accused of depicting all Jews as bourgeois merchants, instead of reaching out to the economically degrading Jewish layers in order to recruit them to communism. The problem addressed by Norden became evident also in the response of the Centralverein representatives, who attacked Heller on the same point from their own side, trying to keep the impoverished Jews away from communism. However, this discussion was conducted mainly among Jews, communists or noncommunists. Even Norden, the most senior communist to comment on the book, was a "Rabbi's son," as formulated by his biographer.[85] The Jewish question did not take a prominent place on the KPD's agenda, especially as the Party was endeavoring to avoid a pro-Jewish public image, facing increasing Nazi popularity among workers.[86] In this respect, Heller's book was a thorn in the eye for the Party, even regardless of its content, as it forced the communists to address the Jewish question in the public sphere. And even worse, it was written by a Jewish Party member.

The problematic reception of *The Decline of Judaism* is reflected also in the journal *Aufbruch* (Departure), which was published by the KPD during 1931–1932, addressing right-wing former soldiers and Nazis in attempt to convert them to communism. While expressing the Party's nationalist line at the time, it hardly engaged with the Jewish question and antisemitism. The publication of Heller's book was announced briefly at page 16 of the February 1932 issue, while noting: "We could warmly recommend this book to our readers. Due to space limits we do not bring a detailed discussion, although it would have been necessary. We will return to that."[87] The book has been never mentioned again.

In 1932 three different articles on the Jewish question were published by German communists, one written by Heller and two by other communists of Jewish origin. Scholars regularly discussed this wave of publications as inspired by *The Decline of Judaism* or as continuing it. Considering the problematic status of Heller's book in the Party, it is more accurate to see them as attempts to repair some of the damage made by the book. The fact that all those publications were written by Jews and appeared in supra-party collections dedicated to the Jewish question, and not in communist publications, implies that the Party authorities made efforts to push the issue out of the communist agenda, back into the Jewish public discourse.[88] As historian Olaf Kistenmacher noted, on the Jewish question the KPD was more "reacting" than "acting,"[89] but not only to Nazis, also to its own members.

Two of the articles were included in a collected volume titled *Clarification: 12 Authors, Politicians on the Jewish Question* (*Klärung: 12 Autoren, Politiker über die Judenfrage*), published in July 1932.[90] One of them was Heller's contribution, and the other was written by a former Zionist writer who had just recently converted to communism, Alfred Kantorowicz. Unlike in *The Decline of Judaism*, Heller opened his essay on "Communism and the Jewish Question" ("Kommunismus und Judenfrage") by stressing the internal Jewish class struggle: "Which Jew? The bourgeois or the proletarian? [. . .] History is a history of class-struggle."[91] That was clearly an apologetic reply to Norden, attempting to satisfy his criticism. Nevertheless, beyond this opening the rest of the piece is a mere summary of Heller's own book.

Kantorowicz, on the other hand, probably on his own initiative, expressed an even more provocative position than Heller's by attributing some advantages to antisemitism in fighting capitalism, and by referring to Nazis and rabbis alike as "enemies of Jewish labor."[92] Maybe as a newcomer in the Party, who wished to demonstrate his rejection of his Zionist past and Jewish origins, Kantorowicz tried to appear as "more catholic than the pope." He was proving himself useful in appealing to the public, whose support stood for competition between communists and Nazis. This was a known communist tactic, though formally disapproved by the Party leadership, a tactic from which Heller distanced himself.[93]

Most intriguing was the third article of 1932, whose author remained anonymous, hiding behind the signature of the Central Committee of the Communist Party of Germany (Zentralkomitee der Kommunistischen Partei Deutschlands [ZK der KPD]). The essay, curiously titled identically to Heller's article from the same year, "Communism and the Jewish Question," was published in another collected volume, *The Jew Is Guilty . . . ?* (*Der Jud' ist schuld . . . ?*), which appeared in September; the volume consisted of contributions from a wider range of political angles, including a piece by the Nazi Ernst Graf von Rewentlow.[94] Historian Edmund Silberner emphasized the importance of the communist article in that volume, as the only document from the Weimar period that expressed a formal position of the KPD on the Jewish question, as it was explicitly signed by the ZK.[95]

While some scholars justly identified much of the historical arguments presented in the article as drawn from *The Decline of Judaism*,[96] others noticed significant differences between these two texts. Enzo Traverso noted that in his book Heller "employed the traditional Marxist conception of antisemitism as a tool of the dominant class to divide the workers." In contrast, he valued the anonymous article as "a precise typology of German antisemitism" and as a more "profound" study.[97] The significant difference between the book and the article was also emphasized by Mario Kessler, who identified each of them as representing a different approach within the KPD toward Nazi antisemitic propaganda in the early 1930s: one, expressed in Heller's book, dismissed it as fraud, whereas the other, displayed by the article, started to take it seriously.[98] Despite the differences, John Bunzl suggested that Otto Heller might have been the author of the article, too.[99] In another place I tended to accept this hypothesis, viewing it as an early change of Heller's views.[100] But now, considering Norden's review, this identification should be revised.

Three ideas expressed in the anonymous article highly resemble Norden's review of Heller: "The communists deny the concept of a unitary Jewry [. . .]. The communist [. . .] knows no Jews as such [*schlechthin*], but only Jewish exploiters and Jewish exploited."[101] Both the emphasis on the "class-struggles within the Jewish communities," as well as the specific wording of Jews (or Judaism) "as such [*schlechthin*]," point to Norden as the author of the article on behalf of the ZK. In coherence with his review, he stressed here that the Jewish question was important to the communists with regard to the "masses of Jewish working population." Another sentence that implies Norden's authorship is: "In Germany the Jews were almost completely stripped [*abgestreift*] of all these remnants [of their nationality]."[102] The verb *abstreifen* (to strip) reminds the reader of Norden's review, where he used it in an unusual form of a verbal noun, *Abstreifung*.[103] The third affirmation of Norden's responsibility for the article was the claim that Zionism was "fighting against the Soviet Union,"[104] the exact claim that he blamed Heller for refraining from in his review. In addition, considering Heller's precarious political status in the Party, he was not likely to have been assigned to write on behalf of the ZK.[105]

As shown by Kistenmacher, who studied the representation of the Jewish question in the main communist newspaper of Germany, "the ZK-declaration refers to the 'Jewish working masses' in Germany, whom *Die rote Fahne* hardly mentions."[106] The ZK was reacting to a problem posed not only by Heller's book, but above all by the rapidly changing circumstances against the background of the economic crisis and social and political turmoil in Germany. Like Heller, the ZK contribution explained the Nazi use of antisemitism as disguising the real reasons for the suffering of the petit bourgeoisie, namely, capitalism. The difference was that the latter was facing a reality in which this instrument turned up as much more efficient.[107] As phrased by historian Thomas Haury: "Completely unlike other statements and resolutions of the Central Committee, it had never appeared in the comprehensive party press—obviously the fear of being denounced as 'squad for protection of Jews' is to be blamed." Compared to Heller's book, the ZK document was "much more adjusted to the situation in Germany and the growing threat from the Nazi party."[108] Unlike Heller, who in his 1932 article bearing the same title, claimed that "a true Jewish question exists only in Eastern and Southern Europe, in the areas of retarded social development";[109] the ZK's "Communism and the Jewish Question" "did not deny the existence of a Jewish question in Germany," as noted by Kessler.[110] The acute problem of the German Jews, according to that article, was that their "economic basis" was "constantly shrinking."[111]

Besides those important differences, it is clear that the ZK article was indeed based on Heller's historical analysis, as it used his terminology of "caste" and "trading-people."[112] The fact that Heller received no credit implies that, even more than confronting his theory, the author wished to politically eliminate Heller himself, against the background of contemporary *Fraktionspolitik* in the KPD.[113] Contrary to the common depiction of Heller as representing the Party line on the Jewish question, it appears that he could not represent it because such a formal line did not even exist when he wrote his book. The anonymous article on behalf of the ZK was not expressing an already existing formal position of the Party leadership on the Jewish question, but forming it from scratch. In doing so, it indeed adopted some elements from *The Decline of Judaism* while rejecting others, and most importantly—while rejecting its author.

Heller tried to improve his position in the Party trough his foreword to the second edition of *The Decline of Judaism*, published in early 1933, where he noted that some of his "colleagues" claimed that the book's title was "misleading." Nevertheless, he decided not to change it, maintaining that the book does not assert the "decline of the Jews as such [*schlechthin*]," but only of "certain social types," the Jewish traders.[114] The formula "the Jews as such [*schlechthin*]" is clearly an appeal for rehabilitation, addressed directly to Norden and the ZK. It was also a reply to another "colleague" of Heller's from the German of branch *Geserd*, Fromm, who pointed out the contradiction between the book's title and its last two-thirds.[115] Following this criticism, wrote Heller, he decided to pay more attention to Jewish inner class-differentiation in the second edition.[116] However, a thorough comparison of the two editions reveals no significant change neither in this regard, nor in any other matter, besides changing the formulation "*Judenpogrom*" to "Arab uprising," while briefly explaining its social background, as demanded by Norden in his review.[117]

Figure 2.1. Books on the Jewish question. From Otto Heller's private collection. Courtesy of the Leibniz Institute for Jewish History and Culture—Simon Dubnow/PGB.

"Trading-People": Is There a Jewish Nation?

The frequent identification of *The Decline of Judaism* as a classic Marxist book is valid only to some extent. A deeper analysis shows that the book significantly defers from previous Marxist works on the Jewish question. The most significant difference was taken for granted by many commentators: while previous Marxists who addressed Jewish matters were reluctant to delve into Jewish history, *The Decline of Judaism* was the first overall Marxist engagement with Jewish history as a main theme.[118] Another difference lies in the terminology through which Heller linked Marxist thought with Jewish history. To that end, he chose a term that was used by Marx to define the economic role of the Jews—"trading-people" (*Handelsvolk*). This concept has been neglected in the Marxist discourse until it was conjured up by Heller. As it was absent from Marx's early and much-cited article "On the Jewish Question" (1844), his only work whose title refers to a Jewish topic, the term was forgotten by his disciples. In bringing that expression back into the discussion, Heller ignited a theoretical dispute among Jewish Marxists of different political streams over the proper application of this term and over the proper Marxist interpretation of Jewish history.

In Marx's later writings, only a few accidental comments relating to Jews are scattered. One of them was hidden between the pages of his voluminous magnum opus, *Das Kapital* (Capital): "Trading-peoples [*Handelsvölker*], properly so called, exist in the ancient world only in its interstices, [. . .] like Jews in the pores of Polish society."[119] This is a very condensed sentence, which includes a new unexplained use of the term "trading-peoples," referring to a vast geographical and temporal sphere ranging from "the ancient world" to (medieval?) "Polish society." This already vague concept is then explicated (or, rather, obscured) by the physiological metaphor of "pores."

Heller was the first Marxist to revive Marx's definition of the Jews as a "trading-people" when he adopted it as a key term in his interpretation of Jewish history. To that end he must have thoroughly scrutinized Marx's writings in order to find some elaboration on that term. And he indeed found it in the third volume of *Das Kapital*, which appeared only after Marx's death. Here Marx repeated the idea that the Jews in Polish society fulfill a similar function to that of ancient trading peoples. He then added: "The trade of the first independent and highly developed trading cities and peoples, as a pure carrying trade [*Zwischenhandel*], rested on the barbarism of the producing peoples between whom they acted as intermediaries."[120] Marx mentioned here the Jews as an equivalent of ancient "trading-people," namely, ethnic groups whose economic function did not lie in the sphere of production, but rather in intermediation between producing societies. According to this view, in precapitalist modes of production, most societies were virtually self-sufficient, while exchange of goods existed only on the margins of the economy.

Relying on this citation, Heller interpreted "producing peoples" of antiquity as the Empires of the Near East in Mesopotamia and Egypt, and "trading-peoples" as the Phoenicians and the Israelites who inhabited the areas between them.[121] According to Heller, "the Jews are neither the first nor the only trading-people in antiquity, but they were the last and only to survive" as such.[122] Unlike other ancient trading peoples, like the Phoenicians, the Greeks, and the Armenians, the Jews forfeited the territory in which they had been the majority, thus they "lost their nation" and became a "caste."[123] For this reason, it was the Jews alone who throughout history continued to exist as a trading people.

Heller did not base his definition of the Jews as a trading people only on Marx's quite incidental mention of this term in a Jewish context. Before Heller, this concept was not particularly identified with Marxist interpretation of Jewish history. To provide Marx's theoretical concept with empiric foundations, Heller relied on "the first economic Jewish historian," the nineteenth-century Reform rabbi from Braunschweig Levi Herzfeld.[124] In his book on the commercial history of the Jews, Herzfeld concluded that "already then [in the first century CE], the Jews outside of Palestine had predominantly become a trading-people [*Handelsvolke*]."[125] Heller defined Herzfeld as "the rabbi who unwittingly became a good materialist," and his book as "the best work on the ancient social history of the Jews."[126] By generalizing it to the entirety of Jewish history, Heller brought to extremity the view of the Jews as a trading people. Nevertheless, in less overarching though still broad applications it was widely accepted by scholars such as the prominent German biblical scholar Julius Wellhausen, the socialist-Zionist economic historian Ignacy Schipper, and many others.[127]

This rather marginal term, which was already obsolete in Marxist discourse, served Heller as a theoretical vehicle to resurrect the status of the Jews as a nation in Marxist terminology in order to substantiate the feasibility of Jewish national autonomy in Birobidzhan. The notion of trading people closed the historical gap of hundreds of years between the old Jewish nation in Palestine and its renewal in Birobidzhan. It provided a materialistic explanation for the survival of Jewish nationality throughout the long exile. If the Jews began their history as a trading people, then they could reforge their national being by forgoing their trade in a designated national territory. The concept of "people" was close enough to "nation," while the supplement of "trading" maintained the obligatory connection to materialist methodology. Employed by Marx himself specifically in a Jewish context, "trading-people" was almost irresistible within Marxist discourse. And indeed, Heller's Marxist critics did not reject the term per se but took exception to its specific application in relation to Jewish history. Their various interpretations reflected different social and political viewpoints.

The Polish Zionist-Marxist historian Raphael Mahler (1899–1977) reviewed Heller's book in two detailed Yiddish articles, titled "Were the Jews Always a Trading-People?" (1934) and "When and How Did the Jews Become a Trading-People?" (1935).[128] In contrast to Heller's hypothesis, Mahler asserted that in antiquity Jews were by no means solely traders, but mainly peasants and artisans, even long after the destruction of Jerusalem by the Romans in 70 CE. Despite his criticism, Mahler did not entirely refute Heller's stance on the Jews as a trading people. According to Mahler, the Jews indeed became a trading people, but only after hundreds of years in exile and only due to exclusion by force, first from agriculture and later from the craft industries. This development occurred, stressed Mahler, only "in Western Europe, [and] only since early Middle Ages."[129] What maintained the Jews' status as a nation in the meantime were their religious and cultural bonds among themselves and to Jerusalem.

Mahler's thesis was in turn challenged by Moyshe Kats (1885–1960), a well-known writer in Communist Yiddishist circles in New York.[130] In 1938–1939, Kats published a long series of articles titled "Problems in Jewish History," in which he analyzed Jewish history from antiquity to the Spanish expulsion. Kats's critique of Mahler was not as a defense of his fellow communist Heller, whom he criticized too; rather, he proposed a third view. Kats accepted Mahler's claim against Heller that ancient Jewry was an occupationally diverse society, but he rejected his explanation of its preservation through religion as an idealistic deviation from the materialistic method. Kats suggested an alternative explanation for Jewish preservation in Diaspora, which might be called "the proselytization theory." According to Kats, even before the destruction of Jerusalem the vast Jewish Diaspora was formed neither out of refugees nor emigrants from Judea, but as a consequence of mass proselytization of urban populations across the Hellenistic and Roman world. Kats saw Judaism as a kind of an ancient protestant religion of certain social strata that he called "the urban democracy," consisting not only of traders, but also of artisans and wage laborers.

Kats explicitly challenged Heller's interpretation of "trading-people," maintaining that even if this term would have been applicable to the ancient Jews of Palestine, Heller's application of it to the different geographical spaces of their diaspora contradicted the materialist method.[131] According to Kats, ancient Jews did not form a nation but a "religious community," based on wider economic distinctiveness than trade alone, which became a "national society" only later due to its foreignness in the Germanic sphere.[132] He called this shift "the process of nationalization."[133] Only with regard to this historical stage did Kats apply Heller's overarching term, "caste," to define the state of the Jews as outcasts in feudal Europe.[134]

At about the same time in which Kats wrote his articles, a young Polish-Jewish intellectual in Brussels, Abram Leon (1918–1944), began writing his own Marxist version of Jewish history. Leon, who left his Zionist youth group of Hashomer Hatzair in favor of the Belgian Trotskyist movement, completed his synthetic historiographic work in late 1942, while being in the underground under the German occupation. He was eventually caught by the Gestapo and sent to his death in Auschwitz.[135] In principle, Leon's thesis resembled Heller's. Interpreting the same citation of Marx, he conceived the Jewish people as a trading people from its very inception.[136] Nevertheless, as a Trotskyist, Leon was compelled to refute the terminology used by a Stalinist such as Heller. Although he had clearly read *The Decline of Judaism*,[137] he did not directly criticize it and instead adopted an alternative term to Heller's "caste," which expressed the same idea and was even closer to Marx's "trading-people": "a people-class."[138] The fact that this term was not coined by Leon himself, but rather adopted from the Zionist social scientist Yakov Leshchinsky, reveals its national subtext.¹³⁹ While refusing to see ancient Jews as a nation, Leon did not deny modern Jewish nationality, which he saw as an outcome of capitalism.¹⁴⁰

Those four Marxist Jewish historiographers—Heller, Mahler, Kats, and Leon—adopted Marx's concept of trading people and applied it in different ways, some of which were confined to very particular eras and regions. However, they all used it to qualify Jewish nationalism. In terms of the late twentieth century, Leon's theory of Jewish nationalism can be defined as "modernist," as he saw nationalism as an altogether modern phenomenon.¹⁴¹ The other three should be categorized as promoting "primordialist" interpretations of Jewish nationalism, with the difference being that Kats identified the emergence of Jewish nationalism in the Middle Ages, whereas Mahler and Heller have extended its existence back to antiquity. Heller, thus, contrary to his common image as a denier of the Jewish nationhood, stood together with the Zionist Mahler at the very primordialist end of the spectrum of Marxist theories of Jewish nationalism.¹⁴²

Respectively, the four intellectuals offered national platforms for the preservation of Jewish existence in modernity. For the Zionist socialist Mahler, the national community of Jewish workers in Palestine was the only solution. Kats proffered a diasporic cultural nationality of a progressive Yiddish-speaking Jewish proletariat, conforming to his American Jewish working-class readership. Even Leon, the least nationalist of them all, did not negate Jewish national self-determination on principle, but rather doubted the chances at it ever being fulfilled in Palestine. He approved of the "opportunity of concentrating in one or more territories," while settling it with his Trotskyist ideal of international revolution through the following formula: "Socialism must limit itself in this sphere [of the national question] to 'letting nature take its course.'"¹⁴³ This stance received legitimacy from Trotsky himself, who expressed a much more empathic approach toward Jewish national self-determination during the thirties than his previous orthodox Marxist position.¹⁴⁴ Similarly, Heller advocated a dual solution of the Jewish question within the borders of the Soviet Union. Alongside the national territorialization in Birobidzhan, he did not resist individual assimilation into the vast Soviet society, declaring (following Lenin) that "socialism has no absolute stance towards the question of assimilation," besides negating forced assimilation.¹⁴⁵

Eventually, except for Mahler, all three other writers adopted one version or another of what might be called "neo-neutralism," or "neo-Bundism," following the "neutralist" stance of the Bund on the national question in the early twentieth century. The Bund faced an ideological dilemma between Jewish nationalism and socialist universalism, which reflected its political dilemma between the Party's standing as an autonomous organization and its affiliation to the Russian Social-Democratic Party.[146] It was the Bundist intellectual and leader Vladimir Medem, who in 1904 suggested "neutralism" as a tactical compromise: "We are not nationalists [. . .]. We are not assimilationists. [. . .] We are not against assimilation, but against the *aspiration* for assimilation, against assimilation as a purpose."[147]

After serving the Bund in that specific historical moment, the neutralist formula had been neglected in favor of a clearer nationalist worldview. This principle neutralism proved useful again in the 1930s, this time for Jewish intellectuals in universalist Marxist movements—Trotskyism and communism—to substantiate their nationalistic turn. As noted, Leon suggested to "let nature take its course" with the future of Jewish nationhood. Kats, for his part, elaborated a Bundist-like concept of diasporic cultural nationalism. And Heller introduced neutrality between assimilation and national autonomy, solving his quandary over the de jure rejection of Jewish nationalism by orthodox Marxism and its de facto recognition through Soviet policy. For obvious political reasons, Heller did not explicitly mention Medem on this matter, though the fact that he knew his work is evidenced in a different context.[148]

Considering the close interrelation between the emergence of modern historiography and national consciousness, the very writing of the history of the Jews as a distinct group implies their definition as a nation.[149] The emergence of Marxist syntheses of Jewish history during the 1930s, following Heller's book, reflected a conciliation of socialist Jews in various political movements with the Jewish national idea, due to the severe crisis of Jewish emancipation and assimilation. Heller, Kats, and Leon were all driven by historical circumstances to conduct a deep theoretical dialogue with the Jewish (and general) nationalist zeitgeist and to incorporate its logic into their thought. This global nationalist trend, which came to prevail among Jews in labor movements in the 1930s, blurred the conventional borders between

Marxism and Jewish nationalism. It reflects a broad acceptance of the merging together of the two worldviews, which the Bund had already established at the beginning of the century, and which the socialist-Zionists had as well, in a different manner. Under the circumstances of the 1930s, this combination was adopted also by Jewish members of non-Jewish socialist movements—non-Jewish Jews like Heller and Leon. This political development required a respective theoretical reconciliation between Marxism and Jewish nationalism, which was enabled through the renewed use of the old Marxian term "trading-people," introduced by Heller in *The Decline of Judaism*.

∽

Unlike the intensive and diverged theoretical and political debate sparked by *The Decline of Judaism* during the first decade after its publication, the postwar scholarly continuation of this debate was one dimensional, reducing the book into a caricature of communist anti-Jewish dogma.[150] Nevertheless, there were two scholars—Shlomo Șirolnikov and Shmu'el Almog—who suggested different readings of *The Decline of Judaism*, implying other, more sophisticated dimensions hidden within the book. Neither could be suspected as being sympathizers of Heller's view. However, in their youth they had both taken part in a short-lived attempt to combine communism with Jewish nationalism (the "Hebrew Communists" in Palestine, 1943–1948).[151] It was probably thanks to this experience that they were more sensitive to the multilayered complexity of Heller's writing. Since they both wrote in Hebrew, their notions were not integrated into the standard scholarly discussion on Heller, which took place mostly in German, and to a lesser extent in English.

The Israeli publicist Șirolnikov, who generally rejected Heller's book, had one reservation: "The only novelty, that he [Heller] could be credited for, is the distinction between Nation and Nationality."[152] Zirolnokov referred to Heller's interpretation of Stalin's article "Marxism and the National Question." On the one hand, Heller relied on the leader's stance, denying the Jews the title of a nation. On the other hand, he held onto Stalin's own rhetorical argument that the Jews had no more than "certain relics of national character."[153] But Heller's move was much more radical than Șirolnikov's assessment.

Without proclaiming to do so, Heller actually inverted Stalin's formulation, interpreting it in a positive manner, as if it was meant that the Jews *do* have a "national character." On this basis, Heller gave the Jews a definition that Stalin did not explicitly attribute to them: "Although the Jews [. . .] are not a nation, they are still a nationality [*Nationalität*]."[154] In that way he facilitated the modern restoration of the ancient Jewish nation in Birobidzhan.

Based on that terminology, Heller's narrative of Jewish history was strikingly nationalistic: "The transformation from a nation to a caste [in antiquity . . .] was the special *national fate* of the Jews."[155] As a caste, "their strict religious unity was actually their economic and *national unity*."[156] "As *one of the oldest nationalities* on earth, owning such a tradition, such a *meaningful cultural past*, [the Jews] should be granted the same equal political rights as a dozen of other nationalities [in the Soviet Union]."[157] Therefore, concluded Heller, "the decline of Judaism" is not "the disappearance of Jewish nationality."[158] On the contrary, thanks to the "endless reservoir of Jewish nationality" in Eastern Europe, "the decline of Judaism is the beginning of the new socialist life of Jewish nationality on a socialist soil."[159]

Through this motion Heller accommodated Stalin's theory of 1913 to the leader's contrasting policy of 1931. The goal of this terminological maneuver was to provide the Soviet policy with a proper Marxist-Stalinist theoretical justification. For that purpose, Heller leaned on a formulation coined by Stalin in 1925 (not in a specifically Jewish context): "The Soviet Union [. . .] enabled the Jews to bring their national culture to a new blossom, *socialist in substance and national in form*."[160] Unwittingly, Heller had generally resurrected, in Marxist theoretical terms, the possibility of the Jews to regain the title of a nation also outside the Soviet Union, as evident in the competing interpretations suggested by Mahler, Kats, and Leon. As Kistenmacher commented, indirectly Heller had even legitimized the Zionist goals: the return to primary production and the creation of a national homeland.[161]

The second Israeli exceptional commentator on *The Decline of Judaism* was Almog, who indicated that the book expressed an atmosphere in which, following the introduction of Birobidzhan, "Jewish nationalism was no longer inherently disqualified" in communist discourse.[162] But while Şirolnikov only reluctantly implied Heller's theoretical-ideological sophistication, Almog appreciated it explicitly.

From his experience as a communist activist and propagandist, Otto Heller learned how to navigate his ship, full of fragile arguments, between the sharp cliffs of the Soviet nationalities policy. He also knew how to balance the opposing positions within the *Evsektsiia*.[163] All these considerations regarded the Soviet Union itself, but the book was written first and foremost for the Jews in the German-speaking countries. [. . .] One should remember that at the time the Jews in Germany became open to communist influence. The economic and political crisis had set the stage for absorbing the communist message, particularly among the youth and the intelligentsia, but also in other layers, as those originated in Eastern Europe. The question whether Judaism had a future was conceived as an actual question, with personal relevancy to every Jew.[164]

Almog was receptive to the need to interpret *The Decline of Judaism* in multiple intertwined contexts, though he himself did not conduct such an interpretation. An interesting fact is that *The Decline of Judaism* was never translated to Russian. It was clearly addressed at German-speaking Jews, who were much more assimilated than most of the Jews in the Soviet Union at the time, attempting to convince them that communism offered the ultimate solution to the Jewish question. To Soviet Jewish citizens, Moscow's nationalities policy was interpreted directly by their own leaders, who did not need any external intervention for that purpose. Nevertheless, the fact that the book was published by a publisher affiliated with the Comintern attests that Heller knew enough of Soviet politics to have his book approved by the Moscow-based Comintern authorities. To Soviet and German-Jewish politics one should also add the inner KPD intrigues, to understand why such an "impeccably orthodox" book in many aspects was nevertheless rejected by the Party authorities, who made "every conceivable difficulty" for the author (as Benjamin correctly guessed).

Only considering Heller's life until writing *The Decline of Judaism*, as it was described in the previous chapter, one can understand how he came to write such an ambivalent book, at the specific historical moment that made it so provocative. Heller's particular life trajectory diverted him from the standard orbit of the non-Jewish Jew. While his envisioned cosmic symmetry between the sunset (*Sonnenuntergang*) of Judaism in the West and its sunrise (*Sonnenaufgang*) in the Birobidzhanian Far East became less and less realistic, it was actually being realized within his own personality. *Der Untergang des Judentums* heralded an *Aufgang des Judentums* in Otto Heller's life.

Chapter 3

In Flight from Two Dictators (1933–1939)

> I am a German. I am a Czech. I am a Jew. I come from a good family. I am a communist . . . Something like this always helps me.
>
> —Egon Erwin Kisch, 1938

On their flight from Nazi Germany, the two Austro-Bohemian KPD traveling journalists of Jewish descent and friends, Otto Heller and Egon Erwin Kisch, ran into each other in Zürich train station.[1] This chance meeting, just like the above-cited bon mot attributed to Kisch,[2] epitomized their intersecting life trajectories. Like other "German-Jewish writers" in exile, these two radically assimilated Jews turned to Jewish themes during the turbulent 1930s.[3] Heller, however, was distinguished in doing so even before going into exile, in *The Decline of Judaism*. Between Heller's two "Jewish books," Kisch published his *Tales from Seven Ghettos* in 1934, dealing, among other things, with past and present persecutions of Jews.[4] So far, they shared a similar fate, but while Kisch eventually reached his safe haven in Mexico, each one of Heller's similar multiple identities made him a victim of persecution. At first, he was banned from Czechoslovakia, as a communist, who, lacking a Czechoslovakian citizenship, was not "Czech" enough. Later he was suspected of not being communist enough, and then forced out of Germany as a communist and as a Jew, though he had not identified himself as a Jew.[5] This chapter will tell of his attempt to find a refuge in the Soviet Union, as a German (dubious-) communist of bourgeois and Jewish origins, and of his fate in France as an Austrian, a communist, and a Jew. During that constant flight, Heller kept intensively contemplating the Jewish question.

This chapter follows Heller's footprints from the period starting with his flight from Germany, shortly after the Nazi rise to power, and ending with the breakout of the Second World War, ten days after he finished writing "The Jew Is to Be Burned" (1939). These years brought about drastic changes in the course of his life, which reflected the turmoil that Europe was thrown into: in Nazi Germany and its accumulating annexed territories; in Stalinist Soviet Union with its so-called Great Purge; in Spain, torn by civil war; and in France, surrounded by fascist powers and flooded with refugees.

From Berlin to Zürich

During 1932 Heller was still relentlessly advocating his *Decline of Judaism* thesis in many assemblies and public debates in Germany and other European countries. That year saw increasing political violence in Germany, on the backdrop of two brutal election campaigns in July and November. Socialists and communists were constantly harassed and attacked by the Nazi paramilitary force of the Sturmabteilung (Storm Detachment [SA]).[6] Heller returned to Berlin from his second journey to the Soviet Far East in November that year.[7] He was now rehabilitated for a low-rank Party position, as "cells-instructor" (*Zelleninstrukteur*).[8] Nevertheless, thanks to *The Decline of Judaism* he was a well-known communist public intellectual of Jewish descent. His wife Emma recalled that in this period Otto "received threat letters and vicious calls on a daily basis."[9] Heller reported a search in their apartment in Berlin-Steglitz.[10] It is unclear if the search was conducted by the SA or by the Prussian police, which by then was already taken over by the conservative nationalists.[11]

During December 1932 and January 1933, Heller held a lecture tour through Switzerland, the Netherlands, Belgium, and the Rhineland in the west of Germany.[12] On his way he even sneaked into Czechoslovakia and lectured in Karlsbad (Karlovy Vary) about "The Struggle in the Far East."[13] On behalf of the "Association of friends of the Soviet Union" (Bund der Freunde der Sowjetunion), he kept advocating Birobidzhan as the ultimate solution to the Jewish question.[14] On January 15 he was still outside Germany, lecturing in

Amsterdam.¹⁵ A week after, on January 22, he gave his last lecture, in Gelsenkirchen, western Germany.¹⁶ Another week later, on January 30, as Hitler was appointed as Reichskanzler, Heller was already back in Berlin. His new book, *Wladi wostok!*, was printed at the last possible moment, in January 1933. But most of the copies fell into the hands of the Nazis and were "destroyed," presumably as part of the book burning of that May.¹⁷

Before his books were burned, Heller himself was already out of Germany, driven out by an earlier fire. On the night of February 27, the Reichstag had been set in flames. Promptly, the SA started rounding up communists, who were collectively blamed for the arson. The following morning, Heller left his apartment and went on hiding in "Red" Wedding, Berlin's communist-dominated district. Meanwhile Emma brought their nine-year-old daughter Lily, as well as their library, to safety in their former hometown of Reichenberg (Liberec), Czechoslovakia.¹⁸ In Wedding, Heller continued his work as cells instructor, now illegally, in the form of underground groups of five.¹⁹ As he had already lost his residence permit in 1926, Heller could not return to Czechoslovakia. On mid-March 1933, he left Germany for Zürich, Switzerland, where his brother Julius lived. In early April he reunited there with his family.²⁰

In Zürich Heller integrated himself into circles of German writers and communists in exile. Besides some "teaching in schools, circles etc.," organized by the Internationale Rote Hilfe (International Red Aid [formerly IAH]) for communist refugees, he worked voluntarily for the publisher of *The Decline of Judaism*, and occasionally wrote for communist newspapers.²¹ As intellectual and social environment he found the "Humm Circle," a leftist, though not exclusively communist, literary club. Rudolf Humm was a Swiss-German novelist, who once a week hosted a group of writers for literary reading and discussions in his home. Among the participants were the Frankfurt-School historian, Karl Wittfogel, on whom Heller relied in *The Decline of Judaism*;²² the German communist and "miner-writer" Hans Marchwitza, who later fought in Spain and exiled to Mexico; and the Italian communist dissident and famous novelist, Ignazio Silone.²³ Unwittingly, Heller was annexed to another "club" of writers, those who were expelled from the Protection Association of German Writers (Schützverband deutscher Schriftsteller [SDS]) as political opponents and Jews alike, among them Kisch, Bruno Frei, and Lion Feuchtwanger.²⁴

Maintaining himself in exile in Zürich was not an easy task, neither emotionally, politically, nor financially. Many issues were simultaneously burning. At the beginning, Heller was still active as the secretary of the Geserd organization for Jewish settlement in the Soviet Union, now banned in Germany. His support of Birobidzhan was joined, maybe for the first time, by an active demonstration of Jewish solidarity, expressed in his care for the fate of his fellow German Jews. On May 5, he wrote to his colleagues in the parallel Soviet organization, Ozet: "What is Ozet doing for the fleeing German Jews???? Are German Jews taken to Birobidzhan? If so, how many??????? And how??? Where to turn??????" The multiple question marks were not typical of Heller's writing. They evident his extreme worry. Besides the physical existence of German Jews, Heller was also troubled with their ideological fate, as the Nazi rise to power gave advantage to his rival "Zionists in Germany," who were "putting on strong agitation"; successfully, bemoaned Heller: "Many emigrate to Palestine."[25]

He reported to Moscow that the German branch of Geserd was practically devastated: "Every connection to the German Geserd has ceased. [Georg] Wegener already went in hiding at the beginning of March and I have not heard from him since. [. . .] Most of the members fled. Almost all *Ostjuden* [sic] were expelled. Young comrades fled or sit in concentration camps." As no answer came from Moscow, Heller repeatedly claimed: "That is a serious scandal! Never before the solution of the Jewish question through the Soviet power had such a tremendous meaning as now. Why are you not doing anything?" Expressing his disappointment in Ozet, Heller's critical tone toward a Soviet institution became dangerous, especially to a politically suspicious communist, as he still was. But he could not hold his tongue: "Are you aware of the political consequences of your inaction?" He mobilized his authoritative historical knowledge: "I do not know what Ozet is undertaking, facing the greatest persecution of Jews that Western Europe has seen since 1500."[26]

Not receiving any answer for almost a year, Heller became completely desperate: "I wrote many letters, never got a response. Many people from different countries are turning to me regarding emigration of German Jews to Birobidzhan and other Jewish settlements in Russia. [. . .] The people that are turning to me think I can do something for them or that I have a saying. I cannot help them, because I am in a bad situation, I am not feeling well."[27] Was he only mentally or also physically "not feeling well"? Perhaps his lungs illness erupted again? Eventually, only in the spring of 1934 Heller was replied to by none other than the chairmen of Ozet, Shimon Dimanshtein. The latter was a very high-ranking Soviet official, and as the former head of the *Evsektsiia*, one of the most senior in Jewish affairs.[28] In *The Decline of Judaism* Heller had quoted him in length, as an authoritative interpreter of Lenin regarding the Jewish question.[29] Nevertheless, Dimanshtein could not meet Heller's expectations: "The question of resettlement from Germany seems particularly difficult." He made it clear that the decision was in the hands of more "leading ranks" than himself.[30]

As Heller repeatedly asked about rescuing "German Jews," and only once in his letters explicitly referred to "*working* German Jews,"[31] Dimanshtein stressed that the question would be decided "class-wise," implying the bourgeois belonging of the vast majority of German Jews.[32] Again, as in the communist critique of *The Decline of Judaism*, Heller's acknowledgment of intra-Jewish class differences was questioned.[33] However, concluded Dimanshtein, "the transfer from Germany to Birobidzhan seems to us [. . .] hardly feasible," especially since the "liquidation of the German Geserd."[34]

Did any doubts regarding the Soviet solution to the Jewish question arise then in Heller's mind, vis-à-vis the grievous situation facing German Jews, including himself, and the inability, or unwillingness of the Soviet authorities to offer them a safe haven? When the Austrian communist journalist and novelist, Lili Körber, visited Birobidzhan in 1934, she addressed the pioneers with the same question: why did they not help the Central European Jews? She reported their answer as follows: "We don't like to take in Western Jews. They are too spoiled and do not want to do pioneer work. [. . . They] are usually intellectuals, fully assimilated and, at least to date, have not found it easily to adopt to our way of life."[35] Her book appeared in 1936. Did Heller read it? Did he recognize the difficulties he himself experienced when he was only travelling Birobidzhan, let alone the idea of settling there? However, after May 1934, there are no further recorded inquiries by Heller on this matter.

Back in May 1933, Heller did not only urge Ozet for help, but also took his own action, setting forth to Paris and Amsterdam. There he agitated for three weeks, against the "persecutions of Jews in Germany," and propagated for Birobidzhan among the German Jewish refugees, who "swamped" France and the Netherlands. For that purpose, he wrote to Ozet that he "urgently need[ed] materials," and as he was not responded to, he begged: "Send me immediately instructions!"[36] It is unknown how Heller financed this trip. In Zürich he barely had any resources, Ozet did not even communicate with him, and the German Geserd did not actually exist anymore.[37] He only received small assistance from the Communist Party of Switzerland.[38] In Amsterdam he was driven around by "young Jewish workers" on their bicycles. "I can only shrug my shoulders," he bitterly wrote to Ozet.[39] Propaganda brochures and newspapers from Birobidzhan arrived from Moscow only a year later.[40] "Thanks for the materials," he briefly replied, "with proletarian greetings."[41]

In Amsterdam Heller was surveilled by German Gestapo agents, who reported to Berlin on his propaganda for boycotting German commodities.

> The Jewish Refugees Committee is cooperating there [in the Boycott Committee]. The communists are naturally trying to play the first role there. As communists, the writer Otto Heller and the journalist Joseph Baruch were sent by this committee as orators across the land. [. . .] Both appear *as Jews in Jewish assemblies, as communists in communist* [assemblies], and *as expelled German journalists in multi-partisan assemblies*. [. . .] The Dutch population's mood is ignited against Germany with intensive tenacity.[42]

The Gestapo's nuanced perception of Heller's multifaceted identity, or—from their point of view—multiple grounds for persecution, is remarkable. Heller was aware of this surveillance, as he asked his Russian addressees: "You can write to this address [in Amsterdam] but do not mention my name."[43] Eventually he was arrested by the Dutch police, who cooperated with the Gestapo, during an assembly in Delft, and deported back to Switzerland.[44]

In between, in Amsterdam Heller also found time to write a preface to the French translation of *The Decline of Judaism*. While announcing that, despite Nazi rise to power, "the conditions under which this book was written have not changed," a change is discernible in his tone nonetheless.

At the moment this book is published in French, the Jewish question—the oldest inventory piece in European history—is once again at the center of the most *burning* current events. For the masses of the German Jewish population, as for the non-Jewish world in general, this is a truly tragic moment. The fact that Germany has been able to become a country of pogroms, and state-run pogroms, so to speak, in a scientific way, is an extremely serious symptom for the bourgeois world.[45]

While reiterating the traditional notion of the Jewish question as a "symptom for the bourgeois world," characteristic to the German original from 1931, a new overtone, which will eventually culminate in the 1939 manuscript, can be already traced here. Now this "symptom" turned out to be "extremely serious" and "tragic," as the events became "burning," a metaphor that will reappear at the heart of "The Jew Is to Be Burned." He also started using another term that will stand at the center of his later work, "the German pogrom."[46] Implicitly Heller tried to excuse his own former underestimation of Nazi antisemitism: "For a long time, as long as Hitler remained in opposition, his active antisemitism was underestimated both in Germany and abroad." Subsequently, Heller exemplified the grievous state of German Jewry through statistical data, concluding that a "struggle [is] engaged by the state for the *annihilation* of German Jews."[47]

And yet, Heller did not disclose any explicit retreat from the argumentations made in *The Decline of Judaism*. He kept on defending his book's title, as he did in the second German edition,[48] despite the fact that by now it has acquired a new horrible connotation.

> In Jewish circles, the author has often been criticized for the very title of this book. This title, it is said, risks, especially nowadays, being interpreted in a Judeophobic sense. But, without even wanting to consider the fact that this book had the great honor of being burned at the Berlin *autodafé*, we immediately say to the French public that this is not about the death of Jews as such, but about the rise and fall of a certain social function, of a social category that has emerged historically.[49]

Heller would also not admit any need to rethink his political stance. Moreover, the more the Zionist propaganda succeeded, his anti-Zionist polemics became fiercer: "What is happening today in Germany will be repeated tomorrow, in another form, in Palestine. The conditions for a conflict between Jews and non-Jews will strengthen in the coming months in all capitalist countries." The conclusion was hence expected: "There is no other solution to the Jewish question but the victory of socialism. The example of Germany proves it."[50] If Heller had any sprouting doubts regarding the attitude of Soviet regime toward the crisis of German Jewry, he concealed them carefully, maybe even from himself.

In an article published several months later Heller demonstrated a gradually increasing understanding that a major shift had occurred in Jewish history. And yet he did not disclose any surprise, but rather projected on the bourgeoisie his own clear surprise: "The bourgeois world is never done with the phenomenon of the Jewish question. Just as the solution seems to be near, then the problem emerges again with double force."[51] It was not his own assimilationist optimism that failed, so he alluded, but that of the German Jewish bourgeoisie. Nevertheless, an unadmitted change of his tone can be heard from between the lines here too. The question of the reasons for the "outbreak of fascist antisemitism," wrote Heller, "must immediately stir all those, who met the event in Germany *as Jews*."[52] If in *The Decline of Judaism*, the Jewish question did not interest him from a Jewish standpoint, as he then claimed,[53] now he implicitly confessed that he "met the events in Germany" as a Jew. Eventually he would delve into the origins of the "outbreak of fascist antisemitism" in "The Jew Is to Be Burned."

The article, peculiarly titled "The Third Kingdom of Israel" ("*Das dritte Reich Israel*"), was aimed against the "flood" of "bourgeois" literature on the Jewish question since the Nazi rise to power, for example, by Leo Baeck, Martin Buber, and Richard Beer-Hofmann.[54] The title, typically provocative, paraphrased the famous German-Jewish writer Lion Feuchwanger, who, just like Heller, was forced to exile Germany and was expelled from its state-sponsored literary community. In 1933 Feuchtwanger advocated a Jewish diasporic nationalism, which affirmed only the spiritual, but not the political dimension of Zionism, calling on a Jewish "hegemony only in the spirit."[55]

Today we experience the third conquest of Palestine. Should this conquest succeed, should it have a sense, then it must be accomplished with other means than those of force. The third Israel has nothing in common with the third Italy or with the Third Reich of the Germans. [. . .] The assignment of the third kingdom of Israel [Die Aufgabe des dritten Reiches Israel] [. . .] can be solved [gelöst] only without force. [. . .] His [the Jewish spiritual nationalism's] sole desire is to dissolve [sich aufzulösen] into a unified world. To dissolve like salt in water, which is solved [gelöst], invisible, nevertheless remains ubiquitous and eternal.[56]

Despite the completely different mind-sets, some resemblances to *The Decline of Judaism* come forward: the critique of Zionism, and the vision of a solution (Lösung) to the Jewish question through dissolution (Auflösung)[57] into a "unified world." It was probably those similarities in particular that urged Heller to sharply differentiate himself from the "bourgeois" Feuchtwanger, by taking his expression "the third kingdom of Israel" out of its context and spinning it into an equation of Jewish nationalism (outside the Soviet Union) and national-socialism.

A second main rival marked by Heller in his article was another celebrated German-Jewish novelist, Alfred Döblin. In 1933 Döblin published a booklet, *Jewish Revival (Jüdische Erneuerung)*, in which he envisioned a spiritual version of Jewish national territorialism.[58] Although Heller was not explicitly mentioned in this pamphlet, the very title can be understood as an antithesis to *The Decline of Judaism*. Already in 1932, Döblin had criticized Geserd as a "supra-party" facade of a communist organization.[59] In *Jewish Revival* Döblin maintained that Birobidzhan could not solve the Jewish problem because in Russia the Jews were assimilating into the general process of proletarianization.[60]

Döblin probably had Heller, among others, in mind when he sarcastically wrote, "Marxists are famous for knowing a lot, some of it is even correct." He implied Heller directly, when he claimed: "If we ignore the forms and formulation which stem from self-hatred, from the mistake regarding trade as the sole factor, [. . .] then the decisive influence of the economic factors remains true."[61] Again, as in the case of Feuchtwanger, it must have been the points in which

Döblin had agreed with him that incensed Heller most of all. His response was harsh: "One can spend sleepless nights when reading something like that." Since Döblin's booklet contains less than a hundred pages, it was not the length that would trouble one's sleep, but the content, which Heller defined as "the dark forest of Döblin's sentences."[62] In his own copy of Döblin's essay, thoroughly marked and commented on, Heller's criticism was much harsher (see figure 3.2). On the page margins, apropos some of the author's most enthusiastic nationalist proclamations, Heller commented: "Fascist!" "Goebbels!" "Sieg Heil!!!"[63]

Alongside the intellectual controversies, Heller was also facing political intrigues. Shortly before he went to serve the communist cause in Amsterdam, old ghosts from Berlin returned to haunt him in Zürich. An anonymous denunciation letter, found in Heller's file in the archives of the Comintern, is dated May 1933. In the letter Heller was accused of maneuvering a failed attempt to win over for

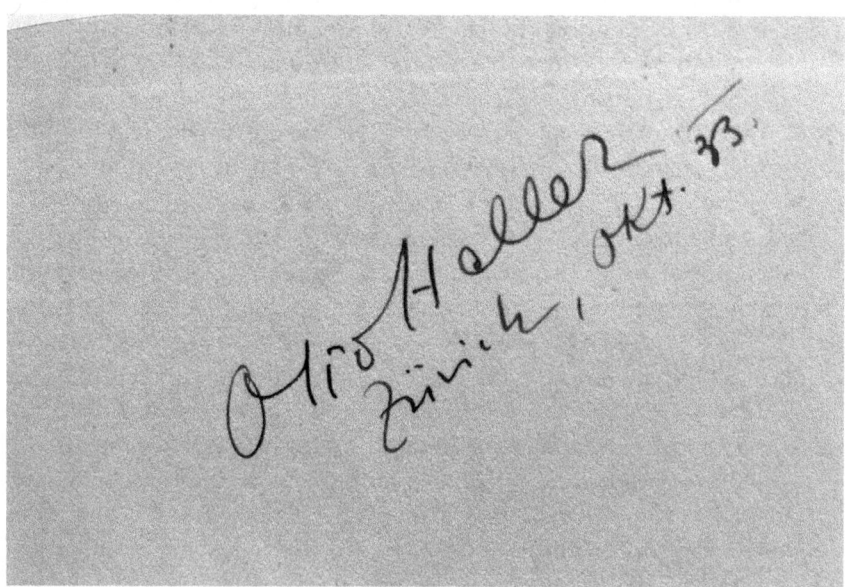

Figure 3.1. Otto Heller's autograph. From his own copy of Alfred Döblin, *Jüdische Erneuerung* (Jewish Revival). Courtesy of the Leibniz Institute for Jewish History and Culture—Simon Dubnow/PGB.

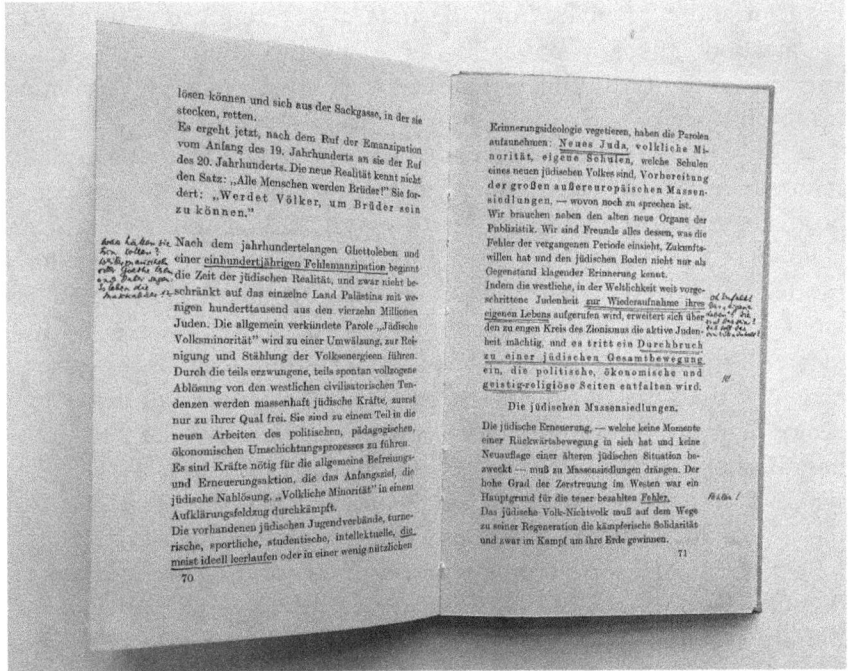

Figure 3.2. Pages from Heller's copy of Alfred Döblin, *Jüdische Erneuerung* (Jewish Revival), with comments in Heller's handwriting. Courtesy of the Leibniz Institute for Jewish History and Culture—Simon Dubnow/PGB.

the conciliators the journal *Information*, which appeared in Zürich in the German language, edited by a certain Tranquilli.[64] Secondino Tranquilli was better known by his pseudonym, Ignazio Silone, as the writer who broke off with the Italian Communist Party in 1930.[65] Heller was blamed for conspiring in that matter with two others: the German writer from the "Humm circle," Marschwitza, with whom Heller had indeed cooperated in Zürich;[66] and with the Swiss rightist communist Jules Humbert-Droz, who was attacked by Stalin himself at the Comintern congress for opposing Thälmann's rehabilitation in 1928.[67] Worst of all, per the anonymous denouncer, Heller had the "stupid impertinence to offer Tranquilli the leadership of the Italian Party in the case that the conciliators would have come to power in the German [Party]."[68] It was this kind of denunciations, common in the communist archives from the time, that brought one researcher to question "the (im-)possibility of friendship" between "German-speaking communist intellectuals of the twentieth century," summing up the history of such friendships as "tragic."[69]

This severe accusation, besides being highly improbable, also is not mentioned in any other existing document, and thus could be disregarded as forged. Nevertheless, it demonstrates that suspicions of *"Versöhnlertum"* (conciliatorism) kept hanging over Heller's head.[70] It is vis-à-vis such suspicions that Heller's bold tone in his letters to Moscow sounds dangerous. It is uncertain whether he was aware of that specific denunciation, but the continuity of the general claims against him must have been known to Heller. In a letter to a senior German communist representative in Moscow, the poet Johaness Becher, whom he comradely addressed as *"Lieber Hans,"* Heller wrote: "Only if we turn against phenomena like the *Information* (to name one local thing), we could achieve serious work. [. . .] The longer the [Nazi] regime holds and the situation of the individuals becomes harder, so could one hold onto subversive phenomena, and the Trotskyist poison could invade the periphery."[71] Heller's fierce reaction against dissident streams was based on his tactic of apologetics. He later claimed that on behalf of the Party he "tracked down" a conciliator named Volk and "succeeded to discover his contact with the small Trotskyist group [. . .] and with the renegades Brentano and Tranquilli [. . .] and [in doing so] rescued important help resources for the Party."[72]

Heller also shared with Becher his difficult situation in Zürich. Professionally he was frustrated: "I wrote two big brochures, which I have no luck with. One is: 'The German Pogrom, its social conditions and its consequences,' lies since July in Seyffardt-Amsterdam, paid and unprinted" (the second brochure was aimed against Döblin).[73] The Seyffardt German-language Dutch publishing house was dissolved in 1934.[74] Heller's brochure, dealing with the Nazi anti-Jewish measures of 1933, remained unpublished. Eventually, it was integrated into "The Jew Is to Be Burned," as a chapter titled "The Meaning of the German Pogrom," only to remain unpublished again.[75] The sad fate of this paper provides further evidence of how Heller had already begun sowing the seeds of his 1939 manuscript in 1933.

As he could not find permanent job and livelihood in Zürich, Heller started seeking other options: "I am politician and journalist, theoretician and propagandist. [. . .] I could achieve much much more, but where and how?" The first place that came to his mind was Paris: "In Paris an 'Institute for the Study of Fascism' was founded, a bit strange to do something like that in P[aris]. I offered [my services] to the people [. . .]. So far I received no answer."[76]

Financially, Heller came to despair in Zürich: "I do not have the quiet for that [theoretical work], because how should I pay for the holes in both pairs of shoes, which are already for three weeks at the shoemaker's, and I cannot collect them, because I do not have the money [. . .]. I help the people as much as I only can, but soon I could not anymore." Yet, the constant stream of persecuted refugees from Germany reminded him that his fate could have been dramatically worse: "One should be ashamed: yesterday came someone from Brandenburg, completely devastated, what sort of funny worries one has! shoe holes! while people are forced to eat their own shit, no one forces us to read our own articles."

His straits, both professional and economic, brought Heller to beg Becher: "An assignment that I can fulfill: please . . ."[77] An assignment arrived soon, but not from Russia, rather from Austria. On February 12, 1934, fights broke out across the land, between the social-democratic militia, the *Schützbund* (protection league), and the fascist regime of Engelbert Dolfuss. The Austrian communists, who were announced illegal already since 1933, took part in the fighting alongside the social-democrats, though a lesser part.[78] In doing so, they anticipated the antifascist "Popular Front" policy, which would be declared by the Comintern only in two years. Emma remembered that Otto strived to join the fighters: "When the *Schützbund* uprising broke out, he immediately tried to go to Austria. Eventually he succeeded, after many difficulties, to reach Vienna in the last hours of the uprising, but had to return to Switzerland of course."[79]

Heller indeed arrived in Austria only on February 17, after the insurrection had been already suppressed, but not as a fighter, rather as a journalist. He was sent by a German communist newspaper in the Swiss exile, the *Rundschau*, as a special reporter to Austria. He later admitted that his reports were criticized by "some comrades," who claimed that he "overrated the Nazis and underestimated the Party."[80] A growing pessimism might have outcropped from between his lines. After losing his third homeland, Germany, to Nazism, he now also had witnessed the loss of his first one to fascism. In the following years, his books were banned in his birthland too, as "printworks that include promotion of prohibited parties."[81]

After he had been deprived of any prospect in Czechoslovakia, Germany, the Netherlands, France, and Austria, now Switzerland too turned its back on Heller. His applications for residence and work permits were denied.[82] Thus, in April 1934, Heller applied to the Central Committee of the KPD, asking for an assignment, hoping that he would not have "to claim any *Rote Hilfe* support." Soon thereafter he received an invitation from Moscow to work for the *Deutsche Zentral Zeitung* ([DZZ], Central German Newspaper), the main German-language organ of the Comintern.[83]

The Soviet Union was definitely not Heller's first choice of asylum. His fears of living there were reflected in a reply he received from Moscow, trying to reassure him regarding the many worries he expressed in an unpreserved letter. The author of the reply, probably Julia Annenkova, the editor of *DZZ*, did not yet know enough to specify Heller's prospected role in the editorial, but promised it would be an "interesting job," and that he would not be used as "technical manpower." He could travel through the land and work for other newspapers too. As Heller also inquired about his wife and daughter, he was advised to come before them, and was informed of a German school in Moscow for Lily. Having asked about "trifles," he received the reply: "no need to bring dishes, everything could be bought in Moscow."[84] Besides worries common to any family in migration, which multiply in the case of refugees, did Heller also fear his political status in Moscow, as a suspected deviant?

Despite the suspicions, the German communist leadership approved Heller's appointment to the *DZZ*, as the editor of the foreign news section, and asked the editorial to cover his travel expenses, for which "he cannot pay."[85] As the Hellers only received train tickets from Moscow, Otto wrote "comrade Julia [Annenkova]" a furious letter, full of exclamation and question marks, revealing his distress.

> You have not sent me any money for travelling and luggage!!! I ask you [*dich*] however to consider, that I, as well as my family [who will travel separately] have at least four days of travel, possibly with two overnight stays (Vienna and Prague). We need luggage, porters, taxi, besides we need to send our stuff from here to M[oscow]. *Where is the*

money from??? I have nothing!!! A typesetter, who travels these days from here to there, receives besides the ticket a daily allowance of 20 Franks and 40 Franks for his luggage. Why not the editor too?? [. . .] How should I eat something until M[oscow]? Pay the luggage-porter?? [. . .] I have no money, nothing.[86]

The Soviet travel standards did not satisfy Heller's Central European bourgeois habits, which as a penniless refugee he could no longer afford himself.

In June, waiting in Zürich for his relocation to Moscow, Heller wrote an introduction to the Polish translation of *The Decline of Judaism*.[87] As in his foreword to the French edition, here too he explicitly declared that "the assumptions upon which this book is based did not change."[88] Yet again, on the implicit level he admitted that much was changed. Comparing to his French foreword, written over a year earlier, Heller's depictions of what was indeed different were even more severe: "these [Jewish] problems [. . .] became in the last years more momentous than ever before, and their influence is anything but theoretical," as the "Jewish problem [*Judennot*]" is worsening in many countries, including Palestine.[89]

One sentence especially reveals a new position: "Against the background of the events in Germany, the basis for existence is tapering and the area for migration is shrinking for the working Jewish masses oppressed by antisemitism."[90] On the level of theory, Heller embraced here for the first time the critique that was targeted at *The Decline of Judaism*, for ignoring the "working and exploited masses of Jewish nationality"[91] (using almost the same wording of his critic regarding the "constantly shrinking" "economic basis" of the Jews).[92] This shift will become central in "The Jew Is to Be Burned."[93] Also anticipating his 1939 manuscript was a bracketed comment criticizing the "ignoramus, who [in the Jewish context] repeatedly compares [the commodities-producing society] with capitalism, which is a complete nonsense."[94] Although Heller did not straightforwardly reject here the linkage between Jews and capitalism, acclaimed in his book, it can be seen as the inception of a doubt that will unfold in his manuscript.[95]

Heller even supported his acknowledgment of "working Jewish masses" with statistics, claiming that "fifty to sixty thousand half or fully proletarian Jews, belonging to the middle-class and intellectual groups, [. . .] were driven out of Germany."⁹⁶ This categorization fit Heller perfectly. From a personal perspective, this new approach reflected Heller's unmediated experience of working-class poverty, which was new to him. It also expressed his most private feeling of helplessness, facing a "shrinking" "area for migration." On July 11, 1934, Heller left Zürich "by command" (*Kommandierung*), as he defined it, on his new mission to the Soviet Union.⁹⁷

In Stalin's Moscow

Shortly after his arrival in Moscow, Heller applied for membership in the All-Soviet Communist Party (Bolsheviks) (Vsesoyuznaya kommunisticheskaya partiya [bol'shevikov], [VKP(b)]), probably to improve his legal status as a refugee in the Soviet Union.⁹⁸ He soon began his work in the *DZZ*, and Emma also started working, in the field of transportation.⁹⁹ She also studied in the communist university for national minorities (KUNMS).¹⁰⁰ At the editorial, Heller met his old comrade from Geserd, Wegener, with whom he had lost contact after the Reichstag Fire.¹⁰¹ Heller's articles at the *DZZ*, published mostly anonymously and occasionally under the pseudonym of Rudolf Kern, followed current international politics, and did not touch on Jewish issues.¹⁰²

A German translator employed in the newspaper, Lily Jergitsch, left one of the liveliest depictions of Heller's work as a journalist.

> His aspiration was to create a newspaper as vibrant as possible, and to fight against its "drought," which appalled him. Since DZZ, like all other newspapers, was allowed to bring only news from TASS [the Soviet news agency], the "vivification" could have existed only in the brilliantly written editorials on foreign politics. In the circles of journalists and writers Heller was respected and appreciated for his excellent journalistic skills. People crowded his regular lectures, [. . .]. His "prophecies" were often fulfilled. [. . .] Heller knew and told more than what was written in the DZZ.¹⁰³

Her impression of him as a person was not as positive: "O.H. was not a pleasant colleague. He had no problem throwing the word 'idiot' at the poor translator [the author herself], who confused the terms ambassador and consul. As a colleague he was not popular."[104] In the atmosphere of mutual denunciations, unpopularity might have been risky. But Heller was playing with fire even more dangerously, as Jergitsch remembered.

> Regarding some events in the Soviet Union he reacted quite critically. It was hard for him to restrain. He often expressed his doubt regarding the forms and manners, in which the socialist competition was implemented in the factories. [. . .] It was striking, that Otto Heller could hardly restrain himself, even regarding Stalin. He even spoke about the cult related to him and asked why he himself does not reject it. I remember: he just came back to the editorial from a visit in Lenin's museum that was just opened. His words were: children, that is more a Stalin museum than a Lenin museum![105]

From late 1934, this kind of behavior became deadly. The assassination of the high-ranking Bolshevik leader, Sergei Kirov, on December 1, provided Stalin with the pretext to launch a wave of show trials against Party members, also known as the Great Terror, or the Great Purge. At first the purges were focused on veteran Bolsheviks, whom Stalin saw as his rivals and accused of treason. Culminating between 1936 and 1938, the purges inflicted hundreds of thousands of Soviet and foreign communist politicians, activists, and intellectuals, who were imprisoned and, in many cases, executed.[106] Usually the victims were blamed for conspiring with so-called deviant factions, such as the Trotskyites, the rightists, and the conciliators.[107]

Three months after Kirov's assassination, in early February 1935, at the editorial Heller reported being sick with high fever, and asked to be hospitalized in a sanatorium.[108] Was it only the Russian winter? Was his old lungs illness triggered? He experienced health problems in at least two of his former visits in the Soviet Union, not necessarily in the winter. Did the sicknesses result only from the stressful situation of being in a foreign land, or against the tense background, unique to the political life in the Soviet Union at the time?

One hint implies a connection with the purges. Heller recovered after two months, discovering that his entry permit to the Comintern headquarters was no longer valid. His editor in-chief, Annenkova, had to apply for a renewal of the permit.[109] Was it just a bureaucratic flaw? Only two weeks later, Heller needed to reject accusations of supporting the conciliators back in 1928, after his name was mentioned in an interrogation conducted against conciliators.[110] This accusation brought him to a "flawed behavior in the assembly of the party group of the DZZ," as Annenkova reported.[111] Could his illness, as well as the delay in renewing his entrance permit, have been caused by that interrogation?

At the beginning of the next winter, in November 1935, Heller was ill again. This time "a lung disease" was explicitly mentioned. A place in a sanatorium was again requested for him.[112] The German journalist Sebastian Haffner, writing of his father's reaction to Nazi oppression, made a distinction, quite sensible for his time: "With people who are used to restraint in word and gesture, some part of the body is invariably affected by severe mental stress. Some have heart attacks in such cases. My father's weakness was his stomach."[113] It seems that Heller's vulnerable organ was his lungs. Originally hurt by political violence, in the First World War, they continued to be susceptible to its near presence.

The next documentation of Heller is only from April 1936, when he was again, or maybe still in hospital. This time the specified reason was "scarlet." A condolence message to a German Party leader was sent on Heller's behalf, not written by his own handwriting.[114] Why could he not write? Many questions regarding Heller's time in Moscow must be left obscure.

In early May his application for membership in the VKP(b) was not yet answered. The party authorities were still gathering more information about his political résumé.[115] Two months later the required information was not yet received.[116] Heller was asked to provide names of referees who would confirm his political liability.[117] He had provided such a list on his arrival in Moscow, already two years ago, which included senior figures such as the Hungarians Béla Kun and Julius Alpári; from Czechoslovakia Bohumír Šmeral, Klement Gottwald, and Antonin Zapotocky; and from the German Party Willi Münzenberg, Wilhelm Pieck, and Walter Ulbricht.[118] This list was apparently no longer sufficient.

During the summer of 1936, Heller understood that his future in the Soviet Union was not secure and openly started seeking a way out. He wrote to the Austrian communist leader Johann Koplenig, suggesting that he would join the Communist Party of Austria (*Kommunistische Partei Österreichs* [KPÖ]) instead of the Soviet Communist Party. Heller offered himself to the Austrian Party in exile, as a coordinator of press work in Switzerland, France, and England. For that purpose, he asked for the Party's help in settling down legally in Zürich. He revealed that this idea was already approved by the Swiss communist Humbert-Droz, which proves their contacts.[119] Heller's move almost succeeded. The Politburo of the Austrian Party decided to accept him. The German and Czechoslovakian Parties, in which Heller was a former member, did not object.[120]

But he was not yet safe. In late July, only a few days after all the approvals were given, Heller was hospitalized again, this time due to "Furunculoses." His physician, Dr. Glaser, asked him awkward questions: what has this comrade done, and why was that comrade arrested? After several days, the doctor himself ceased to arrive at the hospital. Heller found out that he too was arrested.[121]

In early September Heller had not yet managed to leave the country. On the night of September 4, a "secret process" began in Moscow, which was held for several nights until September 8. The purpose of those nocturnal sessions was to purge the KPD-in-exile from opposition groups. During one of the meetings Becher was asked if between 1929 and 1931 he was part of the "*Versöhnlersalon*" (conciliators-saloon). This term brought together the conciliators, among whom Heller's name was mentioned, with a suspicious circle of artists, among whom the painter and designer John Heartfield was named.[122] Heartfield was the brother of the publisher Wiland Herzfelde, to whom Heller would later submit the manuscript "The Jew Is to Be Burned."

Against that background arrests were committed in the *DZZ* editorial, "that back then seemed to us incomprehensible and eerie," recalled Emma.[123] She herself was asked by a certain Robert if Otto was a conciliator.[124] In a Party group assembly it was reported that Heller had contacts with conciliator circles.[125] This purge of the German Party in Moscow brought to the arrest and subsequent execution of many, including some of Heller's closest colleagues at the *DDZ*: the editor, Julia Annenkova, and the editorial members Heinrich Süßkind and Georg Wegener. In addition, a number of senior German communist veterans, such as Heinz Neumann, Hermann Remmele, and many others, lost their lives.[126] As Koestler concluded, "During the Great

Purge, all German communists in Russia with a handful of exceptions, were arrested, deported, or handed over to the Gestapo."[127]

Many of Heller's Russian contacts were eliminated too. Dimanshtein was arrested and executed in 1938.[128] It was probably after learning about Dimanshtein's fate that Heller decided to omit a Dimanshtein quote that had appeared in *The Decline of Judaism* from an otherwise almost identical text in his manuscript, "The Jew Is to Be Burned." In the manuscript Heller reported the dissolvement of local and foreign associations that supported the Jewish colonization, because their "purpose [. . .] was essentially fulfilled."[129] In reality, the activity of these organizations was terminated after "the Jewish population able and willing to farm declined steadily," and many of their "staff members fell victim" to the "purge trials in 1936–37."[130] Almost all the leading Jewish figures in Birobidzhan became victims between 1936 and 1938, which further contributed to the district's decline.[131]

A clear antisemitic undertone accompanied the purges, as the Jewish population of the Soviet Union gradually fell into the category of "enemy nation."[132] Although not yet as bold as it would become in the early 1950s, this undertone was like "distant rolls of thunder warning of a storm to come" that "a very sensitive ear" could have heard.[133] Heller's ear was undoubtedly sensitive to antisemitism, as well as to Soviet politics. He rescued himself at the very last moment. "One day O.H. disappeared," remembered Lily Jergitsch, "no one asked where."[134] On September 8, the last day of the German purge trial, it was reported that "the comrade is out of the country." On this occasion, Heller's "social origin" was not to be forgotten: "bourgeois."[135]

Via Madrid to Paris

While Stalin started implementing, in his own style, the purging principles he had learned from Hitler's "Night of the Long Knives," his public rhetoric turned against Nazi Germany. The Seventh World Congress of the Comintern, held in Moscow in the summer of 1935, abandoned the former "Third Period" policy that marked social-democracy (referred to as "social-fascism") as the "main enemy" of communism. Instead, the Communist International called on a united "Popular Front" of all progressive forces in each country—including the social-democrats—against fascism. During 1936, Popular Front coalitions succeeded to win the elections in France and Spain. On July 17, a military coup broke out in Spain, headed by General Francisco Franco, against the republican Popular Front government. The Spanish Civil War had begun.

By that time, Willi Münzenberg, Heller's former journalistic patron in Berlin, was also on Moscow's purging list. He managed to delay his end, by using the opportunity given to him by the war in Spain. Münzenberg placed himself at the service of the Comintern antifascist propaganda mechanism.[136] In September 1936, the Comintern's executive committee decided to mobilize International Brigades of volunteers among workers of all countries, with the purpose of sending them to Spain to aid the republican troops. The International Brigades were formally a Popular Front initiative, a compound of members of many leftist and democratic political streams, but the organizing core behind this facade was the Comintern. Paris became the key center of recruitment and transport to Spain.[137] There Münzenberg was, and there came Heller.

Heller eluded Moscow at the very last moment. Just like for Münzenberg, the Spanish Civil War offered him a rescue, a new communist assignment outside the Soviet Union. Though not documented, it could have been Münzenberg who helped Heller to get his new posts in Madrid and Paris, as his plan to work for the Austrian Party in Zürich was not accomplished by the time he had to rush out from Moscow. Shortly after arriving in Paris, Heller was sent to Spain, as a propagandist for Radio Madrid.[138] There is no further information on Heller's short stay in the Spanish capital. Koestler, who also volunteered for a Comintern mission in Spain, wrote: "Spain became the rendezvous of the international Leftist bohemia. [. . .] Poets, novelists, journalists [. . .] flocked across the Pyrenees [. . .] 'to be useful,' as the phrase went," for instance, "in one of the numerous radio and propaganda departments."[139] Around a quarter of the over 40,000 volunteers to Spain were of Jewish origins, among them several known German-speaking communist intellectuals, Heller's comrades: Anna Seghers, Alfred Kantorowicz, and E. E. Kisch.[140]

Back in Paris, Heller was recruiting volunteers for the International Brigades. After probably traveling through Czechoslovakia, Emma and Lily joined him in late 1936, not knowing that they would both stay there for the rest of their lives.[141] For many months

Heller oversaw the transportation of Austrian communist volunteers to Spain.[142] In one case he had sent a volunteer, Myron Pasicznyk, to the Rote Hilfe in Zürich, for him to return to Paris with false documents.[143] Another volunteer, Max Stern, remembered how he arrived in a trade-union house in Paris, in February 1937, to join the International Brigades. There he was directed to Heller, who took care of the Austrians. Heller ordered Stern to replace him, because he had to leave for two weeks, Stern did not ask where. For two days he worked by Heller's side, to learn his job: giving the volunteers questionnaires to fill, sending them to medical examinations, arranging accommodation and provision for them, and verifying their political reliability, to avoid penetration of spies or just adventurers lacking in political consciousness. After two weeks Heller returned, and Stern continued to Spain.[144]

In Paris Heller was absorbed by the KPÖ, which had agreed to accept him as a member already in Moscow. He participated as a writer, editor, and in some cases even a cofounder, in several Austrian journals, which came out in Paris in French or German: *Cercle Culturel Autrichien* (Austrian Cultural Circle), *Nouvelles d'Autriche* (Austrian News), *Weg und Ziel* (Way and Goal), *Europäische Stimme* (European Voice), and *Balkan Korrespondenz*.[145] The Hellers lived in Neuilly sur Seine, a rather bourgeois suburb of Paris, which Otto's and Emma's jobs in the press apparently allowed them.[146] This is further evidence of their bourgeois habits, notwithstanding their communist conviction.

Through his journalistic work Heller became acquainted with some of his dearest friends for the years to come. The Hungarian-Austrian communist journalist Árpád Haász, or Albert Haas, who cofounded with him the *Cercle Culturel Autrichien*, would become his close underground associate in Auschwitz.[147] The Austrian unaffiliated writer, Elisabeth Freundlich, was invited to write for the *Nouvelles d'Autriche*, where she met Heller as an editorial member. She worked with him there for about a year, until the war broke and the newspaper was closed.

Like other women who described Heller, Freundlich focused more on his personality than on his *Fraktionspolitik*, a topic the men around him, including Heller himself, seemed obsessed with.

> I learned from Otto Heller to trace the social and historical roots of every event; and he never permitted any linguistic

sloppiness. In this regard he was relentless as the satirist Karl Kraus, his great countryman and much-admired idol.[148] Political slogans obscured our view of reality as much then as they do now. Otto had a horror of thoughtless parroting of hackneyed party rhetoric; he fought it relentlessly and in so doing did not exactly make himself beloved among many party functionaries. [. . .] If he were still alive, our opinions would probably diverge today even more than they did then. But even now, after fifty years, I have the sound of his voice in my ear, I hear his laugh exactly next to me, I hear his ridicule, often hurtful, spurring on my ambition. [. . .] A man of glowing temperament, with an unbridled fighting spirit and great literary gifts. A taciturn, sometimes rude, style of conversation made it hard to recognize right away what a sympathetic and vulnerable heart was beating inside him.[149]

Freundlich seemed to be in love with Heller.[150] But just like the translator who feared him in Moscow, Lily Jergitsch, she noticed his indifference to popularity among his colleagues and political correctness, despite the suspicions that followed him all the way to Paris.

After only two months in France, Heller complained to the editor of *Balkan Korrespondenz*, Richard Stahlmann, that Emma was fired from her work in the Comintern for false accusations of having contacts with Trotskyites. His complaint was reported to Moscow: "According to the explanations I heard from Heller, it could be understood that not only his wife, but also he himself was affiliated with the Trotskyist gang."[151] In Heller's private book collection I found two German booklets by Trotsky. Unlike in all his other books, he did not write his name on the inner cover.[152] Does that imply actual sympathy to Trotskyism, or merely intellectual and political interest? Lacking any other evidence, it is difficult to judge.

Stahlmann himself, however, did not blame him for Trotskyism, but confirmed that although "Heller was very zealous in his [journalistic] work, [. . .] in political matters he is scatterbrained. It was necessary to control him constantly in political matters and to guide him strongly. As far as I knew his weak sides, it was a necessity for him to chatter with all people and I once put him strongly in the frame."[153] Facing such accusations, Heller chose wisely to join the

Austrian Party. His champion in the German Party, Münzenberg, was already surveilled and later haunted down by Soviet apparat men in France, who were most probably responsible for his mysterious death in June 1940.[154]

In the KPÖ Heller had an old friend, Siegfried (Friedel) Fürnberg, who had cofounded with him the German section of the Communist Party in Czechoslovakia.[155] Fürnberg tried, at least to an extent, to protect Heller's name in Moscow: "It became known to the Austrian party that in the past, during his membership in the Czechoslovakian and German parties, Heller had contacts with Trotskyites and conciliators. Although he is not accused of anything by the Austrian party, he was gradually removed from the newspaper [Balkan Korrespondenz]. By the time the war broke only few contributions by him were published."[156] Fürnberg's report might have saved Heller from a worse fate. Outside the Soviet Union, execution by assassination was reserved for senior "traitors," such as Münzenberg and, of course, Trotsky himself. One of the worst punishments that could be imposed on a rank-and-file communist in exile was layoff, which became Heller's fate. His editor simply told the other employees that Heller "was relieved due to budget restrictions."[157] Expulsion from the Party and excommunication was perhaps the one worse penalty, from which he was exempted. Purge trials were not restricted to Soviet territories. Small-scale purges were conducted in communist cells all around the globe. For instance, in the Paris "Institute for the Study of Fascism," to which Heller applied in 1934, occurred one such "Purge in a Teacup," as it was called by Koestler.[158]

An atmosphere of aligning with the strict ideological dictates from Moscow dominated even artistic communist circles. One of them, which became Heller's immediate social environment in Paris, was the "Protection Association of German Writers" (SDS), reestablished in exile by those writers who were expelled from the German, now Nazi-ruled, original organization. In Paris, Heller was regularly lecturing at the association's events.[159] This "was a kind of cultural center for the German émigrés in Paris." As usual in "front"-organizations, the chairman was not communist, but among the most salient members were communist writers like Seghers and Kisch.[160] Koestler portrayed the atmosphere in that club as follows:

> The slogan [of the Soviet Writers' Federation] was: "Write the Truth." [. . .] And there we all sat, Kisch and Anna

Seghers and Regler and Katorowicz and Uhse [. . .] earnestly discussing how to write the truth without writing the truth. With our training in dialectical acrobatics it was not even difficult to prove that all truth was historically class-conditioned, that so-called objective truth was a bourgeois myth, and that "to write the truth" meant to select and emphasize those items and aspects of a given situation which served the proletarian revolution, and were therefore "historically correct."[161]

Such was Heller's intellectual milieu in Paris. But he did not necessarily succumb to this atmosphere.

Figure 3.3. A portrait of Otto Heller. Unknown artist, October 21, 1939. Courtesy of the Papineau-Heller Family Archive (PHFA), Paris.

As his journalistic work was reduced, due to the political suspicions against him, in 1938–1939, Heller "spent much time in the French national library," writing "The Jew Is to Be Burned."[162] In this manuscript, the mantra from his introductions to translations of *The Decline of Judaism* to French and Polish, that nothing has been substantially changed since 1931, did not return.[163] It was not a new edition of his old book, but rather an entirely new one.

While writing his manuscript, Heller studied not only the national history of the Jews (with special emphasis on hatred of Jews since antiquity), but also of the Serbs, Czechs, Slovaks, and Austrians.[164] His interest in Serbian history must have stemmed from his work for the *Balkan Korrespondenz*. But, alongside Czech history, it could have also thrown him back to his encounter with Serb and Czech irredentists during the First World War, and reminded him of the nationalist ideas he learned simultaneously with his exposure to Marxism.[165] Alongside the Slovak, Czech history connected him to his former chosen country of residence, now being gradually annexed by Nazi Germany. Austrian nationalism, as separate from the German, became a hallmark of the KPÖ following the Anschluss.[166] It was under the influence of these national histories that Heller wrote "The Jew Is to Be Burned."

On the morning of November 7, 1938, while Heller might have been sitting in the national library, a young German Jew, son of Polish immigrants, entered the German embassy, located only a one-hour walk from there down the Seine. Seventeen-year-old Herschel Grynszpan, whose family was deported two weeks earlier from Hannover to the Polish border town Zbąszyń, shot the German diplomat Ernst vom Rath. The assassination provided the pretext for the Nazi government to launch the so-called Kristallnacht (Night of the Broken Glass), between November 9 and 10.[167] The November Pogrom, alongside increasing state antisemitism in Eastern Europe and the 1938 anti-Jewish legislation in Hungary and Italy, played an important role in Heller's reassessment of the state of European Jewry: "The Jew Is to Be Burned."[168]

Chapter 4

"The Jew Is to Be Burned" (1939)

> At the crossroads between barbarism and the advancement toward higher forms of social order, it [the Jewish question] arises anew with unprecedented sharpness.
>
> —Otto Heller, 1939

On August 20, 1939, exiled in Paris, Otto Heller finished revising the manuscript of his second book on the Jewish question. The subtitle was already typed: "Studies on the Jewish and Racial Question" ("Studien zur Juden- und Rassenfrage"). He had left the main title undetermined until the very last moment and, only then, twelve days before the outbreak of the Second World War, handwrote the heading that was to become tragically prophetic, both in a general sense and for himself: "The Jew Is to Be Burned" ("Der Jude wird verbrannt") (see figure 4.1). Having written *The Decline of Judaism* in 1931, why did Heller need to write another encompassing book-length work on the same topic—the Jewish question—within less than a decade? This chapter reveals Heller's hitherto virtually unknown manuscript.

Within a few months during 1939, Heller wrote at least three versions of his yet untitled manuscript, all discovered over eighty years later in his daughter's attic. The earliest, found in a folder titled "first transcript," was drafted in "Paris, early 1939."[1] A neighboring folder, simply bearing the name of the intended publishing house, "Malik,"

124 | Radical Assimilation in the Face of the Holocaust

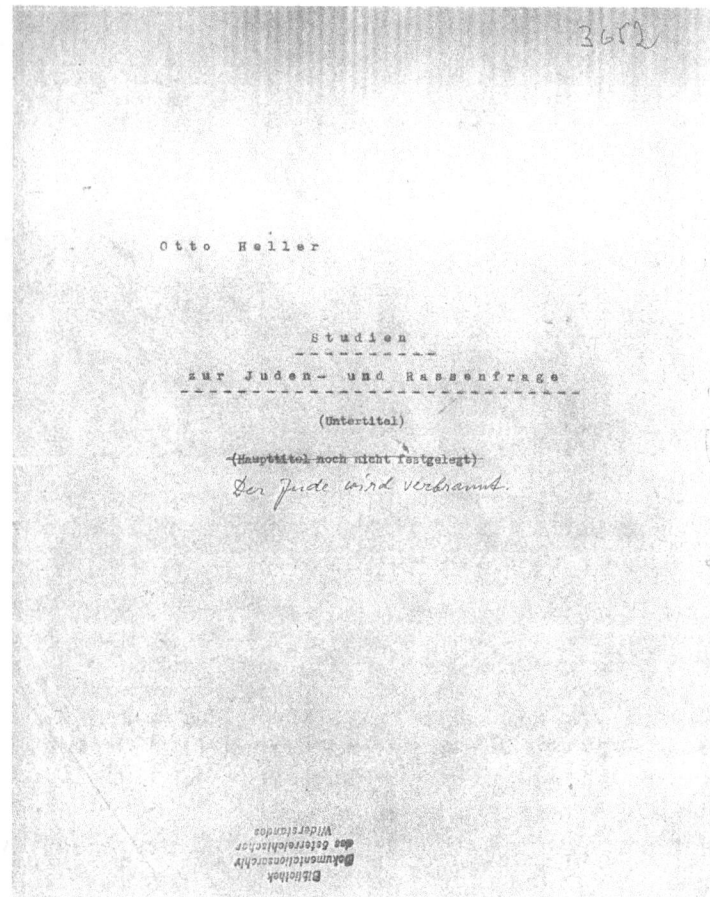

Figure 4.1. Title page of Heller's manuscript "Der Jude wird verbrannt" ("The Jew Is to Be Burned") (Paris, 1939). The main title is handwritten. Courtesy of Dokumentationsarchiv des österreichischen Widerstandes, Vienna: 45920/7.

contains a second draft, probably the one submitted for review by the publisher, Wieland Herzfelde.[2] The latter, a German communist intellectual and publisher, was the founder and long-standing director of Malik Verlag, a private press closely affiliated with the KPD. In 1939, after six years of exile in Europe, Herzfelde reestablished his publishing house in New York, where he received Heller's manuscript from Paris.[3] Emma Heller remembered that "as the Second World

War broke out, the manuscript was ready and the first corrections have already been suggested by Wieland Herzfelde and came back from New York."[4] Actually, by the breakout of the war, Heller had even completed a third version, revised according to some of the publisher's comments, which he finally gave the title "The Jew Is to Be Burned."[5]

The further history of the manuscript is obscure. Considering the circumstances of war, it could not be published. As the Hellers wandered all around France during the war, and from mid-1944 to mid-1945 were all incarcerated in different concentrations camps, it is unclear who kept these illegal documents through the end of the occupation.[6] When Emma and Lily returned to Paris, they apparently found all versions unharmed. In 1947, a single chapter, "What is Race?," was published in an Austrian communist journal.[7] A copy of the final draft might have been collected from Paris by one of Heller's Austrian comrades as early as 1945. However, this copy was "discovered" only in 1967 in the Central Archive of the Communist Party of Austria (Zentrales Parteiarchiv der Kommunistische Partei Österreichs, ZPA der KPÖ).[8] This discovery was probably connected with the oral and written reports provided by Emma Heller during and following her visit in Vienna in 1967.[9] From there the manuscript found its way into the collection of the Documentation Centre of Austrian Resistance (Dokumentationsarchiv des österreichischen Widerstandes, DÖW) in Vienna.[10]

Although most of that time, at least from 1967 if not from 1947, it was lying in archives in Vienna, "The Jews Is to Be Burned" was almost completely ignored, only informatively mentioned by a handful of scholars who encountered it.[11] The only researcher who devoted a brief discussion to this manuscript, the German literary scholar Silvia Schlenstedt, pointed to some significant differences from *The Decline of Judaism*.[12] These differences demand a reevaluation not only of the scholarly image of Heller himself, but of the entire historiography of the communist discourse on the Jewish question.[13] The meaning of "The Jews Is to Be Burned" will unfold in the following discussion, first against the background of the communist literature on the Jewish question from the Nazi era, then with comparison to *The Decline of Judaism* and between the different drafts of the manuscript, and at last through its enigmatically prophetic title.

German Communists on the Jewish Question under Nazism

Heller's book of 1931, *The Decline of Judaism*, was an unwelcomed deviation from the usual reluctance of the KPD to address the Jewish question during the time of the Weimar Republic.[14] This line, based on the rationale that in its struggle against Nazism the party had better not appear to be pro-Jewish, continued well after the Nazi rise to power, when the communists themselves were heavily oppressed by the new regime. The communist literature in the German language, produced during the Nazi period mostly in exile and distributed illegally in Third Reich, continued to pay limited attention to the Jewish question, despite the growing oppression against Jews too. This literature maintained the traditional Marxist concept of antisemitism as a mere deceptive instrument.[15]

According to the communist argument, the Nazi boycott of Jewish businesses on April 1, 1933, did not hurt big Jewish companies, but only small businesses as part of a policy that served big capital, Jewish and "Aryan" alike, at the expense of the lower classes. Thus, antisemitic propaganda was aimed at disguising the true capitalist nature of this campaign from the eyes of the German petty bourgeoisie and proletariat, whom the Nazis pretended to protect against Jewish competition and exploitation.[16] In the first years of the Third Reich, this communist description was not entirely false, as big companies in Jewish ownership were indeed hardly hurt by the Nazi policy. But the logic behind it was different from that identified by the communists: inflicting large-scale Jewish employers would have left many Germans unemployed and hurt the popularity of the Nazis. Additionally, the pressure to take over Jewish property came mainly from small and medium businesses, at least until late 1937.[17]

The communist dismissal of the antisemitic propaganda as a mere deceit, and accordingly their denial of the Jews as essential victims of Nazism, remained intact until the pogrom of November 9, 1938. This outburst of violence against all the layers of Jewish society, followed by confiscations of large Jewish-owned corporations, refuted the earlier communist interpretation of the persecutions against Jews as a mere mask. This, in turn, provoked both theoretical and political responses by representatives of the KPD. Theoretically they attempted to defend the Marxist axiom of the "primacy of economy" over politics, namely the method of reducing political events to expressions of economic interests. This was done by explaining the expropriation of Jewish big capital as a robbery of the Jewish sector of the haute bourgeoisie by its German counterpart.[18] Such an economistic interpretation to the persecution of Jews was demonstrated by Albert Norden in a book published under a pseudonym in Paris.[19] Seven years earlier Heller embraced Norden's criticism of *The Decline of Judaism*.[20] Similarly, he now integrated the latter's new analysis into "The Jews Is to Be Burned." [21] In this respect, Heller's manuscript followed the apologetic theoretical response of the KPD to the events of November 1938.

But it was not the theoretical communist response to the Kristallnacht, but rather the political one, that seemed to invoke Heller to a more substantial shift. The KPD publicly reacted to the pogrom with an intensive, though brief wave of condemning publications. The most salient of them was a formal "Declaration of the Central Committee of the KPD," under the title "Against the Disgrace of the Pogrom against the Jews."[22] According to historian Jeffrey Herf, "this statement was unique in the history of German Communism," which never gave "the Jewish question such a central role," or proclaimed such "solidarity with the Jews."[23] Historian David Bankier explained this unusual wave, both quantitatively and qualitatively, of communist publications as a tactical reaction to the "erosion of ideology in the working class, which was exposed to the flood of antisemitic propaganda and integrated into the ruling Nazi party."[24] And indeed, this short wave of late 1938 did not signify a fundamental shift in the attitude of the communist authorities. A turning point in the communist discourse, not originated in the authorities but in various independent groups of communist exiles, will appear only in 1942, facing the information of mass murder of Jews in Europe.[25]

But for Heller the November pogrom had a more protracted impact. In a folder containing materials that he collected for the writing of "The Jews Is to Be Burned," Heller kept a copy of the Central Committee's announcement, on which he underlined the following sentences: "Help our tortured Jewish fellow citizens by all means!" "Solidarity in sympathy and in assistance for Jewish compatriots."[26] While for the KPD leadership these outcries appeared to be merely instrumental, in Heller's manuscript they found a deeper echo. Completed only in the summer of 1939, well after the public communist protest of November 1938 had declined and prior to that of 1942, Heller revealed a new attitude to the Jewish question in "The Jew Is to Be Burned."

Actually, a few communist publications on the Jewish question preceded the November pogrom, reflecting the atmosphere that had already emerged during a series of smaller and less-known pogroms that took place in Germany in the summer of 1938.[27] These articles tended to be even more sympathetic than those of November, as they were written by communist activists who demonstrated genuine concern, before the Kristallnacht events forced on the Party authorities a public response. One illegal communist booklet, circulated in Germany in the summer of 1938 under the pseudonym Walter Pötsch, denied the identification of Jews with capitalism and emphasized the Jewish contribution to the German culture.[28] Bankier defined this approach as "totally unexpected," as it was "characterized by apologetics typical of the Centralverein deutscher Staatsburger jüdischen Glaubens [Central Association of German Citizens of Jewish Faith], certainly not of communist literature."[29]

Another such essay of summer 1938 was written by Heller's friend and cofounder of the German section of the Communist Party of Czechoslovakia, now active in the Communist Party of Austria, Friedel Fürnberg.[30] Fürnberg's article begins with a Marxist survey of Jewish history, based on Heller's *The Decline of Judaism*. Nevertheless, there are several meaningful differences between Heller's and Fürnberg's Jewish historiographies. Besides emphasizing, like Pötsch, positive contributions by Jews to German and European culture, Fürnberg omitted Heller's key definition of the Jews as a "caste" and paid much more attention to class differences within Jewish society and to Jewish participation in revolutionary movements.[31] Bankier's depiction of Fürnberg as "unlike others of his time, and certainly unlike official Communist interpretation," calls for special attention to "The Jew Is to Be Burned," as a much longer text on the Jewish question, written by a German-speaking communist about a year later.[32]

The texts written by Fürnberg and Pötsch, notwithstanding their distinguished pro-Jewish attitude, should still be understood as part of the limited wave of untypical communist publications focusing on the Jewish question in 1938. Heller's manuscript, though not waving Jewish apologetic flags as high as these two, transcended that wave, both in time and scope. Therefore, it should be positioned differently within the history of the communist reaction to Nazi anti-Jewish policies.

A Manuscript Written "At the Crossroads"

In his introduction to "The Jew Is to Be Burned," Heller conceptualized that historical moment as a "crossroads": "The Jewish question is an organic component of the general abnormality of our society. Above all it affects the great majority of the Jews themselves through distress, misery, and grievance. At the crossroads between barbarism and the advancement toward higher forms of social order, it arises anew with unprecedented sharpness."[33] At first sight, the notion of a "crossroads" is a mere reiteration of Rosa Luxemburg's famous slogan from the time of the First World War: "Capitalist society faces a dilemma, either an advance to Socialism or a reversion to barbarism."[34] But beneath this usual communist rhetoric an innovation was hiding: Heller had now connotated the "crossroads" of "capitalist society" directly to the Jewish question, which "arises anew with unprecedented sharpness." Hence, the metaphor of a "crossroads" bares here a double meaning.

The first meaning is a historical one—Heller's interpretation of that historical moment, on the eve of the Second World War, as another "crossroads between barbarism and [. . .] advancement." The second meaning is historiographic, referring to Heller's writing itself, which reflected an intersection between old and new discourses. On the one hand, this text continued what historian Enzo Traverso called the "traditional Marxist conception," characteristic to *The Decline of Judaism*.[35] This meant seeing the Jewish question as only one of many manifestations of the general social question and antisemitism as a mere primitive reminiscence of "barbarism." On the other hand, here in "The Jew Is to Be Burned," Heller acknowledged the "unprecedented" level of Jewish "misery and grievance," and subsequently identified "National-Socialist race-antisemitism," as the "most gruesome, despicable and dangerous form" of antisemitism.[36] Heller expressed such a dual stance from the very beginning of his manuscript.

> The fact that around one specific people conflicts and controversies of spiritual, economic, and general social nature

are *flared up* [entbrennen] through thousands of years; the fact that this people can preserve intact its existence as an *exceptional* phenomenon through those thousands of years *in the national sense too*; only to become again, finally—in the midst of the process of its dissolvement and transformation—an object and *victim* of a violent crisis; these facts imply *unique* factors and contexts. [. . .] Answers to this question [the Jewish question] are to be looked for in the only place where they are to be found: in the social history of the peoples.[37]

This passage demonstrates three essential motifs in "The Jew Is to Be Burned." The first is the semantic field of fire: conflicts are persistently "flared up" around the Jewish people. This metaphor, appearing already in the title and repeating in many forms along the manuscript, conveys an atmosphere of emergency, which was absent in *The Decline of Judaism*. The second motif is the emphasis on Jewish victimhood, which was also foreign to Heller's published book.

A third aspect is Heller's ambivalent engagement with the notion of the exceptionality of the Jewish people, both in history and in contemporary politics. On the one hand, Jewish history forms "an exceptional phenomenon," that should be explained through "unique factors." This exceptionality was not only socioeconomic but expressed "in the national sense too." Heller's national conception of Jewish history, that was present in a more latent form already in *The Decline of Judaism*, became here explicit. On the other hand, continued Heller, Jewish history should be explained through the same historical factors pertaining the general history all peoples. His previous unequivocal stance, manifested in *The Decline of Judaism*, that "the history of the Jews is not as unique as it seems to be,"[38] was now diluted with a ration of Jewish exceptionalism: "It is the history of three thousand years of wars, exile, persecution, impoverishment [*Verkümmerung*], but also of power, wealth, ascension to the highest spirituality, profound abundance of ideas and spiritual fruitfulness [*geistiger Befruchtung*]."[39]

Likewise, regarding the question of the singularity of the situation of contemporary Jews, with comparison to other victims of Nazism, Heller presented an ambiguous position. In a typical communist, universalist style, he claims that his current work was neither "for [n]or against" the Jews: "We attack anyone who oppresses, persecutes, or humiliates any nation or people. We defend each and every people who become a victim of barbarism." And yet, "nowadays we are defending its Jewish victims *above all*."[40] Unlike *The Decline of Judaism*, where Heller made clear, that "this book is not intended to defend anyone,"[41] in 1939 "defending the Jewish victims" is a declared purpose.

The mixture of similarities and differences between *The Decline of Judaism* and "The Jew Is to Be Burned" is evident straight from the structure of the latter work. The unpublished manuscript encompasses eighteen chapters that can be divided into three main sections. The first chapters, similarly to Heller's published book, constitute a synthetic Marxist interpretation of Jewish history,[42] arranged chronologically from antiquity, "The Origins of Judaism,"[43] via Middle Ages, "The Way through One and a Half Millennia,"[44] up until modernity, "1776–1789–1871."[45] The latter chapter's title discloses a new positive representation of the Jewish role in modern political and social revolutions. Another novelty: a special chapter is devoted to the pejorative image of the *"Talmudjude"* (the Talmud Jew), attempting to dispel this antisemitic myth through engaging with the historical reality of the Talmud, a topic completely ignored in *The Decline of Judaism*.[46]

The second and largest part of the manuscript contains a sociological, historical, and political analysis of antisemitism in Eastern and Central Europe. Compared to Heller's former book, "The Jew Is to Be Burned" allocates much more space for confrontation with the growing threat of race-antisemitism. The discussion on Eastern Europe begins with the history of the antisemitic text, *Protocols of the Elders of Zion*.[47] It continues with a chapter on the contemporary "Burning Questions" concerning the Jews of Eastern Europe.[48] The discussion on German antisemitism begins with the "Predecessors of National-Socialism"[49] in the nineteenth century and reaches the *"Deutsche Pogrom"* ("German pogrom").[50] Various aspects of racism are also discussed, such as the "History of Racism," "Church and Racism," and more.[51]

The three final chapters constitute the third part, dealing with different suggested solutions to the Jewish question, focusing mainly on the debate between the Zionist and Soviet paths.[52] While the historical parts of Heller's two books are similar in structure and scope (though different in content), the two other parts of each of the works substantially differ. As two-thirds of *The Decline of Judaism* is dedicated to the Soviet solution,⁵³ only one chapter deals with antisemitism.⁵⁴ In "The Jew Is to Be Burned," it is the other way around: two-thirds of the text is devoted to inquiry of antisemitism,⁵⁵ while only one chapter focuses on the Soviet Union.⁵⁶ The proportion of the problem to its solution was completely inverted, giving much more weight to the problem in 1939.

The following discussion examines the novelties introduced by "The Jew Is to Be Burned" with comparison to *The Decline of Judaism*, focusing on three interconnected questions that both texts address: (1) What is the relationship between capitalism and the Jews, and how should the Jews be categorized in terms of class? (2) What are the driving forces of antisemitism? And (3) what should be, therefore, the political solution to the Jewish question?

Forerunners or Victims of Capitalism?

One important theoretical innovation in "The Jew Is to Be Burned" was Heller's incorporation of Weberian theory into his own Marxist interpretation of Jewish history.⁵⁷ The importance of this novelty is not only theoretical, but also political. The works of the prominent German sociologist Max Weber (1864–1920) were banned as "reactionary" in the communist world, especially in the Stalinist era.⁵⁸ This raises the question of why Heller chose to explicitly cite Weber's writing in his new manuscript. To address this question, a brief introduction to Weber's polemic with his contemporary German sociologist, Werner Sombart (1863–1941) is required.

Sombart and Weber represent contradictory approaches to the relationship between Jews and capitalism.⁵⁹ Sombart, who emphasized the commercial aspect of capitalism, characterized the Jews as bearers of racial commercial traits originating in their nomadic ancient past. According to Sombart, capitalist commerce, which was foreign to medieval northwestern Europe, was introduced in this region by the forerunners of modern capitalism, the Jews.⁶⁰ As a fierce critic of capitalism, Sombart did not credit the Jews for its promotion, but rather blamed them for this.

In contrast, Weber saw the rational organization of labor as the main feature of modern capitalism and attributed its rise to the Protestant ethos. He saw the Jews as a "pariah capitalist" element, typical of precapitalist societies. Just like *caste*, the term *pariah* was borrowed from traditional Indian society, where it signified the lowest caste in the hierarchy, which was considered outcast. In the Jewish context, Weber's application of this term implied the premodern character of the commercial role fulfilled by the Jews, identifying it as alien to the rational organization of modern capitalism. For Weber, unlike Sombart, the Jewish inclination toward commerce was not a racial trait, rather a product of a gradual historical process.[61] Those two different theoretical frameworks had already been anticipated in Marx's writings.[62] Sombart's attitude is compatible with Marx's early work, "On the Jewish Question," in which he equated Judaism with the bourgeois commercial spirit.[63] Weber's attitude matches Marx's later writings, in which he described the Jews as an ancient or medieval "trading-people" (*Handelsvolk*).[64]

In *The Decline of Judaism*, despite the centrality of the term *caste*, which is close to Weber's "pariah," a latent "Sombartian" tendency is discernible. This became evident where Heller wrote: "The Western Jews were at the very center of the formation of the modern bourgeoisie. Socially and economically they are the first bourgeois [. . .]."[65] Where he emphasized the nomadic element of ancient Israel as a source of Jewish primordial commerce also reminds us of Sombart.[66] Nonetheless, it should be noted that, at the explicit level, Heller rejected Sombart's logic already in his published book: Sombart's "discovery that the Jews are the true creators of modern capitalism" was "based on a confusion of cause and effect."[67] As opposed to Sombart, Heller saw the Jews' integration into Western Europe as a result of the emergence of modern capitalism and not as its cause. And yet his pronounced primordial identification of Jews with commerce in 1931 leaves the reader with the impression of Sombart's influence, even though Heller repudiated it.[68]

Unlike his book's implicit Sombartian tone, Heller's manuscript relied explicitly on Weber's study of *Ancient Judaism* (1923). Here, Heller categorically criticized Sombart's concept of the Jews' "nature," as a "nomadic people" and asks rhetorically: "which people did not wander in its ancient past?"[69] In line with Weber, "The Jew Is to Be Burned" depicts the transformation of the Jews from an agricultural people into a trading caste as a gradual process.[70] In contrast to the almost essentialist depiction in *The Decline of Judaism*, Heller historicized the commercial role of the Jews as having developed during antiquity and was therefore subject to change in modernity. Whereas in his book Heller presented historical Jewry as a proto-bourgeois commercial people, in his manuscript he adopted the unmistakably Weberian terms of "plebian people" and "pariah people," which emphasized the premodern, though not primordial, character of the Jews' economic function.[71]

As for the relationship between Jews and capitalism, Heller's criticism of Sombart became even bolder: "Sombart, who probably knew only capitalist Jews, acknowledged them as inventors of capitalism. But they established it as much as Norwegian fishermen and sailors invented the herring."[72] Contrary to Sombart's view, Jewish history cannot explain the development of capitalism. According to the Heller of 1939, it is the development of capitalism that should explain Jewish history.

This shift, from an implicitly Sombartian argument to an explicitly Weberian one, was targeted against the acute threat posed by the race-antisemitism of the Nazi Reich.[73] Around the publication of his book in 1911, Sombart had been admired by many Jews, despite his anti-Jewish tone. Some were flattered by his attribution of a pioneering role in promoting capitalism to Jews. Others, Zionists in particular, cherished his advocacy of Jewish emigration to Palestine.[74] However, Sombart's support of the Nazi regime since 1934 retrospectively highlighted the antisemitic overtone of his earlier writings.[75] Against this background, Heller distanced himself more clearly from Sombart. Weber's alternative view of capitalism as contradicting the historical economic function of the Jews allowed Heller to explain the attack on the Jews as part of the capitalist nature of Nazism. Heller's relation to Marx's different attitudes toward the Jews also changed in accordance with his new Weberian approach. If in 1931 Heller cited "On the Jewish Question" frequently, while merely dismissing the antisemitic interpretation of that article,[76] in 1939, he tried to avoid this complication by refraining from referencing the text.[77] In "The Jew Is to Be Burned," Weber's theoretical framework complied better with Marx's late concept of "trading-peoples," which was already applied in *The Decline of Judaism*.[78]

Heller was not the only Marxist intellectual to incorporate Weberian theory into his Jewish historiography around 1940. After *The Decline of Judaism*, the first Marxist synthesis of Jewish history, three other such syntheses were written simultaneously: Heller's "The

Jew Is to Be Burned," Moyshe Kats's "Problems in Jewish History," and Abram Leon's *The Jewish Question*.[79] It is striking to observe how, without knowing of each other, Heller, Kats, and Leon underwent parallel processes. Despite writing in different countries (France, the United States, and Belgium, respectively) and in different languages (German, Yiddish, and French), they all found Weber as a necessary complement to Marx at that historical moment.

If Heller adopted Weberian theory in "The Jew Is to Be Burned" without explicitly explaining his rationale, Leon provided a full account of this choice, stating on the eve of the Holocaust: "If the Jews had really played the role that Sombart attributes to them, it would be very difficult to understand why the development of capitalism was such a mortal blow to them."[80] According to Leon, such an understanding was possible only through Weber's conception of the Jews as a "caste in a world otherwise free from castes."[81] As a Trotskyite, Leon was freed from Stalinist taboo on Weber that Heller and Kats were bound to as communists.

Kats was the least explicit of all three in announcing his Weberian inspiration, though it is clearly there. Kats never mentioned Weber's name in his articles, but when he coined the term "urban democracy" to characterize ancient Jews as a social stratum of artisans, traders, and daily wage earners, Weber's "plebian people" resonated.[82] Moreover, by avoiding the term *pariah*, Kats gave the Jews a more respectful status. Kats's Weberian interpretation resembled Heller's in aiming to grant the historical Jews a productive and progressive image, against antisemitic propaganda.[83]

Having rejected the equating of Jews with the bourgeoisie, Heller faced the question of how they should be categorized in terms of class. In his foreword to the second and revised edition of *The Decline of Judaism*, Heller wrote that in response to comments he had received regarding the lack of attention paid to Jewish inner class-differentiation, he would address this matter in the second edition.[84] This promise was not fulfilled in the 1933 edition of the book, but only in the manuscript of 1939: "One should also remember that there are rich and poor Jews, Jewish exploiters and exploited Jews, for whom the Jewish question does not appear in the same form."[85] This time he deeply internalized Norden's criticism from 1932, for overlooking the "working and exploited masses of Jewish nationality" in his book.[86] Here, Heller made use of the Weberian differentiation between "plebs" and "patriciate" among ancient Israel, as well as of his identification of the origins of Diaspora Judaism with a "plebian" heritage. These distinctions allowed Heller not to abandon the urban character that he had already attributed to historical Jewry in *The Decline of Judaism*, while adding to it a laborious and productive aspect.[87] In "The Jew Is to Be Burned," he also stressed elements of social justice in the legislation regarding slavery and landed property in the Book of Deuteronomy as barriers to exploitation.[88]

The strongest expression of this new orientation can be found in the chapter Heller devoted to the Talmud in "The Jew Is to Be Burned." On the one hand, his general portrayal of the Talmud as a conservative legal codex, designed to preserve an isolated caste of traders, reiterated his approach from his book of 1931. On the other hand, Heller now added to it praise for the Talmud's "efforts for social balance and for protecting the economically weak against the rich."[89] He emphasized the productiveness of many rabbinic sages of the Talmud who had been craftsmen and identified elements of class struggle within Talmudic legislation. Moreover, Heller stressed that while the Germanic tribes were still illiterate, Jews already wrote the "most beautiful legends of the Mishna."[90] Alongside the apologetic tone, Heller's positive attitude toward the Jewish traditional text here is remarkable.

In a footnote on the first page of that chapter, he stated that it was based on booklet called *Beams of Light from the Talmud* (see figure 2.1).[91] Long after reading Heller's manuscript, I found this small booklet in his private book collection and learned that he had already obtained it when he was nineteen, on the front line. On the inner cover, replacing another crossed-out name, it is written in pencil: "Otto Heller, im Felde [on the battlefield], 1916." He probably exchanged it for another book with a fellow soldier, and seemed to have read it with interest, as he left pencil marks in some pages and kept it with him through all the subsequent vicissitudes of his life.[92] And yet, though mentioning the Talmud several time in *The Decline of Judaism*, Heller did not directly relate to any specific passage, which he did only in his later manuscript, as if returning to an aspect of his youth, from before leaving Judaism.

Writing about later periods too, Heller paid increased attention to class-differentiation within Jewish society: "The Jews were never a socially unified, amorphous mass. They too were split, within their ghettos, into classes, they too had conservative and progressive currents among them."[93] In all modern revolutions, wrote Heller, Jews had stood on both sides of the barricades: in the French Revolution, in the Spring of Nations, and in the Paris Commune. Many Jews had fought for the sake of freedom, first in the bourgeois liberal camp and later as socialists.[94] As an epigraph at the top of one of his chapters, Heller employed a quote by the French socialist Jean Jaurès, praising the passion for justice embedded in Judaism in order to depict a progressive image of Jewry.[95] "Burning Questions"—the title given by Heller to the chapter on the proletarianization of the Jewish masses in modern Eastern Europe—reveals his attention to the desperate condition of the Jewish lower strata in Poland, Lithuania, Romania, and Hungary.[96] Just like Fürnberg's article of 1938, in "The Jew Is to Be Burned," Heller emphasized class differences within Jewish society. It is thus plausible that the influence of Heller's 1931 book on Fürnberg was no less than Fürnberg's influence on Heller's 1939 manuscript.

Heller's new historical interpretation in "The Jew Is to Be Burned" was designated to refute antisemitic myths, bundling Jews with capitalism, that some of his criticizers had spotted in *The Decline of Judaism*.[97] "Usury was by no means invented by the Jews," stressed Heller against this common prejudice, which received scientific legitimization from Sombart.[98] He maintained that in medieval Eastern Europe the Jews were not the only "trading-people," living "in the pores of Polish society (Karl Marx)." Alongside the Jews, functioning as "merchants" and "craftsmen" were none other than the Germans.[99] For political reasons, Heller could not disclose that he adopted this notion from an Austrian social-democratic journal that appeared in Paris. In an excerpt from this journal, found among the materials Heller collected for his manuscript, he underlined the sentence: "The Germans and the Jews are twin brothers."[100]

While not completely withdrawing his former concept of the Jews as forerunners of capitalism, in "The Jew Is to Be Burned" Heller tempered it significantly, through pointing both to other forerunners as well as to the consequences of capitalism for the Jews themselves: "These conditions [for the emergence of the Jewish question] stem from the [capitalist] economic and social order, whose *co-creators* but also its *victims—this is likely to be ignored*—are *above all* the Jews."[101] Rejecting Sombart's essentialist image of the Jews as capitalists, adopting Weber's conception of a contradiction between capitalism and the

Jews, pointing out internal class-differentiation in Jewish society, and emphasizing Jewish proletarian elements—all these allowed Heller to express much more empathy toward the Jews as the prime victims of capitalism.

Antisemitism: The End or the Beginning?

In *The Decline of Judaism*, as noted by Traverso, Heller "employed the traditional Marxist conception of antisemitism as a tool of the dominant class to divide the workers and mobilize the petty bourgeois masses against the proletariat."[102] This conception included a historical explanation of antisemitism as a medieval remnant that persisted mostly in declining feudal social strata and in semifeudal countries, and which was artificially revived for reactionary political purposes.[103]

In "The Jew Is to Be Burned," Heller did not offer any new theoretical argumentations to explicate the anti-Jewish economic policy in Nazi Germany, which he merely saw as a part of the general process of "concentration of big capital" and "liquidation of the little man."[104] He also did not meet the challenge posed by the pogrom of November 1938, which was clearly aimed against Jews of all classes, but only reiterated Norden's explanation about the rivalry within the haute bourgeoisie, between its Aryan and Jewish sectors.[105] Four days after the completion of the manuscript, in a private letter to his brother-in-law, a textile trader who fled Vienna to London, Heller even sharpened his materialistic analysis. He defined the Nazi regime as "the unlimited dominance of a minimal clique of steel- coal- and bank-magnates," that could "easily expropriate you, other, poor, textile-beggars [*euch andere, arme, Textilschlucker*], for there were all but no Jews in the German heavy industry, as it is known."[106]

Regarding the pogrom itself, Heller expressed in his manuscript a far-reaching optimistic prognosis: Now, that "the Jews have disappeared from the economy," one "cannot blame them any longer for the worsening conditions of life in Germany. [. . .] It [the pogrom] arouses doubts regarding the antisemitic arguments and encourages a rethinking of the political and social purposes connected to the antisemitic incitement, which eventually leads to overt protest."[107] This assessment reflected the orthodox Marxist conception of antisemitism as a declining phenomenon.

Such a revolutionary optimism was commonplace in communist accounts of Nazi Germany. While admitting, in his private letter, that "Germany is definitely not facing the revolution," Heller nevertheless estimated that "Berlin" was experiencing "internal distress," which the regime is no longer capable of handling.[108] He counted many cases of strikes and sabotage conducted by workers and claimed that communist cells, existing "in every street and factory," caused "an enormous nervousness to the Nazis."[109] During the four days between the completion of the manuscript and the writing of this letter, the German-Soviet pact was signed. Heller concluded from the pact that Hitler must turn to a more radical means to suppress the protest, namely, war. In his letter he did not contemplate the implication of that development for the Jews.

Nevertheless, the economic explanation for the anti-Jewish policies in Germany was only one aspect of Heller's interpretation of Nazi antisemitism in "The Jew Is to Be Burned." In another chapter he presented a different approach, a sociological analysis of the reception of antisemitism in German society. This analysis was not original. It was based on the anonymous article of 1932, "Communism and the Jewish Question," which I analyzed here in chapter 2, and suggested that it was written by Albert Norden, the communist harsh critic of *The Decline of Judaism*. That article presented a typology of six social groups that were drawn to antisemitism: (1) artisans and small traders, hurt by the competition of modern industry and wholesale commerce; (2) liberal professions, suffering from a tightening labor market in which Jews were overrepresented; (3) civil servants, who identified Jews with the Republic that had reduced their privileged status; (4) employees of private companies, often employed by Jewish entrepreneurs or managers and threatened by unemployment; (5) peasants, who traditionally saw the Jew as a usurer; (6) university students, who anticipated a future of unemployment.[110] In "The Jew Is to Be Burned," Heller fully adopted this typology, and even developed it at much greater length and detail.[111]

Although those were not Heller's original insights, the fact that he chose to incorporate them into his manuscript is significant. Unlike his superficial acceptance of Norden's criticism in his introduction to the second edition of *The Decline of Judaism*, without profoundly revising the book itself,[112] here Heller appeared to genuinely adopt his criticizer's view. And yet, while explicitly referring, in a different context, to another book by Norden,[113] Heller did not credit the author of the anonymous article, nor the article itself, for the six-group typology. Therefore, it was probably not for reasons of political legitimization that he reiterated this theory.

This social diagnosis of antisemitism was novel in the communist discourse, as it exceeded the notion of antisemitism as a mere declining medieval residue, while demonstrating understanding of its modern nature. In addition, it pointed not only the use of antisemitism as an artificial deceptive political instrument, but also to the social foundations of the success of that use. But even in 1932, those insights were neither original nor new. Quite surprisingly, they resembled Theodor Herzl's Zionist interpretation of antisemitism. As early as 1892, in what is considered his "first article on the Jewish question,"[114] Herzl characterized modern French antisemitism as "a meeting place of the dissatisfied, a saloon of the rejected" elements of society, who were deprived by modernization.[115] In *The Jewish State* (*Der Judenstaat*), Herzl differentiated modern antisemitism from the old religious hatred toward Jews and saw it as a byproduct of emancipation. According to Herzl, the traditional middle-class occupations characteristic of Jews stood in growing competition with the emerging Christian middle-class. Therefore, modern antisemitism "increases day by day and hour by hour among the nations."[116]

Not all Zionist thinkers shared Herzl's understanding of antisemitism. Arthur Ruppin, for example, identified antisemitism with the "hatred of the Jews" that had existed "ever since the beginning of Diaspora."[117] Referencing Ruppin, Heller saw "Zionist propaganda" as based on "the eternity of antisemitism."[118] As shown, this generalization could include neither Herzl nor other Zionists who sought a socioeconomic analysis of the Jewish question, such as Marxist-Zionist Ber Borokhov, who predicted that "progress" would worsen the state of the Jews.[119]

The orthodox Marxist analysis of antisemitism, being based on the belief in progress and subsequently in assimilation as the solution to the Jewish question, hindered an understanding of the modern nature of antisemitism. Zionists, and among them Marxist-Zionists who denied the possibility of solving the Jewish question within European society, were freed from this obstacle and could foresee the worsening of antisemitism. In Shulamit Volkov's terms, the orthodox Marxist conception of antisemitism can be categorized as "continuity" of the old religious hatred for Jews, while Herzl's conception was that of a "break" between the two phenomena.[120]

The anonymous article of 1932 had testified the beginning of a shift in the communist analysis of antisemitism, that culminated in "The Jew Is to Be Burned." This article signified a turn from the conception of "continuity" of antisemitism to the conception of a "break," conceiving antisemitism as a new, severe, and escalating threat. This novel, more "precise" and "profound"—in Traverso's words[121]—social analysis of antisemitism was neither inspired by Herzl nor Zionism, but by the rapid worsening of the same tendency that Herzl identified in its very initial stages. This new analysis of antisemitism was shaped by the impact of the severe deepening of the economic crisis and unemployment from 1931 to 1932, which drew more and more "dissatisfied" Germans, including proletarians, to supporting the Nazi Party. This tendency further exacerbated under the Nazi rule, though more for political than economic reasons.

Now that antisemitism began to threaten communists directly, they started acknowledging its tendency to increase and to analyze it, just as Zionists had been doing for half a century. This acknowledgment did not prevent Heller from continuing to simultaneously view antisemitism as a distraction from class struggle in "The Jew Is to Be Burned."[122] But he now complemented the "traditional Marxist conception" of the political use of antisemitism with a sociological explication of the reasons for its efficiency. In the years before writing his manuscript, this new approach was affirmed by the Nazi rise to power, as well as by six years of persecution of German Jews, which caused Heller to devote an overwhelming portion of the manuscript to antisemitism.[123]

"There Is No Longer a Jewish Question in the Soviet Union"

Those substantial theoretical shifts notwithstanding, the political views expressed by Heller in *The Decline of Judaism* did not turn, and even radicalized in "The Jew Is to Be Burned." His condemnation of Zionism hardened in the years between his two works.[124] Even though he expressed some empathy—or rather, compassion—in both books toward Jewish workers in the socialist colonies in Palestine, he eventually convicted them too as tools in the hands of the reactionary bourgeois World Zionist Organization and British imperialism.[125] Heller endeavored to undermine the feasibility of Zionism as a solution to the Jewish question. As a British imperial instrument, the existence of the Jewish settlement was depended on its utility for British capitalism, so he claimed. Already in his 1931 book Heller pointed to a British shift to orientation on Arab nationalism, expressed by the White Paper of 1930, which limited Jewish immigration and settlement in Palestine. Heller proclaimed it as a "deadly strike" against Zionism.[126]

In 1939 the Jewish settlement was not only still alive, but also significantly larger, after a big wave of Jewish immigration to Palestine that followed the Nazi rise to power. Heller refused to see this as a "triumph of Zionism," and interpreted that migration as a mere flight, not motivated by any national aspirations. Again, he stressed that "Zionism was dealt the deadly strike between 1933 and 1939."[127] This time he meant, besides the Arab Riots that broke out in Palestine in 1936,[128] also the defeat of the Zionists by the Bund in the municipal elections in Warsaw in 1938. He concluded that his "prognosis for Zionism" was "even darker than it was six or seven years ago."[129]

Heller's full support of the Soviet policy toward the Jews also became bolder in "The Jew Is to Be Burned." The manuscript's chapter dealing with this topic was essentially based on *The Decline of Judaism*, albeit with one meaningful exception. In his book Heller described the process in present tense: "The solution to the Jewish question in the Soviet Union *is* not a Jewish problem. It is an issue for the Soviet regime, a problem of the dictatorship of the proletariat."[130] In the manuscript, he changed the tense of this sentence: "The solution to the Jewish question in the Soviet Union *was* not a Jewish problem. (We speak here with full emphasis on the *past tense*. For today, there is no longer a Jewish question in the Soviet Union, neither social nor national.)"[131]

According to Heller, by 1939 the Jewish question had already been resolved in the Soviet Union. This was accomplished in two parallel ways: assimilation in the big cities and national territorialization in agricultural settlements, chiefly in Birobidzhan. Avoiding any preference for either of these solutions, his stance now became even more explicitly "neutralist" than in 1931:[132] "Free social and cultural development of one's own nationality in its own territory [in the Jewish case—Birobidzhan], among other fraternal peoples in full equality and freedom; assimilation according to the individual's free will, without any coercion: this is how the national solution of the Jewish problem takes place, which, socially, has been definitively solved."[133]

Heller's motion toward a more accentuated "neutralism" is another aspect of similarity between "The Jew Is to Be Burned" and the works of Kats and Leon from the same time. It was Leon's follower, the Belgian historian Nathan Weinstock, who (not knowing of Heller's manuscript) defined the admiration of the Soviet Union expressed in *The Decline of Judaism* as "unconditional alliance with Stalinism."[134] The content of the last two chapters in the final version of "The Jew Is to Be Burned," dealing with Zionism and the Soviet Union, seems to affirm the continuity of this alleged unquestionable political loyalty. Nonetheless, Heller's significant changes in the field of theory, as far as freely quoting "reactionary" Weber just like the Trotskyite Leon, put his "unconditional alliance" in question. How could Heller's political loyalty coexist with his evident heterodox theoretical inclination? Did he genuinely believe in 1939 that "there is no longer a Jewish question in the Soviet Union"? A comparison to earlier drafts of the manuscript may suggest an answer.

In the "First Transcript" of "The Jew Is to Be Burned," the chapter about the Jews in the Soviet Union does not exist. It appeared only in the second draft, the one sent to New York, typed in a different typing machine than all other chapters. In this second version, the original chapter title given by Heller, "Solution," was crossed out, and instead a new title was suggested in pencil, in a handwriting that differs from Heller's, probably the publisher's: "The Jews in the Soviet Union." On the last draft of the manuscript, this change was inscribed in Heller's own handwriting (see figure 4.2).

Based on these evidences, the following process can be hypothesized: Heller did not mean to include a chapter on the Soviet solution to the Jewish question in his new book. After some contemplation, and perhaps consultation with comrades or correspondence with the publisher himself, he concluded that for the sake of the book's publication he better add such a chapter. And so, he drafted a short chapter, condensing 200 pages from *The Decline of Judaism* into ten pages, concluding with a citation of Stalin from 1931, in which the Soviet leader condemned antisemitism as "the most dangerous vestige of cannibalism."[135] Stalin's quote was followed by another one, from the French writer Émile Zola, who in 1897 defined antisemitism as "a matter of ignorance and blindness [which would take us] many centuries backwards." And Heller added, as the very last words of his manuscript: "In a society which leads humanity forwards from the darkness of the past to the light of freedom there is no more room for that matter of ignorance and blindness."[136] Following his own experience in the Soviet Union, it is doubtful that Heller was describing the so-called actually existing socialism in the Soviet Union. More likely, he was expressing his utopian wish for a truly humanist kind of socialism. However, even if this chapter was only a requirement of the publisher and not Heller's original intention to express pronounced support of the Soviet Union, it was still the author's own choice to accept it. For the publisher, the chapter's text seemed satisfying, and he was only required to change its title, making the reference to the Soviet Union more visible in the book's table of contents.

There was only one other chapter title that the publisher demanded rephrasing. "Burning Questions," the heading originally given by Heller to the chapter discussing the Jews in Eastern Europe, was switched to "The *Ostjuden* [Jew of Eastern Europe]—Yesterday and Today" (see figure 4.2). The much more optimistic title does not reflect the content of the chapter, which describes the "aggravation of the Jewish question," leading to "hatred toward the Jews," "pogrom[s]," and "ever strengthening calls for their emigration," that was blocked by "closed borders" in the West.[137] In one place in this chapter Heller had typed "in the entire East [. . .] the Jews have virtually not entered agricultural primary production." Right after the words "entire East" he added in handwriting in brackets: "with the exception of the Soviet Union."[138] The title change and the additional correction imply an endeavor to distinguish more clearly between the alleged solution of the Jewish question in the world of "tomorrow," the Soviet East, and the "Burning Questions" regarding the acute distress of the Jews in the rest of the East, representing "yesterday."

"No Matter! The Jew Is to Be Burned"

The contradiction between Heller's theoretical innovation and political dogmatism in "The Jew Is to Be Burned" was revealed not only

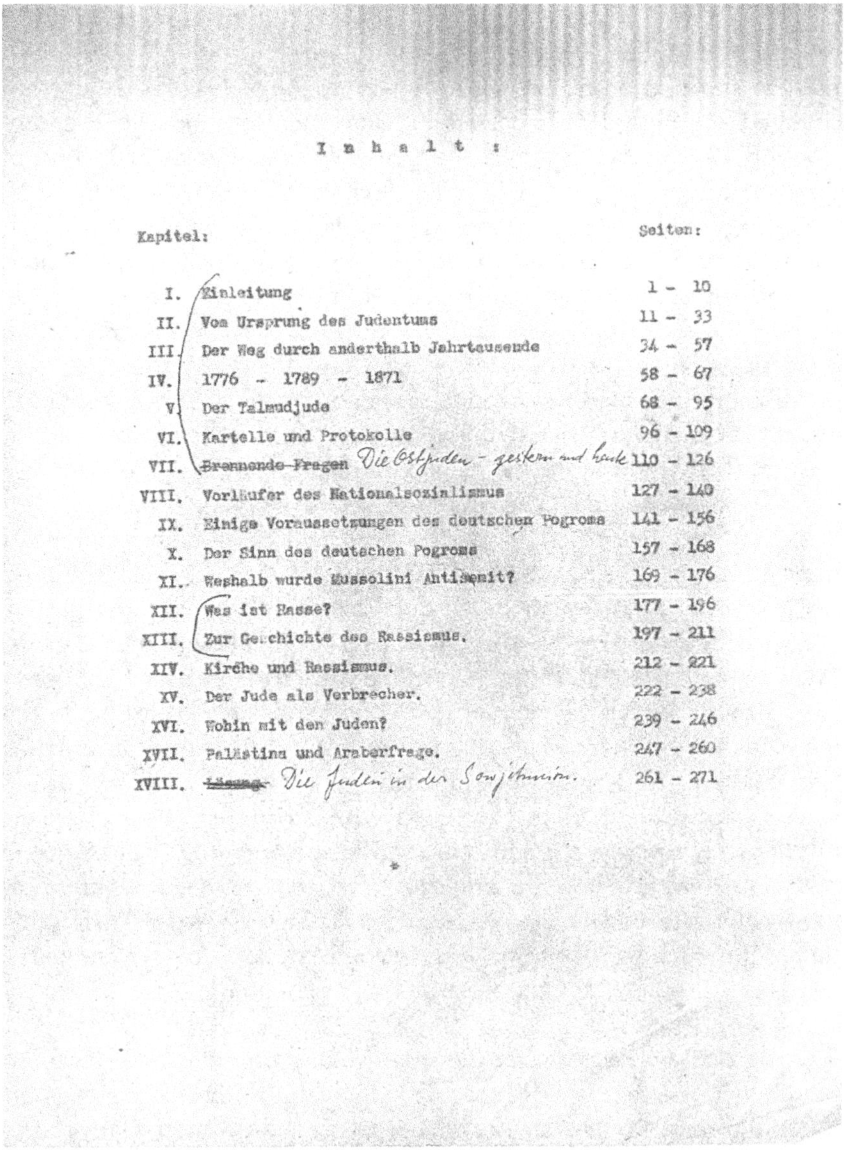

Inhalt:

Kapitel:		Seiten:
I.	Einleitung	1 – 10
II.	Vom Ursprung des Judentums	11 – 33
III.	Der Weg durch anderthalb Jahrtausende	34 – 57
IV.	1776 – 1789 – 1871	58 – 67
V.	Der Talmudjude	68 – 95
VI.	Kartelle und Protokolle	96 – 109
VII.	~~Brennende Fragen~~ *Die Ostjuden – gestern und heute*	110 – 126
VIII.	Vorläufer des Nationalsozialismus	127 – 140
IX.	Einige Voraussetzungen des deutschen Pogroms	141 – 156
X.	Der Sinn des deutschen Pogroms	157 – 168
XI.	Weshalb wurde Mussolini Antisemit?	169 – 176
XII.	Was ist Rasse?	177 – 196
XIII.	Zur Geschichte des Rassismus.	197 – 211
XIV.	Kirche und Rassismus.	212 – 221
XV.	Der Jude als Verbrecher.	222 – 238
XVI.	Wohin mit den Juden?	239 – 246
XVII.	Palästina und Araberfrage.	247 – 260
XVIII.	~~Lösung~~ *Die Juden in der Sowjetunion.*	261 – 271

*

Figure 4.2. Table of contents from Heller's manuscript "Der Jude wird verbrannt" ("The Jew Is to Be Burned") (Paris, 1939). Two chapter titles are altered in Heller's handwriting. Courtesy of Dokumentationsarchiv des österreichischen Widerstandes, Vienna: 45920/7.

concerning the past and the present, but also the future. In his 1939 manuscript, Heller clung to his previous prognosis of *The Decline of Judaism* through assimilation. As if six years of Nazi rule had not changed anything, Heller persisted: "Since the Jews' bourgeois emancipation, assimilation is a decisive fact in Western Europe, which even the interlude of fascist racism will not change."[139] This optimistic disregarding of Nazism as a mere "interlude" in the process of Jewish assimilation in Western Europe stands in bold contrast with the manuscript's pessimistic title, which has neither reference nor explanation within the book itself. Nowhere in the text did Heller predict the burning of Jews. On the contrary, he saw the November Pogrom, namely, the burning of synagogues and not of Jews, as the climax of antisemitic violence, that signaled an end to Jewish persecutions, for it unmasked the true nature of Nazi antisemitism as a tool for class oppression. Why then "The Jew Is to Be Burned"?

The sentence "The Jew is to be burned" was taken from Gotthold Ephraim Lessing's famous 1779 play, *Nathan the Wise*. The plot, set in medieval Jerusalem after the Christians had lost the city to the Muslim conqueror Saladin, presents a conflict between Christians, Muslims, and Jews. During this conflict, the narrow-minded, anti-Jewish patriarch of Jerusalem repeatedly demands the execution of the main Jewish protagonist, Nathan, refuting all pleas and arguments: "No matter! The Jew is to be burned."[140] Eventually, the patriarch's wish is not fulfilled. The play ends with an idyllic scene of fraternity between the main characters of all three religions, excluding the patriarch, emphasizing Lessing's enlightened message of interreligious tolerance and harmony. Heller particularly chose the patriarch's demand, which proved to be vain in the play, as if to say: The patriarch's ghost is now conjured up, casting a shadow over 160 years of German enlightenment.

A comparison between the titles Heller gave his two works on the Jewish question reveals another dimension to the theoretical shift he underwent. *The Decline of Judaism* presents an impersonal process of "decline," attributed to a deterministic force: "The iron march of history."[141] Contrarily, "the Jew is to be burned" is a phrase attributed to a person, be it the patriarch of Jerusalem, a modern antisemite, or Hitler. That title was compatible with the different philosophy of history that Heller introduced in "The Jew Is to Be Burned": "There is no historical law for the development of peoples."[142] While in his book Heller held onto Stalin's deterministic interpretation of Historical Materialism, in the manuscript he ascribed a much bigger role to human agency. Even if the supposed result of the "decline" and the "burning" is the same—the disappearance of the Jews—the contrasting interpretations of the process leading to that result reflect opposing evaluations. If "decline" was—in Heller's eyes in 1931—an optimistic prospect of full integration, being burned was an extremely pessimistic, even catastrophic prognosis.

Probably by coincidence, albeit a striking one, Heller chose the exact phrase recited by Herzl half a century earlier in the very same Paris. Immediately following his conceptualization of antisemitism as the "saloon of the dissatisfied," Herzl put into the mouths of the "dissatisfied" the exclamation: "No matter! The Jew is to be burned."[143] Heller was certainly unfamiliar with Herzl's journalistic report of 1892, but exactly for that reason this coincidence is symptomatic of Heller's theoretical shift to a pessimistic view of antisemitism. If, in 1931, Judaism could still be seen by Heller as peacefully "declining" through assimilation, by 1939 "Burning Questions" were threatening to burn the Jews themselves.

Heller might have picked up the allusion to Lessing's play from a poem, published in November 1938 in the *Deutsche Zentralzeitung*, the German-language Comintern weekly for which he was working in Moscow in the mid-1930s.[144] The poem, also titled "The Jew Is to Be Burned," was written by the German-Jewish communist writer Klara Blum. In her poem, Blum drew analogy between two scenes: the burning at the stake of a Jew named Isaak in Worms in 1306, for refusing to convert to Christianity; and the burning alive of a Jewish doctor in Danzig (Gdańsk) in 1938, during the events of the November Pogrom. In both cases, as stressed by the poet in a repeating verse, the victim was "blamed for being a son of the Jewish people." A leftist hallmark of the poem is reflected through one salient difference between the equivalent burnings: While nobody came for Isaac's help, in Danzig some German patients, who owed their lives to their Jewish physician, tried to rescue him, and were pushed back by the perpetrators.[145] The message was clear: "Hitler is not Germany."[146] On the other hand, emphasizing the mutual belonging of a medieval Jew and an assimilated Jewish doctor in modern Germany to the same "Jewish people," was not common in the communist literature. Like Heller, Blum repeatedly wrote on Jewish topics and antisemitism, and was constantly suspected of deviations from the Party line.[147] The inclusion of such a poem in a communist journal was a typical manifestation of the short wave of communist sympathetic publications of November 1938.

Beyond communist circles, neither Heller nor Blum were unique in turning to Lessing's expression or, more generally, to metaphors borrowed from the semantic field of fire in the context of European Jewry in the 1930s. The German Zionist newspaper *Jüdische Rundschau* already had cited the phrase "the Jew is to be burned," after the burning of books in May 1933.[148] The reknowned Jewish historian Simon Dubnov alarmed people in the mid-1930s by saying, "The House of Israel is in flames."[149] The same atmosphere was conveyed in 1938, in the famous song by the Polish Yiddish poet Mordechai Gebirtig, *"Undzer shtetl brent!"* (Our town is burning), written following the pogrom in the town of Przytyk.[150] Such infernal images were traditionally portrayed by Jewish nationalists, to stress the state of emergency of their people. In 1897, Herzl and Dubnov initiated two different Jewish national movements, Zionism and Autonomism. Gebirtig was a member of the socialist autonomist Jewish workers' movement in Poland, the Bund.[151] Among the communists, Heller was almost alone in presenting such a catastrophic prospect significantly after November 1938, and well before the initiation of the "Final Solution" in late 1941.

Historian Hermann Weber argued that following the Stalinization of the KPD, "ideological justification and concealment replaced the efforts to engage in theoretical reflection."[152] In Heller's manuscript, "The Jew Is to Be Burned," a heavy curtain of "ideological justification" indeed concealed his "theoretical reflection," but did not replace it altogether. Heller obscured his new independent and subversive theoretical reflections on Jewish history and on the contemporary Jewish question behind obligatory pro-Soviet apologetic phrases. Through Max Weber's theory, Heller's awareness of the collision between capitalism and the traditional economic role of the Jews in Europe had become much clearer. His enhanced understanding of class-differentiation in Jewish society sharpened his acknowledgment of the "Burning Questions" concerning the vast Jewish proletariat in Eastern Europe. Delving into the history of antisemitism and race theory he grasped the lethal threat posed by Nazi race-antisemitism. The actual anti-Jewish policy implemented by the Nazis led him to express sympathy, and even national solidarity with his fellow "bourgeois" German Jews. As a result of all this, he concluded that the future held a horrible tragedy for European Jewry: "The Jew Is to Be Burned."

The title did not stem from the manuscript's political dimension, but rather from the theoretical one. In the equilibrium between political fidelity and theoretical deviance in the manuscript, the title tips the scales to the side of the latter. Though retrospectively the title gained a chilling prophetic meaning, one cannot claim that Heller's manuscript predicted Nazi crematoria. Nevertheless, he presented a strong pessimistic feeling of a coming disaster that was not expressed openly in the text due to his political obligation to revolutionary optimism. Heller encoded and sublimated his anxiety into the theoretical field. But his restrained dread sprang through the title, which was chosen at the last moment. Perhaps it happened in such haste that it brought Heller to abandon his habitual caution in his writing. Or

Figure 4.3. Otto Heller, unknown date. Courtesy of the Papineau-Heller Family Archive (PHFA), Paris.

perhaps it was formulated as a thoroughly thought-out sophisticated hint to the informed reader.

∼

Heller's two major works on the Jewish question, *The Decline of Judaism* (1931) and "The Jew Is to Be Burned" (1939), are significantly different, but only in their theoretical aspects. Heller's political stances, his harsh criticism of Zionism and admiration of the Soviet Jewish policy, remained unchanged, and even sharpened in the second work. How can this dichotomy, between his political rigidity and theoretical flexibility, be explained? If he was heterodox enough to openly use the theory of "reactionary" Weber, why did he not express a similar openness in the political sphere?

The duality of "The Jew Is to Be Burned," holding together theoretical innovation with political dogmatism, should be traced back to Heller's intensive experiences in the years after 1933, as described in the previous chapter, and especially in Paris, where the manuscript was written. His new acknowledgment of antisemitism as a severe and worsening threat was gradually unfolding during six years of escalating persecutions of Jews, in which he himself became a persecuted refugee. His new emphases on class differentiations within Jewry and on the Jewish proletariat can be attributed not only to the general rapid impoverishment of the Jews in Central and Eastern Europe, but also to Heller's own new experience of poverty.

Heller's new inclination to Jewish solidarity can be seen as a reflection of the unique example of Jewish Popular Front in France and Spain. Even during the "Popular Front" period, Jewish nationality was still formally denied by the Comintern, and hence Jews were not supposed to form a Popular Front of their own, rather they were expected to join the fronts of the respective peoples among whom they were living. In June 1938, against the insistence of the Bund in Poland not to cooperate with other Jewish political streams, Dubnov called: "Jewry also needs such a 'Popular Front' to fight growing antisemitism and worldwide reaction."[153]

But in France, flooded with Jewish immigrants and refugees from every political stream, the Popular Front policy led to "nationalization," not only of the French Communist Party (*Parti Communiste Français* [PCF]), but also of the Jewish communists. Starting from

1936, under Léon Blum's Popular Front government, a distinct "Jewish Popular Front" was established, uniting communists, Bundists, and left-wing Zionists. This coalition focused on combating antisemitism. The Spanish Civil War provided a further unifying cause.[154] The Jewish Popular Front in France triggered the establishment of a Yiddish-speaking company within the International Brigades.[155] Heller's proximity to this exceptional case of a Jewish Popular Front must have had its impact on his writing.

Besides Heller's capability of theoretical innovation, his "unconditional alliance with Stalinism,"[156] also demands an explanation, facing many developments that should have challenged it. Already since 1937, the French and the German Popular Fronts were in shambles. The Yiddish section of the PCF was formally dissolved, as part of a wide anti-Trotskyist purge in all language-sections, which contributed to a growing disillusionment of the Popular Front.[157] In Spain the communists, supported by Soviet advisers, brutally oppressed other groups in the republican camp, such as Anarchists and Trotskyites. Behind the Popular Front and International Brigades terror was outcropping.[158]

Heller's vision of Birobidzhan was also challenged. If in 1931 the Jewish settlement was still a new and promising project, as early as 1932 Heller mildly expressed certain dissatisfaction with the pace of its development.[159] In 1936, Joseph Leftwich, a leading Jewish territorialist writer in London, could have already described Heller's optimistic 1931 prognosis of Birobidzhan as an "auto-suggestive psychological state."[160] By 1937, according to the statistics Heller himself provided, there were only 25,000 Jews living in the autonomous district,[161] whereas the government's plan had been to reach 150,000 by that time.[162] Heller's stronger emphasis in "The Jew Is to Be Burned" on assimilation rather than on Birobidzhan as the solution to the Jewish question, compared to his approach in *The Decline of Judaism*, can be interpreted as another sign of unadmitted disappointment.[163]

If in 1931, Stalin's dictatorship was still new and not yet completely overt and aggressive, by 1939, the regime's repression against the Soviet population in general and Jewish life in particular had become clearer. During the 1930s, most Jewish cultural institutions in the Soviet Union were closed by the regime. The purges became a massive bloodshed and among their victims were many of Jewish origins, including Jewish leaders in Birobidzhan. However, Heller was neither the only communist, nor the only communist of Jewish descent, who kept faith with the Soviet Union despite all this. Some of the information was indeed obscured behind masks of secrecy, deception, and propaganda. But as a prominent journalist in Moscow at the launch of the terror, who himself had to flee due to the threat of purges, Heller could have not been blind to the actual occurrences. It should also be recalled that besides almost losing his life, he had lost his livelihood twice, for being mistrusted by his own movement: in Berlin in 1928–1929 and in Paris in 1938–1939.

How could Heller's political loyalty, typed into his 1939 manuscript, coexist with his repeated criticism of the communist establishment in the previous years: starting from his furious 1933 letters from Zürich and Amsterdam to Ozet, and witnessed by Jergitsch in Moscow in the mid-1930s, and by Stahlmann and Freundlich in Paris toward the end of the decade?[164] Even if while writing *The Decline of Judaism* Heller was still a true believer, it would be hard to assume that when he wrote "The Jews Is to Be Burned" his faithfulness was still naive. Why did he not leave the Party? Heller did not address this question in his writings.

Others from similar backgrounds who did break off with communism under similar circumstances explained how difficult it was to let go of that movement. Koestler told of himself: "I no longer had friends outside the party. It had become my family, my nest, my spiritual home. Inside it, one might quarrel, grumble, feel happy or unhappy; but to leave a nest, however cramping and smelly it seemed sometimes, had become unthinkable."[165] This total dedication of many years of one's life in communism, brought with it "the true-believer's insurmountable horror of excommunication."[166]

Silone went on further, equating communism to a religion: "For me to join the Party of Proletarian Revolution was not just a simple matter of signing up with political organization; it meant conversion, a complete dedication. Those were still the days when to declare oneself a Socialist or a Communist was equivalent to throwing oneself to the winds, and meant breaking with one's parents and not finding a job."[167] According to Koestler and Silone, the devotion to communism was first of all social and emotional. Koestler stressed that the Stalinist crimes were known to him and to his comrades: "Though we wore blinkers, we were not blind, and even the most fanatical among us could not help noticing that all was not well in our movement." Intellectuals tended to confront this awareness through rationalization: "We were never tired of telling each other—and ourselves—that the party could only be changed from the inside, not from the outside."[168]

Communism had its special appeal for intellectuals.[169] "They were not 'typical' converts," suggested the British socialist Richard Crossman, "being people of quite unusual sensitivity, they made most abnormal Communists, [. . .]. They had a heightened perception of the spirit of the age, and felt more actually than others both its frustrations and its hopes." Crossman wondered: "How could these intellectuals accept the dogmatism of Stalinism?"[170] Koestler's answer, based on his own experience was: "You could resign from a club and from the ordinary sort of party if its policy no longer suited you; but the Communist Party was something different: it was the incarnation of the will of history itself."[171] And thus, so formulated Koestler the inner voice of the critical communist: "Shut your mouth tight, swallow your bile and wait for the day [. . .] after the defeat of the enemy and victory of World Revolution. [. . .] Until that day you had to play the game—confirm and deny, denounce and recant, eat your words and lick your vomit; it was the price you had to pay for being allowed to continue feeling useful, and thus keep your perverted self-respect."[172] Heller could not even have always shut his mouth tight. And yet, he was not willing to forgo the feeling of usefulness and meaningfulness given to him by communism, for almost two decades already. In addition, the Party was his social milieu and a source of livelihood, as unstable as it was. Those were crucial factors, especially in exile.

For Koestler, as for many others, the Hitler-Stalin pact from August 23, 1939, was the straw that broke the camel's back. Until then, "in spite of everything, the Soviet Union still represented our last and only hope on a planet in rapid decay."[173] Münzenberg, who had already been expelled from the Party in May 1938,[174] denounced Stalin publicly for the first time only after the Soviet invasion to Poland, in September 1939. Münzenberg defined the Soviet leader as a "traitor" to the revolution, while announcing a "struggle against Hitler and Stalin" for "German freedom," and publishing a list of forty German communists murdered in the purges.[175] He paid for that with his life.

Heller had completed his revision of the manuscript "The Jew Is to Be Burned" three days before Molotov and Ribbentrop signed their agreement in Moscow. Heller did not translate his growing unease with the Soviet Union, sublimated and coded into the heterodox theoretical aspects of his manuscript, into conscious political criticism. In a letter to his brother-in-law, dated August 24, 1939, Heller justified the pact as a necessary defensive tactic for the Soviet Union against the capitalist and fascist joint interest in its fall. He characterized the socialist country as a state "with a totally different social structure, which does not conduct wars of conquest," not interested in the "division" of any land, and "wants to help Poland" against Hitler.[176] What did he think when three weeks later, according to the secret protocol of the pact, the Red Army invaded Poland, which was divided between Hitler and Stalin? It is unknown.

From that point in time onward, besides a few private letters with hardly any political content and several coauthored underground reports, we have no other writings by Heller himself. The Comintern intelligence reports could only tell that "when the war broke out, Heller's political position was correct," and that "in political matters Heller was making a good impression."[177] Stalin's alliance with Hitler did not break Heller's allegiance to communism. Only later it was reported that during the war, though it is unclear when exactly, he "was excluded from the party" for "incorrect political views."[178] While Heller's political obedience remained undetermined, how did his conception of the Jewish question continue to evolve? From September 1, 1939, he no longer had either the quiet or the time for theoretical contemplation. His further biography, during the catastrophe, must follow his deeds.

Chapter 5

In Fight (1940–1945)

Sometimes the pen can dig deeper than the spade.

—Otto Heller, 1940

The writers would write. I didn't start as a writer and will not end as one.

—Otto Heller, 1941

Heller's life had not only begun, in Koestler's words, as a "typical case-history of a Central-European member of the intelligentsia," but it continued as such into "the totalitarian age," when "it was entirely normal for a writer, an artist, politician or teacher with a minimum of integrity to have several narrow escapes from Hitler and/or Stalin, to be chased and exiled, and to get acquainted with prisons and concentration camps." "Finally," added Koestler, "it was quite normal for six million Jews to end their lives in a gas chamber."[1] Though himself a Jew, Koestler did not draw a direct line from the "typical" life trajectory of an intellectual to what became a "normal" death for a Jew. In Heller's biography, those two histories are inseparable. That close connection was, in itself, characteristic of the non-Jewish Jew in the age of catastrophe.

Heller's contradicting identities, the "non-Jewish" and the "Jew," intersected and confronted one another through the question that was said to be directed to him amid the Death March, "if he still," after

Auschwitz, "held onto the conception expressed" in *The Decline of Judaism*.[2] Gutman, who recounted this question, could not know that, already by 1939, in "The Jew Is to Be Burned," Heller had altered his conception. If the "years of persecution," as historian Saul Friedländer defined 1933–1939, brought about a shift in Heller's understanding of the Jewish question, did the far more disastrous "years of extermination" (1939–1945) result in a respectively more radical change? This chapter follows his annals in those catastrophic years, first in occupied France, and subsequently as a prisoner in Auschwitz.

Resistance in France

After running from Hitler and then from Stalin, Heller was arrested as an alleged supporter of both dictators. Following the German-Soviet pact of August 23, 1939, German and Austrian communist refugees in France became suspected as a fifth column. As Germans or Austrians, they were identified with the Third Reich and as communists with its allied Soviet Union. On September 1, the Wehrmacht attacked Poland, launching the Second World War. Two days later, Britain and France declared war on Nazi Germany. Now all Germans and Austrians, communists or not, Jews or not, were treated as subjects of an enemy state and arrested.[3]

To handle the large numbers of interns, French authorities used sport facilities. On September 7, Heller was brought to Colombes stadium in Paris. On September 18, a day after the Soviet Union had fulfilled its part in the secret protocol of the pact and invaded Poland from the east, Heller was transferred to an internment camp in Meslay-du-Maine, in northwestern France.[4] From a comrade who was confined with him, Walter Stein, Emma heard about his time there: "In the fifteenth group, which included fifty Austrian emigrants and other ex-Austrians, there were about ten communists. Through his story-telling-skill, O.H knew how to keep this group's moral high, under bad living conditions—fifty cm straw bed for each."[5] During Heller's captivity, Emma and Lily were supported by Otto's friend and former colleague from *Nouvelles d'Autriche*, Elisabeth Freundlich, and her parents.[6]

In January 1940, Heller was liberated, thanks to his registration since March 1938 as an "ex-Austrian." This status was created by the French state after the Anschluss, to make a distinction between anti-Hitler Austrians and Austrian Nazis living in France.[7] The suspicions by fellow communists followed Heller from Berlin through Moscow to Paris. In March 1940, a Czechoslovakian delegate to the Comintern reported: "Heller is a typical intellectual, very volatile, with a sharp satirical [and] often negative critique, a talented journalist, who was not free from petit bourgeois tendencies."[8]

On May 10, 1940, Germany invaded France. On the eve of the attack, Heller was still desperately trying to write and publish. He still advocated for the power of writing, as he wrote in a letter to his

Figure 5.1. Otto Heller, unknown date. Courtesy of the Papineau-Heller Family Archive (PHFA), Paris.

brother-in-law from May 9: "Sometimes the pen can dig deeper than the spade."[9] The events of the next morning further undermined his writing prospects. During the storming of the German army, as the roads southward were clogged with fleeing civilians, Freundlich met the Hellers on the road, coming by foot from Paris.[10] But Otto's flight did not last long, as now all foreigners who had been released, thanks to anti-Nazi credentials, were rearrested.[11]

Heller was sent with a company of foreign laborers, including many Austrians who had fought in the Spanish Civil War, to Langlade, near Nîmes, in the south of France. Emma and Lily had to continue without him for some weeks, wandering around with no stable accommodation. In June, after the armistice with Germany and now under the French collaborative government of Vichy, a part of the labor company, including Heller, was demobilized on the condition that they cultivate the land. In early July, they squatted in an old falling farmstead in Langlade, and, by the end of the month, Emma and Lily rejoined him there. The communal farm became a home for some two dozen of refugees and an underground hub for Austrian antifascists, among them Heller's friend, Albert Haas.[12]

Forty-two-year-old Heller was now doing, maybe for the first time in his life, physical work. Freundlich was impressed to witness "Otto Heller, whom many unjustly imagine to be a typical intellectual, helpless outside his discussions with like-minded comrades, outside the world of books and writings, proved to be a fantastic organizer."[13] This was as close as he ever came to his ideal of the Jewish pioneer in the collective farms of Birobidzhan. He proudly wrote to Freundlich: "Our life here on the farm is difficult, but at least it has meaning. We have helped many and done something. We didn't kiss up to anyone; we felt at home, at least. The farm makes headway, we have found a way to feed ourselves."[14] Heller was also proud to share that another such farm was established near Toulouse, after their example.[15]

And still, he did not neglect his intellectual activity and used his time in Langlade for learning English and reading. In a small bundle of notes from that period, he inscribed brief summaries and short quotes from the books he read, probably those available, mainly in French history and German philosophy. Among those papers, there is a small note citing one sentence from the reknown Jewish historian and national activist, Simon Dubnov. The quote from Dubnov's *The Modern History of the Jewish People* (*Die neueste Geschichte des jüdischen Volkes*), does not address Jewish history, but "the German society," which, despite reaching the "apogee of spiritual and technical culture," could not overcome "the level of a half constitutional police-state, with many traits of the monarchist military-despotism."[16] Though apparently still interested in Jewish history, Heller found one of Dubnov's insights on non-Jewish history to be the most illuminating and relevant for his time.

While living on the farm, in November 1940, Otto and Emma Heller were granted admission to Mexico by Gilberto Bosques, the Mexican consul in Marseille, who clandestinely helped veterans of the International Brigades escape France.[17] Under Lázaro Cárdenes's presidency, Mexico provided shelter to several thousands of outstanding political refugees and writers, including the writer Heinrich Mann. Some of Heller's German-speaking communist comrades, such as Bruno Frei, Alfred Kanterowich, Hans Marchwitza, Anna Seghers, and Egon Erwin Kisch, were already there. About half of the political refugees in Mexico were Jews.[18]

Thus, the Hellers came to obtain the precious visa, longed for by many refugees, as described by Seghers in her novel *Transit*.[19] But, as in the novel, whenever one required document was attained, other complications showed up, making it useless. When the Hellers' application for visas was submitted, probably by one of their friends in Mexico, Lily was written under her parents' papers. By the time it was approved, she had reached the age in which she needed her own papers, so her visa was delayed. Freundlich recalled that Otto and Emma refused to leave without their daughter.[20] In his only preserved letter to a close woman friend, rare in its emotional frankness, Heller told Freundlich of his other reasons to stay in France.

> I am not an armchair warrior, and I condemn the useless scribblers, who do nothing but a) emigrate and b) write about what others do. What, then, should I do? Move to Marseille, sit in a coffeehouse and wait? And live on what? [. . .] What then should I do? Let everything drop here and "make a departure," like all the people in Marseille? Understand this: I know very well that I must prepare myself to leave, for the string on which we hang is stretched more and more [. . .]. We have 200 kg of potatoes here in the farm, seeds, meat, etc. Should I throw that all away? [. . .]

> I have had all of Mexico up to my ears. It is difficult in Europe, but it is my continent, my homeland, my affairs. What shall I do in Mexico? Write? About what others are doing in Europe? The writers would write. I didn't start as a writer and will not end as one. Believe me: my lettuce is more interesting than all the pickled cabbage written by the Ex-Ex-Austrians in Mexico. [. . .] We have roots that are too deep, and the earth is firm, but shifting. We cannot get free. Not with the legs, because not with the heart. The brain is—as is known—an inhibiting organ. Also the heart, particularly when it is directly connected to the brain. Leaving has become a profession. I have no vocation for it. Now my closest friends want me to prepare to leave. Therefore and only therefore do I prepare myself to go. Halfheartedly? No. Without a single atom of my heart. When I get the letters and telegrams from there my breath always catches: what effort, what care, what immense costs for my friends and colleagues![21]

Heller explained his reluctance to emigrate through his commitment to his European cultural roots, to political concrete action as opposed to mere writing, and specifically to his activity in the collective farm. Although these arguments could have been genuine at that point in time, previous letters show that he did attempt to emigrate. On May 9, 1940, Heller announced that he would register his family for immigration to the United States, expressing his regret for not doing so two years earlier.[22] Perhaps this was part of his motivation to learn English. However, the German invasion of France the following day undermined this intention.

Freundlich herself managed to flee to the United States. Before departing she said farewell to Heller: "'Take care,' he said when we parted, and his voice sounded raw, and then we embraced one another for a heartbeat. [. . .] I was silent and secretly wiped my eyes. My heart was heavy, but I didn't realize it was to be our last meeting."[23] From the United States, Freundlich tried to arrange for the Hellers' visas that would include Lily, but failed. She then endeavored to at least help by sending food, which was also a complicated operation. She could only send money to Portugal, to be used there to buy cans of sardiness that were then sent to France.[24] These were very expensive and took some eight weeks to arrive, as mentioned in a letter from Heller's brother in Zürich, who modestly financially supported the family.[25] "Only after the war did I find out," recalled Freundlich, "that it had been these few ridiculous cans of sardines which had provided provisions for Otto's daughter Lily so she had been able to manage the long walk to school."[26]

Nevertheless, some financial help was also received from Heller's other siblings, Karl (now Charles) Heller and Hanni Askonas, who had immigrated to the New York and London, respectively.[27] All that help must have been crucial for the Hellers, especially as—adding to all their existing difficulties—Otto had a bicycle accident, which neutralized him while his leg was in a cast, as Lily remembered.[28] The financial support from Heller's family raises questions about Emma's depictions of Otto's relationship with them as very tense ever since his turn to socialism two decades earlier.[29] Had the tension already been alleviated by then? Or was it the stressful situation that helped them put aside old conflicts? Or perhaps Emma's assessment was exaggerated in the first place, reflecting her own difficulties with her husband's family? Regardless, the Hellers' support became even more important after Otto was arrested again.

In April 1941, the inhabitants of the farm were denounced to the Vichy police for engaging in clandestine activity. Heller, Haas, and other members of the group were arrested and accused of high treason.[30] Their trial was held in October in front of a military tribunal in Montauban. One of the arrestees, Gerty Schindel, would later reveal that a former fighter in Spain, who did not live on the farm but often visited and brought food, was the informer. In contrast to his betrayal, Schindel distinguished the solidarity among the group members, who did not throw the blame on one another.[31] She believed that, although the French Communist Party hired "excellent lawyers" for them, "what [. . .] brought about a turn in the trial and influenced the judges [. . .], was Otto Heller's speech. Otto Heller did not only speak a classical French, but was also highly educated. As a writer he had always stood for justice and human dignity." In his defense statement, Heller stressed that the defendants did not resist fascism only for Austria, "but also for a free democratic France." Then, said Schindel, "I could see the change in the faces of the judges."[32] "By his plea," she told Max Stern, whom Heller had recruited to the International Brigades in 1937, Heller "had contributed decisively to the acquittal of almost all defendants."[33] Only a handful of them were sentenced for several years in prison.[34]

But Heller, although among the acquitted, was not liberated. On November 3, 1941, he was interned in a camp in La Vernet, under the category of "undesirable aliens."[35] There are reasons to believe that the "undesirability" of many of those interns was their Jewishness. At the time, out of 47,000 imprisoned foreigners, 40,000 were Jews.[36] In La Vernet, Heller was registered as a writer and an Austrian Jew. In the list of inmates, it was noted that he was in a good physical condition, and that he brought with him four books, one briefcase, two passports, photos, and "papers."[37]

If Heller had used some of these "papers" to write any memoirs or letters, none survived. Arthur Koestler was imprisoned in La Vernet at an earlier time in the same section C in which Heller was held,[38] designated "for those without any definite charge on their record, but who were 'suspects' either in the political or criminal line." Koestler left a detailed description of that camp, located at the foot hill of the Pyrenees: "The first impression on approaching it was of a mess of barbed wire and more barbed wire. It ran all round the camp in a three-fold fence and across it in various directions, with trenches running parallel."[39] "It had the reputation of a penal colony, and deserved it," concluded Koestler.[40] Although La Vernet was a far worse place than the previous temporary detainment facilities in which Heller had already been held, it did not compare to the concentration camps in the German Reich. And still, when Heller was brought to La Vernet, he had not yet experienced Auschwitz. Koestler wished that the reader's knowledge of German concentration camps would not shade the atrocities of La Vernet.

> The standard of comparison in the treatment of human beings having crashed to unheard-of depths, every complaint sounded frivolous and out of place. The scale of sufferings and humiliations was distorted, the measure of what a man can bear was lost. In Liberal-Centigrade, Vernet was the zero-point of infamy; measured in Dachau-Fahrenheit it was still 32 degrees above zero. In Vernet beating-up was a daily occurrence; in Dachau it was prolonged until death ensued. In Vernet people were killed for lack of medical attention; in Dachau they were killed on purpose. In Ver-

net half of the prisoners had to sleep without blankets in 20 degrees of frost; in Dachau they were put in irons and exposed to the frost.[41]

Not only in Vichy France was Heller tagged as a "suspect" of unproven political crimes, in Moscow, the suspicions against him never ceased: "Was he a serious conciliator or a Trotskyite? [. . .] It is uncertain."[42] Nevertheless, in La Vernet, he applied to the KPÖ organization in the camp and was rehabilitated by the Party, perhaps due to his contribution to his comrades' acquittal in court.[43] Again, the Austrian Party was more merciful to him.

From within the camp, Heller endeavored to use his visa to be transferred to a camp of foreign citizens in Les Milles, near Marseille, the sole transit camp in France for those to be expelled.[44] And indeed, on February 11 or 12, 1942, after more than three months in La Vernet, Heller was moved to a camp in Brebant, and from there, on March 3, to Les Milles.[45]

As in La Vernet, Heller hardly left any written trace from his time in Les Milles. Although it was considered an easier camp, the writer Lion Feuchtwanger (whom Heller criticized in his 1934 article), titled his memoir from his own internment of Les Milles, *The Devil in France: My Encounter with Him in the Summer of 1940*.

> The whole area was enclosed on two of its sides by a brick wall, on the other two, by an earthwork or terrace, all thoroughly fenced in with barbed wire and guarded by sentries. [. . .] Looking into the main building from the yard through one of the great doors, one saw nothing but a huge black hole. [. . .] The whole place reminded one of a catacomb. [. . .] Dust, dust everywhere! We were obliged to spend a large part of our time on the inside of this building. There we slept, there we had our meals. We depended on those rooms whenever it rained or whenever, as happened frequently in that part of France, the wind was strong and turned the yards into one great dust cloud. [. . .] We were given a little straw for our bedding, and the rest was left to us. There were no chairs, no benches, no tables, nothing but piles of defective bricks. Out of these we tried to build seats and tables, but they would always fall apart.[46]

> There were more than a thousand of us, [. . .]. Most of us were Jews. [. . .] Work was given us. We were obliged to move the bricks about, piling them up now here, now there. We trundled them around in wheelbarrows and then, at the command of a sergeant, tossed them from hand to hand and stacked them up in neat rows. The work was not really hard. What irritated and angered us was its utter fatuousness. There was no reasonable purpose behind the order—the authorities intended simply to keep us busy.[47]

From Les Milles, Heller wrote to his sister that he was starving. Depicting his work in construction for a bowl of soup and five francs a day, he asked her to send him money.[48] In April, funds were approved for him to sail to the United States, which, by this time, was no longer feasible.[49] On July 8, 1942, it was reported that Heller disappeared from Les Milles.[50] After four months, he had somehow managed to escape.[51]

Whether his emigration efforts were entirely frustrated or he actively decided to stay, following his escape, Heller did not head south to the port of Marseille, but rather north, to join the fight against Nazi Germany. After crossing the border from Vichy into the occupied part of France Heller reached Paris, where he established contact with the resistance organization Austrian National Front (Front National Autriche).[52] In October 1942, he was among some fifty Austrian communists who formed, by an order from Moscow, the Austrian Freedom Front (Österreichische Freiheitsfront).[53] Through this group, he joined the Travail Allemand ([TA], German Work), a section of the French Resistance, created in the summer of 1941 by German and Austrian refugees for anti-Nazi propaganda.[54] TA published bulletins titled *Der Soldat am Mittelmeer* (The Soldier in the Mediterranean) and *Der Soldat am Westen* (The Soldier in the West), aimed at weakening the morale of German troops on French territories. The information for the publications was obtained mostly through Radio Moscow and German People's Broadcast (*Deutscher Volksender*) and then written down by several comrades, among them Heller.[55] TA also included a "Girls-Group," destined to influence German and Austrian soldiers, which was led in northern France by Gerty Schindel, among others.[56]

Heller was sent by the TA to infiltrate a unit of the Wehrmacht in Lille, near the Belgian border. Under the false identity of a Raymond Brunet, he passed himself off as an interpreter, as did some other dozen members of the organization in different places. That enabled Heller to inform French Resistance groups of German troop movements and to distribute illegal issues of *Der Soldat am Westen* among the soldiers.[57] Heller's former recruit to the International Brigades, Max Stern, distinguished that "as a well-known communist intellectual of Jewish origins he was in high risk."[58] Franz Marek, one of the leaders of the KPÖ in northern France, retrospectively considered it "irresponsible" to appoint an "old and gifted writer" for this mission.[59] Marek described Heller as having "contacts, nimble, versatile, wrote some brochures."[60] According to Marek, in the espionage work within the Wehrmacht, Heller became "specialized on intellectual types, whom he could impress with his high and universal education, so he could more easily get into a conversation with." Marek stressed that Heller "came although he was not the youngest and although he owned some visas, that could allow him to travel to Cuba or Mexico."[61] Heller's daughter, Lily, was also proud to tell how her father, "facing the possibility of moving to America [. . .] he decided [. . .] to join the resistance which was growing in the north."[62] If she was the reason that the family did not leave to Mexico, then Lily either did not know or knew, but preferred not to mention it.

While Heller was disguised as a Wehrmacht interpreter in the north, Emma and Lily, now living in Collonges au Mont d'Or, near Lyon, were also active in the resistance, distributing illegal publications.[63] It is doubtful they had any contact with him, and it is also unclear if they or he knew that on November 6, Heller's mother and sister, Emma Steinhaus, along with her husband Oscar, who had fled Austria to France, were all sent from Drancy camp, near Paris, to Auschwitz and murdered there.[64]

On December 23, 1943, in his apartment in Lille, Heller was arrested by the Gestapo.[65] There are several different versions regarding the identity of the informer who disclosed Heller, together with other TA people in the area, but he probably came from inside the organization.[66] Heller was imprisoned in the Gestapo prison in Fresnes, Paris, and tortured during his interrogation.[67] He was accused of

166 | Radical Assimilation in the Face of the Holocaust

Figure 5.2. Lily Heller, unknown date. Courtesy of the Papineau-Heller Family Archive (PHFA), Paris.

undermining the work of the German army, distributing pamphlets, prohibited networking, and collecting military information for the resistance.[68] On an unknown date, he was convicted by a military tribunal and condemned, according to one version, to ten years of labor, according to another, to death.[69]

Meanwhile, on June 24, 1944, Emma and twenty-year-old Lily were also arrested, caught in their home in Collonges au Mont d'Or with convicting materials.[70] From their interrogators, they learned about Otto's arrest.[71] "It was the Gestapo," told Lily, "that gave us news about him and showed us a photo of him in prison with a shirt stained with blood, dated to March 44."[72] As they were transferred to Fresnes, Emma contemplated asking the Gestapo to see Otto, but decided "that I am not allowed to do it, that this is dishonorable."[73]

She tried once to obtain paper to write him a letter, but failed. In August, as the front came closer, and the prison regime was somewhat loosened, Emma and Lily tried once to shout his name from the window. They later learned that he was already gone.[74]

From all of his time in occupied France, between 1940 and 1944, Heller did not leave any account of his political views or any theoretical work. He left the writing to "the writers," devoting himself to acts of resistance.[75] Other communist writers of Jewish descent in France, especially those of foreign origins, addressed the Jewish question during the war. They tended to blur the unique treatment of Jews by the Nazis, by equating Jewish suffering with French suffering.[76] Under German occupation, communist references to antisemitism in France still held the traditional Marxist interpretation, similar to Heller in *The Decline of Judaism*, depicting it as a reactionary medieval remnant and as an antirevolutionary diversion.[77] By that time, having already written "The Jew Is to be Burned," Heller shifted his understanding of antisemitism, and now saw it as an escalating threat to Jewish existence and to humanity.[78] He could not yet know that, although he did not wish to "end" "as a writer,"[79] in Auschwitz he was destined to write again. Moreover, on his return to writing, he would be forced to confront the Jewish question, this time in its most horrifying sense.

Underground in Auschwitz

On July 25, 1944, as Allied armies were already marching into France, Heller was transferred from the Gestapo jail to Drancy.[80] On the 31st he was deported, on one of the last transports from France, convoy number 77, to Auschwitz.[81] Two weeks later, on August 15, Emma and Lily were deported to the women concentration camp Ravensbrück, northern to Berlin.[82] Lily believed that her father's deportation to Auschwitz was the substitute to his death sentence, which was practically almost equivalent.[83] Arriving in Auschwitz in early August, out of 1,310 deportees who were with Heller on the convoy, 836 were sent directly to the gas chambers.[84]

By that time, Auschwitz was already a fully developed center of the Nazi system, filling two major tasks: a main operative vehicle for "the final solution of the Jewish question"; and a huge concentration and forced labor camp for political prisoners from all over Europe. The Auschwitz conglomerate by then reached its full measures, encompassing more than forty subcamps. The main camp, known as Auschwitz I, located in the Silesian town of Oświęcim, was inhabited mostly with political prisoners. Auschwitz II was built only a few miles away, in the village Brzerzinka, or Birkenau, according to its German name. This was the main site of mass murder, containing four complexes of gas chambers and crematoria. Next to them stood long rows of barracks, populated primarily by Jewish prisoners, who were excluded from the death transports and chosen for imprisonment and forced labor.[85] In total, in August 1944 over 100,000 prisoners were incarcerated in Auschwitz camps system.[86]

The Czech-Jewish communist and a resistance activist in Auschwitz, Viktor Lederer (1905–?), remembered how one day, "in our oblong room with three-storied bunks the block-clerk entered with a middle-sized faint man," who presented himself as Otto Heller.[87] Lederer, who had heard of Heller as a famous communist writer in his own homeland, was excited to meet him in person.[88] Lederer testified: "Maybe it was already in the same evening, however in every following evening he told us, not about himself, his family, and his friends, but rather about the struggle of our [the Czechoslovakian], the French, and the Austrian Communist Parties."[89] Lily also learned after the war from her father's fellow inmates that despite "working for most of the time, in between he found the way to distract his comrades with lectures."[90] According to Lederer, Heller often related to the victims of the gas chambers: "I feel their death and misery as if I died myself." Lederer also attributed to Heller the following confession, recited from his memory.

> Above all I am a communist, that is exactly why I wrote the book *The Decline of Judaism*. Yet Hitler and all that I experience here have educated me more profoundly. Exactly because I am a Jew I must take part in the fight against Fascism, against antisemitism, whose increasing insanity originated in class-hatred, the ferocity of reckless egoists. Here in Auschwitz I received the most sorrowful proof of Lenin's truth, that antisemitism is a lightning arrester for the dissatisfaction of the masses. Yet this lightning arrester

does not protect Nazism from the wrath of humanity, demanding social justice, freedom, and peace.[91]

Lederer had put into Heller's mouth two very different positions. On the one hand, Heller is cited as saying "I am a Jew," a self-perception that he has never pronounced in writing, and as deeply identifying with the Jewish victims of Auschwitz. On the other hand, he was allegedly sticking to conventional communist slogans regarding antisemitism as a mere instrument, characteristic of *The Decline of Judaism*. At the beginning his motivation for fighting stems from his Jewishness, and at the end from universal humanistic values. Although these positions are not necessarily contradictory, they were usually considered as such in communist circles. Written some years after the events, Lederer's account cannot be taken as given. Hence, it cannot answer the question how Heller's Jewish perception was shaped by his experience in Auschwitz. Nevertheless, as it was clearly written for a communist newspaper, it was more likely to be biased toward the communist side, which gives certain credibility to Heller's alleged Jewish self-identification.

The Polish-Jewish historian of the resistance in Auschwitz, Ber Mark, believed that Heller underwent a substantial change in the camp: "After being educated by cruel experience, [he] conducted a soul-searching [Mark used the Hebrew religiously loaded idiom, ḥeshbon ha-nefesh], and approached the Jewish national idea." In Auschwitz, claimed Mark, Heller "drew closer to Polish Jewry," and subsequently "went through a revision of his worldview."[92] Heller, concluded Mark, "had completely changed and became a nationalist Jew."[93] This assessment, significantly more far-reaching than Lederer's, is not supported by direct evidence. The question of Heller's relation to his Jewishness and to the Jewish Holocaust in Auschwitz shall be now examined through his only textual footprints from the camp, his writings for the prisoners' underground.

Shortly after his arrival in the camp, Heller encountered Albert Haas, whom he knew from his exile in France.[94] Haas was probably the one who introduced Heller into conspiratorial activity in the camp.[95] Heller joined the international resistance organization of prisoners in Auschwitz, known as Auschwitz Fighting Group (Kampfengruppe Auschwitz [KGA]). The underground leadership consisted of political prisoners interned in Auschwitz I, where Heller was most likely dwelling as well.[96] There is no record of the total number of prisoners who participated in the underground activity, which must have been fluctuating constantly. Estimations range between several hundreds and several thousands.[97]

KGA was formed already during 1943 as a coordination of various national and political underground groups. The initiative came from the Austrian group, headed by the communist Hermann Langbein. The commander of KGA was the Polish socialist Józef Cyrankiewicz (1911–1989). Besides the Austrian and Polish groups, a German group took important part in the leadership. Czech, French, Russian, and Yugoslavian groups were also active, though not represented in KGA central committee.[98] Several Jewish underground groups formed contacts with KGA, including a big group of Sonderkommando prisoners, whose forced labor was in operating the crematoria in Birkenau and handling the corpses.[99] For that they were virtually isolated from the rest of the camp.[100] To which of the national groups did Heller belong? In some testimonies he was identified as a Czech.[101] Arriving after the formation of the international joint force, and thus probably not belonging to any specific former national group, Heller could have been equally categorized through each of the other components of his compound identity, as German, Austrian, or Jewish. Formally considered a political prisoner and a Jew, his camp uniform must have been labeled with both a red and a yellow triangle.[102]

One of the main aspects of resistance in Auschwitz was to maintain "contact with the world," "to inform the world about the crimes being committed," and to carry out "intelligence work for the Allies."[103] Information was gathered in the camp by KGA's "propaganda-political service," responsible of composing brochures, memoranda, and resolutions. These were addressed both to the camp's prisoners and the outside world, aiming to dispel the mist of secrecy, deception, and propaganda surrounding the camp. Alongside sections dealing with military preparations for uprising (that never occurred), organizational matters, communication, and arranging escapes, the propaganda department played a central role in the underground's activity, providing the materials to be smuggled outside the camp. While some information was conveyed by escapees, most of it was delivered through civilian workers in the camp and in the factories connected to it, by the Polish resistance movement in the area and sometimes even by Germans.[104]

The materials dispatched by KGA reached the Kraków-based underground organization Aid to Concentration Camp Prisoners (Pomoc Więźniów Obozów Koncentracyjnych, PWOK), where it was edited in the form of bulletins, each titled "Periodical Report." These were among the sources for the earliest publications about the true nature of Auschwitz that reached the world outside occupied Poland.[105] Thirteen such reports survived, consisting of some sixty-five pages, and covering the period from February to October 1944.[106] Heller probably participated in the writing of the last five reports, composed from August onward.

The leading members of the propaganda service of KGA were Cyrankiewicz, Haas, Alfred Klahr, Bruno Baum, and Heller.[107] The fact that the chief commander of the organization, Cyrankiewicz, took under his direct responsibility the editorial work attested the importance of this activity to the underground. Before his arrest in Auschwitz, in September 1942, Cyrankiewicz was a prominent underground activist of the Polish Socialist Party (Polska Partia Socjalistyczna [PPS]) in Kraków and an officer in the Home Army, the national Polish underground front, which included the socialists, while opposing the communists.[108] Since Poles were majority in the underground, it was clear to the leadership of KGA that the chief commander should be a Pole. As a Home Army officer, Cyrankiewicz could maintain the communication with the outside world, which was mediated through the Polish Home Army to the Government-in-Exile in London, in which the PPS was represented. As such, he was accepted by a wide range of Polish circles in Auschwitz, and able to bridge the deep differences with the KGA, for example between Polish nationalists and German communists.[109]

Another internal tension that increasingly occupied Cyrankiewicz was between Jews and non-Jews in the underground, who faced radically different situations. Every passing day increased the chances of the Jews being murdered, especially the Sonderkommando prisoners, who were frequently liquidated. For the non-Jews, contrarily, every passing day increased their chances of survival until the liberation. Cyrankiewicz's policy was to postpone the uprising plans, keeping them only for case of general liquidation of all inmates in the camp.¹¹⁰ For undermining the Jewish efforts to revolt Cyrankiewicz was ascribed antisemitic resentment, or at least lending his ear to that of the right-wing Polish groups within the underground, who observed the ongoing extermination of the Jews with content.¹¹¹

Cyrankiewicz was exceptional among his subordinates on the propaganda service. He was not just the only socialist and the only Pole, but also the only one without Jewish origins. Heller, Klahr, Haas, and Baum were all German-speaking communists, born to Jewish families, typical "non-Jewish Jews." Mark criticized Baum, the only one of them who retrospectively documented their activity in Auschwitz, for not referring to Heller, Haas, and all the other Jewish activists in the resistance as Jews, rather merely by their civil nationalities.¹¹² How did those communists of Jewish descent relate to their Jewishness in Auschwitz? An answer to this question can be searched for in the Periodical Reports they wrote. As these reports were written and edited jointly, Heller's part in them can be inferred only after considering the role of his colleagues.

Albert Haas (1896–1967) had originated from Hungary, where he participated in the 1918 revolution. After the suppression of the revolution, he had to flee the country and joined the Communist Party of Austria, for which he worked as a journalist until the Anschluss of 1938, which pushed him again into exile, in Paris. In 1943, after two years of imprisonment in France, Haas was deported to Auschwitz, where he became a prominent figure within the French Resistance group and a leading member of the underground cell of prisoners enslaved in Union and Deutschen Ausrüstungswerke (DAW) factories.¹¹³

Alfred Klahr (1904–1944) and Heller were never simultaneously present in Auschwitz, since Klahr escaped the camp in late June 1944, while Heller arrived only in early August. Klahr was an Austrian communist journalist, a member of the Central Committee of the Communist Party of Austria, and one of the leading theoreticians of the Austrian nationalism.¹¹⁴ In Auschwitz he was a member of the Austrian resistance group that cofounded KGA. In January 1944, when all Jewish prisoners stood for a deadly selection, Klahr demanded from the KGA leadership to provoke a general mutiny in the camp, against the murder of Jewish prisoners. The members of the central committee of the organization, who were all non-Jewish, did not accept Klahr's demand. They thought that at the time, an uprising did not have a chance, and that it would result in the murder of many prisoners.[115] In June 1944, together with a Polish comrade, Klahr carried out a successful escape from Auschwitz. The two reached Warsaw shortly before the outbreak of the Polish uprising in the city, during which Klahr was shot to death.[116] Klahr's escape must have left a void in the editorial work. Considering Haas's previous acquaintance with Heller, it is reasonable to assume that the former recruited the latter to fill Klahr's place.[117] Did Heller informally replace Klahr as a "Jewish voice" within the editorial? I shall return to this hypothesis later on.

Bruno Baum (1910–1971) was active in the communist youth organization in Berlin, and ever since his arrest in 1935 was held captive in prisons and concentration camps. After being transferred to Auschwitz in April 1943, he joined the resistance movement.[118] In October 1944, he became a member of the KGA central committee, responsible for political matters.[119] Baum's role in the underground editorial was decisive, both as a participant as well as a documenter of its activity. His book, *Resistance in Auschwitz* (*Widerstand in Auschwitz*) includes the most detailed account of the propaganda service in general and of Heller's part in particular.

> Our greatest task was to convey, in letters or reports, what was happening in the camp. The enormous gassings [. . . were] not believed even by those who had fought against Hitler illegally for many years and knew the infinite atrocities of the Nazis. We, who knew that Auschwitz is the largest human extermination site that has ever existed in the world, knew that we can only be helped if the world would know what is happening [. . .]. We obtained connection [to Kraków] and tried to bring to publicity some materials about the conditions and the mass murder in the camp. [. . .] From Kraków it was sent to a Polish representative in London. We knew for sure that we were being heard, but the London broadcaster, like the world press, did not bring our news. We were again disappointed that we were not believed. Even in these places our reports sounded too fantastic. It was not until mid-1944, when the advance of the Soviet Army left the British with no other option but to establish the second front, that large-scale publications began. [. . .] In order to give that work a solid basis, we

created an editorial committee consisting of our Austrian comrades Arbert [sic] Haas and Otto Heller. These comrades collected material, wrote speeches and essays [. . .].

Comrade Heller had to put his material together at his commando and therefore his most important concern was bringing it into the camp, by using toothpaste tubes, in which the articles, written on thin paper, could be stored easily. A similar method was used by Haas. The finished speeches, articles, etc. came to me afterwards and were usually checked by me during the night shift in the small laundry workshop [. . .]. From me the material came to Cyrankiewicz, who transported it on. From mid-1944 onwards we sent something at least twice a week. Now the tragedy of Auschwitz went through the world. I think it is no exaggeration to say that most of the Auschwitz propaganda that was spread over the world around this time was written by us in the camp ourselves. [. . .] We sent documents [. . .], by which to prove the completely monstrous mass extermination.[120]

Baum attributes a pivotal role in the writing process to both Heller and Haas. The central part of the two was confirmed by another member of the underground central committee, the Pole Tadeusz Hołuj.[121] Nonetheless, the much more detailed depiction of Heller's work in Baum's report, given earlier than Hołuj's, raises a question about the division of labor between the two "Austrian comrades." While Heller was active only in the editorial, Haas had much wider responsibilities within the resistance. Could he have taken an equal part in the editorial work?

Lederer, who oversaw the inner communication of the underground, was one of the closest eyewitnesses to Heller in the camp.[122] The two were assigned together to forced labor at the "disinfection commando" (*Schädlingsbekämpfung Kommando*), which handled chemicals for production of pesticides by factories of the German concern I. G. Farben, located in Auschwitz. Lederer testified that it was through Haas that Heller received the instruction to write articles about the life in Auschwitz and the solidarity of "progressive" prisoners in the camp. Lederer became acquainted with this task as Heller asked for his assistance in correcting his articles and guarding the place of writing.[123] According to this description, Heller was the main writer, while Haas was the coordinator and intermediator with the leadership. In another account Heller was defined as the "editor of the underground news" (*Redakteur der konspiratorischen Nachrichten*) and Haas as an activist in the organization.[124]

Hence, a more accurate tracking of the chain of information within the "editorial" should be as follows: the information, gathered from various underground members around the camp, was conveyed by Haas to Heller, who compiled the first drafts of the reports. Klahr was not mentioned in Baum's description since when the latter entered his position the former was already out of the camp. It is plausible that Klahr had fulfilled a similar role to that later performed by Heller. Haas was the liaison, who transferred Heller's texts to Baum, perhaps contributing some of his own input. Baum was the political authority, responsible for the adjustment of the reports to the current political agenda of the leadership. Baum's revised versions were handed over to Cyrankiewicz, who edited the final formulation in Polish. His messages were subsequently edited by PWOK in the form of the Periodical Reports in Polish, which is the only version preserved.

The Periodical Reports followed the current of events in the camp, focusing on several recurring themes: the prisoners' demand to be entitled to human rights; the atrocities executed in the camp and the identity of their perpetrators; the threat of liquidation of the camp and murder of all prisoners; and the mass murder of Polish prisoners, perceived as a plan to "'exterminate' the Poles" ("ausroten" [sic] Polaków).[125] Another topic the reports repeatedly dealt with was the extermination of Jews, who were deported to Auschwitz from all over Europe for that purpose. What messages did the authors of the reports wish to convey regarding the purposes of the camp? How did they conceive the relation between its two different functions, as a concentration camp for political prisoners and as an extermination camp for Jews? Which dimension received more attention and emphasis, and thus was more crucial for them to alert the world about? Investigating the relation between universalist and particularistic interpretations of the Holocaust[126] in the secret messages might be revealing regarding Heller's position.

The first underground publication after Heller's arrival in the camp was a "Resolution of the Political Prisoners."[127] Lederer's memory of Heller being asked to write about the life of the "progressive" prisoners in the camp implies that Heller's might have already been involved in its formulation.[128] The trigger for publishing this document originated in the trial of the German generals involved in the attempt to assassinate Hitler on July 20, 1944. The Nazi judge accused one of the defendants for his intention, in case of successful coup d'état, to arrest the SS crews guarding the concentration camps, and to release the prisoners. According to the judge, the general intended to "release purely criminal elements."[129] In response, the authors of the resolution wished to clarify that

> in German concentration camps, the number of criminal offenders, exclusively German, does not exceed 5% of the total number of prisoners; they are indeed professional criminals—murderers and thieves. [. . .] This already small percentage of professional criminals has recently been reduced to almost zero, because all those capable of serving were sent to the front [. . .]. In German concentration camps there are now 99 percent *political prisoners of all nations*, fighting for freedom. There are French, Belgians, Dutch, Italians, Germans, Austrians, Czechs, Poles, Romanians, Serbs, Hungarians, Bulgarians, Greeks, Norwegians, Jews. There are representatives of all social strata of these nations.[130]

Having asserted that, the authors addressed the "free world" in a plea "for the rights of political prisoners." Moreover, they identified themselves "as soldiers" of their respective nations, who "demand to be treated as soldiers—we demand human rights, the rights of prisoners of war in captivity." Obviously, the authors of the resolution did not expect the Nazis to grant them human rights. They emphasized the moral and symbolic significance of an international recognition of their rights as "an expression of a common fight for the freedom of nations, for the freedom of the world, for *Human* dignity."[131] Nonetheless, they stressed that they were not asking for "philanthropic" aid, rather to be treated as "a part of the fight against Hitlerism itself, in which we, the prisoners, are not some kind of ballast, but simply a front section. [. . .] Any plans for military assistance for us must include the concept of using our forces in the military sense and including them in the general fight."[132] After expressing his disappointment that London had ignored the group's earlier reports, as they must have "sounded too fantastic," Baum reported that "we now wrote a Resolution of the Prisoners in the German Concentration Camps, and we had the joyful satisfaction of hearing ourselves from abroad while secretly listening."[133]

The next report, from September 16, 1944, an exceptionally long one, contained a list of SS staff from Auschwitz and their respective crimes.[134] Heller's role in composing this report is unclear, since a similar list was already sent during the first half of 1944, but the original of the earlier one did not survive.[135] However, the September report probably included a more detailed and updated list. It began with an unequivocal demand: "We send more detailed descriptions of the henchmen of Auschwitz. All data is authentic beyond any doubt. It will be very much appreciated if London will announce *death sentences* for them *as soon as possible*."[136] Already the first list was revealed to the world in a BBC broadcast, which added that the Allies had passed death sentences against all the SS men named in the list.[137] Cyrankiewicz reported with satisfaction to the Polish underground that "the announcement [. . .] had such an effect on those sentenced that some of them suffered breakdowns."[138] Though the immediate goal of the report—announcement of death sentences—was obtained, the impact of these threats is questionable. Contrary to Cyrankiewicz's satisfaction, in a following report the editorial admitted its frustration in face of the "continuing gassing," without "political rationale" or any attempt by the Germans "to cover themselves up": "The Germans are now destroying themselves, [. . .] murdering without paying attention to the consequences of these crimes, and the consequences will be terrible for them."[139] Retrospectively it might be even claimed, that the threats merely achieved the opposite end, by pushing the perpetrators deeper into the moral abyss they were already in. Having been criminalized and sentenced to death, they had nothing more to lose. Their bond to the Nazi regime became a matter of life and death. Continuing serving the Reich was now their only, rather desperate, chance of survival. They were chained by the criminal fraternity.[140]

Extraordinarily, in October 1944, KGA reported on an event that took place far away from Auschwitz, in concentration camp Buchenwald, in Germany. It mentioned the death of two prominent German leftist leaders, allegedly during a British bombing of Buchenwald: the socialist Rudolf Breitscheid and the communist Ernst Thälmann.[141]

The latter was the leader of the KPD who tried to distance Heller from the Party back in Berlin.[142] Ever since 1933 Thälmann was incarcerated in various concentration camps. According to the report, it was the Nazis who bombed the concentration camp and falsely accused the British. Buchenwald was actually attacked by the American air force, and whereas Breitscheid was probably indeed killed by the air raid, Thälmann was executed a week earlier. The Nazis used the bombing as a pretext to announce him as one of its victims.[143] The fact that no later than early October 1944, the underground in Auschwitz knew about the bombing that occurred in late August in a distanced concentration camp evidence its impressive intelligence capability, considering the conditions in which it operated. Whether deliberately or unwittingly distorting the facts, the propaganda section used this information to serve two purposes: emphasizing the leftist political affiliation of the concentration camps' prisoners; and alarming of a potential liquidation plan in Auschwitz.

As the Red Army was advancing into Poland, the underground reported its worries about a prospective plan to liquidate all the prisoners by the retreating Nazis. The resistance was informed that Otto Moll, the notorious commander of the crematoria, was ordered to prepare operational plans. On September 6, Cyrankiewicz reported to Kraków about "Action Moll," a plan to destroy the camp by bombing it from the air.[144] The October report announced: "This large-scale attempt to erase these traces by final murder is a new proof of the decisive bestiality of Hitlerism, which the free world cannot allow."[145] The message reached London on October 10, and the BBC broadcasted a warning against the liquidation plan, issued by the British and United States governments. Radio Moscow also published the plan. The German government promptly denied the reports.[146] Since an order to liquidate camp prisoners was not issued before late January 1945, the warning could be seen as a preemptive act on the side of the underground, based on terrifying rumors that spread in the camp.[147] Referring to a different scenario—evacuation of the camp— one of the reports alluded particularly to the assumed future of the Jewish prisoners in that case: "The fate of most of the remaining Jews is clear to those who know German bestiality."[148]

The Periodical Reports do not offer an unequivocal answer to the question who should be seen as the main victims of Auschwitz? Their attitude toward the Jewish aspect—namely, to the crucial role of this camp in the "Final Solution"—was dual. On the one hand, sometimes the mass murder of Jews was imperatively presented as no more than one among other crimes perpetrated in the camp. On the other hand, some of the reports paid special attention to the mass murder of Jews in Birkenau.

The conceptualization of the extermination of Jews as merely one of many atrocities taking place in Auschwitz was exemplified by accusing the camp's commander, Rudolf Höss, of "abusing and mass murdering 106,000 registered prisoners, 12,600 Russian prisoners of war, and one million Jews deported from all over Europe, murdered by asphyxiation by gas."[149] In another place, near the end of a detailed list of cases of killing prisoners, under the title "100,000 murdered," "more than one million gassed from Jewish transports" was casually mentioned, without being calculated into the sum, although by that it would have been drastically increased, making a much more shocking impression.[150] It appears that in such cases the authors were careful not to place the Jewish victims at the forefront.

Nevertheless, there were also cases of special attention paid to the fate of the Jews in Auschwitz. The most salient example of focus on the Jewish catastrophe in Auschwitz was the reporting of the extermination of Hungarian Jewry, between May and July 1944, prior to Heller's arrival in the camp. A "special Appendix" to the May report dealt with "Action Höss," named after the former commander of the Auschwitz complex, now in charge of this extremely intensive killing operation.[151] In the June report, which unregularly devoted three of its four pages to this subject, it was stressed: "The monstrous crime continues, it is gaining force."[152] The reports from May and June described in detail the mechanism of industrial murder. The authors felt they must appeal to the skeptical reader: "It all sounds fantastic, but it is true!"[153] They sealed this chapter with a call for the remaining Jews out there: "Wake up fiercely, decisively. Do not die with impunity! Those! [sic] who went to their death are screaming at the future transports of Jews—fight! Sell your life dearly! We all go to our death anyway. Let the world, that cannot yet know about these atrocities, hear about the act of despair. Let there be a new Warsaw Ghetto. Fight everywhere, on the transport, on unloading and on your way to the gas plant, on your way to death."[154] Such a call for the Jews to resist as Jews was unique in the history of non-Jewish resistance movements. It can be most certainly ascribed to Klahr, who in January had already aspired to an uprising. However, such a mutiny did not take place, and the murderous action continued uninterrupted. In mid-July, a few days after the almost complete cessation of transports from Hungary, the underground counted over 300,000 victims.[155]

Heller arrived in Auschwitz after the transports from Hungary ended, when the pace of extermination significantly decreased. Nevertheless, he witnessed the murder of 65,000 Jews from Lodz alone during August, which could have not pass through without leaving a stark imprint, especially on a newcomer, who did not experience "Action Höss."[156] The bulletin from September reported that the "Gassing Continues."

> The Birkenau gasworks and crematoria continue to fulfill their monstrous task, regardless of the fast approaching justice system. The Jews of Lodz ghetto have been gassed and burned recently, thus eliminating the last remnants. 12.9 this year a transport from Krosno [Poland] brought 300 Jewish children, who were immediately gassed and burned. Even nowadays, despite the evacuation plans, Jewish transports from the east and recently from France, Belgium, and the Netherlands are coming. The retreating Hitlerist torturer is taking the Jews and continues to send them to death. The war situation does not improve the grave condition of the Jews, but rather, judging by the events, speeds up their elimination.[157]

Later, in October, a passage titled "The Gassing Still Continues" counted the murdered Jews from Theresienstadt, Hungary, Lodz, and Buchenwald, stressing that "sick and *healthy* Jews" alike were gassed.[158] Another noteworthy comment from that period relates to an Allied bombing in the area of the camp: "Unfortunately, forty prisoners, *including twenty-three Jews*, died."[159] As historian Dan Diner had put it, relating to a different situation in Flossenbürg, the authors had differentiated here "between death to death"—between the death of Jewish and non-Jewish prisoners in the same bombing. "What is the essence of this difference?" asked Diner. "The answer stems from the unique character of the specific collective death that the Nazis had imposed upon all Jews, only for their origin. And that death was absolute."[160] Assuming that Heller took a major role

SPRAWOZDANIE OKRESOWE
/ od 1.IX.1944 do 2o.IX.1944/
KOMUNIKAT SPECJALNY

OŚWIĘCIM

Warszawa w Oświęcimiu

Propaganda niemiecka krzyczy o opiece nad ewakuowanymi z Warszawy, krzyczy o obozie w Pruszkowie zorganizowanym w celu niesienia "pomocy wysiedlonym" z gruzów. Z 14-tu bloków transportowych obozu pruszkowskiego, mie szczących każdy około 3.500m ludzi, odeszły trzy transporty do Ravensbrück - do Stutthofen /pod Gdańskiem/ i w kierunku Gliwitz - Wrocławia. Część kobiet i dzieci odesłano do Piotrkowa Trybunalskiego.
Do Oświęcimia przyjechały bezpośrednio z Pruszkowa transporty ludności warszawskiej w wagonach z eskortą wojskową.

I. transport 12.8.1944 mężczyźni 2.000
                      kobiet   3.200
II.   "   4.9.1944 mężczyzn 3.000
                      kobiet   1.150
III.   "   14.9.1944 mężczyzn
                      i kobiet   900

Ludność Warszawy wśród ciężkiej walki , otoczona bagnetami niemieckimi wyszła z miasta, ratując swe życie, wierząc w obietnice niemieckie. Część tych ewakuowanych znalazła "schronienie" w strasznych murach Oświęc mia. W Wciągnięci na listę t.zw. "Zivil-häftlingów" /więźniowie cywilni/ otrzymują numerację obozową i odżywienie więźnia obozu bez dodatku tygodniowego, t.zw. "zulagi" /Zulaga - dwa razy w tygodniu po pół bochenka chleba i plaster kiełbasy/. Warunki stają się coraz gorsze - straszliwa ciasnota, niedostateczne ubranie przy zbliżających się zimnych jesiennych dniach, brak lekarstw, powtarzające się wypadki dyfterii, tyfusu, szkarlatyny. Zmarło już 15-tu ludzi. Więźniowie z Warszawy są odseparowani od reszty obozu, by przypadkiem nie przeciekały wiadomości o wypadkach warszawskich
Obozy koncentracyjne przyjęły obecnie "gości" w swoje mury, przyjęły ludzi, którym niemcy przed całym światem nietykalność, wolność i opiekę za pewnili. Gdzież te zapewnienia? Skazani wraz z mieszkańcami obozów giną po woli, o ile zbrodniarz hitlerowski nie zechce gwałtownie i szybko likwidować. Wolny świat dowiaduje się o tym i musi przez swoje instytucje ingerować. Międzynarodowy Czerwony Krzyż, państwa demokratyczne upomnieć się muszą o nowe ofiary hitleryzmu - ostro i bezwzględnie grozić.

Bombardowanie obozu

W ramach ogolnego ataku samolotów amerykańskich w dniu 13.9.1944 na zakłady przemysłowe I.G. Farben w Dworach, obrzucili lotnicy bombami także pewne urządzenia obozowe.
W Auschwitz I. zniszczono w obrębie "wielkiej postenketty" dwa baraki zamieszkałe przez SS, w których znalazło śmierć 15-tu S-manów, 28-miu jest ciężko rannych. Nie odszukana jeszcze pewna część leży pod gruzami. Należy zauważyć, że baraki te schowane były poprostu między barakami w których ustawicznie pracują więźniowie. Zniszczono również 1 barak "Bekleidungs werkstätte", w którym niestety znalazło śmierć 40-tu więźniów - z tych 23 Żydów - i zostało 65-ciu ciężko rannych. 13-cie osób pozostało jeszcze pod gruzami - przypuszczalnei nie żyją.
W Auschwitz II. spadły tylko 2 bomby, jakkolwiek lotnictwo miało tu godniejsze cele do niszczenia - krematoria gazowe. Jedna z bomb uszkodziły tor i nasyp kolejowy bocznicy prowadzącej do krematorium, druga zniszczyła znajdujący się między torami schron, zabijając około 30-tu robotników cywilnych

Figure 5.3. Underground Periodical Report from 1.IX to 20.IX, 1944, 1. Issued by Aid to Concentration Camp Prisoners (PWOK), based on information smuggled from Auschwitz by the international prisoners' underground. Archiwum Państwowego Muzeum Auschwitz-Birkenau w Oświęcimiu (APMA-B), Materiały Ruchu Oporu, vol. VII, 459–60, D-RO/91, inventory number 72786.

W Auschwitz III. spadły bomby na Bunę - Dwory, wykonywując właściwy ph plan zniszczenia w fabrykach benzyny, wodociągach i halach maszyn.

Gazowanie trwa ...

Gazownie i krematoria Birkenau spełniają nadal swą potworną czynność bez względu na zbliżający się szybko wymiar sprawiedliwości. Gazuje się i pali ostatnio Żydów łódzkich z ghettam likwidując w ten sposób ostatnie resztki. 12.9.br. przywieziono transport 300 dzieci żydowskich z pod Krosna, które natychmiast zostały zagazowane i spalone. Jeszcze obecnie - mimo planów ewakuacyjnych - przychodzą transporty żydowskie ze wschodu i ostatnio z Franji, Belgii i Holandii. Oprawca hitlerowski wycofując się zabiera Żydów przezbaczając ich w dalszym ciągu na śmierć. Sytuacja wojenna nie wpływa na polepszenie dóli żydowskiej, raczej sądząc z wypadków przyśpiesza jeszcze ich likwidowanie.

Ewakuacja

stabilizacja frontu wschodniego przyczyniła się w znacznym stopniu do osłabienia transportów ewakuacyjnych, nie mniej jednak niemcy licząc się z ofensywą sowiecką zechcą usunąć niewygodnych świadków swych zbrodni zapobiec niebezpieczeństwu na wypadek uwolnienia obozu /wyzyskanie sił obozu w akcji wojskowej/, przez wysłanie przedewszystkim elementu najniebezpieczniejszego - Polaków i Rosjan - w głąb kraju. Ogólna cyfra Polaków - 8.450 mężczyzn i 7.070 kobiet - ma zostać wywieziona w ciągu najbliższych 3-ch tygodni.

20.IX.1944 P.W.O.K.

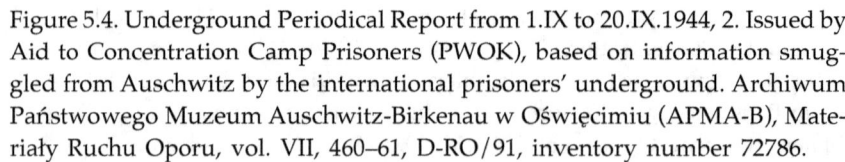

Figure 5.4. Underground Periodical Report from 1.IX to 20.IX.1944, 2. Issued by Aid to Concentration Camp Prisoners (PWOK), based on information smuggled from Auschwitz by the international prisoners' underground. Archiwum Państwowego Muzeum Auschwitz-Birkenau w Oświęcimiu (APMA-B), Materiały Ruchu Oporu, vol. VII, 460–61, D-RO/91, inventory number 72786.

in composing the reports from August onward, those remarks can be attributed to him.

The collective composition of the reports precludes a definite differentiation between the contributions of their various authors. Nevertheless, some cautious conclusions can be drawn from the existing documents, considering the background of their authors and the context of their production. Cyrankiewicz seemed to play an intermediary role, both within the resistance movement and to the outer world. He sought to appease all involved parties: left and right wing, Jews and non-Jews, the Polish government-in-exile and the politically diverged Allies. It is reasonable to assume that while the other "editorial members"—all German-speaking communists—were responsible for the leftist character of the reports, it was Cyrankiewicz's role to moderate those expressions and temper them with components of consensual "democracy" and Polish nationalism.

What weight did the "non-Jewish Jews" in the editorial gave to the Jewish Holocaust, among the other crimes perpetrated in Auschwitz? Baum's view can be inferred from his postfactum account, *Resistance in Auschwitz*, which was based on drafts written shortly after the events, during 1945–1946.[161] Baum was criticized for diminishing the role of Jews, both as the main victims of the extermination camp and as participants in the resistance.[162] This critique is exaggerated. Baum paid special attention to Auschwitz's role as an extermination camp for Jews, even before its role against political prisoners.[163] He emphasized that the underground included not only political prisoners, but also "many Jews who had only come to the camp because they were Jews."[164] He told of the Jewish groups organized within the resistance: "we [. . .] had the best experiences with them."[165] Other testimonies affirm Baum's personal role in establishing contacts with them.[166] It can therefore be hypothesized that before being handed over to Cyrankiewicz, Baum's versions were more attentive to the fate of the Jews in Auschwitz than the final reports. The earlier link in the chain, before Baum, was Haas, who seemed to have a lesser role in the writing itself. As there is also no evidence of any special attention on his part to Jewish issues, before, during, or after the war, neither for better nor for worse, his effect on the content of the reports in this respect can be disregarded.[167]

Assuming that Klahr and Heller were responsible for most of the preedited written materials, we are now left with the question what was the difference between the reports written during Klahr's "term" in the editorial (February–June 1944) and Heller's (August–October 1944)? From a quantitative point of view, "Jew," "Jews," or "Jewish" appeared much more frequently in the earlier period. Nevertheless, from the qualitative aspect, the completely different courses of events in each subperiod must be also considered. During Klahr's presence in the camp the transportation of Jews into the camp and their murder was much more intensive. Thus, Klahr, although not inclined to express his Jewish belonging before Auschwitz, raised the voice of protest particularly against the murder of Jews. In Heller's time, though other pressing issues came forward in the reports—the "Resolution of the Political Prisoners," the SS-men list, and "Action Moll"—the extermination of Jews was still reported, despite its lesser intensity, and even in notably nuanced and empathic manner.

The periodical reports cannot provide a definite account of the development of Heller's view on the Jewish question in Auschwitz. And yet, as the most intimate documentation of Heller from this period, the reports allow me to carefully conclude that in the camp Heller was not as alienated from Jews and Jewishness as assumed by Gutman and many others.[168] Alongside his communist comrades of Jewish descent, he attempted to expose to the world the annihilation of the Jewish people, perpetrated in front of their eyes in Auschwitz. They expressed their universalist worldview by presenting the mass murder of Jews as one among the many crimes of Auschwitz. At the same time, they were attentive to the unique Jewish dimension of the place. Even without full knowledge of the ongoing Holocaust as a whole, they gave voice to the Jewish victims of Auschwitz by acknowledging their exceptional fate as the only group brought to the camp exclusively to be murdered. The entanglement of those two viewpoints in the reports shows that in the eyes of those authors, their particular concern for the Jewish fate did not contradict their universalistic conviction.

On October 7, 1944, the Jewish prisoners of the Sonderkommando revolted, attacked their guards, set one crematorium on fire, and began to escape. This revolt broke out despite disapproval of the KGA leadership and without its cooperation.[169] In the last underground bulletin, reporting on the revolt, the Jewish identity of the participants of that "successful mass escape [which] caused fear among the SS" was not mentioned.[170] After reporting on the Sonderkommando revolt, in October 1944, no more Periodical Reports appeared. The resistance movement members were forced deeper into the underground, facing what they expected to be a "fury and [. . .] bloody retaliation against all political prisoners."[171] A thorough and cruel investigation was indeed carried out, but none of the central interrogated—four young Jewish women, who smuggled gunpowder to the rebels—disclosed any other resistance activist.[172]

Cyrankiewicz himself continued dispatching short messages, up until the evacuation in January 1945, which dealt mostly with technical topics: communication channels, arrangements for escapes, requests for food packages, preparations for the evacuation, statistical data of the camp, and so on.[173] The lack of more substantial information regarding the events in the camp, which would have facilitated the issuing of further Periodical Reports, should be explained primarily by the aggressive investigation against the underground movement, which must have terminated the editorial work. In his last messages Cyrankiewicz ignored the continuing arrival of Jewish transports to the gas chambers, which lasted until late October.[174] This could be explained either by lack of information or by lack of interest. However, in the absence of the other four editorial members, Heller among them, the underground no longer reported the Jewish tragedy of Auschwitz.

∽

There are only few, contradicting testimonies of Heller's fate after Auschwitz. Together with most other prisoners who survived until then, he was evacuated from the camp as part of the notorious Death Marchs in January 1945.[175] He was brought to Mauthausen and from there to one of its subcamps, in Ebensee, Upper Austria. Heller was registered as "interpreter" and in national terms he was categorized, this last time, as a *"Deutsches Reich Jude"* (a Jew from the German Reich).[176] Still in Ravensbrück, in March 1945, Lily and Emma met "a women friend who came from Auschwitz [and] told us that in January he [Otto] was still in good health. That was a great relief for us." It was only much later, back in Paris, that they "realized that at that time [March] he was about to die." After their liberation from Ravensbrück, Lily and Emma applied to the Unitarian Service Committee for humanitarian aid, reporting what they had probably heard from survivors, that "the Gestapo searched after him [Otto] in the camp to shoot him."[177] The committee simply concluded that he "has been shot by the Germans."[178] His acquaintance from the Austrian communist resistance, Margarete Schütte-Lihotzky, reported on rumors that the SS shot Heller in Ebensee.[179]

A Jewish underground member from Auschwitz, Mordekhai Hileli, testified that arriving in Mauthausen he met Heller, who "knew the area well" and told him, with a trace of prisoners' gallows humor: "The view here is beautiful, but in the winter months it will be hard for us, because of the abundant rains. We could not survive in these conditions." "Unfortunately," added Hileli, "he was right. Near the block entrance, during the rollcall, Heller collapsed, grabbed my arm and passed away."[180] Another anonymous comrade told that in early February Heller was brought, "very weak, suffering from phlegmon at the leg," to the hospital in Ebensee camp, where the two shared a bed. In that bed he witnessed Heller dying and heard his last words: "My poor wife, my poor daughter—mom."[181] In 1951 after several years of sickness and financial difficulties, Emma joined a French group to visit the place of death of her beloved life companion.[182]

According to the formal report on his death register card, issued by the camp's hospital, Heller perished on March 26, 1945, at 8:35 a.m., due to "phlegmon at the right leg. Infected wound at the big toe."[183] Cases of executions reported as death of medical reasons were not uncommon in Nazi camps. Whether by a bullet or the result of sickness and starvation, Heller was murdered for being a communist and a Jew alike. His body must have been burned in the camp's crematorium. And with him, his last thoughts on the Jewish question, were burned to ashes.

Figure 5.5. Emma and Lily after the liberation, unknown date. Courtesy of the Papineau-Heller Family Archive (PHFA), Paris.

Epilogue
The Road Not Taken

> Émigré German Jews are like a new tribe: Having forgotten how to be Jews, they are learning it all over again. They are unable to forget that they are German, and they can't lose their Germanness. They are like snails with two shells on their back.
>
> —Joseph Roth, 1937

Born into a Central European bourgeois acculturated Jewish family on the eve of the twentieth century, it is no surprise that in his youth Otto Heller decided to forget how to be a Jew, taking the path of radical assimilation. Like many others of his generation, Heller rebelled against both his bourgeois and his Jewish origins, becoming a radical leftist intellectual, a non-Jewish Jew. Some non-Jewish Jews noticed the Jewish shell on their back during the "years of persecution" (1933–1939). Many others recognized it only facing the "years of extermination" (1939–1945). For some, the process was much longer. Bruno Frei, Heller's friend and comrade with whom he shared a similar worldview and life trajectory (though escaping Europe in 1941), embraced Jewish nationalism in the late 1960s, following the antisemitic excess in the Soviet Bloc and the Six-Day-War.[1] Others never revoked their opposition to Jewish belonging. Albert Norden, Heller's communist critic who later settled in the GDR, remained a radical assimilationist and a fervent anti-Zionist until his last day and even sharpened his stance after 1967.[2]

Heller's return to his repressed Jewishness began even prior to 1933. It was a gradual process, latent at the beginning and still indecisive at the end. Though he never went as far as supporting Zionism, he came to a unique position among his fellow non-Jewish Jews. Against the background of the Stalinization of the KPD in the late 1920s and early 1930s, he experienced suspicion and rejection within his own movement. Though primarily a political process of purging opposing fractions, it also carried the whiff of de-Judaization, attempting to impart a more "proletarian" as well as German national image to the Party.

This biography shows it was against the background of his demotion within the Party that Heller came to write *The Decline of Judaism* (1931). Therefore, he could not have represented any formal Communist Party line, as it was frequently maintained in scholarship. Moreover, such a line did not even exist, as the Party attempted to avoid the Jewish question. Heller's book actually subverted this policy of avoidance. Deprived of his central position in the communist press, he became a traveling reporter in the Soviet Union, where he encountered for the first time both the Yiddish-speaking working-class Jewish masses of Eastern Europe, as well as the Soviet project of creating Jewish national territorial autonomy in Birobidzhan. While holding onto his assimilationist view regarding his Central European homelands, he discovered a new national path for Jewry, which, at this stage, he saw as restricted to the Soviet Union. Thus, Heller's book not only expressed the previous rejection of his Jewishness, but also his renewed attention to it. As a specialist on the Jewish question, he became a peculiar non-Jewish Jew.

The years between *The Decline of Judaism* and "The Jew Is to Be Burned" (1939) brought about a further significant transformation in Heller's view on the Jewish question. The Nazis' rise to power and the escalating persecution of Jews in Central Europe; growing antisemitism in Poland and other East European countries; the Arab riots in Palestine; the oppression of Jewish public life in the Soviet Union; and the antisemitic undertone of the Great Purge—all of these raised the Jewish question to a new, far more acute and dangerous level than ever before. As a haunted refugee himself, fleeing from both Hitler and Stalin, Heller experienced the "Jewish question" firsthand. Against this backdrop, he adopted the Weberian concept of the Jews as victims of capitalism, emphasized the distress of the ever-impoverished Jewish proletariat, and recognized antisemitism as a severe and worsening danger. He demonstrated solidarity with his fellow persecuted German Jews, even the bourgeois among them, and, thus, practically acknowledged a worldwide and socially stratified Jewish nationhood.

Being persecuted as a Jew, Heller now realized his existential position of "being a Jew," though he has not yet endorsed it. Following the publication of *The Decline of Judaism*, Heller declared that the Jewish question did not interest him from a Jewish standpoint.[3] Having written "The Jew Is to Be Burned," this claim appears less credible. Interestingly, these two rare book-length accounts of the Jewish question written by a communist, gradually approached their only predecessor, *Rome and Jerusalem* (1862), which manifested Moses Hess's full endorsement of Jewish nationalism. It was not by chance that the most prolific communist theoreticians of the Jewish question came from Jewish origins. Heller's theoretical endeavor reflected his own struggle with these very origins. At the same time, he was struggling with his commitment to communism too. Many independent testimonies demonstrate Heller's growing unease with the communist leadership and policies. And yet, he had never broken off with the conviction that played such a crucial rule throughout all of his adult life.

However, on one issue Heller never deviated from the communist convention: he remained a harsh critic of Zionism. Albeit significant, the shift in his thought toward Jewish national solidarity was limited to the theoretical sphere and did not bear political implications. A parallel political shift in the communist world was postponed by the Molotov-Ribbentrop pact, signed only three days after Heller's manuscript was completed, which placed communists around the globe in an uncomfortable position, in general, and with regard to the Jewish question, in particular. It was only June 22, 1941, the day of the German abrupt invasion of Soviet Union, that "transformed many of these [Soviet] 'non- Jewish Jews' (according to Isaac Deutscher's notorious formulation) into Soviet Jews suddenly aware of their origins—and proud of being Jewish."[4] This assessment of the shift within Soviet Jewry, presented by historian Saul Friedländer, is also valid for many Western non-Jewish Jews (leaving aside his moral judgment of the term).

New political attitudes among communists began to appear after the German attack and especially vis-à-vis the information on the mass murder of Jews, which started surfacing in late 1941. By that time, Heller was already moving alternately between underground work and various internment facilities, and thus could hardly leave written traces of his reaction to this information. The new political line was prescribed neither by the Soviet Union nor by the KPD's Moscow-based formal leadership, which only briefly denounced the mass murder of Jews among other Nazi crimes, only in late 1942.[5] Revisions of the communist approach to the Jewish question were instead initiated independently by several dispersed German-speaking communist exiles. The first manifestations of the new trend, in the form of calls of alarm against the Nazi scheme to annihilate European Jewry, were pronounced by the Austrian-Jewish communist Jakob Rosner (known by his pseudonym G. Hausner), exiled in Sweden, and from communists from the Sudetenland, exiled in London, already since late 1941.[6]

In the sphere of theory, a German book published in Moscow in 1941 by the Austrian communist in exile Ernst Fischer, presenting a Marxist analysis of racism, included a chapter on "the Jewish question."[7] This chapter begins by highlighting the Jewish question among other demonstrations of racism: "The question of race appears in present-day Europe first of all in the form of the Jewish question."[8] Most of his discussion, focusing on Jewish history, follows the outlines of *The Decline of Judaism*, while integrating elements presented by Heller only in "The Jew Is to Be Burned," such as Weberian rejection of Jewish responsibility for capitalism and emphasis on intra-Jewish class differentiation.[9] Since the author could have not read Heller's unpublished manuscript, he must have arrived—two year later than Heller—at similar conclusions, facing the worsening course of events.

The British communist of Austrian-Jewish origins, Israel Panner, took this new historical narrative one step forward, supplementing it with new political proclamations. In 1942 he published the booklet titled *Anti-Semitism and the Jewish Question*, under the pen name I. Rennap (his name reversed).[10] The publication drew legitimation through an introduction by the communist member of the British parliament, William Gallacher, who described the author as "a Jew who loves his own people, who suffers when his people suffer."[11] While drawing much of his historical narrative and interpretation of antisemitism from Heller's 1931 book, Panner supplemented it, in the spirit of 1942, with the call to all Jews to "unite as Jews."[12]

The most salient representative of a new communist attitude to the Jewish question was Paul Merker (1894–1969), the leader of *Freies Deutschland* (Free Germany), a group of German communist exiles in Mexico. Historian Jeffrey Herf defined Merker as "an unusual German Communist" for his intense writing about the Holocaust in real time (since 1942), his recognition of the uniqueness of Jewish suffering, and his support for Jewish national rights and the establishment of a Jewish state in Palestine, as well as for his demand for automatic compensation for every Jewish victim of the Nazis at the expense of the future German state.[13] Before fleeing to Mexico in 1942, Merker had been a leading figure in the German communist underground in France from 1939.[14] Contact between him and Heller is plausible. Heller's Mexican visa imply a connection to Merker's group. Heller's new approach to the Jewish question, as expressed in his Paris manuscript, might have been discussed with Merker during their common stay in France.

The formation of the Jewish Anti-Fascist Committee by the Soviet government in 1942 further encouraged these novel trends among communists, because it was understood by many Jews, within and outside the Soviet Union, as a Soviet recognition of a worldwide Jewish nation. Nonetheless, for the Soviet leadership, it was merely an instrument of war propaganda, which was tightly supervised not to exceed its formal purposes of rallying support and raising money abroad for the Soviet Union's war efforts.[15]

Further examples of the tendency to lend support for Jewish nationalism were also evident outside German-speaking communist circles, though only in later years. In 1944, the leader of the Communist Party of the United States, Earl Browder, called for the establishment of a Jewish nation-state after the war.[16] Inspired by him, a group of Jewish communists in the Land of Israel seceded from the formerly binational (Jewish and Arab) Communist Party of Palestine and formed a "Hebrew Communist" movement in 1945.[17] Among the young members of this faction were Shlomo Şirolnikov and Shmu'el Almog, who later presented the most nuanced interpretations of the complex relationship between Marxism and Jewish nationalism in *The Decline of Judaism*.[18]

After the war, some of the German communist emigrants who returned from Western countries stressed the role of racial antisemitism as the "core of the fascist world view."[19] Merker and other returnees brought their new attitude with them to the Soviet Occupation Zone of East Germany, later to become the GDR, actively advocating recognition and restitution for the Jews as a distinct group of victims of Nazism.[20] Communist sympathy toward Jewish nationalism culminated the 1947 speech of the Soviet ambassador to the United Nations, Andrei Gromyko, in favor of establishing a Jewish nation-state in Palestine. Though this support was designated to promote Soviet interests in the Middle East, the far-reaching acknowledgment of Jewish national rights by this high-ranking official made an impression of a historical Soviet recognition of Jewish nationalism beyond the borders of the Soviet Union.[21]

The years between 1942 and 1947 can be seen as an "interim period" of reconciliation between communism and worldwide Jewish nationalism.[22] Nevertheless, this brief gracious moment was followed by an aggressive antisemitic campaign within the Soviet Bloc, which gave the period between 1948 and 1952 its reputation as "the Black Years" in the history of the Jews in communist countries.[23] It was during this time that Merker paid a heavy price for his pro-Jewish and pro-Zionist sentiments. He was accused of being an agent in the services of the United States and Israel, was put on trial, and sentenced to prison.[24]

Retrospectively, the change that Heller underwent throughout the 1930s anticipated a wider political trend that emerged in the communist world only during the 1940s. Written under the impression of a historic "crossroads," "The Jew Is to Be Burned" signifies a divergence of two different communist roads regarding the Jewish question. During the 1930s, and most boldly in 1939, Heller started paving a road that eventually turned out to be "the road not taken" (using Robert Frost's metaphor) in communist history. In comparison to orthodox Marxism, which was still the mainstream in the communist world during the 1940s and beyond, this road was "the one less traveled by" (Frost). However, Heller did not take this road as far as the communist supporters of Jewish nationalism of the wartime. Compared to them, Heller was much more cautious not to wave the Jewish national flag too high and refrained from signaling any support for Zionism. But while Merker and others expressed their sympathy to Jewish nationalism only in remote places of refuge and only after the

Holocaust had already erupted, Heller made his shift on European soil during "the catastrophe before the catastrophe" (1938–1939).[25]

Communism and Jewish nationalism converged in Heller's life for the last time "on the snowy roads of Silesia and Austria," when he was approached by Zionist activists amid the Death March. If they indeed asked Heller "if he still," after Auschwitz, "held onto the conception expressed" in *The Decline of Judaism*, and if he was even capable of answering such a question under such circumstances, it is impossible to reconstruct his exact answer. Had Heller lived another month to see liberation, he could have shared the conclusions he had drawn from "merciless history."[26] We might then have learned to what extent he "became a nationalist Jew" following his "cruel experience," as Ber Mark wanted to believe.[27]

While Heller's reply will probably remain forever unknown, his biography illuminates not only the development of his conception of the Jewish question up until his last anguished days, but also sheds new light on the question itself. In his formulation of that question from the Death March, Yisra'el Gutman exemplified the common view of Heller's book as an attempt to prove "that a Jewish nation does not exist and have never existed."[28] This reading was shaped both by Gutman's own Zionist resentment of communism, as well as by the collapse of the reconciliatory trend of the 1940s back into the traditional rivalry between communism and Jewish nationalism during the Cold War. Reflecting the prevailing Israeli and Western interpretations of *The Decline of Judaism*, Gutman's argument disguised the actual content of the book: Heller's claim that a Jewish nation *did* exist and *will* exist. The discovery of "The Jew Is to Be Burned" reveals that, by 1939, Heller's inclination toward Jewish nationalism had become even stronger.

The development of Heller's attitude toward the Jewish question during the Second World War is the hardest to reconstruct due to scant evidence. While in Auschwitz, according to one testimony, he expressed a profound identification with the Jewish victims, and for the first time since he left Judaism in 1917, he declared "I am a Jew."[29] If he indeed pronounced these words, it should be seen as a moment of existential upheaval, in which he endorsed for the first time his "Jewish being." The secret underground reports smuggled from the camp imply that at the very least, Heller perceived the Jews as victims of an unprecedented attempt of total genocide, and at the same time as one among many other groups who became victims of Nazism. In other words, he integrated particularistic and universalist interpretations of the Holocaust, as a witness to crimes that were still unfolding.

During those years of persecution and extermination, many assimilated Jews were compelled to rethink their former distancing from Jewish belonging. Those here called "non-Jewish Jews" were among the most radical assimilationists and thus faced this dilemma with accentuated sharpness. Many of them, though definitely not all, moved along the spectrum of "non-Jewish Jewishness" toward a more particularistic "Jewish" belonging, while holding on to their "non-Jewish" universalism. Such a movement transcended the habitual dichotomy between the two positions. It signified a departure from the view of universalism and Jewish (or any other) particularity as mutually exclusive. As the catastrophe was unfolding, Heller and others came to see that, on the contrary, the liberation of the Jews and the liberation of humankind are mutually reinforcing.

Facing the growing antisemitism and escalating persecution that culminated in the Holocaust, Otto Heller became an exceptionally Jewish "non-Jewish Jew." It was exactly this inherent tension between Heller's typicality as a radically assimilated Jew and his uniqueness as one who made the Jewish question his primal vocation, that make him the epitome of that dialectical synthesis of particularism and universalism.

Notes

Prologue

1. Bruno Frei, "Marxist Interpretations of the Jewish Question," *Wiener Library Bulletin* 35–36, no. 28 (1975), 4.

2. Israel Gutman, *Men and Ashes: The Story of Auschwitz-Birkenau* (Merḥavya: Sifriat Poalim, 1957), 130 [Hebrew].

3. Mordekhai Hileli, "Ha-Maḥteret ha-Ṣiyonit be-Oshviṣ," Moreshet Archive, 9-1-3/45/1400, 33 [Hebrew]; Florian Freund, *Die Toten von Ebensee. Analyse und Dokumentation der im KZ Ebensee umgekommenen Häftlinge 1943–1945* (Vienna: Braintrust, 2010), 95, 149.

4. Gutman, *Men and Ashes*, 130.

5. Otto Heller, *Der Untergang des Judentums. Die Judenfrage, ihre Kritik, ihre Lösung durch den Sozialismus* (Vienna, Berlin: Verlag für Literatur und Politik, 1931).

6. Edmund Silberner, *Kommunisten zur Judenfrage. Zur Geschichte von Theorie und Praxis des Kommunismus* (Opladen: Westdeutscher Verlag, 1983), 274.

7. Mario Kessler, *On Anti-Semitism and Socialism: Selected Essays* (Berlin: Trafo, 2005), 57–58.

8. Shmu'el Almog, "Shlilat ha-Ṣiyonut o 'Shqi'at ha-Yahadut,'" *Le'umiut, Ṣiyonut, Antishemiyut: Masot u-Meḥqarim* (Jerusalem: Ha-Sifriya Ha-Ṣiyonit, 1992), 86 [Hebrew]. On the public debate around the book, see ch. 2.

9. See detailed discussion in ch. 2.

10. Besides all references mentioned above and below, there are also: Bruno Frei, *Socialismus und Antisemitismus* (Vienna/Munich/Zürich: Europaverlag, 1978), 11–13; Jost Hermand, "Juden in der Kultur der Weimarer Republik," in *Juden in der Weimarer Republik*, ed. Walter Grab and Julius H. Schoeps (Stuttgart/Bonn: Burg, 1986; Studien zur Geistesgeschichte, Bd. 6), 23; Karin Hartewig, *Zurückgekehrt: Die Geschichte der jüdischen Kommunisten in der DDR* (Cologne/Weimar/Vienna: Böhlau, 2000), 32–35; Mario Kessler, "Sozialismus und Zionismus in Deutschland 1897–1933," in *Juden und deutsche Arbeiterbewegung bis 1933*, ed. Ludger Heid and Arnold Paucker (Tübingen:

Mohr, 1992), 100–1; Mario Kessler, "Die KPD und der Antisemitismus in der Weimarer Republik," *Utopie Kreativ* 173 (2005), 230–31; Robert S. Wistrich, *From Ambivalence to Betrayal: the Left, the Jews, and Israel* (Lincoln: University of Nebraska Press, 2012), 292, 305.

11. Shlomo Na'aman, "Reshit ha-Yerivut beyn ha-Marqsizm la-Ṣiyonut ha-Soṣyalistit." *Iyunim Bitqumat Yisra'el*, 2 (1992), 34 [Hebrew]. Heller was not murdered in Auschwitz, but rather in Ebensee, a subcamp of Mauthausen (see ch. 5). In a different context Na'aman adimitted that "after Auschwitz the concept of 'the decline of Judaism' was often understood wrongly." Shlomo Na'aman, *Marxismus und Zionismus* (Gerlingen: Bleicher, 1997), 176.

12. Me'ir Talmi, *Ha-She'ela ha-Le'umit ve-Hameṣi'ut ha-Yehudit be-Yameynu* (Merḥavya: Sifriat Poalim, 1956), 24 [Hebrew].

13. Gutman, *Men and Ashes*, 130.

14. Eike Geisel, *Triumph des guten Willens. Gute Nazis und selbsternannte Opfer. Die Nationalisierung der Erinnerung* (Berlin: Tiamat, 1998), 143. On Herbert Baum's group see John M. Cox, *Circles of Resistance: Jewish, Leftist and Youth Dissidence in Nazi Germany* (New York: Lang, 2009).

15. George L. Mosse, "German Socialists and the Jewish Question in the Weimar Republic," *Leo Baeck Institute Yearbook* 16 (1971), 140.

16. Silvia Schlenstedt, "Versteckte Unglücke und Freisetzten von Erinnerung Zeichen des Selbstverständnisses sozialistischer Autoren jüdischer Herkunft in der deutschen Literatur nach 1945," in *The Jewish Self-portrait in European and American Literature*, ed. Hans-Jürgen Schrader, Elliott M. Simon, and Charlotte Wardi (Berlin: De Gruyter, 1996), 172.

17. Walter Laqueur, *A history of Zionism* (New York: Schocken, 1989), 428–29. My emphasis.

18. Susie Linfield, *The Lion's Den: Zionism and the Left from Hannah Arendt to Noam Chomsky* (New Haven and London: Yale University Press, 2019), 301.

19. Julius Carlebach, *Karl Marx and the Radical Critique of Judaism* (London: Routledge and Kegan Paul, 1978), 206.

20. Carlebach, *Karl Marx and the Radical Critique*, 208.

21. Silberner, *Kommunisten zur Judenfrage*, 277.

22. See Eva Reichmann-Jungmann, "Der Untergang des Judentums," *Der Morgen* 8, no. 1 (April 1932): 64–72. Reprinted in her book *Größe und Verhängnis deutsch-jüdischer Existenz: Zeugnisse einer tragischen Begegnung* (Heidelberg: Schneider, 1974): 38–45.

23. Robert M. Wistrich, "Marksizm ve-Le'umiyut Yehudit (Hashorashim ha-Teoretiyim la-Imut)," *Ba-Sha'ar* 138, 2 (March-April 1978), 119–20 [Hebrew]. See also Hans-Helmuth Knütter, *Die Juden und die deutsche Linke in der Weimarer Republik 1918–1933* (Düsseldorf: Dorste, 1971), 175. On Kautsky's thesis see later on in the Prologue.

24. Thomas Haury, *Antisemitismus von links: kommunistische Ideologie, Nationalismus und Antizionismus in der frühen DDR* (Hamburg: Hamburg Ed., 2002), 259. Citing from *Der Untergang des Judentums*, 174.

25. Olaf Kistenmacher, *Arbeit und "jüdisches Kapital." Antisemitische Aussagen in der KPD-Tagesyeitung* Die Rote Fahne *während der Weimarer Republik* (Bremen: Edition Lumière, 2016), 13.

26. *Der Untergang des Judentums*, 361, cited by Kistenmacher, *Arbeit und "jüdisches Kapital,"* 229; see also, 320.

27. Aharon David Gordon, *Ha-Uma ve-ha-A'avoda* (Jerusalem: Ha-Sifriya ha-Ṣiyonut, 1953), 134 [Hebrew].

28. Derek J. Penslar, *Shylock's Children: Economics and Jewish Identity in Modern Europe* (Berkeley, Los Angeles, London: University of California Press, 2001), 205–16.

29. John Bunzl, *Klassenkampf in der Diaspora: Zur Geschichte der jüdischen Arbeiterbewegung* (Vienna: Europa, 1975), 21; Alfredo Bauer, *Kritische Geschichte der Juden*, vol. 1 (Essen: Neue Impulse, 2005), 49.

30. Mario Kessler, *Zionismus und internationale Arbeiterbewegung* (Berlin: Akademie Verlag, 1994), 165.

31. Shlomo Ṣirolnikov, *Ha-Dialeqtiqa shel Mahapekhat Yisra'el* (Tel Aviv: Cheriqover, 1982), 99 [Hebrew]; Almog, "Shlilat ha-Ṣiyonut," 87. For further discussion, see the end of ch. 2.

32. Konstantin Baehrens, "Antisemitismus als 'Fetischisierung': Monographien von Otto Heller, Ernst Ottwalt and Hans Günter um 1933," in *Judentum und Arbeiterbewegung: Das Ringen um Emanzipation in der ersten Hälfte des 20. Jahrhunderts*, ed. Markus Börner, Anja Jungfer and Jakob Stürmann (Berlin, Boston: De Gruyter, 2018), 324. See also Silberner, *Kommunisten zur Judenfrage*, 275; Kessler, *Zionismus und internationale Arbeiterbewegung*, 164.

33. See below in ch. 1.

34. A. N. (Albert Norden), "Der Untergang des Judentums," *Die Rote Fahne*, 30 (February 2, 1932), 10; see in detail in ch. 2.

35. Otto Heller,"Der Jude wird verbrannt" [Typoskript, 1939], DÖW, 45920/7.

36. Dietrich Schlenstedt, "Auf der Suche nach den Gründen der Barbarei. Wolfgang Heise auf der Berliner Historiker-Konferenz 1961," in *Nachkriegsliteratur als öffentliche Erinnerung. Deutsche Vergangenheit im europäischen Kontext*, ed. Helmut Peitsch (Berlin/Boston: De Gruyter, 2018), 186.

37. Felix Weltsch, "Die Mystik des Warenhandels," *Jüdische Rundschau* 37, no. 9 (February 2, 1932): 41.

38. Tom Navon, "'The Jew Is to Be Burned': A Turning Point in the Communist Approach to the Jewish Question on the Eve of Catastrophe," *Jewish History* 34 (2021): 331–59. See also ch. 4.

39. Todd Endelman, *Leaving the Jewish Fold: Conversion and Radical Assimilation in Modern Jewish History* (Princeton: Princeton University Press 2015), 6. See also 16, 298. On Heller, see ch. 1.

40. Jonathan Frankel and Dan Diner, "Introduction. Jews and Communism: The Utopian Temptation," in *Dark Times, Dire Decisions: Jews and Communism*, ed. Jonathan Frankel and Dan Diner (Studies in Contemporary Jewry, Vol. 20; New York: Oxford University Press, 2004), 3–12.

41. Isaac Deutscher, "The Non-Jewish Jew," in *The Non-Jewish Jew and Other Essays* (London: Verso, [1958] 2017), 30.

42. Deutscher, "The Non-Jewish Jew," 38.

43. "The Jew in Modern Society: A Conversation with Isaac Deutscher," *Jewish Quarterly* 13, no. 4 (48) (Winter 1966): 8. This interview was later adapted as an article, under the title "Who Is a Jew?," in *The Non-Jewish Jew and Other Essays*, 43–46.

44. Deutscher, "The Jew in Modern Society," 9.

45. Paul Hanebrink, *A Specter Haunting Europe: The Myth of Judeo-Bolshevism* (Cambridge: Harvard University Press, 2018); Stanisław Krajewski, "Jews, Communism, and the Jewish Communists," in *Jewish Studies at the CEU. I. Yearbook, 1996–1999* ed. András Kovács (Budapest: Central European University, 2000), 115–30.

46. Deutscher, "The Jew in Modern Society," 7.

47. Deutscher, "The Non-Jewish Jew," 31. Emphasis in original.

48. This is an allusion to Marx. See ch. 2.

49. JeanPaul Sartre, *Anti-Semite and Jew*, trans. George J. Becker (New York: Schocken, [1944] 1976), 71.

50. Avi Sagi, *To Be a Jew: Joseph Chayim Brenner as a Jewish Existentialist*, trans. Batya Stein (London and New York: Continuum, 2011), 119.

51. Jean Améry, "On the Necessity and Impossibility of Being a Jew," in *At the Mind's Limits: Contemplations by a Survivor on Auschwitz and its Realities*, trans. Sidney and Stella P. Rosenfeld (Bloomington: Indiana University Press, 1980), 94.

52. Deutscher, "The Non-Jewish Jew," 31.

53. Adam M. Weisberger, *The Jewish Ethic and the Spirit of Socialism* (New York: Peter Lang, 1997); Philip Mendes, *Jews and the Left: The Rise and Fall of a Political Alliance* (New York: Palgrave Macmillan, 2014), 12–15; Adam Sutcliffe, *What Are Jews For? History, Peoplehood, and Purpose* (Princeton: Princeton University Press, 2020), 241–63.

54. Michael Waltzer, "The Strangeness of Jewish Leftism," in *Jews and Leftist Politics: Judaism, Israel, Antisemitism and Gender*, ed. Jack Jacobs (Cambridge, UK: Cambridge University Press, 2017), 30.

55. David Cesarani, *The Left and the Jews, the Jews and the Left* (London: Labour Friends of Israel, 2004), 5, 68.

56. Jaff Schatz, *The Generation: The Rise and Fall of the Jewish Communists of Poland* (Berkeley: University of California Press, 1991), 11–19, 47–52.

57. Jack Jacobs, "Introduction," in *Jews and Leftist Politics*, ed. Jack Jacobs, 1.

58. Ezra Mendelsohn, *On Modern Jewish Politics* (New York, Oxford: Oxford University Press, 1993), 141–45.

59. Percy S. Cohen, *Jewish Radicals and Radical Jews* (London: Academic Press, 1981).

60. Arthur Liebman, *Jews and the Left* (New York: J. Wiley, 1979), 4–26; Waltzer, "The Strangeness of Jewish Leftism," 36; Mendes, *Jews and the Left*, 5–12.

61. Cesarani, *The Left and the Jews*, 52–59, 79; Shoshana Dietz, *Jewish-Marxist* "(Re)presentations: A Study of German and Russian Jewish Writers During the Interwar Period" (PhD diss., University of Texas at Austin, 1995), 143–50.

62. *Der Untergang des Judentums*, 11–12.

63. Holly Case, *The Age of Questions* (Princeton: Princeton University Press, 2018), 12–17, 115–34.

64. See Jacob Toury, "The Jewish Question: A Semantic Approach," *Leo Baeck Institute Yearbook*, 11 (1966), 85–106.

65. Abraham Léon, *La Conception Materialiste de la Question Juive* (Paris: EDI, [1946] 1968). In English translation: Abram Leon, *The Jewish Question: A Marxist Interpretation* (New York: Pathfinder, 2020)—all further refernces are to this edition unless specified otherwise. On Leon see in ch. 2. See also Enzo Traverso, *The Marxists and the Jewish Question: The History of a Debate, 1843–1943*, trans. Bernard Gibbons (Atlantic Highlands: Humanities Press, 1994).

66. See, for example, Joshua M. Karlip, *The Tragedy of a Generation: The Rise and Fall of Jewish Nationalism in Eastern Europe* (Cambridge, MA, and London: Harvard University Press, 2013), 5–10.

67. Edmund Silberner, *The Anti-Semitic Tradition in Modern Socialism* (Jerusalem: Hebrew University, 1953); Robert S. Wistrich, *Revolutionary Jews from Marx to Trotsky* (London: Harrap, 1976); Carlebach, *Karl Marx and the Radical Critique of Judaism*; W. D. Rubinstein, *The Left, the Right, and the Jews* (New York: Universe Books, 1982).

68. Jack Jacobs, *On Socialists and 'The Jewish Question' after Marx* (New York: New York University Press, 1992); Traverso, *The Marxists and the Jewish Question*; see also his revised edition: Enzo Traverso, *The Jewish Question: History of a Marxist Debate*. trans. Bernard Gibbons (Leiden: Brill, 2018); Lars Fischer, *The Socialist Response to Antisemitism in Imperial Germany* (New York: Cambridge University Press, 2007); Jan Rybak, "Marxismus, jüdischer Nationalismus und Zionismus: Historische Analyse eines angespannten Verhältnisses," *Chilufim* 20 (2016): 3–32.

69. Colin Shindler, *Israel and the European Left: Between Solidarity and Delegitimization* (New York: Continuum, 2012); Wistrich, *From Ambivalence to Betrayal*; Linfield, *The Lion's Den*; Alessandra Tarquini, ed., *The European Left*

and the Jewish Question, 1848–1992: Between Zionism and Antisemitism (Cham: Palgrave Macmillan, 2021).

70. Frankel and Diner, "Introduction. Jews and Communism," 11. And see Tom Navon, "Marxism and Zionism," in *Routledge Handbook on Zionism*, ed. Colin Shindler (London: Routledge, forthcoming).

71. Karl Marx, "On the Jewish Question," in *The Marx-Engels Reader*, ed. Robert Tucker (New York: Norton, [1844] 1978), 26–52; Fischer, *The Socialist Response to Antisemitism*, 56–102. The question of whether Marx's "On the Jewish Question" should be read as an antisemitic text has been exhaustively discussed. For a recent discussion, see Robert Fine and Philip Spencer, *Antisemitism and the Left: On the Return of the Jewish Question* (Manchester: Manchester University Press, 2017), 31–40; Shlomo Avineri, *Karl Marx: Philosophy and Revolution* (New Haven: Yale University Press, 2019), 41–54.

72. Karl Marx, *Grundrisse: Foundations of the Critique of Political Economy*, trans. Martin Nicolaus (Harmondsworth: Penguin, [1857–1858] 1984), 253, 486; Karl Marx, *Capital*, vol. 1, in Karl Marx and Friedrich Engels, *Collected Works*, vol. 35 (New York: International Publishers, [1867] 1975), 90; Chad Alan Goldberg, "The Two Marxes: From Jewish Domination to Supersession of the Jews," *Journal of Classical Sociology*, 15, no. 4 (2015): 415–34. For further discussion, see chs. 2 and 4.

73. Karl Kautsky, *Nationalität und Internationalität*, Ergänzungshefte zur Neuen Zeit 1 (January 18, 1908), 7.

74. J. V. Stalin, "Marxism and the National Question," *Works*, vol. 2 (Moscow: Foreign Languages Publishing House, [1913] 1953), 307–10.

75. Friedrich Engels, "Über den Antisemitismus," *Arbeiterzeitung* 19 (May 9, 1890).

76. V. I. Lenin, "Anti-Jewish Pogroms," *Collected Works* (Moscow, [1919], 1972), vol. 29, 252–53.

77. August Bebel, *Sozialdemokratie und Antisemitismus* (Berlin: Buchhandlung Vorwärts, [1893] 1906), 27.

78. Traverso, *The Marxists and the Jewish Question*, 195; *Der Untergang des Judentums*, 128–34.

79. The "First Period" (1917–1924) in the policy of the Comintern was characterized by revolutionary attempts throughout Europe; the "Second Period" (1924–1928) by the stabilization of "Socialism in one country"; and the third (1928–1935) was aimed especially against social-democracy under the catchphrase "social-fascism." On the "Fourth Period" (1935 until the dissolving of the Comintern in 1943), marked by the idea of "Popular Front" uniting communists with other parties in every country against fascism, see ch. 4.

80. Gutman, *Men and Ashes*, 130.

81. Kevin Morgan, "Parts of People and Communist Lives," in *Party People, Communist Lives: Explorations in Biography*, ed. Kevin Morgan (London: Lawrence and Wishart, 2001), 9–11.

82. Dagi Knellessen and Felix Pankonin, "Einführung," Schwerpunkt Jüdische Lebenswege im 20: Jahrhundert—Neue Perspektive der Biographieforschung, *Jahrbuch des Dubnow-Instituts* 16 (2017), 294, 298.

83. Knellessen and Pankonin, "Einführung," 294.

84. Emma Heller, "Biographie d'Otto Heller," January 28, 1967, DÖW, 3834.

85. Otto Heller (Rudolf Kern), "Biographie," July 7, 1936, RGASPI, 495-187-2896-033–035; Rich. Kern (Otto Heller), "Lebenslauf," n.d., RGASPI, 495-187-2896-063b; Rich. Kern (Otto Heller), Formular zwecks Besorgung des Parteiausweis von der Zentrale der KPD für den Eintritt in die WKP(B), July 26, 1934, RGASPI, 495-187-2896-063; Otto Heller, "Fragebogen," Moscow, May 30, 1932, RGASPI, 495-187-2896-079; O.H., "Erganzung zu meiner Biografie vom 7. Juli 1936," RGASPI, 495-187-2896-037.

86. Volker R. Berghahn, "Structuralism and Biography: Some Concluding Thoughts on the Uncertainties of a Historiographical Genre," in *Biography between Structure and Agency: Central European Lives in International Historiography*, ed. Volker R. Berghahn and Simone Lässig (New York: Berghahn, 2008), 244.

87. APMAB, RMM, vol. 7, 416–81 [Polish]. See Tom Navon, "News from Auschwitz: The International Underground's Secret Reports and the Jewish Holocaust," *Yad Vashem Studies* 51, no. 1 (2023): 53–87.

88. Emma Heller, "Biographie d'Otto Heller," January 28, 1967, DÖW, 3834; Lily Heller to Unitarian Service Committee [French], Paris, July 18, 1946, PHFA; Babette Gross, *Willi Münzenberg: eine politische Biografie* (Stuttgart: Deutsche Verlags-Anstalt, 1967), 175; Bericht von Lily Jergitsch, DÖW, 3834; Elisabeth Freundlich, *The Traveling Years*, trans. Elizabeth Pennebaker (Riverside, CA: Ariadne Press, [1975] 1999), 66–73; "Aus: Interview mit Gerty Schindel über den Hochverratsprozess gegen Wiederstandkämpfer in Montauban 1941, 1983," in *Österreicher im Exil Frankreich, 1938–1945. Eine Dokumentation*, ed. Ulrich Weinzierl (Vienna: Österreichischer Bundesverlag, 1984), 187–89.

89. Erna Stahlmann an Emma Heller, October 28, 1966, PHFA; Erna Stahlmann an Lily Heller, February 3, 1966, PHFA.

90. "Genossin Erna Stahlmann," *Neues Deutschland* 22, no. 316 (November 16, 1967): 2.

Chapter 1

1. Geburtsbuch der Israelitische Kulturgemeinde Wien, IKGW, T 1897, 309, no. 3081. Some lexicons mistakenly mention Heller's birthplace as Brünn (today, Brno, in the Czech Republic).

2. *Adolf Lehman's allgemeiner Wohnungs-Anzeiger nebst Handels- und Gewerbe-Adressbuch für die k.k. Reichs-Haupt- und Residenzstadt Wien* (Vienna,

1900), vol. 2, 415; *Adolf Lehman's Adressbuch*, 1910, vol. 2, 423; Marsha Rozenblit, *The Jews of Vienna, 1867–1914: Assimilation and Identity* (Albany: SUNY Press, 1983), 78; Nathan Marcus, "Address Book: Vienna through the Eyes of the Viennese," in *Vienna 1900: Blooming on the Edge of an Abyss*, ed. Sharon Gordon and Rina Peled (Jerusalem: Carmel, 2019), 42 [Hebrew].

3. Otto Heller (Rudolf Kern), "Biographie," July 7, 1936, RGASPI, 495-187-2896-033; Emma Heller, "Biographie d'Otto Heller," January 28, 1967, DÖW, 3834, 1.

4. *Adolf Lehman's Adressbuch*, 1910, vol. 1, 371. *Neue Freie Presse*, 18044 (17.11.1914), 11, 18; *Grazer Tagblatt*, 24, 308 (November 24, 1914), 14.

5. Albert Lichtbau, "Ambivalent Modernity: The Jewish Population of Vienna," *Quest, Issues in Contemporary Jewish History* 2 (October 2011): 182.

6. Emma Heller to Monsieur le Général de Michaux, Président de la Commission Supérieur Interministérielle de Criblage, Ministère de l'Intérieur (Direction de la Sûreté Nationale), 29.11.1939, Archives nationales de France, 21119, Heller Otto, AN-19940451-102, dossier no. 8796, 22. Brought by Leonard Wilhelm, "Biography of Otto Heller" (2016–2017), Convoi77, https://en.convoi77.org/deporte_bio/heller-otto/ (retrieved on April 1, 2021). Most of the Bohemian locations mentioned here had both German and Czech names. While recognized today by their Czech names, I will use primarily the German ones, since those were used by Heller as a German-speaker. The Czech names will be mentioned in brackets at first occurrence.

7. Rozenblit, *The Jews of Vienna*, 17.

8. Robert S. Wistrich, *Socialism and the Jews: The Dilemmas of Assimilation in Germany and Austria-Hungary* (Rutherford, NJ: Fairleigh Dickinson University Press, 1982), 184.

9. Rozenblit, *The Jews of Vienna*, 78.

10. Anna L. Staudacher, *"meldet den Austritt aus dem mosaischen Glauben." 18000 Austritte aus dem Judentum in Wien, 1868–1914: Namen-Quellen-Daten* (Vienna: Lang, 2009), 239.

11. Rozenblit, *The Jews of Vienna*, 127, 148–50.

12. Hans Hellmer, "Für einen österreichischen Freiheitskämpfer: In memoriam Otto Heller," *Grazer Volkszeitung* 1, no. 123 (October 18, 1945), 3.

13. *Neue Freie Presse*, 18044 (November 17, 1914), 18.

14. Rich. Kern (Otto Heller), "Lebenslauf," n.d., RGASPI, 495-187-2896-063b.

15. Rozenblit, *The Jews of Vienna*, 99–100, 103, 105–7, 122–25.

16. Rich. Kern (Otto Heller), "Lebenslauf," n.d., RGASPI, 495-187-2896-063b.

17. Moshe Zimmermann, "Juden jugendbewegt," in *Aufbruch der Jugend. Deutsche Jugendbewegung zwischen Selbstbestimmung und Verführung* (Nuremberg: Germanischen Nationalmuseums, 2013), 107–12.

18. Otto Heller (Rudolf Kern), "Biographie," July 7, 1936, RGASPI, 495-187-2896-033; Rich. Kern (Otto Heller), "Lebenslauf," n.d., RGASPI, 495-187-2896-063b.

19. Stefan Zweig, *The World of Yesterday* (London: Cassell, 1943), 33.
20. Zweig, *The World of Yesterday*, 13–32.
21. Wistrich, *Socialism and the Jews*, 177; Lichtbau, "Ambivalent Modernity," 173.
22. Wistrich, *Socialism and the Jews*, 262–70.
23. Wistrich, *Socialism and the Jews*, 300.
24. Yuval Rubovitch, "Austro-Marxism: Socialism Discovers Nationalism," in *Vienna 1900*, ed. Gordon and Peled, 80.
25. Sigmund Freud to Wilhelm Fliess, October 15, 1897, in *The Complete Letters of Sigmund Freud to Wilhelm Fliess, 1887–1904*, ed. Jeffrey M. Masson (Cambridge: Harvard University Press, 1985), 271–72.
26. Carl E. Schorske, *Fin-de-Siècle Vienna: Politics and Culture* (New York: Alfred A. Knopf, 1979), 134.
27. Schorske, *Fin-de-Siècle Vienna*, xxvii, 117.
28. Theodor Herzl to Baron Leitenberger, January 26, 1893, cited by Schorske, *Fin-de-Siècle Vienna*, 157.
29. Jacobs, *On Socialists and "The Jewish Question,"* 89.
30. Theodor Herzl, diary entry from 1893, cited in Schorske, *Fin-de-Siècle Vienna*, 161.
31. Luise and Dieter Hecht, "Between Two Funerals: Viennese Jews between the Liberal Faith and the National Question," in *Vienna 1900*, ed. Gordon and Peled, 199.
32. Rich. Kern (Otto Heller), "Lebenslauf," n.d., RGASPI, 495-187-2896-063b.
33. Otto Heller (Rudolf Kern), "Biographie," July 7, 1936, RGASPI, 495-187-2896-033.
34. Wistrich, *Socialism and the Jews*, 207. See also 297, 327.
35. *Der Untergang des Judentums*, 130–31; "Der Jude wird verbrannt," 139–40.
36. Michele Battini, *Socialism of Fools: Capitalism and Modern Anti-Semitism*, trans. Noor Mazhar and Isabella Vergnano (New York: Columbia University Press, 2016), 7; William I. Brustein and Louisa Roberts, *The Socialism of Fools? Leftist Origins of Modern Anti-Semitism* (New York: Cambridge University Press, 2015), 2; Michael Lerner, *The Socialism of Fools: Anti-Semitism on the Left* (Oakland, CA: Tikkun Books, 1992), vi; Mario Kessler, *Antisemitismus, Zionismus und Sozialismus: Arbeiterbewegung und jüdische Frage im 20. Jahrhundert* (Mainz: Decaton, 1994), 98; Wistrich, *Socialism and the Jews*, 252, and 270–75; Fine and Spencer, *Antisemitism and the Left*, 45, 63 n. 3.
37. Andrew G. Whiteside, *The Socialism of Fools: Georg Ritter von Schoenerer and Austrian Pan-Germanism* (Berkeley: University of California Press, 1975), 89, 338 n. 27.
38. Cited by Wistrich, *Socialism and the Jews*, 265. See also 269.
39. Wistrich, *Socialism and the Jews*, 237–39, 343–48.

40. Engelbert Pernerstorfer, "Zur Judenfrage," *Der Jude*, 1, no. 5 (August 1916), 315. Translated by Wistrich, *Socialism and the Jews*, 346 (Wistrich wrongly referred to 313).

41. Koestler, *The Invisible Writing*, 39.

42. Gertrud Pickhan, *"Gegen den Strom." Der Allgemeine Jüdische Arbeiterbund "Bund" in Polen 1918–1939* (Leipzig: Schriften des Simon-Dubnow-Instituts Leipzig, 1; Stuttgart, Munich: Deutsche Verlags-Anstalt, 2001), 61; Bunzl, *Klassenkampf in der Diaspora*, 101; Mario Kessler, "Parteiorganisation und nationale Frage: Lenin und der Jüdische Arbeiterbund 1903–1914," in *Lenin: Theorie und Praxis in historischer Perspektive*, ed. Theodor Bergmann, Wladislaw Hedeler, Mario Kessler, and Gert Schäfer (Mainz: Decaton, 1994), 225.

43. Nora Levin, *While Messiah Tarried: Jewish Socialist Movements, 1871–1917* (New York: Schocken Books, 1977), 359–61.

44. Stalin, "Marxism and the National Question."

45. Rybak, "Marxismus, jüdischer Nationalismus und Zionismus," 18.

46. Ian Kershaw, *Hitler, 1889–1936: Hubris* (London, New York: Penguin, 2001), 60–67.

47. Brigitte Hamann, *Hitler's Vienna: A Portrait of the Tyrant as a Young Man* (London: Tauris, 2010), 347–53; quote from 347.

48. *Neue Freie Presse*, 18044 (November 17, 1914), 18.

49. Schorske, *Fin-de-Siècle Vienna*, 203. See also xxvi, 191, 199.

50. Rich. Kern (Otto Heller), "Lebenslauf," n.d., RGASPI, 495-187-2896-063b.

51. Marsha L. Rozenblit, *Reconstructing a National Identity: The Jews of Habsburg Austria during World War I* (Oxford: Oxford University Press, 2001), 3–4.

52. Otto Heller (Rudolf Kern), "Biographie," July 7, 1936, RGASPI, 495-187-2896-033.

53. Zweig, *The World of Yesterday*, 33.

54. Rich. Kern (Otto Heller), "Lebenslauf," n.d., RGASPI, 495-187-2896-063b; see also Emma Heller, "Biographie d'Otto Heller," January 28, 1967, DÖW, 3834, 1.

55. Hans Hellmer, "Für einen österreichischen Freiheitskämpfer. In memoriam Otto Heller," *Grazer Volkszeitung*, 1, 123 (October 18, 1945), 3.

56. Emma Heller, "Biographie d'Otto Heller," January 28, 1967, DÖW, 3834, 1.

57. Otto Heller (Rudolf Kern), "Biographie," July 7, 1936, RGASPI, 495-187-2896-033.

58. Otto Heller, in "Schriftsteller über Karl Marx," *Internationale Literatur* 2, no. 4 (1933): H. 2, 182.

59. Otto Heller, "Fragebogen," Moskau, May 30, 1932, RGASPI, 495-187-2896-079.

60. Rich. Kern (Otto Heller), "Lebenslauf," n.d., RGASPI, 495-187-2896-063b; Emma Heller, "Biographie d'Otto Heller," January 28, 1967, DÖW, 3834, 1

61. Geburtsbuch der Israelitische Kulturgemeinde Wien, IKGW, T 1897, 309, no. 3081.

62. Otto Heller (Rudolf Kern), "Biographie," July 7, 1936, RGASPI, 495-187-2896-033.

63. Emma Heller, "Biographie d'Otto Heller," January 28, 1967, DÖW, 3834, 1. In the area of Verdun German and Austrian units were attacked by American gas warfare. See Richard S. Faulkner, *Muese-Argonne 26 September–11 November 1918* (Washington, DC: Center of Military History, United States Army, 2018).

64. Rich. Kern (Otto Heller), "Lebenslauf," n.d., RGASPI, 495-187-2896-063b.

65. "Otto Heller," Universitätsarchiv Wien, Phil. Nationale, SS 1918—WS 1919/20.

66. Yekhiel Hirshhoyt, "Mahler, Rafael," in *Leksikon far der nayer literatur*, ed. Shmuel Niger and Yankev Shatski (New York: Alveltlekhn yidishn kulturkongres veraynikt mit Tsika, 1963), vol. 5, 393–97 [Yiddish]; R. M. [Raphael Mahler], "Geshikhte un folk," *Yunger Historiker* 1 (1926): 12–17 [Yiddish].

67. Wistrich, *Socialism and the Jews*, 187.

68. Rich. Kern (Otto Heller), "Lebenslauf," n.d., RGASPI, 495-187-2896-063b.

69. "Otto Heller," Universitätsarchiv Wien, Phil. Nationale, SS 1918—WS 1919/20.

70. Hans Hellmer, "Für einen österreichischen Freiheitskämpfer. In memoriam Otto Heller," *Grazer Volkszeitung* 1, no. 123 (October 18, 1945): 3.

71. Hans Hautmann, *Geschichte der Rätebewegung in Österreich 1918–1924* (Vienna, Zürich: Europaverlag, 1987), 19, 165–66.

72. Rich. Kern (Otto Heller), "Lebenslauf," n.d., RGASPI, 495-187-2896-063b; Otto Heller (Rudolf Kern), "Biographie," July 7, 1936, RGASPI, 495-187-2896-033.

73. Otto Heller, "Fragebogen," Moskau, May 30, 1932, RGASPI, 495-187-2896-079; Rich. Kern (Otto Heller), "Lebenslauf," n.d., RGASPI, 495-187-2896-063b.

74. Hautmann, *Geschichte der Rätebewegung*, 17–18.

75. Hautmann, *Geschichte der Rätebewegung*, 359.

76. Rich. Kern (Otto Heller), "Lebenslauf," n.d., RGASPI, 495-187-2896-063b.

77. Hautmann, *Geschichte der Rätebewegung*, 359–60.

78. Rich. Kern (Otto Heller), "Lebenslauf," n.d., RGASPI, 495-187-2896-063b.

79. Otto Heller, "Ein Jahr Republik: Eine Vortragsdisposition," *Bildungsarbeit: Blätter für das Bildungswesen der deutschösterreichischen Sozialdemokratie*, 5–6 (December 1919), 1.

80. Otto Heller, "Geschichte von einem demokratischen Kuvert," *Der rote Soldat* 10, no. 1 (January 1928): 8.

81. Rich. Kern (Otto Heller), "Lebenslauf," n.d., RGASPI, 495-187-2896-063b.

82. Otto Heller (Rudolf Kern), "Biographie," July 7, 1936, RGASPI, 495-187-2896-033. My emphasis.
83. Emma Heller, "Biographie d'Otto Heller," January 28, 1967, DÖW, 3834, 1.
84. Otto Heller (Rudolf Kern), "Biographie," July 7, 1936, RGASPI, 495-187-2896-033.
85. Emma Heller, "Biographie d'Otto Heller," January 28, 1967, DÖW, 3834, 1.
86. Rubovitch, "Austro-Marxism," in *Vienna 1900*, ed. Gordon and Peled, 95–96.
87. Otto Heller, "Fragebogen," Moskau, May 30, 1932, RGASPI, 495-187-2896-079.
88. Otto Heller (Rudolf Kern), "Biographie," July 7, 1936, RGASPI, 495-187-2896-033, 034.
89. Rich. Kern (Otto Heller), "Lebenslauf," n.d., RGASPI, 495-187-2896-063b; Zdenek Suda, *Zealots and Rebels: A History of the Ruling Communist Party of Czechoslovakia* (Stanford: Hoover, 1980), 40.
90. Otto Heller (Teplitz), "Klassenkampf, Kulturkampf, Wahlkampf. Eine Rededisposition," *Bildungsarbeit: Blätter für das Bildungswesen der deutschösterreichischen Sozialdemokratie*, 1 (January 1920), 27. Emphasis in original.
91. Heller, in "Schriftsteller über Karl Marx," *Internationale Literatur* 2. no. 4 (1933): H. 2, 182. Compare to Koestler, *The Invisible Writing*, 39: "It was one of our undisputed articles of faith that members of the working-class, regardless of their level of intelligence and education, would always have a more 'correct' approach to any political problem than the learned intellectuals."
92. Kopecky (Vertretung des Z.K.d.KPTsch beim EKKI) an die Kaderabteilung des EKKI, March 28, 1940, RGASPI, 495-187-2896-015.
93. Suda, *Zealots and Rebels*, 3.
94. "Wer sind die Führer der deutsch-böhmischen Sozialdemokratie?" *Wienerwald-Bote*, 23, 37 (September 9, 1922), 2.
95. Wistrich, *Socialism and the Jews*, 182.
96. Cited by Suda, *Zealots and Rebels*, 24.
97. Jan Gerber, "'Rote Assimilation.' Judentum und Kommunismus im mittleren und östlichen Europa (1917–1968)," in *Judentum und Arbeiterbewegung*, eds. Markus Börner, Anja Jungfer, and Jakob Stürmann, 187–89; Jan Gerber, "Imperial Residuals: A New Perspective on the Slánský Trial" (unpublished manuscript).
98. Suda, *Zealots and Rebels*, 46–47.
99. Rich. Kern (Otto Heller), "Lebenslauf," n.d., RGASPI, 495-187-2896-063b; Otto Heller, "Fragebogen," Moskau, May 30, 1932, RGASPI, 495-187-2896-079; Emma Heller, "Biographie d'Otto Heller," January 28, 1967, DÖW, 3834, 1; Siglinde Bolbecher, "Heller, Otto," *Lexikon der österreichischen Exilliteratur* (Vienna: Deuticke, 2000), 296; on Fürnberg see in chapters 3 and 4.

100. Rich. Kern (Otto Heller), "Lebenslauf," n.d., RGASPI, 495-187-2896-063b; Otto Heller (Rudolf Kern), "Biographie," July 7, 1936, RGASPI, 495-187-2896-033.

101. *Die Aufgaben der proletarischen Jugendorganisation im Kampfe um die Diktatur des Proletariats: Eine Erwiderung an die sozialdemokratischen Jugendführer* (Teplitz-Schönau: Junge Welt, 1920), 3.

102. Rich. Kern (Otto Heller), "Lebenslauf," n.d., RGASPI, 495-187-2896-063b.

103. Ladislav Cabada, *Intellectuals and the Communist Idea: The Search for a New Way in Czech Lands from 1890 to 1938* (Lanham: Lexington Books, 2010), 65–66.

104. Emma Heller, "Biographie d'Otto Heller," January 28, 1967, DÖW, 3834, 1; A memoir by Emma Heller's sister in-law, n.d., PHFA.

105. Meldungen, Lieberc Archive.

106. Rich. Kern (Otto Heller), "Lebenslauf," n.d., RGASPI, 495-187-2896-063b; A. Neurath, "Zum Falle Heller," *Vorwärts*, June 26, 1926, 4; Otto Heller (Rudolf Kern), "Biographie," July 7, 1936, RGASPI, 495-187-2896-034; Vladimir Ruda, "Die Arbeiterpresse von Liberec" (an excerpt from an unknown newspaper, 1984?), PHFA; Suda, *Zealots and Rebels*, 23–24.

107. Meldungen, Lieberc Archive; Otto Heller, "Zu Biographie Heller," n.d., RGASPI, 495-187-2896-036; Marriage certificate, August 10, 1922 (original in Czech), PHFA; authorized translation to French from June 6, 1947, DAVCC, dossier d'Otto Heller, AC-21P-462307.

108. Suda, *Zealots and Rebels*, 55–56.

109. Paul E. Zinner, *Communist Strategy and Tactics in Czechoslovakia, 1918–1948* (London and Dunmow: Pall Mall, 1963), 47–48.

110. Otto Heller (Rudolf Kern), "Biographie," 7.7.1936, RGASPI, 495-187-2896-034. In 1929 Hais broke off with communism and joined the Social-Democratic Party—Zinner, *Communist Strategy and Tactics in Czechoslovakia*, 48–50.

111. Ben Fowkes, "To Make the Nation or to Break It: Communist Dilemmas in Two Interwar Multinational States," in *Bolshevism, Stalinism and the Comintern*, ed. LaPorte, Morgan, and Worley, 215.

112. Suda, *Zealots and Rebels*, 67–68; Zinner, *Communist Strategy and Tactics in Czechoslovakia*, 39–42.

113. O.H. an die Kader-Abteilung des EKKI, Moscow, April 10, 1935, RGASPI, 495-187-2896-048. See also A. Neurath, "Zum Falle Heller," *Vorwärts*, June 27, 1926, 4–5.

114. Otto Heller (Rudolf Kern), "Biographie," July 7, 1936, RGASPI, 495-187-2896-034.

115. Inge Diersen, "Heller, Otto," *Lexikon sozialistischer deutscher Literatur: Von den Anfängen bis 1945* (Halle: VEB Verlag Sprache und Literatur, 1963), 211.

116. Rich. Kern (Otto Heller), "Lebenslauf," n.d., RGASPI, 495-187-2896-063b.

117. Otto Heller (Rudolf Kern), "Biographie," July 7, 1936, RGASPI, 495-187-2896-034.
118. Emma Heller, "Biographie d'Otto Heller," January 28, 1967, DÖW, 3834, 1.
119. "Vom Tage," *Die Rote Fahne* [Vienna] 9, no. 132 (June 30, 1926): 3; "Wie es zur Ausweisung des Genossen Heller kam," *Vorwärts*, June 18, 1926, 3.
120. "Genosse Otto Heller erhält keine Einreiseerlaubnis," *Vorwärts*, June 17, 1926, 3.
121. Otto Heller, "Ein 'Raubmörder' ersucht höflichst um seinen Prozess. Offener Brief an die Zentralprokurator der tschechoslowakischen Republik in Brünn," *Vorwärts*, June 23, 1926, 5.
122. "Zum Abschied," *Vorwärts*, June 17, 1926, 3; Rich. Kern (Otto Heller), "Lebenslauf," n.d., RGASPI, 495-187-2896-063b.
123. Emma Heller, "Biographie d'Otto Heller," December 28, 1967, DÖW, 3834, 2.
124. Gerber, "Imperial Residuals."
125. Rich. Kern (Otto Heller), "Lebenslauf," n.d., RGASPI, 495-187-2896-063b; Otto Heller (Rudolf Kern), "Biographie," July 7, 1936, RGASPI, 495-187-2896-034.
126. Sean McMeekin, *The Red Millionaire: A Political Biography of Willi Münzenberg, Moscow's Secret Propaganda Tsar in the West* (New Haven: Yale University Press, 2005), 194.
127. Rolf Surmann, *Die Münzenberg-Legende: Zur Publizistik der Revolutionären Arbeiterbewegung 1921–33* (Cologne: Prometh, 1983), 120–21. John Green wrongly maintained that Münzenberg had already purchased this newspaper in 1922. John Green, *Willi Münzenberg: Fighter against Fascism and Stalinism* (London and New York: Routledge, 2020), 160–61.
128. Willi Münzenberg to Wi./K., Berlin, August 16, 1926, Bundesarchiv, RY1/1388, 40.
129. Otto Heller (Rudolf Kern), "Biographie," July 7, 1936, RGASPI, 495-187-2896-034.
130. McMeekin, *The Red Millionaire*, 201–2, 214; Surmann, *Die Münzenberg-Legende*, 124.
131. Emma Heller to Robert [?], Moscow, September 23, 1936, RGASPI, 495-187-2896-044.
132. Otto Heller (Rudolf Kern), "Biographie," July 7, 1936, RGASPI, 495-187-2896-034; Otto Heller, "Fragebogen," Moskau, May 30, 1932, RGASPI, 495-187-2896-079.
133. Knütter, *Die Juden und die deutsche Linke in der Weimarer Republik*, 203–4; Silberner, *Kommunisten zur Judenfrage*, 265.

134. Whether analyzed as a political, social, or everyday history, and whether accepting the term *Stalinization* or not, the overall picture of centralization and subordination is clear. For different approaches see: Hermann Weber, *Die Wandlung des deutschen Kommunismus: Die Stalinisierung der KPD in der Weimarer Republik* (Frankfurt a.M.: Europäische Verlagsanst, 1971); Ossip K. Flechtheim, *Die KPD in der Weimarer Republik* (Hamburg: Junius, 1986), 151–228; Klaus-Michael Mallmann, *Kommunisten in der Weimarer Republik: Sozialgeschichte einer revolutionären Bewegung* (Darmstadt: Wissenschaftliche Buchgesellschaft, 1996), 77–83; Bert Hoppe, *In Stalins Gefolgschaft: Moskau und die KPD 1928–1933* (Oldenbourg: Wissenschaftsverlag, 2011), 358–59. For a recent survey of the historiographical debate see Norman LaPorte, Kevin Morgan, and Matthew Worley, "Introduction: Stalinization and Communist Historiography," in *Bolshevism, Stalinism and the Comintern*, ed. LaPorte, Morgan, and Worley, 1–21.

135. Koestler, *The Invisible Writing*, 309; Hoppe, *In Stalins Gefolgschaft*, 359.

136. Flechtheim, *Die KPD in der Weimarer Republik*, 182.

137. Hoppe, *In Stalins Gefolgschaft*, 54.

138. Weber, *Die Wandlung des deutschen Kommunismus*, 186.

139. Flechtheim, *Die KPD in der Weimarer Republik*, 198, 204, 207–8, 215–17; Weber, *Die Wandlung des deutschen Kommunismus*, 193, 235.

140. Flechtheim, *Die KPD in der Weimarer Republik*, 199–200. See also Weber, *Die Wandlung des deutschen Kommunismus*, 199–210.

141. Flechtheim, *Die KPD in der Weimarer Republik*, 200.

142. Weber, *Die Wandlung des deutschen Kommunismus*, 222–37.

143. Rich. Kern (Otto Heller), "Lebenslauf," n.d., RGASPI, 495-187-2896-063b.

144. Otto Heller (Rudolf Kern), "Biographie," July 7, 1936, RGASPI, 495-187-2896-034, 35.

145. "Information: Heller, Otto" [Russian], July 20, 1942, RGASPI, 495-187-2896-002-002o6; Ulbricht an der Kaderabteilung, June 6, 1942, RGASPI, 495-187-2896-011. The leading conciliator Ernst Meyer, was indeed editing the *Die Welt am Abend* for several months during 1924, but it was before the newspaper became formally affiliated with the party and before Heller arrived in Berlin. Florian Wilde, *Ernst Meyer (1887–1930)—vergessene Führungsfigur des deutschen Kommunismus: Eine politische Biographie* (diss., University of Hamburg, 2013), 399–404. Green had wrongly attributed his appointment to Münzenberg. Green, *Willi Münzenberg*, 161.

146. KPČ = Communist Party of Czechoslovakia, in a mixed German-Czech acronym.

147. O.H. an die Kader-Abteilung des EKKI, Moscow, April 10, 1935, RGASPI, 495-187-2896-049. My emphasis.

148. Weber, *Die Wandlung des deutschen Kommunismus*, 237.

149. O.H. an die Kader-Abteilung des EKKI, Moscow, April 10, 1935, RGASPI, 495-187-2896-048; Kazmarchuk, "Summary of a message from Josef Meisel, 11.2.1945" [Russian], March 27, 1946, RGASPI, 495-187-2896-004–005.

150. Otto Heller (Rudolf Kern), "Biographie," July 7, 1936, RGASPI, 495-187-2896-034, 35; O.H. an die Kader-Abteilung des EKKI, Moscow, April 10, 1935, RGASPI, 495-187-2896-049.

151. Otto Heller (Rudolf Kern), "Biographie," July 7, 1936, RGASPI, 495-187-2896-034, 35.

152. O.H. an die Kader-Abteilung des EKKI, Moscow, April 10, 1935, RGASPI, 495-187-2896-049. Emphasis in original.

153. Gross, *Willi Münzenberg*, 175.

154. McMeekin, *The Red Millionaire*, 220–21.

155. "Heller, Otto," *Österreicher Kultur und Literatur der 20er Jahre*, https://litkult1920er.aau.at/litkult-lexikon/heller-otto/ (retrieved on September 13, 2020).

156. Gross, *Willi Münzenberg*, 175.

157. Otto Heller, "Mit Eisbrecher Krassin nach Sibirien," *Der drohende Krieg*, 2, 12 (December 1, 1929), 412–14.

158. *Sibirien: Ein anderes Amerika* (Berlin: Universum-Bucherei für Alle, 1930), 10–11. See also Peggy Lohse, "Deutsche in Sibirien (1). Wie Otto Heller die Neue Welt im Osten entdeckte," *Russia Beyond*, June 18, 2016, https://de.rbth.com/deutschland_und_russland/menschen/2016/06/18/deutsche-in-sibirien-1-wie-otto-heller-die-neue-welt-im-osten-entdeckte_603967 (retrieved on April 19, 2021).

159. *Sibirien*, 218–19.

160. *Sibirien*, 221.

161. *Sibirien*, 225–26.

162. *Sibirien*, 229–30.

163. Koestler, *The Invisible Writing*, 66–67.

164. Otto Heller, "Fragebogen," Moskau, May 30, 1932, RGASPI, 495-187-2896-078.

165. *Sibirien*, 12; McMeekin, *The Red Millionaire*, 208–9. See also Surmann, *Die Münzenberg-Legende*, 156, 159.

166. Rich. Kern (Otto Heller), "Lebenslauf," n.d., RGASPI, 495-187-2896-063b; Surmann, *Die Münzenberg-Legende*, 121; McMeekin, *The Red Millionaire*, 263.

167. Rich. Kern (Otto Heller), "Lebenslauf," n.d., RGASPI, 495-187-2896-063b; "Sibirien, das Sowjetamerika," *Die Rote Fahne* [Vienna], 13, 65 (March 16, 1930), 12.

168. "Aus der Steuerpraxis der Gemeinde Wien," *Die Rote Fahne* [Vienna], 13, 142 (June 18, 1930), 5.

169. Ernest Hamburger, "One Hundred Years of Emancipation," *Leo Baeck Institute Year Book*, 14, 1 (1969), 50–51.

170. Hoppe, *In Stalins Gefolgschaft*, 364; Flechtheim, *Die KPD in der Weimarer Republik*, 218.

171. Haury, *Antisemitismus von links*, 253–55. See also David Bankier, "The German Communist Party and Nazi Antisemitism, 1933–1938," *Leo Baeck Institute Year Book*, 32 (1987), 326–27; Silberner, *Kommunisten zur Judenfrage*, 265–74; Traverso, *The Jewish Question*, 145–50; Mosse, "German Socialists and the Jewish Question," 123, 136–37; Conan Fischer, *The German Communists and the Rise of Nazism* (London: Macmillan, 1991), 59–63; Cox, *Circles of Resistance*, 63–66.

172. Horst Duhnke, *Die KPD von 1933 bis 1945* (Cologne: Kieperheuter and Witsch, 1972), 21, 30; Bankier, "The German Communist Party and Nazi Antisemitism," 340.

173. Koestler, *The Invisible Writing*, 39.

174. O.H. an Robert Neumann, March 27, 1929, DÖW, 11548/12. Other parts of the letter were published in Franz Stadler, ed., *Robert Neumann: Mit eigener Feder. Aufsätze. Briefe. Nachlassmaterialien* (Innsbruck, Vienna, Bozen: Studien Verlag, 2013), 442–43.

175. See ch. 2.

176. Heckert, Deutsche Vertretung beim EKKI, Bescheinigung, June 25, 1930, RGASPI, 495-187-2896-080.

177. Koestler, *The Invisible Writing*, 75.

178. On the "paradigm of assimilation" see Traverso, *The Jewish Question*, 70–80.

179. Terry Martin, *The Affirmative Action Empire: Nations and Nationalism in the Soviet Union, 1923–1939* (Ithaca: Cornell University Press, 2001), 1–18. The quotation is from p. 10.

180. Martin, *The Affirmative Action Empire*, 319.

181. Martin, *The Affirmative Action Empire*, 43–44.

182. Nora Levin, *The Jews in the Soviet Union since 1917: Paradox of Survival* (New York: New York University Press, 1988), vol. 1, 120–51; William Orbach, "A Periodization of Soviet Policy towards the Jews," *Soviet Jewish Affairs* 12, no. 3 (1982): 45.

183. Martin, *The Affirmative Action Empire*, 23–27.

184. Cited by Levin, *The Jews in the Soviet Union*, vol. 1, 285.

185. Jacob Lvavi (Babitzky), *The Jewish Colonization in Birobijan* (Jerusalem: The Historical Society of Israel, 1965), 40–45 [Hebrew]; Chimen Abramsky, "The Biro-Bidzhan Project, 1927–1959," in *The Jews in Soviet Russia since 1917*, ed. Lionel Kochan (Oxford: Oxford University Press, 1978), 70–71; Levin, *The Jews in the Soviet Union*, vol. 1, 283; Benjamin Pinkus, *The Jews of the Soviet Union: The History of a National Minority* (Cambridge, UK: Cambridge University Press, 1988), 73–76; Robert Weinberg, *Stalin's Forgotten Zion: Birobidzhan and the Making of a Soviet Jewish Homeland* (Berkeley: University of California Press, 1998), 21–23; Antje Kuchenbecker, *Zionismus ohne Zion. Idee und Geschichte eines*

jüdischen Staates in Sowjet-Fernost (Dokumente, Texte, Materialien: Zentrum für Antisemitismusforschung der Technischen Universität Berlin, vol. 32; Berlin: Metropol, 2000), 240–42; Martin, *The Affirmative Action Empire*, 44.

186. *Der Untergang des Judentums*, 174.

187. *Der Untergang des Judentums*, 336.

188. Zvi Gitelman, *Jewish Nationality and Soviet Politics: The Jewish Sections of the CPSU, 1917–1930* (Princeton: Princeton University Press, 1972), 426–33; Lvavi, *The Jewish Colonization in Birobijan*, 54–56; Levin, *The Jews in the Soviet Union*, vol. 1, 285–86.

189. Gitelman, *Jewish Nationality and Soviet Politics*, 472–76; Martin, *The Affirmative Action Empire*, 26.

190. Harold B. Segel, "Introduction," in *Egon Erwin Kisch, the Raging Reporter: A Bio-Anthology* (West Lafayette: Purdue University Press, 1997), 3–4.

191. *Der Untergang des Judentums*, 294. My emphasis.

192. *Der Untergang des Judentums*, 296. My emphasis. Bogdan Chmelnicky was the Cossack leader who led the attacks against Jews in 1648. Symon Petliura and Anton Denikin were Ukrainian "White" (anticommunist) generals, whose troops committed mass-murders of Jews during the postrevolutionary civil war (1917–1922).

193. *Encyclopedia of Camps and Ghettos, 1933–1945* (Bloomington and Indianapolis: Indiana University Press, 2012), vol. 2, 1621–23.

194. *Der Untergang des Judentums*, 303–4.

195. Kiril Federman, *The Holocaust in the Crimea and the North Caucasus* (Jerusalem: Yad Vashem, 2016), 42, 407–417.

196. Koestler, *The Invisible Writing*, 66.

197. *Der Untergang des Judentums*, 297. My emphasis.

198. *Der Untergang des Judentums*, 300. On Kalinin see ibid., 220–21.

199. *Der Untergang des Judentums*, 307–8. My emphasis.

200. Jonathan Dekel-Chen, *A Common Camp? Jewish Agricultural Cooperativism in Russia and the World, 1890–1941* (Jerusalem: Magnes, Yad Tabenkin, 2008), 149–60 [Hebrew].

201. *Der Untergang des Judentums*, 313–14.

202. *Der Untergang des Judentums*, 226–38; Kessler, *On Anti-Semitism and Socialism*, 57–58.

203. *Der Untergang des Judentums*, 314–15. My emphasis. See also Kistenmacher, *Arbeit und "jüdisches Kapital,"* 208.

204. *Der Untergang des Judentums*, 320–21.

205. *Der Untergang des Judentums*, 327.

206. *Der Untergang des Judentums*, 329. My emphasis. See also Otto Heller, "Beim Grossrabbiner von Buchara," *Die Linkskurve*, 3, 4 (April 1931), 15–17.

207. See *Der Untergang des Judentums*, 316: "In Baku, due to the heat, I had no possibility to preoccupy myself especially with Jewish questions."
208. *Der Untergang des Judentums*, 323–24.
209. *Der Untergang des Judentums*, 330.
210. *Der Untergang des Judentums*, 372.
211. *Der Untergang des Judentums*, 330.
212. Masha Gessen, *Where the Jews Aren't: The Sad and Absurd Story of Birobidzhan, Russia's Jewish Autonomous Region* (New York: Nextbook, Schocken, 2016), 50.
213. Gessen, *Where the Jews Aren't*, 61.
214. *Der Untergang des Judentums*, 333. The translation of this sentence is partially based on Sabine Bergler, "Observations and Travel Reports by Austrian Communists on Red Zion," in *Genosse. Jude: Wir wollten nur das Paradies auf Erden/Comrade. Jew: We only Wanted Paradise on Earth*, ed. Gabriele Kohlbauer-Fritz and Sabine Bergler (Vienna: Amalthea, 2017), 131.
215. *Der Untergang des Judentums*, 334.
216. *Der Untergang des Judentums*, 337–38.
217. *Der Untergang des Judentums*, 345.
218. *Der Untergang des Judentums*, 354–55.
219. *Der Untergang des Judentums*, 357–58.
220. *Der Untergang des Judentums*, 360.
221. *Der Untergang des Judentums*, 359.
222. *Der Untergang des Judentums*, 374.
223. Carola Tischler, *Flucht in die Verfolgung: Deutsche Emigranten im sowjetischen Exil—1933 bis 1945* (Münster: LIT, 1996), 56.
224. Mosse, "German Socialists and the Jewish Question," 139.
225. Tischler, *Flucht in die Verfolgung*, 56; Mosse, "German Socialists and the Jewish Question," 139.
226. At the time Münzenberg seemed to have provided Heller also with other occasional jobs: Manager of the local department of Berlin am Morgen and press manager of his production company, Prometheusfilm—Rich. Kern (Otto Heller), "Lebenslauf," n.d., RGASPI, 495-187-2896-063b.
227. Otto Heller, "Grundsätzliches zum Antisemitismus," 3, 8 (August 1931); *Die Wende*, 4, 7 (October 1932); Rich. Kern (Otto Heller), "Lebenslauf," n.d., RGASPI, 495-187-2896-063b; "Untergang des Judentums," *Die Rote Fahne* [Vienna], 15, 19 (January 22, 1932), 4.
228. "Die Mazzoth-Aktion für Rußland," *Jüdische Rundschau*, 35, 36 (December 5, 1931), 224; *Geserd*, 3, 2–3 (February-March 1931); Otto Heller (Rudolf Kern), "Biographie," July 7, 1936, RGASPI, 495-187-2896-035.
229. "Wir gefallen Otto Heller nicht," *Jüdische Rundschau*, 36, 87 (November 10, 1931), 519. Heller's article, "Jüdische Nationalsozialisten," was published

in *Neue Montagszeitung*, on September 11, 1931. A copy of this issue currently cannot be found.

230. Directory of teachers 1931–1932, in Andreas Peglau, "Die Marxistische Arbeiterschule MASCH," *Anregungen zum (selbst)bewussten Leben*, https://andreas-peglau-psychoanalyse.de/die-marxistische-arbeiterschule-masch/ (retrieved on April 19, 2021).

231. Fürenberg to anonymous, June 13, 1932, RGASPI, 495-187-2896-077.

232. *Wladi Wostok! der Kampf um den Fernen Osten* (Berlin: Neuer Deutscher Verlag, 1932); *Auf zum Baikal! Der sozialistische Aufbau in Ostsibirien und die Fantasien des Herrn Kamaitzi* (Moscow: Verlagsgenossenschaft Ausländischer Arbeiter in der UdSSR, 1933); *Das Geheimnis der Mandschurei* (Hamburg, Berlin: Hoym, 1932); *Die rote Fahne am Pazifik. Zehn Jahre Sowjetmacht im Fernen Osten* (Moscow: Verlagsgenossenschaft Ausländischer Arbeiter in der UdSSR, 1933).

233. "Der Aufmarsch der Milliarden. Brief aus Ostsibirien, dem Lande der unbegrenzten Möglichkeiten," *Inprekor*, 12, 57 (July 12, 1932), 1800 (1799–1800). Reprinted in *Die Rote Fahne* [Vienna], July 24, 1932, 9.

234. *Wladi Wostok*, 201–2.

235. Bergler, "Observations and Travel Reports by Austrian Communists on Red Zion," 131.

236. *Der Untergang des Judentums*, 373.

237. Lvavi, *The Jewish Colonization in Birobijan*, 90. According to other data the apogee was 23 percent—Bergler, "Observations and Travel Reports by Austrian Communists on Red Zion," 139.

238. Lvavi, *The Jewish Colonization in Birobijan*, 344–45.

239. Bergler, "Observations and Travel Reports by Austrian Communists on Red Zion," 139; see ch. 4.

240. Schorske, *Fin-de-Siècle Vienna*, 169.

241. Wistrich, *Socialism and the Jews*, 220.

Chapter 2

1. Interview with Yeḥi'el Harari, Kibbutz Eyn-Shemer, Israel, 1964, Moreshat Archive, 6-1-62/1/13, 25.

2. Elkana Margalit, *"Hashomer Hatsair": From a Youth Community to Revolutionary Marxism, 1919–1936* (Tel Aviv: University of Tel Aviv, 1971), 189–93 [Hebrew].

3. "Vermischtes: Die Freie Jüdische Volkshochschule," *Jüdische Rundschau* 37, no. 9 (February 2, 1932): 44. On Heller's expulsion from Czechoslovakia see ch. 1.

4. *La Fin Du Judaïsme*, trans. Marcel Ollivier (Vendôme, Paris: Impr. des Presses universitaires de France, 1933); *Zmierzch Żydostwa*, trans. Tadeusz Zabłudowski (Warsaw: M. Fruchtman, 1934); *Der Untergang des Judentums: Die*

Judenfrage, ihre Kritik, ihre Lösung durch den Sozialismus (Vienna/Berlin: Verlag für Literatur und Politik, 1933). Henceforth, references are to the first edition unless specified otherwise.

5. "Juden im Urwald," *Berlin am Morgen*, December 3–14, 1930; "Das verwunschene Volk. Die asiatischen Juden—Das Getto von Turkestan," *Die Welt am Abend*, October 15, 1930, 1–2; "Beim Grossrabbiner von Buchara," *Die Linkskurve* 3, no. 4 (April 1931): 15–17; "Grundsätzliches zum Antisemitismus," *Geserd* 3, no. 8 (August 1931); *Die Welt am Abend*, December 12, 1931; "An Ekshn," *Tshernovitzer bleter* 105 (December 13, 1931): 2 [Yiddish]; "Az antisemitizmes és a faj kerdésé," *Korunk* (1932): 81–90.

6. Liberals: Sigmund Reis, *Der Orden Bne Briss. Mitteilungen d. Großloge für Deutschland VIII. U.O.B.B*, 11, 11 (December 1931), 178; Eva Reichmann-Jungmann, "Der Untergang des Judentums," *Der Morgen* 8, no. 1 (April 1932): 64–72. Religious: *Bayerische Israelitische Gemeindezeitung* 8, no. 7 (April 4, 1932): 102–3. Zionist center: s.n., "Getarnter Prospekt," *Jüdische Rundschau* 36, no. 99–100 (December 28, 1931): 581; Samu Halpern, *Die Stimme* 5, no. 212 (January 28, 1932): 6. Zionist left: W. S., "Antwort an Otto Heller," *Der Jüdische Arbeiter* 9, no. 2 (February 4, 1932): 7–8. Zionist right: "Das komunistische Schlagwort vom 'Untergang des Judentums,' " *Die neue Welt* 6, no. 231 (February 19, 1932): 1.

7. Eli Strauss, *Geht das Judentum unter?* (Vienna: Zionistische Landeskomitee für Österreich, 1933); Salomon Goldelman, *Löst der Kommunismus die Judenfrage? Rote Assimilation und Sowiet-Zionismus* (Vienna: H. Glantz, 1937).

8. Communist: Bruno Frei, "Der Untergang des Judentums," *Die Weltbühne* 28, no. 1 (January 5, 1932): 14–17. Social democrat: Otto Mänchen-Helfen, "Otto Heller, 'Der Untergang des Judentums,' " *Die Gesellschaft* 2, no. 11 (November 1932): 461–62. Marxist Zionist: Raphael Mahler, "Tsi zenen di yidn ale mol geven a handelsfolk?" *YIVO Bleter* 7 (1934): 20–35; Mahler, "Tsi zenen di yidn," "Ven un vi azoy zenen di yidn geven a handelsfolk?" *YIVO Bleter* 8 (1935): 27–43 [Yiddish]. Unaffiliated Marxist: Erich Fromm, "Otto Heller: Der Untergang des Judentums," *Zeitschrift für Sozialforschung Leipzig* 1 (1932): 438.

9. "Untergang des Judentums," *Die Rote Fahne* [Vienna] 15, no. 19 (January 22, 1932): 4; "Vortrag Otto Heller: Der Untergang des Judentums," *Prager Tagblatt* 37, no. 24 (January 28, 1932), 7; *Die Wende* 5, no. 1 (January 1933); Goudsmit (secretary of the "Komitee zum Studium der Judenfrage im Zusammenhang mit der Kolonisation," Amsterdam), "Otto Heller: Die Judenfrage und die Kolonisation" (translated from Dutch to German by S. Diamant, the committee's treasurer), January 15, 1933, PHFA; Olim, "Die Lösung der Judenfrage in der Sowjet-Union," *Bayerische Israelitische Gemeindezeitung* 8, no. 4 (February 15, 1932): 55–56.

10. Helmut Eschwege, *Fremd unter meinesgleichen: Erinnerungen eines Dresdner Juden* (Berlin: Linke, 1991), 21–22; "Berliner Kalender: Klub junger Zionisten," *Jüdische Rundschau* 36, no. 82 (October 23, 1931): 494.

11. "Ortsgruppen: Frankfurt a.M.," *Jüdische Rundschau* 36, no. 98 (December 18, 1931): 576; "Ortsgruppen. Dresden (Poale Zion)," *Jüdische Rundschau*, 37, no. 15 (February 23, 1932): 73; "Ortsgruppen. Düsseldorf," *Jüdische Rundschau* 37, no. 36 (May 6, 1932): 172; "Ortsgruppen. Nürnberg-Fürth," *Jüdische Rundschau* 37, no. 87 (November 1, 1932): 424.

12. Knut Bergbauer, "'Wider die Rote Assimilation': Die Auseinandersetzungen über Sozialismus, Kommunismus und Zionismus in der jüdischen Jugendbewegung Deutschlands," in *Jugend im Kalten Krieg: zwischen Vereinnahmung, Interessenvertretung und Eigensinn*, ed. Meike Sophia Baader and Alfons Kenkmann (Göttingen: V&R Unipress, 2021), 227.

13. Arno Lustiger, *Stalin and the Jews: The Red Book. The Tragedy of the Jewish Anti-Fascist Committee and the Soviet Jews* (New York: Enigma, 2003), 62; *Yahudiligin Cokusu: Yahudi Sorunu, Yahudi Sorununun Elestiri, Sosyalizm'le Cozumu*, trans. Suheyla-Saliha N. Kaya (Istanbul: Inter Yayinlari, 1992).

14. Silberner, *Kommunisten zur Judenfrage*, 277; George L. Mosse, "German Socialists and the Jewish Question in the Weimar Republic," *Leo Baeck Institute Yearbook*, 16 (1971), 140–41, 149; Schlenstedt, "Versteckte Unglücke," 173–74.

15. Further central aspects of *The Decline of Judaism*—Heller's interpretations of the relationship between Jews and capitalism and of antisemitism—will be elaborated in comparison with his later manuscript "The Jew Is to Be Burned" (in ch. 4).

16. For a review of the scholarly discussion on *The Decline of Judaism*, see the Prologue.

17. *Der Untergang des Judentums*, 12.

18. *Der Untergang des Judentums*, 9–110.

19. For a detailed analysis of various aspects in Heller's Jewish historiography, see Tom Navon, *Marxist Interpretations of Jewish History* (Jerusalem: Zalman Shazar Center, 2023) [Hebrew].

20. *Der Untergang des Judentums*, 111–25.

21. *Der Untergang des Judentums*, 126–50.

22. *Der Untergang des Judentums*, 151–74.

23. See further discussion in the Prologue and in ch. 4.

24. *Der Untergang des Judentums*, 5–150.

25. *Der Untergang des Judentums*, 175–288.

26. See in the Prologue.

27. *Der Untergang des Judentums*, 77, 85.

28. *Der Untergang des Judentums*, 204–5.

29. *Der Untergang des Judentums*, 289–376. On Heller's journey see in detail in ch. 1.

30. *Der Untergang des Judentums*, 372–74.

31. For scholarship on *The Decline of Judaism* see in the Prologue.

32. Erich Fromm, "Otto Heller: Der Untergang des Judentums," *Zeitschrift für Sozialforschung Leipzig* 1 (1932): 438.

33. W. R–ck., "Eine Aussprache über den 'Untergang des Judentums,'" *C.V.-Zeitung*, 9, 9 (February 26, 1932), 78. Reading Fromm's notion of the contradiction between the book's title and its content, the Israeli historian Silberner wondered why the book was not titled "The Decline of Jewish Commerce." Silberner, *Kommunisten zur Judenfrage*, 275–76.

34. S.n., "Getarnter Prospekt," *Jüdische Rundschau* 36, no. 99–100 (December 28, 1931): 581. My emphases.

35. Felix Theilhaber, *Der Untergang der deutschen Juden: Eine volkswirtschaftliche Studie* (Munich: Reinhardt, 1911).

36. Bestand Büchergestell am 13. January 1949, PHFA, 11.

37. Arthur Ruppin, *Die Juden der Gegenwart. Eine sozialwissenschaftliche Studie* (Berlin: S. Calvary, 1904), 176, 245, mentioned in *Der Untergang des Judentums*, 84, 90, 93, 161. Jacob Klatzkin, *Probleme des Judentums* (Berlin: L. Schneider, 1930), 46, 51, mentioned in *Der Untergang des Judentums*, 109–10, 119–20, 123–25. Regarding the similarity of Heller's argumentation to that of Ruppin and Theilhaber, see Michael Brenner, *Prophets of the Past: Interpreters of Jewish History*, trans. Steven Rendall (Princeton and Oxford: Princeton University Press, 2010), 161–62, 253n18.

38. Silberner, *Kommunisten zur Judenfrage*, p. 277; Mosse, "German Socialists and the Jewish Question," 140–41, 149; Silvia Schlenstedt, "Versteckte Unglücke," 173–74.

39. Strauss, *Geht das Judentum unter?*, 22, 26.

40. H. Rosenblum, "Entartung auf beiden Seiten," *Die neue Welt*, 6, no. 249 (June 24, 1932): 1–2.

41. Felix Weltsch, "Die Mystik des Warenhandels," *Jüdische Rundschau* 37, no. 9 (February 2, 1932): 42. See also Bruno Frei, "Marxist Interpretations of the Jewish Question," *Wiener Library Bulletin* 35/36, no. 28 (1975): 3–4.

42. Dr. H. Hofmann, "Die ökonomische Judenfrage," *Der Jüdische Arbeiter* 9, no. 2 (February 5, 1932): 4.

43. Hofmann, "Die ökonomische Judenfrage," 5.

44. Goldelman, *Löst der Kommunismus die Judenfrage?*, 207. The starting point of Goldelman's book is a critique of Heller's book. Goldelman, *Löst der Kommunismus die Judenfrage?*, 9–13, 278.

45. Mosse, "German Socialists and the Jewish Question," 140–41.

46. *Abwehr-Blätter* 42, no. 1/2 (February 1932), cited by Mosse, "German Socialists and the Jewish Question," 141.

47. Fritz Aronstein, "'Der Untergand des Judentums': Bemerkungen zu dem Buch von Otto Heller und zu einem kontradiktorischen Abend," *C.V.-Zeitung* 9, no. 9 (February 26, 1932): 77. "Proletarianization" was discussed

as a real threat within Jewish circles in Berlin against the background of the economic crisis. See Gabriel Alexander, "The Jews of Berlin under the Impact of the Economic Crisis," in *Weimar Jewry and the Crisis of Modernization, 1918–1933*, ed. Oded Heilbronner (Jerusalem: Magnes, 1994): 122–51 [Hebrew].

48. Fritz Aronstein, "'Der Untergand des Judentums': Bemerkungen zu dem Buch von Otto Heller und zu einem kontradiktorischen Abend," *C.V.-Zeitung* 9, no. 9 (February 26, 1932), 78.

49. Reichmann-Jungmann, "Der Untergang des Judentums," *Der Morgen* 8, no. 1 (April 1932): 66.

50. S.n., "Getarnter Prospekt," *Jüdische Rundschau* 36, no. 99–100 (December 28, 1931), 581.

51. Sigmund Reis, *Der Orden Bne Briss: Mitteilungen d. Großloge für Deutschland VIII. U.O.B.B* 11, no. 11 (December 1931): 178.

52. Georg Wegener, "Otto Heller: Der Untergang des Judentums," *Mittelungensblatt der Gesellschaft zur Förderung des Jüdischen Siedlungswerkes in der UdSSR (Geserd)* 4, no. 1 (January 1932).

53. N.N., "Untergang des Judentums," *Die Rote Fahne* [Vienna], December 13, 1931, 10. Emphases in original.

54. "Zum Vortrag Otto Heller," *Die Rote Fahne* [Vienna], January 26, 1932, 5.

55. *Lenin über die Judenfrage* (Moscow: Verlagsgenossenschat ausländischer Arbeiter in der UdSSR, 1932), 7.

56. "Verirrte Jugend," *Die neue Welt* 6, no. 239 (April 15, 1932): 3–4.

57. Y.B., "Oto Heler: der untergang funem yidntum," *Tshernovitzer bleter*, 105 (December 13, 1931), 3–4 [Yiddish].

58. Hermann Peczenik, "Jüdische Kolonisation in der Sowjetunion: Ein Vorwort," in M. Alberton, *Biro-Bidschan, die Judenrepublik* (Leipzig-Wien: E. Prager, 1932), 7; Ya'akov Ṣvi Qolton, *Le-She'elat ha-Yehudim u-Fitrona* (Tel Aviv, 1932) [Hebrew]; F. Fürnberg, "Die Judenfrage und der Antisemitismus," *Die Kommunistische Internationale* (September 1938): 905–19; I. Rennap, *Anti-Semitism and the Jewish Question* (London: Lawrence and Wishart, 1942). See also Mosse, "German Socialists and the Jewish Question," 139–40; Arno Lustiger, "German and Austrian Jews in the International Brigade," *Leo Baeck Institute Yearbook*, 35 (1990), 310; Silberner, *Kommunisten zur Judenfrage*, 275; Kessler, *On Anti-Semitism and Socialism*, 23; Almog, "Shlilat ha-Ṣiyonut," 86; Shmu'el Dotan, *Adumim: Ha-Miflaga ha-Qomunistit be-Eereṣ Yisra'el* (Kfar Saba: Shavna ha-Sofer, 1991), 229 [Hebrew].

59. Max Horkheimer, "The Jews and Europe," in *Critical Theory and Society. A Reader*, ed. Stephen Eric Bronner and Douglas MacKay Kellner (New York, London: Routledge, [1939] 1989): 77–94. See Jack Jacobs, *The Frankfurt Scholl, Jewish Lives, and Antisemitism* (New York: Cambridge University Press, 2015), 44–46.

60. Wilhelm, "Biography of Otto Heller," n8.
61. Otto Mänchen-Helfen, "Otto Heller, 'Der Untergang des Judentums,'" *Die Gesellschaft* 2, no. 11 (November 1932): 461–62. Heller responded to this critique, accusing the author in distorting statistics regarding the Soviet Union. "Hinrichtung eines 'Kritikers,'" *Berlin am Morgen*, November 22, 1932, 5.
62. Traverso, *The Jewish Question*, 70–80.
63. Frei, "Marxist Interpretations of the Jewish Question," 3–4. A similar reservation expressed Mosse, "German Socialists and the Jewish Question," 139.
64. Gershom Scholem, *Walter Benjamin: The Story of a Friendship* (New York: New York Review of Books, 2003), 225.
65. Walter Benjamin to Gerhard Scholem, December 20, 1931, in *The Correspondence of Walter Benjamin, 1910–1940* (Chicago: University of Chicago Press, 1994), 388.
66. Kessler, *On Anti-Semitism and Socialism*, 23. See also ch. 1.
67. Bruno Frei, "Der Untergang des Judentums," *Die Weltbühne* 28, no. 1 (January 5, 1932): 15.
68. Paul Held, "Otto Heller: 'Der Untergang des Judentums,'" *Inprekor*, 11, 112 (27.11.1931), 2552.
69. Georg Wegener, "Otto Heller: 'Der Untergang des Judentums,'" *Geserd* 4, no. 1 (January 1932). On *Geserd*, see ch. 1, and on Wegener ch. 3.
70. Baehrens, "Antisemitismus als 'Fetischisierung,'" 324.
71. Kessler, *Zionismus und internationale Arbeiterbewegung*, 164.
72. Kistenmacher, *Arbeit und "jüdisches Kapital*," 11. *Die Weltbühne* (The World-stage) was an unaffiliated leftist journal, *Internationale Pressekorrespondenz* (International Press-correspondence) was published by the Comintern, and *Mittelungensblatt* (News-page) by *Geserd*. Other supportive communist references, mentioned above in the former section of this chapter, were published in Vienna.
73. Albert Norden, *Ereignisse und Erlebtes* (Berlin: Dietz, 1981), 266; Norbert Podewin, *Der Rabbinersohn im Politbüro: Albert Norden—Stationen eines ungewöhnlichen Lebens* (Berlin: Edition Ost, 2001), 96, 109; Mario Kessler, *Westemigranten. Deutsche Kommunisten zwischen USA-Exil und DDR* (Vienna, Cologne, Weimar: Böhlau, 2019), 507; Kistenmacher, *Arbeit und "jüdisches Kapital*," 285, 322–23.
74. A.N. [Albert Norden], "Der Untergang des Judentums," *Die Rote Fahne* [Berlin], 30 (June 2, 1932), 10.
75. A.N., "Der Untergang des Judentums." My emphasis.
76. Georg Wegener, "Otto Heller: Der Untergang des Judentums," *Geserd* 4, no. 1 (January 1932).
77. *Der Untergang des Judentums*, 152–53.
78. "Presseschau," *Jüdische Rundschau* 37, no. 13 (February 16, 1932), 63.
79. A.N. [Albert Norden], "Der Untergang des Judentums," *Die Rote Fahne* [Berlin], 30 (February 6, 1932), 10.

80. Karl-Heinz Hädicke, "Verlag für Literatur und Politik (VLP)," in *Lexikon sozialistischer Literatur. Ihre Geschichte in Deutschland bis 1945*, ed. Simone Barck and Reinhard Hillich (Stuttgart/Vienna: Metzler, 1994), 484–85.

81. Peter Huber, "The Central Bodies of the Comintern: Stalinization and Changing Social Composition," in *Bolshevism, Stalinism and the Comintern: Perspectives on Stalinization, 1917–53*, ed. Norman LaPorte, Kevin Morgan, and Matthew Worley (New York: Palgrave Macmillan, 2008), 69. See ch. 1.

82. On Münzenberg, see ch. 1.

83. Koestler, *The Invisible Writing*, 382.

84. Konrad Kwiet, "Historians of the GDR on Antisemitism," *Leo Baeck Institute Year Book*, 21 (1976), 178. See also Reinhard Rürup, *Emanzipation und Antisemitismus. Studien zur "Judenfrage" der bürgerlichen Gesellschaft* (Frankfurt am Main: Fischer Taschenbuch, 1975), 50–51.

85. Podewin, *Der Rabbinersohn im Politbüro*.

86. Haury, *Antisemitismus von links*, 256; See in detail in ch. 1.

87. *Aufbruch. Kampfblatt im Sinne des Leutnants a.D. Richard Scheringer* 2, no. 1/2 (February 1932), 16. Reprinted in *Aufbruch. Dokumentation einer Zeitschrift zwischen den Fronten*, ed. Hans Coppi and Susanne Römer (Koblenz: Verlag Fölbach, 2001). I am thankful to Gideon Botsch for this source and insight.

88. Silberner, *Kommunisten zur Judenfrage*, 279, 283; Kistenmacher, *Arbeit und "jüdisches Kapital,"* 283–84, 290, 293, 310.

89. Kistenmacher, *Arbeit und "jüdisches Kapital,"* 284.

90. "Jüdische Bibliography," *Israelitisches Familienblatt* 34, no. 28 (July 14, 1932): 14.

91. Heller, "Kommunismus und Judenfrage," in E. Johannsen et al., *Klärung. 12 Autoren, Politiker über die Judenfrage* (Berlin: W. Kolk, 1932), 82.

92. Alfred Kanterowicz, "Liquidation der Judenfrage," in E. Johannsen et al., *Klärung*, 157.

93. Kistenmacher, *Arbeit und "jüdisches Kapital,"* 291, see also 13, 284, 311–12; *Der Untergang des Judentums*, 198.

94. "Kommunismus und Judenfrage," in *Der Jud' ist schuld . . . ? Diskussionsbuch zur Judenfrage* (Basel/Leipzig/Berlin/Vienna: Zinnen Verlag, 1932), 272–86; *Die Wahrheit* 37 (September 9, 1932): 3. About the Nazi contribution see Günter Walden, *Ignoranten und Rassisten: Die Bedeutung des Antisemitismus für den Aufstieg der NSDAP in der Weimarer Republik* (Norderstedt: Books on Demand, 2020), 365–70.

95. Silberner, *Kommunisten zur Judenfrage*, 279.

96. Silberner, *Kommunisten zur Judenfrage*, 283; Knütter, *Die Juden und die deutsche Linke in der Weimarer Republik*, 175.

97. Traverso, *The Marxists and the Jewish Question*, 195. On this analysis of antisemitism, see detail in ch. 4.

98. Mario Kessler, *Die SED und die Juden—zwischen Repression und Toleranz. Politische Entwicklungen bis 1967* (Berlin: Akademie, 1995), 22.
99. Bunzl, *Klassenkampf in der Diaspora*, 24n35.
100. Navon, "The Jew Is to Be Burned," 349–50.
101. "Kommunismus und Judenfrage," 276.
102. "Kommunismus und Judenfrage," 280, 283–84.
103. A.N. [Albert Norden], "Der Untergang des Judentums," *Die Rote Fahne* [Berlin], 30 (February 6, 1932), 10. I thank my friend and colleague Martin Jost for his help in deciphering this word.
104. "Kommunismus und Judenfrage," 285.
105. See ch. 1.
106. Kistenmacher, *Arbeit und "jüdisches Kapital,"* 285, 302–3, 321. "Kommunismus und Judenfrage," 283–84.
107. Kistenmacher, *Arbeit und "jüdisches Kapital,"* 290–91.
108. Haury, *Antisemitismus von links*, 256.
109. Heller, "Kommunismus und Judenfrage," 91; Silberner, *Kommunisten zur Judenfrage*, 279.
110. Kessler, *Zionismus und internationale Arbeiterbewegung*, 164.
111. "Kommunismus und Judenfrage," 277.
112. "Kommunismus und Judenfrage," 278. Regarding the latter term, see in detail below, in the next section of this chapter.
113. See ch. 1.
114. *Der Untergang des Judentums* (2nd ed.), 7.
115. Erich Fromm, "Otto Heller: Der Untergang des Judentums," *Zeitschrift für Sozialforschung Leipzig* 1 (1932): 438; in 1931–1932 Fromm was the editor of the association's journal, *Mittelungensblatt der Gesellschaft zur Förderung des Jüdischen Siedlungswerkes in der UdSSR*.
116. *Der Untergang des Judentums* (2nd ed.), 7.
117. *Der Untergang des Judentums*, 163; *Der Untergang des Judentums* (2nd ed.), 163; A.N. [Albert Norden], "Der Untergang des Judentums," *Die Rote Fahne* [Berlin], 30 (February 6, 1932), 10. See also Kistenmacher, *Arbeit und "jüdisches Kapital,"* 284–85, 322–23.
118. Navon, *Marxist Interpretations of Jewish History*.
119. Marx, *Capital*, vol. 1, 90.
120. Karl Marx, *Capital*, vol. 3, trans. David Fernbach (London: Penguin, [1894] 1981), 447–48.
121. *Der Untergang des Judentums*, 45.
122. *Der Untergang des Judentums*, 44.
123. *Der Untergang des Judentums*, 47.
124. Salo Baron, "Levi Herzfeld: The first Jewish Economic Historian," in *History and Jewish Historians: Essays and Addresses* (Philadelphia: Jewish Publication Society of America, 1964), 333–34.

125. Levi Herzfeld, *Handelsgeschichte der Juden in Altertum* (Braunschweig: J. H. Meyer, 1879), 274.

126. *Der Untergang des Judentums*, 31, 33.

127. Tom Navon, "*Handelsvolk*: Marx's View of the Jews as a Trading-People and Its Implications," *Critique: Journal of Socialist Theory*, 96 (forthcoming).

128. Raphael Mahler, "Tsi zenen di yidn ale mol geven a handelsfolk?" *YIVO Bleter* 7 (1934): 20–35; Raphael Mahler, "Ven un vi azoy zenen di yidn geven a handelsfolk?" *YIVO Bleter* 8 (1935): 27–43 [Yiddish].

129. Mahler, "Ven un vi azoy zenen di yidn geven a handelsfolk?," 41.

130. For a biographic sketch by Paul Novick, see in Moyshe Kats, *Moyshe Kats bukh* (New York: Moyshe Kats bukh komitet, 1963), 9–24 [Yiddish].

131. Moyshe Kats, "Farvus hoben zikh di yidn antvikelt in a shtotisher bafelkerung?" *Der Hamer* 11, no. 10 (October 1938), 50 [Yiddish]. Mahler raised a similar claim: Mahler, "Ven un vi azoy zenen di yidn geven a handelsfolk?," 28.

132. Moyshe Kats, "Fun a religiezer gemainde tsu a natzionaler gemainshaft," *Der Hamer* 11, no. 11 (November 1938): 48–57 [Yiddish].

133. Kats, "Fun a religiezer gemainde," 53.

134. Moyshe Kats, "Di idishe kaste," *Der Hamer* 12, no. 2 (February 1963), 48–57 [Yiddish].

135. For a biographic sketch by Ernst Germain [Mandel], see Leon, *The Jewish Question*, 291–312.

136. Leon, *The Jewish Question*, 60.

137. Leon, *The Jewish Question*, 283.

138. Leon, *The Jewish Question*, 57. See Hal Draper, *Karl Marx's Theory of Revolution* (New York: Monthly Review, 1977), vol. 1, 591.

139. Yakov Leshchinsky, "The Development of the Jewish People over the Last 100 Years," trans. Robert Brym, *East European Jewish Affairs* 50 ([1928] 2020): 236. Leon cited this article by Leshchinsky in his book but did not attribute to him the term "people-class."

140. Leon, *The Jewish Question*, 63.

141. The most salient modernist theories of nationalism were presented by Ernst Gellner, *Nations and Nationalism* (Ithaca: Cornell University Press, 1983); Eric J. Hobsbawm, *Nations and Nationalism since 1780: Programme, Myth, Reality* (Cambridge: Cambridge University Press, 1990); and Benedict Anderson, *Imagined Communities: Reflections on the Origin and Spread of Nationalism* (New York: Verso, 1991).

142. The most salient primordialist theories of nationalism were presented by Anthony D. Smith, *The Nation in History: Historiographical Debates about Ethnicity and Nationalism* (Cambridge: Polity Press, 2000); and Adrian Hastings, *The Construction of Nationhood: Ethnicity, Religion, and Nationalism* (Cambridge: Cambridge University Press, 2001).

143. Leon, *The Jewish Question*, 288. See also Traverso, *The Jewish Question*, 195.

144. Joseph Nedava, *Trotsky and the Jews* (Philadelphia: Jewish Publication Society of America, 1971), 216–26.

145. *Der Untergang des Judentums*, 209. See further in ch. 4.

146. Henry Tobias, "The Reassessment of the National Question," in *Essential Papers on Jews and the Left*, ed. Ezra Mendelsohn (New York: New York University Press, 1997), 109–10; Yoav Peled, *Class and Ethnicity in the Pale* (London: Palgrave Macmillan, 1989), 58–61; Moshe Mishkinsky, "Vladimir Medem—ha-Ish be-Tnu'ato," in *Yehudim be-Tnu'ot Mahapkhaniot*, ed. Eli She'alti'el (Jerusalem: Shazar, 1983), 71–72 [Hebrew]; Roni Gechtman, "National-Cultural Autonomy and "Neutralism': Vladimir Medem's Marxist Analysis of the National Question, 1903–1920," *Socialist Studies* 3, no. 1 (May 1, 2007): 69–92.

147. Vladimir Medem, "Di sotzialdemokratye un di natzionale frage," *Tsum tsavntsiksten yortsayt* (New York: Amerikaner reprezentants fun Algemeynem Yidishn Arbeter-Bund in Poyln, [1904] 1943), 189 [Yiddish]. Emphasis in original.

148. *Der Untergang des Judentums*, 201.

149. Generally, see Eric Hobsbaum, "Introduction: Inventing Traditions," in *The Invention of Traditions*, ed. Eric Hobsbaum and Terence Ranger (Cambridge: Cambridge University Press, 1983), 12–14. In the Jewish context see David N. Myers, *Re-Inventing the Jewish Past: European Jewish Intellectuals and the Zionist Return to History* (New York: Oxford University Press, 1995), 13–16.

150. See in the Prologue.

151. More details on this group see in the Epilogue.

152. Ṣirolnikov, *Ha-Dialeqtiqa shel Mahapekhat Yisra'el*, 99.

153. Stalin, "Marxism and the National Question," 310.

154. *Der Untergang des Judentums*, 208.

155. *Der Untergang des Judentums*, 14. My emphasis.

156. *Der Untergang des Judentums*, 57–58. My emphasis.

157. *Der Untergang des Judentums*, 223. My emphasis.

158. *Der Untergang des Judentums*, 18.

159. *Der Untergang des Judentums*, 20, 23.

160. *Der Untergang des Judentums*, 218–19. My emphasis indicates Stalin's formulation within Heller's text; see Jacob Miller, "Soviet Theory on the Jews," in *The Jews in Soviet Russia since 1917*, ed. Kochan, 56. This is based on the *Communist Manifesto*, by Marx and Engels: "Though not in substance, yet in form, the struggle of the proletariat with the bourgeoisie is at first a national struggle."

161. Kistenmacher, *Arbeit und "jüdisches Kapital*," 306, referring to *Der Untergang des Judentums*, 156.

162. Almog, "Shlilat ha-Ṣiyonut," 87.

163. The Jewish Section of the Soviet Communist Party, whose members were divided—until its dissolution in 1930—between supporters of Jewish settlement in Ukraine and in Birobidzhan. See ch. 1.

164. Alomog, "Shlilat ha-Ṣiyonut," 86.

Chapter 3

1. Otto Heller, "Aus Brief an E. E. Kisch," *Neue Deutsche Blätter* 2, no. 5 (June 1935), 282.

2. Kisch is said to have said so to the Austrian-Jewish writer Friedrich Torberg in Paris in 1938. Quoted from "Egon Erwin Kisch (1885–1948)," *Frankfurter Rundschau*, April 5, 2005, https://www.fr.de/politik/egon-erwin-kisch-1885-1948-11727841.html. A slightly different version is cited by Marcus G. Patka, *Egon Erwin Kisch: Stationen im Leben eines streitbaren Autors* (Vienna: Böhlau, 1997), 407. I thank Anja Jungfer for the information regarding this quotation.

3. Klaus Hermsdorf, "'Deutsche-jüdische' Schriftsteller? Anmerkungen zu einer Literaturdebatte des Exils," *Zeitschrift zur Germanistik* 3, no. 3 (August 1982): 278.

4. Egon Erwin Kisch, *Tales from Seven Ghettos*, trans. Edith Bone (London: Anscombe, [1934] 1948).

5. See ch. 1.

6. Flechtheim, *Die KPD in der Weimarer Republik*, 225.

7. *Wladi Wostok*, 7. See ch. 1.

8. Otto Heller (Rudolf Kern), "Biographie," July 7, 1936, RGASPI, 495-187-2896-035.

9. Emma Heller, "Biographie d'Otto Heller," January 28, 1967, DÖW, 3834, 2.

10. Otto Heller (Rudolf Kern), "Biographie," July 7, 1936, RGASPI, 495-187-2896-035. The address is known from: A memoir by Emma Heller's sister in-law, n.d., PHFA; Rich. Kern (Otto Heller), Formular zwecks Besorgung des Parteiausweis von der Zentrale der KPD für den Eintritt in die WKP(B), July 26, 1934, RGASPI, 495-187-2896-063.

11. Flechtheim, *Die KPD in der Weimarer Republik*, 224.

12. Rich. Kern (Otto Heller), "Lebenslauf," n.d., RGASPI, 495-187-2896-063b; Goudsmit (secretary of the "Komitee zum Studium der Judenfrage im Zusammenhang mit der Kolonisation," Amsterdam), "Otto Heller. Die Judenfrage und die Kolonisation" (translated from Dutch to German by S. Diamant, the committee's treasurer), January 15, 1933, PHFA; *Die Wende* 5, no. 1 (January 1933).

13. "Wahrheit über Rußland, Aus einem Gespräch mit Otto Heller," *Karlsbader Tagblatt* 285 (December 13, 1932), 2.

14. Otto Heller (Rudolf Kern), "Biographie," July 7, 1936, RGASPI, 495-187-2896-035.
15. S. Diamant an Otto Heller, January 15, 1933, PHFA.
16. Otto Heller (Rudolf Kern), "Biographie," July 7, 1936, RGASPI, 495-187-2896-035.
17. Rich. Kern (Otto Heller), "Lebenslauf," n.d., RGASPI, 495-187-2896-063b; Otto Heller (Rudolf Kern), "Biographie," July 7, 1936, RGASPI, 495-187-2896-035.
18. Emma Heller, "Biographie d'Otto Heller," January 28, 1967, DÖW, 3834, 2.
19. Otto Heller (Rudolf Kern), "Biographie," July 7, 1936, RGASPI, 495-187-2896-035. On the initial illegal organization of the KPD see Duhnke, *Die KPD von 1933 bis 1945*, 115; Koestler, *The Invisible Writing*, 28.
20. Otto Heller (Rudolf Kern), "Biographie," July 7, 1936, RGASPI, 495-187-2896-035; Rich. Kern (Otto Heller), "Lebenslauf," n.d., RGASPI, 495-187-2896-063b; Meldungen, Liberec archive; A memoir by Emma Heller's sister in-law, n.d., PHFA.
21. Rich. Kern (Otto Heller), "Lebenslauf," n.d., RGASPI, 495-187-2896-063b; Rich. Kern (Otto Heller), Formular zwecks Besorgung des Parteiausweis von der Zentrale der KPD für den Eintritt in die WKP(B), July 26, 1934, RGASPI, 495-187-2896-063; Emma Heller, "Biographie d'Otto Heller," January 28, 1967, DÖW, 3834, 2.
22. *Der Untergang des Judentums*, 24, 29–30, 138.
23. R. J. Humm, *Bei uns im Rabenhaus: Aus dem literarischen Zürich der Dreissigerjahre* (Zürich/Stuttgart: Fretz and Wasmuth, 1963), 15–20; Koestler, *The Invisible Writing*, 339–341. Koestler arrived in Zürich and joined the circle only in 1935, after Heller was already not there.
24. "Leon Feuchtwanger ausgeschlossen," *Der jüdische Arbeiter*, July 4, 1933, 3.
25. Heller an Ozet, May 5, 1933, GRAF, 9498/1/425, 60. I thank Carola Tischler for sharing with me her copies of Heller's correspondence from the Ozet files in GRAF.
26. Heller an Ozet, May 23, 1933, GRAF, 9498/1/425, 59.
27. Heller an Ozet, March 16, 1934, GRAF, 9498/1/425, 12.
28. Arkadi Zeltser, "Dimanshtein, Semen Markovich," *The YIVO Encyclopedia for Jews in Eastern Europe*, https://yivoencyclopedia.org/article.aspx/Dimanshtein_Semen_Markovich (accessed on June 15, 2021).
29. *Der Untergang des Judentums*, 229–30.
30. Dimanshtein to Heller [Russian], n.d., GRAF, 9498/1/425, 58. Dimanstein's undated letter should be probably dated to April 1934, as in March Heller was still complaining that he did not receive any answer.
31. Heller an Ozet, March 16, 1934, GRAF, 9498/1/425, 12. My emphasis.
32. Dimanshtein to Heller [Russian], n.d., GRAF, 9498/1/425, 58.
33. See ch. 2.

34. Dimanshtein to Heller [Russian], n.d., GRAF, 9498/1/425, 58.

35. Lili Körber, *Begegnungen in Fernen Osten* (Budapest: Biblios, 1936), 316–17. Cited by Bergler, "Observations and Travel Reports by Austrian Communists on Red Zion," 134.

36. Heller an Ozet, May 5, 1933, GRAF, 9498/1/425, 60; Heller an Ozet, May 23, 1933, GRAF, 9498/1/425, 59; O.H. an die Kader-Abteilung des EKKI, Moscow, April 10, 1935, RGASPI, 495-187-2896-050.

37. Otto Heller an das Internationale Büro der V.R.S. zu Moskau [Johannes Becher], November 27, 1933, AdK, 1272.

38. Otto Heller (Rudolf Kern), "Biographie," July 7, 1936, RGASPI, 495-187-2896-035.

39. Heller an Ozet, May 23, 1933, GRAF, 9498/1/425, 59.

40. Bljumberg to Heller [Russian], n.d., GRAF, 9498/1/425, 11. This undated letter should have been sent in April 1934, as Heller's reply is from May 2, and it could be assumed that he responded promptly.

41. Heller to Ozet, May 2, 1934, GRAF, 9498/1/425, 10.

42. "Ermittlungen in Holland" (Gestapo Bericht), Berlin, May 30, 1933, Bundesarchiv, R58/3414, 2. My emphasis.

43. Heller an Ozet, May 5, 1933, GRAF, 9498/1/425, 60.

44. Otto Heller (Rudolf Kern), "Biographie," July 7, 1936, RGASPI, 495-187-2896-035; Rich. Kern (Otto Heller), "Lebenslauf," n.d., RGASPI, 495-187-2896-063b.

45. Otto Heller, "Préface a l'édition Française" (May 1933), *La Fin Du Judaïsme*, 7–8. My emphasis.

46. Heller, "Préface a l'édition Française," 10.

47. Heller, "Préface a l'édition Française," 7. My emphasis.

48. Heller, *Der Untergang des Judentums* (2nd ed.), 7. See ch. 2.

49. Heller, "Préface a l'edition Française," *La Fin Du Judaïsme*, 9.

50. Heller, "Préface a l'edition Française," 10.

51. Otto Heller, "Das dritte Reich Israel: zur Literatur über die Judenfrage," *Neue Deutsche Blätter* 1, no. 5 (January 1934), 304.

52. Heller, "Das dritte Reich Israel," 305. My emphasis.

53. Felix Weltsch, "Die Mystik des Warenhandels," *Jüdische Rundschau* 37, no. 9 (February 2, 1932), 41.

54. Heller, "Das dritte Reich Israel," 304, 306.

55. Lion Feuchtwanger, "Nationalismus und Judentum," in Lion Feuchtwanger and Arnold Zweig, *Die Aufgabe des Judentums* (Paris: Verlag des Europäischen Merkur, 1933),. 39.

56. Feuchtwanger, "Nationalismus und Judentum," 41–42.

57. *Der Untergang des Judentums*, 74, 80.

58. Adam Rovner, "Promised Lands: Alfred Döblin as a Territorialist Ideologue," *Maarav*, spring 2012, http://maarav.org.il/english/2012/04/29/promised-lands-alfred-doblin-as-a-territorialist-ideologue-adam-rovner/.

59. "Zionismus und Kommunismus," *Jüdische Rundschau* 37, no. 9 (February 2, 1932), 41.
60. Alfred Döblin, *Jüdische Erneuerung* (Amsterdam: Querido, 1933), 50.
61. Döblin, *Jüdische Erneuerung*, 25.
62. Heller, "Das dritte Reich Israel," 312.
63. Heller's handwritten comments in Döblin, *Jüdische Erneuerung*, 75. Heller's copy was found in PHFA, and currently to be found in Heller's collection at the Dubnow Institute library in Leipzig. Klaus Müller-Salget identified between the lines of Heller's article, "Das dritte Reich Israel," without knowing his private copy, an "accusation that he [Döblin] had allowed himself to be infected by fascism." Klaus Müller-Salget, "Alfred Döblin und das Judentum. Aus Anlass seines 125. Geburtstages," *Literaturkritik.de*, https://literaturkritik.de/id/6305 (retrieved May 18, 2021). See also Jost Hermand, *Engagement als Lebensform: Über Arnold Zweig* (Berlin: Ed. Sigma, 1992), 111–12.
64. Anonymous an L.K., May 6, 1933, RGASPI, 495-187-2896-070–073.
65. Ignazio Silone, in *The God that Failed*, ed. Richard Crossman (London: Hamish Hamilton, 1950), 76.
66. "Kurzer Bericht über sie Situation der deutschen revolutionären Literatur-Bewegung" (J. Becher? 1934?), Bundesarchiv, RY1/674, 10.
67. Hoppe, *In Stalins Gefolgschaft*, 55. See ch. 1.
68. Anonymous an L.K., June 5, 1933, RGASPI, 495-187-2896-070.
69. Doris Danzer, *Zwischen Vertrauen und Verrat: deutschsprachige kommunistische Intellektuelle und ihre sozialen Beziehungen (1918–1960)* (Göttingen: V and R Unipress, 2012), 537, 541.
70. See in ch. 1.
71. Otto Heller an das Internationale Büro der V.R.S. zu Moskau [Johannes Becher], November 27, 1933, AdK, 1272.
72. O.H. an die Kader-Abteilung des EKKI, Moscow, April 10, 1935, RGASPI, 495-187-2896-050. On Trotskzism see the Prologue.
73. Otto Heller an das Internationale Büro der V.R.S. zu Moskau [Johannes Becher], November 27, 1933, AdK, 1272.
74. "J. L. Willem Seyffardt," *Nieuwsblad voor den Boekhandel*, 108, 19 (May 14, 1941), 330–31.
75. "Der Jude wird verbrannt," 157–61.
76. Otto Heller an das Internationale Büro der V.R.S. zu Moskau [Johannes Becher], November 27, 1933, AdK, 1272. On the "Institute for the Study of Fascism," see Koestler, *The Invisible Writing*, 296–307.
77. Otto Heller an das Internationale Büro der V.R.S. zu Moskau [Johannes Becher], November 27, 1933, AdK, 1272.
78. Walter Baier, *Das Kurtze Jahrhundert. Kommunismus in Österreich. KPÖ 1918 bis 2008* (Vienna: Steinbauer, 2009), 38–40; Historische Kommission beim ZK der KPÖ, *Geschichte der Kommunistische Partei Österreichs: 1918–1955. Kurzer Abriss* (Vienna: Globus, 1977), 149–52.

79. Emma Heller, "Biographie d'Otto Heller," January 28, 1967, DÖW, 3834, 2.

80. O.H., "Erganzung zu meiner Biografie vom 7. July 1936," RGASPI, 495-187-2896-037.

81. "Warnung vor Verkauf usw. vor Druckwerken, die eine Förderung verbotener Parteien beinhalten," *Oesterreichische Buchhändler-Correspondenz* 76, no. 131 (December 14, 1935), 195; 77, 15 (June 20, 1936), 80.

82. Emma Heller, "Biographie d'Otto Heller," January 28, 1967, DÖW, 3834, 2.

83. Otto Heller (Rudolf Kern), "Biographie," July 7, 1936, RGASPI, 495-187-2896-035.

84. Anonymous to Heller, Moscow, May 16, 1934, RGASPI, 495-187-2896-065. Only the first page is to be found in Heller's dossier in the Comintern archive, so the sender's details are missing.

85. Heckert to Grinco, June 22, 1934, RGASPI, 495-187-2896-066; Müller to Smoljanski, Moscow, June 22, 1934, RGASPI, 495-187-2896-047. See also, Klaus Jarmatz and Simone Barck, "Die 'Deutsche Zentralzeitung,'" in *Exil in der UdSSR* (Leipzig: Philipp Reclam, 1989), Bd. 1, S. 170; Simone Barck, "Eine unbekannte Bibliographie der DZZ: Zur Ambivalenz einer kulturhistorischen Quelle," in *Verratene Ideale. Zur Geschichte deutscher Emigration in der Sowjetunion in den 30er Jahren*, ed. Oleg Dehl, Natalja Mussienko, and Simone Barck (Berlin: Trafo, 2000), 320–21.

86. Heller an Julia [Annenkova], May 5, 1934, RGASPI, 495-187-2896-064. Emphasis in original.

87. Otto Heller, "Przedmowa do Wydania Polskiego" (June 1934), *Zmierzch Żydostwa*, 21.

88. Heller, "Przedmowa do Wydania Polskiego," 14.

89. Heller, "Przedmowa do Wydania Polskiego," 15.

90. Heller, "Przedmowa do Wydania Polskiego," 19.

91. A. N. [Albert Norden], "Der Untergang des Judentums," *Die Rote Fahne* [Berlin], 30 (February 6, 1932), 10.

92. "Kommunismus und Judenfrage," 277.

93. See in detail in chs. 2 and 4.

94. Heller, "Przedmowa do Wydania Polskiego," 15.

95. See ch. 4.

96. Heller, "Przedmowa do Wydania Polskiego," 16.

97. Rich. Kern (Otto Heller), Formular zwecks Besorgung des Parteiausweis von der Zentrale der KPD für den Eintritt in die WKP(B), July 26, 1934, RGASPI, 495-187-2896-063.

98. Rich. Kern (Otto Heller), Formular zwecks Besorgung des Parteiausweis von der Zentrale der KPD für den Eintritt in die WKP(B), July 26, 1934, RGASPI, 495-187-2896-063.

99. Keller an Tschernomordik, September 9, 1936, RGASPI, 495-187-2896-045.

100. Emma Heller and Robert [?], Moscow, September 23, 1936, RGASPI, 495-187-2896-044.

101. Tischler, *Flucht in die Verfolgung*, 60.

102. For example, Rudolf Kern [Otto Heller], "Bei den Männern mit den grünen Mützen," *DZZ* 11, no. 37 (February 14, 1936): 4; Kern [Otto Heller], "Die deutschen Rotarmisten," *DZZ* 11, no. 44 (February 23, 1936): 1.

103. Bericht von Lily Jergitsch (1975), DÖW, 3834, 1.

104. Bericht von Lily Jergitsch, 3.

105. Bericht von Lily Jergitsch, 2.

106. Stephen Koch, *Double Lives: Spies and Writers in the Secret Soviet War of Ideas against the West* (New York: Free Press, 1994), 133.

107. Reinhard Müller, "Einleitung," in Georg Lukács, Johannes R. Becher, Friedrich Wolf et al., *Die Säuberung. Moskau 1936: Stenogramm einer geschlossenen Parteiversammlung*, ed. Reinhard Müller (Reinbek bei Hamburg: Rowohlt, 1991), 10.

108. O.H. to J. I. Annenkowa (DZZ), Moscow, February 2, 1935, RGASPI, 495-187-2896-056.

109. J. Annenkowa an die deutsche Vertretung beim EKKI, March 28, 1935, RGASPI, 495-187-2896-055.

110. O.H. an die Kader-Abteilung des EKKI, Moscow, April 4, 1935, RGASPI, 495-187-2896-048.

111. J. Annenkowa an die deutsche Vertretung beim EKKI, March 28, 1935, RGASPI, 495-187-2896-055.

112. Deutsche Vertretung beim EKKI an Brandt, Moscow, November 1, 1935, RGASPI, 495-187-2896-060.

113. Sebastian Haffner, *Defying Hitler: A Memoir*, trans. Oliver Pretzel (Lexington, Plunkett Lake Press, 2014), 142.

114. Heller an Pieck, April 8, 1936, Bundesarchiv, NY4007/12, 68.

115. Fritz Weber (Deutsche Vertretung beim EKKI) to Grewe (DZZ), Moscow, May 1, 1936, RGASPI, 495-187-2896-061.

116. Fritz Weber (Deutsche Vertretung beim EKKI) to Grewe (DZZ), Moscow, June 29, 1936, RGASPI, 495-187-2896-062.

117. Fritz Weber to Heller, January 7, 1936, RGASPI, 495-187-2896-054.

118. Rich. Kern (Otto Heller), Formular zwecks Besorgung des Parteiausweis von der Zentrale der KPD für den Eintritt in die WKP(B), July 26, 1934, RGASPI, 495-187-2896-063.

119. O.H. to J. Koplenig, n.d. (probably summer 1936), RGASPI, 495-187-2896-042.

120. Wieden (vertretung des ZK.der KPOe beim EKKI) an die Kaderabteilung, June 26, 1936, RGASPI, 495-187-2896-040; Pieck an den Verbindungdienst

des Sekretariats des EKKI, July 10, 1936, RGASPI, 495-187-2896-027; Friedrich (Vertretung des Z.K.d.KPTsch beim EKKI) an Robert (Kaderabteilung des EKKI), July 21, 1936, RGASPI, 495-187-2896-039.

121. O.H. to Annenkowa, Moscow, July 27, 1936, RGASPI, 495-187-2896-038.
122. Lukács et al., *Die Säuberung*, 146.
123. Emma Heller, "Biographie d'Otto Heller," January 28, 1967, DÖW, 3834, 3.
124. Emma Heller an Robert, Moscow, September 23, 1936, RGASPI, 495-187-2896-044.
125. Keller, September 27, 1936, RGASPI, 495-187-2896-025.
126. Reinhard Müller, "Einleitung," in Lukács et al., *Die Säuberung*, 10. Regarding Wegener see Tischler, *Flucht in die Verfolgung*, 60.
127. Koestler, *The Invisible Writing*, 131.
128. Zeltser, "Dimanshtein."
129. "Der Jude wird verbrannt," 266. Dimanshtein's quote is in *Der Untergang des Judentums*, 181.
130. Allan L. Kageda, "American Jews and the Soviet Experiment: The Agro-Joint Project, 1924–1937," *Jewish Social Studies* 43, no. 2 (Spring 1981), 155.
131. Bergler, "Observations and Travel Reports by Austrian Communists on Red Zion," 139–40.
132. Martin, *The Affirmative Action Empire*, 344. See also Mario Kessler, "Der Stalinsche Terror gegen jüdische Kommunisten 1937/1938," in *Kommunisten verfolgen Kommunisten stalinistischer Terror und "Säuberungen" in den kommunistischen Parteien Europas seit den dreißiger Jahren*, ed. Hermann Weber and Dietrich Staritz (Berlin: Akad.-Verl., 1993): 87–102. See also, Gennadi Kostyrchenko, *Out of the Red Shadows: Anti-Semitism in Stalin's Russia* (Amherst, NY: Prometheus books, 1995); Louis Rapoport, *Stalin's War against the Jews: The Doctors' Plot and the Soviet Solution* (New York: Free Press, 1990), 41–54.
133. Arkady Vaksberg, *Stalin against the Jews*, trans. Antonina W. Bouis (New York: Alfred A. Knopf, 1994), 82–83.
134. Bericht von Lily Jergitsch (1975), DÖW, 3834, 3.
135. Würz, September 8, 1936, RGASPI, 495-187-2896-026.
136. Koch, *Double Lives*, 265–77; McMeekin, *The Red Millionaire*, 285.
137. Lisa A. Kirschenbaum, *International Communism and the Spanish Civil War: Solidarity and Suspicion* (New York: Cambridge University Press, 2015), 84.
138. Emma Heller, "Biographie d'Otto Heller," January 28, 1967, DÖW, 3834, 3; Edgar Schütz, *Österreichische JournalistInnen und PublizistInnen im Spanischen Bürgerkrieg 1936–1939: Medienpolitik und Presse der Internationalen Brigaden* (Vienna: LIT, 2016), 278; DÖW ed., *Für Spaniens Freiheit: Österreicher an der Seite der Spanischen Republik 1936–1939* (Vienna: Österreichischer Bundesverlag, Vienna-Munich, Jugend und Volk, 1986), 391; Lustiger, "German and Austrian Jews in the International Brigade," 311; Martin Sugarman, *Against Fascism: Jews*

who served in the International Brigade in the Spanish Civil War, July 1, 2016, https://www.jewishvirtuallibrary.org/jews-who-served-in-the-international-brigade-in-the-spanish-civil-war (accessed on June 17, 2021), 108, 124.

139. Koestler, *The Invisible Writing*, 398.

140. Konrad Kwiet and Helmut Eschwege, *Selbstbehauptung and Widerstand: Deutsche Juden in Kampf um Existenz und Menschenwürde 1933–1945* (Hamburg: Christians, 1984), 101–3; Sugarman, *Against Fascism*, 2, 125, 128.

141. Emma Heller, "Biographie d'Otto Heller," January 28, 1967, DÖW, 3834, 3. Emma remembered arriving in Paris only in 1937, but according to contemporary documentation she was already there in November 1936; Schiller to the cadre department of the Comintern [Russian], November 5, 1936, RGASPI, 495-187-2896-024.

142. Academy of Sciences of the Soviet Union, *International Solidarity with the Spanish Republic 1936–1939* (Moscow: Progress Publishers, 1976), 45.

143. "Aus: Einvernahme des Myron Pasicynyk bei der Gestapo Wien betreffend seine Tätigkeit bei der Organisierung der Grenzübertritte von Spanienfreiwilligen, 9/10 Juli 1940," in DÖW (Hg.), *Für Spaniens Freiheit*, 107.

144. Max Stern, *Geschichte wird gemacht: Vom Lehrlingsstreik 1919 zum Freiheitsbataillon 1945* (Vienna: Globus, 1988), 72–76.

145. Schiller to the kader department of the Comintern [Russian], November 5, 1936, RGASPI, 495-187-2896-024; A. Müller, "Betrifft Heller, Otto," September 7, 1937, RGASPI, 495-187-2896-023; Schilling, "Information über Otto Heller," June 4, 1942, RGASPI, 495-187-2896-012.

146. Certificate de domicile, August 21, 1939; Acte de deces, January 6, 1948, DAVCC, dossier d'Otto Heller, AC-21P-462307.

147. Willi Weinert, "1938–1945," in *Die Kommunistische Partei Österreich: Beiträge zu ihrer Geschichte und Politik* (Vienna: Globus, 1987), 319. On Haas see in ch. 5.

148. This is the only reference to Karl Kraus as a source of inspiration for Heller. Although Kraus is not mentioned in any of Heller's preserved texts, he did hold in his possession a few of Kraus's books, as well as numerous issues of the journal he edited, *Die Fackel* (The Torch)—Bestand Büchergestell am January 13, 1949, PHFA. It also makes sense that Heller was influence by this fin-de-siècle Viennese satirist. They were both considered by some contemporaries as "self-hating Jews." See Paul Reitter, *The Anti-Journalist: Karl Kraus and Jewish Self-Fashioning in Fin-de-siècle Europe* (Chicago: University of Chicago Press, 2008), 69–106.

149. Freundlich, *The Traveling Years*, 67–68.

150. So hypothesized also Erich Hackl, "Die Namen der Dinge: Salut für Elisabeth Freundlich," *Kommune* 3 (2001), 64.

151. Schiller to the kader department of the Comintern [Russian], November 5, 1936, RGASPI, 495-187-2896-024.

152. Leo Trotzki, *Probleme der Entwicklung der Soviet Union* (Berlin: Bulletin der Russischen Opposition [Bolschewiki-Leninisten], 1931); Trotzki, *Die spanische Revolution und ihre drohenden Gefahren* (Berlin: Grylewicz, 1931). Both booklets were found in PHFA.

153. "Information: Heller, Otto" [Russian], July 20, 1942, RGASPI, 495-187-2896-002–002 06. Richard Stahlmann was the husband of Erna Stahlmann, who later intended to write a biography of Heller. See the Prologue.

154. Koch, *Double Lives*, 299–320; McMeekin, *The Red Millionaire*, 295–307.

155. Emma Heller, "Biographie d'Otto Heller," January 28, 1967, DÖW, 3834, 1; Siglinde Bolbecher, "Heller, Otto," *Lexikon der österreichischen Exilliteratur* (Vienna: Deuticke, 2000), 296. On Fürnberg see in chs. 1 and 4.

156. Fürnberg (Vertretung des Z.K.der KPOe. beim EKKI) an die Kaderabteilung, December 31, 1940, RGASPI, 495-187-2896-020.

157. Schilling, "Information über Otto Heller," June 4, 1942, RGASPI, 495-187-2896-012.

158. Koestler, *The Invisible Writing*, 308–18.

159. Dieter Schiller, Karlheinz Pech, Regine Herrmann, and Manfred Hahn, *Exil in Frankreich* (Kunst und Literatur im antifaschistischen Exil 1933–1945 in Sieben Bände, vol. 7; Leipzig: Reclam, 1981), 136, 365. One example of a lecture given by Heller is "From Abbé Grégoire to Rosenberg: the Racial Question in the French Revolution." "Otto Heller spricht im SDS," *Deutsche Volkszeitung* 4, no. 28 (June 1939): 7.

160. Koestler, *The Invisible Writing*, 283.

161. Koestler, *The Invisible Writing*, 471.

162. Emma Heller, "Biographie d'Otto Heller," January 28, 1967, DÖW, 3834, 3.

163. *La Fin Du Judaïsme*, 8; *Zmierzch Żydostwa*, 14.

164. Heller's working materials, PHFA.

165. See in ch. 1.

166. Alfred Klahr, *Zur österreichischen Nation* (Vienna: Globus, 1994).

167. Saul Friedländer, *The Years of Persecution, 1933–1939* (New York: Harper Collins, 1997), 268–70.

168. "Der Jude wird verbrannt," 110–26, 161–75. See in detail in ch. 4.

Chapter 4

1. "Der Jude wird verbrannt," 1. Niederschrift, PHFA, 10.

2. "Malik," PHFA.

3. Susanne Schulz, "Malik-Verlag," in *Lexikon sozialistischer Literatur. Ihre Geschichte in Deutschland bis 1945*, ed. Simone Barck and Reinhard Hillich (Stuttgart/Weimar: Metzler, 1994): 311–14.

4. Emma Heller, "Biographie d'Otto Heller," January 28, 1967, DÖW, 3834, 3.
5. This version, also found in PHFA, is identical with that existing in DÖW, 45920/7.
6. See ch. 5.
7. Otto Heller, "Was ist Rasse?" *Weg und Ziel* 10 (1947): 729ff.
8. Willi Weinert, "Aus dem Archiv: Otto Heller," *Alfred Klahr Gesellschaft Mitteilungen* 1 (March 1998), 7.
9. "Otto Heller. Gedächtnisprotokoll, aufgenomen mit seiner Witwe, Emmi Heller," November 10, 1966, PHFA; Emma Heller, "Biographie d'Otto Heller," January 28, 1967, DÖW, 3834; Erna und Richard Stahlmann an Emma Heller, Ostern 1967, PHFA.
10. Otto Heller, "Der Jude wird verbrannt" [Typoskript], DÖW, 45920/7. All references are to this version, unless otherwise mentioned.
11. Bunzl, *Klassenkampf in der Diaspora*, 18n, 22n24; Schütz, *Österreichische JournalistInnen und PublizistInnen im Spanischen Bürgerkrieg 1936–1939*, 280; Weinert, "Aus dem Archiv," 7. For more on the archival history of the manuscript, see here in the Foreword.
12. Schlenstedt, "Versteckte Unglücke," 174–76.
13. Navon, "The Jew Is to Be Burned."
14. See in chs. 1 and 2.
15. See the Prologue.
16. Jeffrey Herf, "German Communism, the Discourse of 'Antifascist Resistance,' and the Jewish Catastrophe," in *Resistance against the Third Reich*, ed. Michael Geyer (Chicago: University of Chicago Press, 1994): 257–94; Bankier, "The German Communist Party and Nazi Antisemitism."
17. Peter Hayes, "Big Businesses and 'Aryanization' in Germany 1933–1939," *Jahrbuch für Antisemitismusforschung* 3 (1994): 254–81.
18. Bankier, "The German Communist Party and Nazi Antisemitism," 338.
19. Hans Behrend [Albert Norden], *Die wahren Herren Deutschlands* (Paris: Prométhée, 1939); also published in English as *The Real Rulers of Germany* (London: Lawrence and Wishart, 1939), 105–16.
20. See ch. 2.
21. "Der Jude wird verbrannt," 161–64.
22. "Gegen die Schmach der Judenpogrom. Erklärung der Zentralkomitees der KPD," *Die rote Fahne: Sonderausgabe gegen Hitlers Judenpogrom* (November 1938), 1.
23. Herf, "German Communism," 264.
24. Bankier, "The German Communist Party and Nazi Antisemitism," 340.
25. See the Epilogue.
26. Heller had a slightly different version of this proclamation, titled "Gegen die Schande der Judenpogrom. Erklärung der Zentralkomitees der KPD," cut from an unknown publication (67–68), in "Der Jude wird verbrannt,"

Materialien, PHFA. The translation to English is taken from Herf, "German Communism," 264.

27. Bankier, "The German Communist Party," 336–37.

28. Walter Pötsch, *Die Grundlagen des jüdischen Volkes: Eine notwendige Abrechnung* (Breslau: Pötsch, 1938).

29. Bankier, "The German Communist Party and Nazi Antisemitism," 338.

30. Siegfried Fürnberg, "Die Judenfrage und der Antisemitismus," *Die Kommunistische Internationale* 9 (1938): 905–19. On Fürnberg's relationship with Heller, see chs. 1 and 3.

31. Fürnberg, "Die Judenfrage und der Antisemitismus," 906–13.

32. Bankier, "The German Communist Party and Nazi Antisemitism," 338.

33. "Der Jude wird verbrannt," 4.

34. Rosa Luxemburg, *The Crisis in the German Social-Democracy (The "Junius" Pamphlet)* (New York: Socialist Publication Society, 1919), 18. Though Luxemburg attributed that phrase to Engels, it probably originated from Kautsky.

35. Traverso, *The Marxists and the Jewish Question*, 195.

36. "Der Jude wird verbrannt," 6.

37. "Der Jude wird verbrannt," 1–2. My emphases.

38. *Der Untergang des Judentums*, 18.

39. "Der Jude wird verbrannt," 5.

40. "Der Jude wird verbrannt," 6. My emphasis.

41. *Der Untergang des Judentums*, 6.

42. For a detailed discussion on Heller's Jewish historiography see Navon, *Marxist Interpretations of Jewish History*.

43. "Der Jude wird verbrannt," 11–33.

44. "Der Jude wird verbrannt," 34–57.

45. "Der Jude wird verbrannt," 58–67.

46. "Der Jude wird verbrannt," 68–95. This expression became the title of an antisemitic book from 1871 by August Röhling, *Der Talmudjude. Zur Beherzigung für Juden und Christen aller Stände* (Münster: Russell, 1871). See Wistrich, *Socialism and the Jews*, 208.

47. "Der Jude wird verbrannt," 96–109.

48. "Der Jude wird verbrannt," 110–26.

49. "Der Jude wird verbrannt," 127–40.

50. "Der Jude wird verbrannt," 141–68.

51. "Der Jude wird verbrannt," 177–238.

52. "Der Jude wird verbrannt," 239–71.

53. *Der Untergang des Judentums*, 175–376.

54. *Der Untergang des Judentums*, 126–50.

55. "Der Jude wird verbrannt," 96–238.

56. "Der Jude wird verbrannt," 261–71.
57. Schlenstedt, "Versteckte Unglücke," 175.
58. Johannes Weiss, *Weber and the Marxist World*, trans. Elizabeth King-Utz and Michael J. King (London and New York: Routledge and Kegan Paul, 1986), 16.
59. Yuri Slezkine, *The Jewish Century* (Princeton: Princeton University Press, 2019), 53–57; Jerry Muller, *Capitalism and the Jews* (Princeton: Princeton University Press, 2010), 46–61.
60. Werner Sombart, *The Jews and Modern Capitalism*, trans. M. Epstein (Glencoe: Free Press, [1911] 1951), 323.
61. Max Weber, *The Protestant Ethic and the Spirit of Capitalism*, trans. Talcott Parsons (New York: Scribner, [1904–1905] 1958), 165–66; Max Weber, *Ancient Judaism*, trans. Hans Gerth and Don Martindale (Glencoe: Free Press, [1917–1919] 1952), 345; Max Weber, *General Economic History*, trans. F. H. Knight (New York: Greenberg, [1923] 1927), 196, 358–60.
62. Chad Alan Goldberg, *Modernity and the Jews in Western Social Thought* (Chicago: University of Chicago Press, 2017), 64, 72, 104–6; Daniel Gutwein, "Beyn ha-Yehudim ve-ha-Qapitalizm be-Tfisato shel Marks: me-Zombart le-Veber," *Zion* 55, no. 4 (1990): 419–48 [Hebrew]. On Sombart and early Marx, see Jonathan Karp, "Kopf ohne Körper? Wirtschaftsgeschichte jüdischen Lebenswelten," in *Kapitalismusdebatten um 1900. Über antisemitisierende Semantiken des Jüdischen*, ed. Nicolas Berg (Leipzig: Leipziger Universitätverlag, 2011), 63.
63. Marx, "On the Jewish Question."
64. Marx, *Grundrisse*, 253, 486; Marx, *Capital*, vol. 1, 90. On the concept of "trading-people," see in detail in ch. 2.
65. *Der Untergang des Judentums*, 74.
66. *Der Untergang des Judentums*, 27; Sombart, *The Jews and Modern Capitalism*, 326–30.
67. *Der Untergang des Judentums*, 19. For some other critical remarks on Sombart, see *Der Untergang des Judentums*, 58, 74, 103.
68. Traverso, *The Jewish Question*, 188; Carlebach, *Karl Marx and the Radical Critique of Judaism*, 209.
69. "Der Jude wird verbrannt," 12.
70. "Der Jude wird verbrannt," 12–13, 20, 27–28.
71. "Der Jude wird verbrannt," 17, 19, 31; Weber, *Ancient Judaism*, 3, 364.
72. "Der Jude wird verbrannt," 7.
73. Schlenstedt, "Versteckte Unglücke," 175. It is interesting to note that one researcher, who did not know of Heller's manuscript, criticized *The Decline of Judaism* relying on Weber's theorization of Jewish history. Marcel R. Marcus, "A Critique of Marxist Analysis of Jewish History" (MA Thesis, University of Newcastle upon Tyne, 1984), 108–9.

74. Penslar, *Shylock's Children*, 165–70.
75. Abram L. Harris, "Sombart and German (National) Socialism," *Journal of Political Economy* 50, no. 6 (December 1942): 805–35; Sutcliffe, *What Are Jews For*, 149–52.
76. *Der Untergang des Judentums*, 5, 15–16, 18–19, 77, 120.
77. Except for two accidental references to "On the Jewish Question": "Der Jude wird verbrannt," 39, 58.
78. See ch. 2.
79. On Kats and Leon see ch. 2.
80. Leon, *The Jewish Question*, 186.
81. Weber, *General Economic History*, 358, cited by Leon, *The Jewish Question*, 186.
82. Moyshe Kats, "Farvus hoben zikh di yidn antvikelt in a shtotisher bafelkerung?" *Der Hamer* 11, no. 10 (October 1938), 53.
83. Moyshe Kats, "Der yidisher kheylek in der eyropeysher kultur fun mitelalter," *Der Hamer* 12, no. 6 (June 1939): 49–57 [Yiddish].
84. *Der Untergang des Judentums* (2nd ed.), 7.
85. "Der Jude wird verbrannt," 4.
86. A.N. [Albert Norden], "Der Untergang des Judentums," *Die Rote Fahne* [Berlin], 30 (February 6, 1932), 10. See ch. 2.
87. "Der Jude wird verbrannt," 27–28; Weber, *Ancient Judaism*, 21–23.
88. "Der Jude wird verbrannt," 20–21.
89. "Der Jude wird verbrannt," 81.
90. "Der Jude wird verbrannt," 73.
91. "Der Jude wird verbrannt," 68.
92. J. Stern (Rabinner), *Lichtstrahlen aus dem Talmud* (Leipzig: Philipp Reclam, 1886). The booklet was found in Heller's collection in PHFA.
93. "Der Jude wird verbrannt," 60.
94. "Der Jude wird verbrannt," 61–67.
95. "Der Jude wird verbrannt," 58.
96. "Der Jude wird verbrannt," 100–26.
97. See ch. 2.
98. "Der Jude wird verbrannt," 4.
99. "Der Jude wird verbrannt," 110.
100. Othmar Jesser, "Berichte aus Oesterreich," *Der sozialistische Kampf* (February 1939), 45, in "Der Jude wird verbrannt," Materialien, PHFA.
101. "Der Jude wird verbrannt," 3. My emphases.
102. Traverso, *The Marxists and the Jewish Question*, 195.
103. *Der Untergang des Judentums*, 128–34. See also Traverso, *The Jewish Question*, 54–64.
104. "Der Jude wird verbrannt," 157–68.
105. "Der Jude wird verbrannt," 161–64; Behrend [Norden], *The Real Rulers of Germany*, 105–16.

106. Otto Heller an Rudi Askonas, August 28, 1939, PHFA, 1.
107. "Der Jude wird verbrannt," 167–68.
108. Otto Heller an Rudi Askonas, August 28, 1939, PHFA, 1.
109. Otto Heller an Rudi Askonas, 3.
110. [Albert Norden], "Kommunismus und Judenfrage," 274–76. Regarding the latter group, university students, Norden himself might have drawn his analysis from an earlier article by Heller, in which he analyzed the proliferation of antisemitism among students. Otto Heller, "Der Jud' ist schuld!" *Der rote Student* 2, no. 7 (November-December 1931): 144–46.
111. "Der Jude wird verbrannt," 149–56.
112. See ch. 2.
113. "Der Jude wird verbrannt," 161.
114. Alex Bein, "Ma'amaro ha-Rishon shel Herṣl be-She'elat ha-Yehudim," in *Im Herṣl u-ve-Iqvotav* (Tel Aviv: Masada, 1954), 14–18 [Hebrew].
115. Theodor Herzl, "Französische Antisemiten" [August 31, 1892], *Neue Freie Presse* 10067 (September 3, 1892): 1–2, quotation from p. 2. As the matter of fact, the analysis of the German social-democrat August Bebel from 1893 was not far from Herzl's. The difference between them was in the prognosis. Whereas Bebel predicted the decline of the social conditions that enhanced antisemitism, Herzl anticipated their ascendance. Bebel, *Sozialdemokratie und Antisemitismus*, 27, cited in *Der Untergang des Judentums*, 128–31. See also Traverso, *The Jewish Question*, 59–60, and here, in the Prologue.
116. Theodor Herzl, *The Jewish State* (New York: Dover, [1896] 1988), 90. Herzl's *Judenstaat* is usually translated as *The Jewish State*, but it should be noted that the literal translation is "The State of the Jews."
117. Arthur Ruppin, *The Jews in the Modern World* (London: Macmillan, 1934), 243. In earlier editions, Ruppin still held with the same interpretation as Herzl: "Antisemitism is as old as emancipation." Arthur Ruppin, *Die Juden der Gegenwart: Eine sozialwissenschaftliche Studie* (Berlin: Jüdischer Verlag, 1920), 175. The change in his views might be understood against the background of the escalation of antisemitism.
118. *Der Untergang des Judentums*, 157.
119. Ber Borokhov, "Le-She'elat Ṣiyon ve-Teritorya" [in Hebrew], *Ktavim*, vol. 1 (Tel Aviv: Hakibbuty Hameuchad, [1905] 1955), 37.
120. Shulamit Volkov, *Germans, Jews, and Antisemites: Trials in Emancipation* (Cambridge: Cambridge University Press, 2006), 67–82.
121. Traverso, *The Marxists and the Jewish Question*, 195.
122. "Der Jude wird verbrannt," 146–49.
123. The shift in Heller's appreciation of antisemitism can be seen as parallel to the famous shift in Horkheimer's view, but while the latter still disregarded antisemitism in 1939 and paid more attention to it only in 1944, Heller had undergone this change already from 1931 to 1939. See Horkheimer, "The Jews and Europe"; Max Horkheimer and Theodor W. Adorno, *Dialectic*

of Enlightenment: Philosophical Fragments, trans. Edmund Jephcott (Stanford: Stanford University Press, [1944] 2002), pp. 137–72; Dan Diner, "The Limits of Reason: Max Horkheimer on Antisemitism and Extermination," *Beyond the Conceivable: Studies on Germany, Nazism, and the Holocaust* (Berkeley: University of California Press, 2000), 97–116.

124. *Der Untergang des Judentums,* 151–74; "Der Jude wird verbrannt," 247–60.

125. *Der Untergang des Judentums,* 167–68; "Der Jude wird verbrannt," 252.

126. *Der Untergang des Judentums,* 163.

127. "Der Jude wird verbrannt," 259.

128. "Der Jude wird verbrannt," 256.

129. "Der Jude wird verbrannt," 260.

130. *Der Untergang des Judentums,* 177. My emphasis.

131. "Der Jude wird verbrannt," 263. My emphasis.

132. On "neutralism" see ch. 2.

133. "Der Jude wird verbrannt," 270.

134. Nathan Weinstock, "Introduction," in Abram Leon, *The Jewish Question: A Marxist Interpretation* (New York: Pathfinder, 1970), 33.

135. J. V. Stalin, "Anti-Semitism" (January 12, 1931), *Works,* vol. 13 (Moscow: Foreign Languages Publishing House, 1954), 30. Cited in "Der Jude wird verbrannt," 271. This announcement of Stalin was published only in 1936.

136. Émile Zola, *Nouvelle Campagne* (Paris: Bibliothèque Charpentier, 1897), 203. Cited in "Der Jude wird verbrannt," 271.

137. "Der Jude wird verbrannt," 112–15.

138. "Der Jude wird verbrannt," 113.

139. "Der Jude wird verbrannt," 269.

140. Gotthold Ephraim Lessing, *Nathan der Weise* (Munich: Wilhelm Goldmann, [1779] 1960), 98. I follow the English translation by Guenther Reinhardt: Gotthold Ephraim Lessing, *Nathan the Wise* (New York: Barron's Educational Series, 1950), 86.

141. *Der Untergang des Judentums,* 91.

142. "Der Jude wird verbrannt," 12.

143. Herzl, "Französische Antisemiten" [August 31, 1892], *Neue Freie Presse* 10067 (September 3, 1892), 2.

144. See ch. 3.

145. Klara Blum, "Der Jude wird verbrannt," *DZZ,* 75 (November 24, 1938), 3.

146. This slogan was phrased by the Social-Democratic leader, and future chancellor of West Germany, Willi Brandt, "Hitler ist nicht Deutschland" (September 28, 1938), *Berliner Ausgabe* (Bonn: Dietz, 2002), vol. 1, 375–86.

147. Thomas Lange, "Emigration nach China. Wie aus Klara Blum Dshu Bailan wurde," *Exilforschung* 3 (1985): 339–48. I thank Konstantin Baehrens for informing me of Klara Blum and her poem.

148. "Fanal und Besinnung," *Jüdische Rundschau* 38, no. 38 (June 25, 1933), 1.

149. Sophie Dubnov-Erlich, *The Life and Work of S. M. Dubnov: Diaspora Nationalism and Jewish History*, trans. Judith Vowles (Bloomington: Indiana University Press, 1991), 218.

150. Mordecai Gebirtig, "Our Town Is Burning," *The Holocaust Encyclopedia* (United States Holocaust Memorial Museum), https://encyclopedia.ushmm.org/content/en/song/our-town-is-burning (retrieved December 12, 2021).

151. On the Bund, see in ch. 1.

152. Hermann Weber, "The Stalinization of the KPD: Old and New Views," in *Bolshevism, Stalinism and the Comintern*, ed. LaPorte, Morgan and Worley, 40.

153. Dubnov-Erlich, *The Life and Work of S. M. Dubnov*, 229.

154. Renée Poznanski, "On Jews, Frenchmen, Communists, and the Second World War," in *Dark Times, Dire Decisions*, ed. Frankel and Diner, 170–73.

155. David H. Weinberg, *A Community on Trial: The Jews of Paris in the 1930s* (Chicago: University of Chicago Press, 1977), 121–36; Gerben Zaagsma, *Jewish Volunteers, the International Brigades and the Spanish Civil War* (London: Bloomsbury, 2017), 34–35.

156. Weinstock, "Introduction," 33.

157. Poznanski, "On Jews, Frenchmen, Communists," 173–74.

158. Kirschenbaum, *International Communism and the Spanish Civil War*, 118; McMeekin, *The Red Millionaire*, 296; Koch, *Double Lives*, 267.

159. *Wladi wostok*, 201–2. See ch. 1.

160. Joseph Leftwich, *What Will Happen to the Jews?* (London: Robert Anscombe, 1936), 137.

161. "Der Jude wird verbrannt," 268.

162. Walter Laqueur, "Zionism, the Marxist Critique and the Left," *Israel, the Arabs and the Middle East*, Irving Howe and Carl Gershman, eds. (New York: Quadrangle, 1972), 31–33.

163. Schlenstedt, "Versteckte Unglücke," 174.

164. See ch. 3.

165. Koestler, *The Invisible Writing*, 287.

166. Koestler, *The Invisible Writing* 300.

167. Ignazio Silone, in *The God that Failed*, ed. Richard Crossman, 98.

168. Koestler, in *The God that Failed*, ed. Richard Crossman, 65.

169. Richard Crossman, "Introduction," in *The God that Failed*, ed. Richard Crossman, 2–3.

170. Crossman, "Introduction," 6.

171. Koestler, *The God that Failed*, 65.

172. Koestler, *The God that Failed*, 66.

173. Koestler, *The Invisible Writing*, 474. See also Poznanski, "On Jews, Frenchmen, Communists," 173–74.

174. McMeekin, *The Red Millionaire*, 294. Koch maintained it had happened behind the scenes already in May 1937. Koch, *Double Lives*, 305.

175. McMeekin, *The Red Millionaire*, 302–3; Koch, *Double Lives*, 308–10.

176. Otto Heller an Rudi Askonas, August 24, 1939, PHFA, 1, 5.

177. Schilling, "Information über Otto Heller," June 4, 1942, RGASPI, 495-187-2896-012; "Information: Heller, Otto" [Russian], July 20, 1942, RGASPI, 495-187-2896-002–002o6.

178. Kazmarchuk, "Summary of a message from Josef Meisel, 11.2.1945" [Russian], March 27, 1946, RGASPI, 495-187-2896-004–005.

Chapter 5

1. Koestler, *The Invisible Writing*, 520–21.

2. Gutman, *Men and Ashes*, 130.

3. Regina M. Delacor, "From Potential Friends to Potential Enemies: The Internment of 'Hostile Foreigners' in France at the Beginning of the Second World War," *Journal of Contemporary History* 35, no. 3 (July 2000): 361–68; Koestler, *The Invisible Writing*, 510.

4. Otto Heller, brief chronological notes (August 1939–November 1940), PHFA.

5. Emma Heller, "Biographie d'Otto Heller," January 28, 1967, DÖW, 3834, 3–4.

6. Freundlich, *The Traveling Years*, 68.

7. Liberation certificate of January 19, 1940: Archives nationales de France: AN-19940451-102, dossier no. 8796: Heller Otto, p. 9, brought by Wilhelm, "Biography of Otto Heller." The release was made possible also thanks to personal recommendations from French professors and journalists who collaborated with him. Raymond Lyon [French], October 10, 1939, PHFA; Emma Heller, "Biographie d'Otto Heller," January 28, 1967, DÖW, 3834, 4.

8. Kopecky (Vertretung des Z.K.d.KPTsch beim EKKI) an die Kaderabteilung des EKKI, March 28, 1940, RGASPI, 495-187-2896-015 and 495-187-2896-001.

9. Otto Heller to Rudi Askonas, Neuilly sur Seine [French], May 9, 1940, PHFA.

10. Freundlich, *The Traveling Years*, 70.

11. Saul Friedländer, *The Years of Extermination, 1939–1945* (New York: Harper Collins, 2007), 109–10.

12. Otto Heller, brief chronological notes (August 1939–November 1940), PHFA; Otto Heller to Rudi Askonas [French], Langlade, June 18, 1940, PHFA; Emma Heller, "Biographie d'Otto Heller," January 28, 1967, DÖW, 3834, 4; Otto Heller to Elisabeth Freundlich, March 15, 1941, cited in Freundlich, *The Traveling Years*, 72; see also 66 and 73.

13. Freundlich, *The Traveling Years*, 66.
14. Otto Heller to Elisabeth Freundlich, March 15, 1941, cited in Freundlich, *The Traveling Years*, 72.
15. Freundlich, *The Traveling Years*, 73.
16. Simon Dubnow, *Die neueste Geschichte des jüdischen Volkes: Das Zeitalter der ersten Emanzipation (1789–1815)* (Berlin: Jüdischer Verlag, 1930), vol. 3, 39, cited by Heller in "Divers," PHFA.
17. Gilberto Bosques to Emma Heller [French], November 27, 1940, PHFA.
18. Daniela Gleizer, *Unwelcome Exiles: Mexico and the Jewish Refugees from Nazism, 1933–1945* (Leiden, Boston: Brill, 2014), 194–98; Otto Heller, brief chronological notes (August 1939–November 1940), PHFA.
19. Anna Seghers, *Transit*, trans. James A. Galston (Boston: Little, Brown, 1944).
20. Freundlich, *The Traveling Years*, 70.
21. Otto Heller to Elisabeth Freundlich, March 15, 1941, cited in Freundlich, *The Traveling Years*, 71–72.
22. Otto Heller to Rudi Askonas, Neuilly sur Seine [French], May 9, 1940, PHFA.
23. Freundlich, *The Traveling Years*, 70.
24. Freundlich, *The Traveling Years*, 71.
25. Ernst Heller (Zurich) an Lily Heller, November 24, 1941, PHFA. See also his letters to Emma and Lily from April to September 1942, PHFA.
26. Freundlich, *The Traveling Years*, 71.
27. Public Notary, State of New York, October 4, 1941, PHFA.
28. Lily Heller to Unitarian Service Committee [French], Paris, July 18, 1946, PHFA.
29. See ch. 1.
30. Emma Heller, "Biographie d'Otto Heller," January 28, 1967, DÖW, 3834, 4–5; Tilly Spiegel, *Österreicher in der belgischen und französischen Resistance* (Vienna: Europa Verlag, 1969), 43–44; Schütz, *Österreichische JournalisInnen und PublizisInnen im Spanischen Bürgerkrieg*, 281–82; Freundlich, *The Traveling Years*, 73.
31. "Aus: Interview mit Gerty Schindel über den Hochverratsprozess gegen Wiederstandkämpfer in Montauban 1941, 1983," in *Österreicher im Exil Frankreich, 1938–1945: Eine Dokumentation*, ed. Ulrich Weinzierl (Vienna: Österreichischer Bundesverlag, 1984), 187–89.
32. "Aus: Interview mit Gerty Schindel," 189.
33. Stern, *Geschichte wird gemacht*, 74.
34. Freundlich, *The Traveling Years*, 73.
35. Emma Heller, "Biographie d'Otto Heller," January 28, 1967, DÖW, 3834, 4–5.
36. Friedländer, *The Years of Extermination*, 170.

37. Internierte und Deportierte des Lagers Vernet, Bundesarchiv, SgY9/64, Nr. 158.

38. Internierte und Deportierte des Lagers Vernet; Ernst Heller (Zurich) and Lily Heller, November 24, 1941, PHFA.

39. Arthur Koestler, *The Scum of the Earth* (London: Eland, [1941] 2012), 85.

40. Koestler, *The Invisible Writing*, 509.

41. Koestler, *The Scum of the Earth*, 84.

42. "Information" [Russian], January 1, 1941, RGASPI, 495-187-2896-013–014.

43. Kazmarchuk, "Summary of a message from Josef Meisel, 11.2.1945" [Russian], March 27, 1946, RGASPI, 495-187-2896-004–005.

44. Emma Heller, "Biographie d'Otto Heller," January 28, 1967, DÖW, 3834, 5; Wilhelm, "Biography of Otto Heller."

45. Ministre des Anciens Combattants et Victimes de Guerre à Ministre de l'Intérieur, September 12, 1952, DAVCC, dossier d'Otto Heller, AC-21P-462307; Internierte und Deportierte des Lagers Vernet, Bundesarchiv, SgY9/64, Nr. 158. I thank Enrico Lucca for his help with the French documents.

46. Lion Feuchtwanger, *The Devil in France: My Encounter with Him in the Summer of 1940* (Los Angeles: University of Southern California, [1941] 2009), 39–40.

47. Feuchtwanger, *The Devil in France*, 18–19.

48. Otto Heller to "Sister," Aix-en-Provence, April 28, 1942, PHFA.

49. Unitarian Service Committee to Otto Heller [French], Marseille, April 30, 1942, PHFA; Ernst Heller to Lily, June 3, 1942, PHFA.

50. Ministre des Anciens Combattants et Victimes de Guerre à Ministre de l'Intérieur, September 12, 1952, DAVCC, dossier d'Otto Heller, AC-21P-462307.

51. Emma Heller, "Biographie d'Otto Heller," January 28, 1967, DÖW, 3834, 5.

52. Hans Hellmer, "Für einen österreichischen Freiheitskämpfer. In memoriam Otto Heller," *Grazer Volkszeitung* 1, no. 123 (November 18, 1945): 3; Emma Heller, "Biographie d'Otto Heller," January 28, 1967, DÖW, 3834, 5.

53. Kristina Schweig-Pfoser and Ernst Schwanger, "Einleitung," in *Österreicher im Exil Frankreich*, ed. Weinzierl, 28; Weinert, "1938–1945," 321; Baier, *Das Kurtze Jahrhundert*, 69–75.

54. Hans Hellmer, "Für einen österreichischen Freiheitskämpfer. In memoriam Otto Heller," *Grazer Volkszeitung* 1, no. 123 (October 18, 1945), 3; Emma Heller, "Biographie d'Otto Heller," January 28, 1967, DÖW, 3834, 5; Poznanski, "On Jews, Frenchmen, Communists," 180.

55. Walter Vesper, "Mit Parteiauftrag nach dem Süden," in *Résistance: Erinerungen deutscher Antifaschisten*, ed. Dora Schaul (Berlin: Dietz, 1985), 236.

56. Weinert, "1938–1945," 320.

57. Antuan Lehr (Front National Autrichien), "Attestation" [French], November 7, 1966, PHFA; Marcel Mugnier, Attentation, June 20, 1950, DAVCC, dossier d'Otto Heller, AC-21P-462307; Stern, *Geschichte wird gemacht*, 74; Emma Heller, "Biographie d'Otto Heller," January 28, 1967, DÖW, 3834, 5.

58. Stern, *Geschichte wird gemacht*, 74.

59. Maximilian Graf, Sarah Knoll, Ina Markova and Karlo Ruzicic-Kessler, *Franz Marek: Ein europäischer Marxist. Die Biographie* (Berlin: Mandelbaum, 2019), 82; Weinert, "1938–1945," 320.

60. Niederschrift des mündlichen Berichts des Gen. Franz Marek, Vienna, January 22, 1959, Bundesarchiv, SgY30/1082, Bl. 34–46, 5.

61. Interview mit Gen. Fran[z] Marek, Österreich, Bundesarchiv, SgY30/1082, Bl. 45.

62. Lily Heller to Unitarian Service Committee [French], Paris, July 18, 1946, PHFA.

63. Emma Heller an die Kaderabteilung des Z.K. der K.P.Ö, "Bericht über meine Verhaftung und die Verhöre im Juni 1944 in Lyon," Vienna, May 15, 1952, PHFA, 1.

64. Serge Klarsfeld, *Memorial to the Jews Deported from France, 1942–1944: Documentation of the Deportation of Victims of the Final Solution in France* (New York: Beate Klarsfeld Foundation, 1983), 339, 342.

65. Emma Heller, "Biographie d'Otto Heller," January 28, 1967, DÖW, 3834, 5. "Demande d'attribution du titre de déporté resistant," DAVCC, dossier d'Otto Heller, AC-21P-462307, 1.

66. Niederschrift des mündlichen Berichts des Gen. Franz Marek, Vienna, January 22, 1959, Bundesarchiv, SgY30/1082, Bl.34–46, 6; Sally Gringold, Bericht, Bundesarchiv, RY61/11, Bl. 24–31, 5; A memoir by Emma Heller's sister-in-law, n.d., PHFA.

67. Emma Heller an die Kaderabteilung des Z.K. der K.P.Ö, Vienna, "Bericht über meine Verhaftung und die Verrhöre im Juni 1944 in Lyon," Vienna, May 15, 1952, PHFA,. 5; "Demande d'attribution du titre de déporté resistant," DAVCC, dossier d'Otto Heller, AC-21P-462307, 4; Lily Heller to Unitarian Service Committee [French], Paris, July 18, 1946, PHFA; Hans Hellmer, "Für einen österreichischen Freiheitskämpfer. In memoriam Otto Heller," *Grazer Volkszeitung* 1, no. 123 (October 10, 1945), 3.

68. Demande d'attribution du titre de déporté resistant, DAVCC, dossier d'Otto Heller, AC-21P-462307, 5.

69. Marcel Mugnier, Attentation, June 20, 1950, DAVCC, dossier d'Otto Heller, AC-21P-462307; Demande d'attribution du titre de déporté resistant, DAVCC, dossier d'Otto Heller, AC-21P-462307, 4.

70. Emma Heller an die Kaderabteilung des Z.K. der K.P.Ö, "Bericht über meine Verhaftung und die Verhöre im Juni 1944 in Lyon," Vienna, May 15, 1952, PHFA, 1.

71. Emma Heller, "Bericht über meine Verhaftung," 5.

72. Lily Heller to Unitarian Service Committee [French], Paris, July 18, 1946, PHFA.

73. Emma Heller an die Kaderabteilung des Z.K. der K.P.Ö, Vienna, "Bericht über meine Verhaftung und die Verhöre im Juni 1944 in Lyon," Vienna, May 15, 1952, PHFA, 10.

74. Emma Heller an die Kaderabteilung des Z.K. der K.P.Ö, Wien, "Bericht über meine Verhaftung und die Verhöre im Juni 1944 in Lyon," Vienna May 15, 1952, PHFA, 11.

75. Otto Heller to Elisabeth Freundlich, March 15, 1941, cited in Freundlich, *The Traveling Years*, 72.

76. Renée Poznanski, "Jewish Communists in France during World War II: Resistance and Identity," in *Jewish Histories of the Holocaust: New Transnational Approaches*, Omer Bartov and Norman J. W. Goda, eds. (New York, Oxford: Berghahn Books, 2014), 218–21.

77. Poznanski, "On Jews, Frenchmen, Communists," 178.

78. See ch. 4.

79. Otto Heller to Elisabeth Freundlich, March 15, 1941, cited in Freundlich, *The Traveling Years*, 72.

80. Cahiers de mutation de Drancy, Mémorial de la Shoah: FRAN107/F/9/5788/0053/L. Brought by Wilhelm, "Biography of Otto Heller."

81. "Demande d'attribution du titre de déporté resistant," DAVCC, dossier d'Otto Heller, AC-21P-462307, 4; Klarsfeld, *Memorial to the Jews Deported from France*, 589.

82. Emma Heller an die Kaderabteilung des Z.K. der K.P.Ö, Wien, "Bericht über meine Verhaftung und die Verhöre im Juni 1944 in Lyon," Vienna, May 15, 1952, PHFA, 11.

83. Lily Heller to Unitarian Service Committee [French], Paris, July 18, 1946, PHFA; Hans Hellmer, "Für einen österreichischen Freiheitskämpfer: In memoriam Otto Heller," *Grazer Volkszeitung* 1, no. 123 (October 18, 1945): 3.

84. Klarsfeld, *Memorial to the Jews Deported from France*, 589. The men from this transport received prisoner numbers from B3673 to B3963 (Heller's number is unknown). By 1945 there were 214 survivors left (Klarsfeld, *Memorial to the Jews Deported*, 585). See also, "History and Make Up of the Convoy," *Convoi 77*, https://convoi77.org/en/les-deportes/histoire-du-convoi/ (last access October 8, 2020).

85. Yisrael Gutman, "Auschwitz: An Overview," in *Anatomy of the Auschwitz Death Camp*, Yisrael Gutman and Michael Berenbaum, eds. (Bloomington: Indiana University Press, 1994): 5–33.

86. Tadeusz Iwaszko, "Reasons for Confinement in the Camp and Categories of Prisoners," in *Auschwitz 1940–1945: Central Issues in the History of the Camp; vol. II: The Prisoners—Their Life and Work*, ed. Wacław Długoborski

and Franciszek Piper, trans. William Brand (Oświęcim: Auschwitz-Birkenau State Museum, 2000), 40–42.

87. Viktor Lederer, "Erinnerungen an Otto Heller," an excerpt from an unknown newspaper (most probably a communist German-language newspaper in Czechoslovakia), found in PHFA.

88. Viktor Lederer, "Wspomnienia z Oświęcimia," APMAB, Studies Collection, vol. 69, 231–32.

89. Viktor Lederer, "Erinnerungen an Otto Heller," an excerpt from an unknown newspaper, PHFA.

90. Lily Heller to Unitarian Service Committee [French], Paris, July 18, 1946, PHFA.

91. Viktor Lederer, "Erinnerungen an Otto Heller," an excerpt from an unknown newspaper, PHFA.

92. Ber Mark, *Megiles Oyshvits* (Tel Aviv: Yisroel-bukh, 1977), 87 [Yiddish]. See in English translation: Ber Mark, *The Scrolls of Auschwitz*, trans. Sharon Neemani (Tel-Aviv: Am Oved, 1985), 48.

93. Mark, *Megiles Oyshvits*, 119; Mark, *The Scrolls of Auschwitz*, 69.

94. Dr. Arpad Haas, "Erklärung," Vienna, November 25, 1947, PHFA. On Haas see ch. 3 and the previous section of this chapter.

95. Viktor Lederer, "Wspomnienia z Oświęcimia," APMAB, Studies Collection, vol. 69, 231.

96. Henryk Świebocki, *Auschwitz 1940–1945: Central Issues in the History of the Camp; vol. IV: The Resistance Movement*, trans. William Brand (Oświęcim: Auschwitz-Birkenau State Museum, 2000), 129.

97. Tzipora Hager Halivni, "The Birkenau Revolt: Poles Prevent a Timely Insurrection," *Jewish Social Studies* 51, no. 2 (1979): 153n117; Philip Friedman, *Oshvientshim* (Buenos Aires: Tsentral farband fun Poylishe Yidn in Argentine, 1950), 192 [Yiddish].

98. Świebocki, *Auschwitz*, vol. 4, 103–27; Józef Garliński, *Fighting Auschwitz: The Resistance Movement in the Concentration Camp* (Los Angeles: Aquila Polonica, 2018), 279–310.

99. Mordekhai Hileli, "Ha-Maḥteret ha-Ṣiyonit be-Oshviṣ," Moreshet archive, 9-1-3/45/1400; Świebocki, *Auschwitz*, vol. 4, 116–21; Mark, *The Scrolls of Auschwitz*, 67–99; Gutman, *Men and Ashes*, 118–64.

100. Gideon Greif, *We Wept without Tears: Testimonies of the Jewish Sonderkommando from Auschwitz* (New Haven: Yale University Press, 2005).

101. Tadeusz Hołuj, APMAB, Collection of Testimonies, vol. 37, 32; Viktor Lederer, "Erinnerungen an Otto Heller," an excerpt from an unknown newspaper, PHFA.

102. Iwaszko, "Reasons for Confinement in the Camp and Categories of Prisoners," 27.

103. Świebocki, *Auschwitz*, vol. 4, 13–16.

104. Świebocki, *Auschwitz*, 132–33, 224–29, 267–71.
105. Marin Gilbert, "What Was Known and When," in *Anatomy of the Auschwitz Death Camp*, Yisrael Gutman and Michael Berenbaum, eds. (Bloomington: Indiana University Press, 1994), 549; David Engel, *Facing a Holocaust: The Polish Government-in-Exile and the Jews, 1943–1945* (Chapel Hill: University of North Carolina Press, 1993), 286–87n121.
106. APMAB, RMM, vol. 7, 416–81 [Polish]. See Navon, "News from Auschwitz."
107. Świebocki, *Auschwitz*, vol. 4, 132–33.
108. Świebocki, *Auschwitz*, vol. 4, 103–4.
109. Garliński, *Fighting Auschwitz*, 353–54, 371–72; Hager Halivni, "The Birkenau Revolt," 123–30.
110. Gideon Greif and Itamar Levin, *Revolt in Auschwitz: The Uprising of the Sonderkommando in the Gas Chambers, 7.10.1944* (Rishon le-Șion: Miskal, 2017), 81–82, 100, 103, 123, 158–159, 165–166 [Hebrew]; Mark, *The Scrolls of Auschwitz*, 136–37.
111. Halivni, "The Birkenau Revolt," 140.
112. Mark, *The Scrolls of Auschwitz*, 69–70; referring to Bruno Baum, *Widerstand in Auschwitz* (Berlin: VVN, 1949), 33.
113. Tadeusz Hołuj, APMAB, Collection of Testimonies, vol. 37, 32. Union and Deutschen Ausrüstungswerke (DAW) were among the German ammunition industries that exploited Auschwitz prisoners in forced labor.
114. Martin Krenn and Michael Tatzber-Schebach, "Alfred Klahr (1904–1944). Neue Forschungen zu seiner Biographie," *Alfred Klahr Gesellschaft Mitteilungen* 19, no. 2 (June 2012): 1–10; Günther Grabner, "Zur Biografie von Alfred Klahr," in *Zur österreichischen Nation*, 190–203; Hilde Koplenig, "Alfred Klahr (1904–1943)," *Zeitgeschichte* no. 4 (1976): 97–111.
115. Hermann Langbein, *People in Auschwitz*, trans. Harry Zohn (Chapel Hill: University of North Carolina Press, 2004), 115. On the members of the central committee of KGA see Świebocki, *Auschwitz*, vol. 4, 129–30.
116. Krenn and Tatzber-Schebach, "Alfred Klahr," 6–7; Grabner, "Zur Biografie von Alfred Klahr," 201–3; Koplenig, "Alfred Klahr," 102.
117. Viktor Lederer, "Wspomnienia z Oświęcimia," APMAB, Studies Collection, vol. 69, 231.
118. Mario Niemann and Andreas Herbst, eds., *SED-Kader—die mittlere Ebene: biographisches Lexikon* (Paderborn/Munich/Vienna/Zürich: Schöningh, 2010), 100–1.
119. Świebocki, *Auschwitz*, vol. 4, 129–30.
120. Baum, *Widerstand in Auschwitz*, 32–34. The PWOK reports appeared twice a month at the most. It is possible that materials were sent from the camp to Kraków more frequently and were gathered in the periodical reports.
121. Tadeusz Hołuj, APMAB, Collection of Testimonies, vol. 37, 38.

122. Baum, *Widerstand in Auschwitz*, 29. Baum called him *Hans* Lederer, but it is almost beyond doubt Viktor Lederer, who plausibly had both a German name and a Slavic name.

123. Viktor Lederer, "Wspomnienia z Oświęcimia," APMAB, Studies Collection, vol. 69, 231–32.

124. Adam Lutwak, "Die Auschwitzfront," APMAB, Studies Collection, vol. 16, 57.

125. "Sprawozdanie za okres [Periodical Report] od 20.IV do 5.V.1944" [Hereafter: PR from . . . to . . .], APMAB, RMM, vol. 7, 433. Quotation marks in original. The German verb "ausrotten" (to exterminate) appears in original within the Polish text, spelled mistakenly "asuroten."

126. Dan Michman, "Particularist and Universalist Interpretations of the Holocaust," in *Beyond "Ordinary Men": Christopher R. Browning and the Holocaust Historiography*, Thomas Pegelow-Kaplan, Jörgen Matthäus and Mark W. Hornburg, eds. (Paderborn: Ferdinand Schöningh, 2019), 269–86.

127. PR from 1.VIII to 1.IX.1944: "Stwierdzenie o obozach koncentracynych" (Statement about the Concentration Camps), APMAB, RMM, vol. 7, 455–56; "Rezolucja więźniów politycznych" (Resolution of the Political Prisoners), August 1944, APMAB, RMM, vol. 2, 86–90; Świebocki, *Auschwitz*, vol. 4, 133n365.

128. Viktor Lederer, "Wspomnienia z Oświęcimia," APMAB, Studies Collection, vol. 69, 231–32.

129. "Resolution of the Political Prisoners," APMAB, RMM, vol. 2, 86.

130. "Resolution of the Political Prisoners," 86–87. Emphasis in original.

131. "Resolution of the Political Prisoners," 87. Emphasis in original.

132. "Resolution of the Political Prisoners," 90.

133. Baum, *Widerstand in Auschwitz*, 33.

134. "Katy Oświęcimia" (Auschwitz Henchmen), September 16, 1944, APMAB, RMM, vol. 7, 462–71; Irena Paczyńska, *Grypsy z Konzentrationslager Auschwitz Józefa Cyrankiewicza i Stanisława Kłodzińskiego* (Kraków: Wydawn. Uniw. Jagiellońskiego, 2013), CIII; Nr. 165, 476–87; Świebocki, *Auschwitz*, vol. 4, 279n695, 327.

135. Świebocki, *Auschwitz*, vol. 4, 279.

136. "Auschwitz Henchmen," APMAB, RMM, vol. 7, 462. Emphasis in original. "*More* detailed" might be in relation to the lost list from early 1944.

137. Świebocki, *Auschwitz*, vol. 4, 279n695. See also Henryk Świebocki, *London Has Been Informed . . . : Reports by Auschwitz Escapees*, trans. Michael Jacobs and Laurence Weinbaum (Oświęcim: Auschwitz-Birkenau State Museum, 1997), 86–87.

138. APMAB, RMM, vol. 2, 75, cited by Świebocki, 327. On July 28, 1944, the BBC broadcasted another warning for "German criminals," based

on a report from Auschwitz, Pawiak, Majdanek, and Ravensbrück (Świebocki, *Auschwitz*, vol. 4, 326–27). Compare Baum, *Widerstand in Auschwitz*, 36.

139. PR from 5.V to 25.V.1944, APMAB, RMM, vol. 7, 439.

140. David Bankier, *The Germans and the Final Solution: Public Opinion under Nazism* (Oxford, UK, Cambridge, US: Blackwell, 1992), 101–15, 139–56; Dieter Pohl, "Das NS-Regime und das Bekanntwerden seiner Verbrechen," Dieter Pohl and Frank Bajohr, *Der Holocaust als offenes Geheimnis: Die Deutschen, die NS-Führung und die Alliierten* (Munich: C. H. Beck, 2006), 112, 118, 120–23, 128–29; Michael Geyer, "'There Is a Land Where Everything Is Pure: Its Name Is Land of Death.' Some Observation on Catastrophic Nationalism," in *Sacrifice and National Belonging in Twentieth-Century Germany*, ed. Greg Eghigian and Matthew Paul Berg (College Station: Texas A&M University Press, 2002), 131–32.

141. PR from 20.IX to 5.X.1944, APMAB, RMM, vol. 7, 476.

142. See ch. 1.

143. Harry Stein, "Buchenwald—Stammlager," in *Der Ort des Terrors, Bd. 3: Sachsenhausen, Buchenwald* (Munich: C. H. Beck, 2006), 339; Nikolaus Wachsmann, *KL: die Geschichte der nationalsozialistischen Konzentrationslager* (Munich: Siedler, 2016), 674–75.

144. Paczyńska, *Grypsy z Konzentrationslager Auschwitz*, Nr. 153, 450–52. For a partial translation to English, see Świebocki, *Auschwitz*, vol. 4, 340–41.

145. PR from 20.IX to 5.X.1944, APMAB, RMM, vol. 7, 476.

146. Świebocki, *Auschwitz*, vol. 4, 328.

147. Daniel Blatman, *The Death Marches: The Final Phase of Nazi Genocide*, trans. Chaya Galai (Cambridge: Harvard University Press, 2011), 126–27; Świebocki, *Auschwitz*, vol. 4, 328. See also Garliński, *Fighting Auschwitz*, 381–83.

148. PR from 5.V to 25.V.1944 (26.5.1944), APMAB, RMM, vol. 7, 439.

149. "Auschwitz Henchmen," APMAB, RMM, vol. 7, 462.

150. PR from 1.II to 1.III.1944 (March 26, 1944), APMAB, RMM, vol. 7, 418–19. This formulation was further distributed in the Polish underground press, even in socialist organs: Klaus-Peter Friedrich, *Der nationalsozialistische Judenmord und das polnisch-Jüdische Verhältnis im Diskurs der polnischen Untergrundpresse (1942–1944)* (Marburg: Herder, 2006), 202–3.

151. Special Appendix to PR from 5.V to 25.V.1944, APMAB, RMM, vol. 7, 440–43.

152. PR from 25.V to 15.VI.1944, APMAB, RMM, vol. 7, 444–46. Quote from p. 444; Paczyńska, *Grypsy z Konzentrationslager Auschwitz*, CXXIV.

153. PR from 25.V to 15.VI.1944, APMAB, RMM, vol. 7, 445. Exclamation mark in original.

154. PR from 25.V to 15.VI.1944, 446.

155. PR from 15.VI to 15.VII.1944, APMAB, RMM, vol. 7, 451.

156. Laura Crago, "Łódź," in *Encyclopedia of Camps and Ghettos*, vol. 2, 81.

157. PR from 1.IX to 20.IX.1944, APMAB, RMM, vol. 7, 460–61.
158. PR from 5.X to 15.X.1944, APMAB, RMM, vol. 7, 480. Emphasis in original.
159. PR from 1.IX to 20.IX.1944, APMAB, RMM, vol. 7, 460. My emphasis.
160. Dan Diner, "On the Faculty to Differentiate: Auschwitz and Dresden," *Tabur: Yearbook of European History, Society, Culture and Thought* 1 (2008), 66 [Hebrew].
161. Bruno Baum, "Bericht über die Tätigkeit der KP im Konzentrationslager Auschwitz" (an initial report, written at the latest in June 1945), "Unser Widerstand in Auschwitz" (the book's manuscript, written at the latest during 1946), Bundesarchiv, RY1/468.
162. Mark, *The Scrolls of Auschwitz*, 69–70; Hartewig, *Zurückgekehrt*, 462–65.
163. Baum, *Widerstand in Auschwitz*, 11. That stands in contrast to Hartewig's claim that "although Auschwitz was a center for murder of Jews, in the first third of his book Baum says nothing about Jewish prisoners" (Hartewig, *Zurückgekehrt*, 463).
164. Baum, *Widerstand in Auschwitz*, 13.
165. Baum, *Widerstand in Auschwitz*, 28.
166. Mordekhai Hileli, "Ha-Maḥteret ha-Ṣiyonit be-Oshviṣ," Moreshet Archive, 9-1-3/45/1400, 16–17; Gutman, *Men and Ashes*, 151.
167. Maria Bianca Fanta, *Die Arbeiter der Feder: Journalistinnen und Journalisten der kommunistischen Parteizeitung "Österreichische Volksstimme" und die Zäsuren ihrer Lebensgeschichten (1945–1956)* (Andrássy Gyula Deutschsprachige Universität Budapest: Dissertation, 2014), 144; Botos János, "Árpád Haász (1896–1967)," *Pártélet* 31, no. 7 (July 1986): 88–90. His birth certificate confirms his Jewish origins—Állami anyakönyvek, 1895–1975: Őriszentpéter (Vas county) Registry Office in Szekszárd at the Archives of Tolna County. I thank Eva Vadasz for her help with the Hungarian documents.
168. See the Prologue.
169. Greif and Levin, *Revolt in Auschwitz*, 165–66.
170. PR from 5.X to 15.X.1944, APMAB, RMM, vol. 7, 481; Paczyńska, *Grypsy z Konzentrationslager Auschwitz*, Nr. 181, 530–32. For a partial translation to English, see Świebocki, *Auschwitz*, vol. 4, 341. Contrary to that report, telling of 500 escapees, none of the rebels in that incident succeeded to escape.
171. PR from 5.X to 15.X.1944, APMAB, RMM, vol. 7, 481.
172. Greif and Levin, *Revolt in Auschwitz*, 209.
173. Paczyńska, *Grypsy z Konzentrationslager Auschwitz*, 532–98.
174. Danuta Czech, "Calendar," in *Auschwitz 1940–1945: Central Issues in the History of the Camp, vol. V: Epilogue*, ed. Wacław Długoborski and Franciszek Piper, trans. William Brand (Oświęcim: Auschwitz-Birkenau State Museum, 2000), 218–20.
175. Gutman, *Men and Ashes*, 130.

176. Zeitgeschichte Museum Ebensee, AMM Y 36, AMM Y 43: lists of prisoners. Heller's prisoner number in Mauthausen was 119829.

177. Lily Heller to Unitarian Service Committee [French], Paris, July 18, 1946, PHFA.

178. An English appendix to Lily Heller's French letter to the Unitarian Service Committee, Paris, July 18, 1946, PHFA.

179. Margarete Schütte-Lihotzky, *Errinerungen aus dem Widerstand: Das kämpferische Leben eine Architektin von 1938–1945* (Vienna: Pormedia, 2014), 25. I thank Sophie Hochhäusel for informing me of this memoir.

180. Mordekhai Hileli, "Ha-Maḥteret ha-Ṣiyonit be-Oshviṣ," Moreshet Archive, 9-1-3/45/1400, 30–31. According to this testimony, Heller died in Mauthausen, which is clearly wrong. Hileli, who was also removed later to Ebensee ("Ha-Maḥteret ha-Ṣiyonit be-Oshviṣ," 32), might have switched the places.

181. Selma [Österreichische Freiheitfront] an Lilly Heller, n.d., PHFA.

182. Emma Heller an die Kaderabteilung des Z.K. der K.P.Ö, Wien, "Bericht über meine Verhaftung und die Verhöre im Juni 1944 in Lyon," Vienna, May 15, 1952, PHFA, 12.

183. Yad Va-Shem Archive, O.41-139: Card file of Jews who perished in the Ebensee camp hospital, 1944–1945 ("Phlegmone cruris dextri. Vulnus infectum hallucis dextri"); Red Cross, Certificate of Incarnation, DAVCC, dossier d'Otto Heller, AC-21P-462307. See also See also Bundesarchiv, DO1/32543 Bd. 2: Totenliste KZ Mauthausen, 54; Freund, *Die Toten von Ebensee*, 149; *Gedenkbuch Berlins der jüdischen Opfer des Nationalsozialismus* (Berlin: Hentrich, 1995), 477.

Epilogue

1. Jan Gerber, *Die große Allianz: Juden, die Arbeiterbewegung und die Linke, 1848–1968* (unpublished manuscript).

2. Hartewig, *Zurückgekehrt*, 567–68.

3. Felix Weltsch, "Die Mystik des Warenhandels," *Jüdische Rundschau* 37, no. 9 (February 2, 1932), 41.

4. Friedländer, *The Years of Extermination*, 249.

5. Herf, "German Communism," 270.

6. David Bankier, "'Ha-Germanim ha-Ḥofshiyim' ve-ha-Qehila ha-Yehudit be-Meqsiqo: le-Reshit ha-Maga'im beyn ha-Qomunizm ve-ha-Ṣiyonut be-Shnot ha-Arba'im," in *Hitler, the Holocaust and German Society: Allied and Aware* (Jerusalem: Yad Vashem, 2007), 271–73 [Hebrew].

7. Ernst Fischer, *Die fascistische Rassentheorie* (Moscow: Verlag für fremdsprachige Literatur, 1941), 31–45. I am grateful to Wulf D. Hund from the University of Hamburg for drawing my attention to this book.

8. Fischer, *Die fascistische Rassentheorie*, 31.
9. Fischer, *Die fascistische Rassentheorie*, 41, 43.
10. Rennap, *Anti-Semitism and the Jewish Question*.
11. William Gallacher, "Introduction," in Rennap, *Anti-Semitism and the Jewish Question*, 11.
12. Rennap, *Anti-Semitism and the Jewish Question*, 114. See also Marcus, *A Critique of Marxist Analysis of Jewish History*, 187–88n45.
13. Herf, "German Communism," 270–81, quotation from 277. See also Bankier, "Ha-Germanim ha-Ḥofshiyim," 279–81.
14. Herf, "German Communism," 276.
15. Gennady Estraikh, "The Life, Death, and Afterlife of the Jewish Anti-Fascist Committee." *East European Jewish Affairs* 48, no. 2 (2018): 139–48; Shimon Redlich, *Propaganda and Nationalism in Wartime Russia: The Jewish Antifascist Committee in the USSR, 1941–1948* (Boulder: East European Quarterly, 1982).
16. James G. Ryan, *Earl Browder: The Failure of American Communism* (Tuscaloosa and London: The University of Alabama Press, 1997), 225.
17. Carmit Gai, *Standing Alone: The Story of the Hebrew Communists, 1943–1949* (Ben Shemen: Keter, 2019) [Hebrew].
18. See ch. 2.
19. Stephan Heymann, cited by Jan Gerber, "Sieger der Geschichte: Auschwitz im Spiegel der Geschichtswissenschaft und Geschichtspolitik der DDR," in *Trotz und wegen Auschwitz: Antisemitismus und nationale Identität nach 1945*, ed. Christoph Beyer (Münster: Unrast, 2004), 29.
20. Phillip Graf, "Twice Exiled: Leo Zuckermann (1908–85) and the Limits of the Communist Promise," *Journal of Contemporary History* 56, no. 3 (2021): 766–88.
21. Jeffrey Herf, *Israel's Moment: International Support for and Opposition to Establishing the Jewish State, 1945–1949* (Cambridge: Cambridge University Press, 2022), 145–47, 254–55.
22. Following the term coined in a different context by Dan Diner, "Zwischenzeit 1945 bis 1949: Über jüdische und andere Konstellationen," *Aus Politik und Zeitgeschichte* 65, 16/17 (2015): 16–20.
23. Alfred D. Low, *Soviet Jewry and Soviet Policy* (New York: Columbia University Press, 1980), 81–87; Zvi Gitelman, *Anti-Semitism in the USSR: Sources, Types, Consequences* (New York: Synagogue Council of America, 1974), 18.
24. Mario Kessler, "Anti-Semitism against a Non-Jew: The Case of Paul Merker 1952–1953," in Mario Kessler, *Anti-Semitism and Socialism*, 149–66.
25. Dan Diner, "The Catastrophe before the Catastrophe," in *Beyond the Conceivable: Studies on Germany, Nazism, and the Holocaust* (Berkeley: University of California Press, 2000): 78–94.
26. Gutman, *Men and Ashes*, 130.

27. Mark, *Megiles Oyshvits*, 48, 119; Mark, *The Scrolls of Auschwitz*, 48, 69. Mark's evaluation of Heller reflected the process he himself underwent. See Tom Navon, "At the Crossroad between Communism and Jewish Nationalism: Ber Mark as a Historian of Premodern Jewish Society," *East European Jewish Affairs* 52, no. 2/3 (forthcoming).

28. Gutman, *Men and Ashes*, 130.

29. Viktor Lederer, "Erinnerungen an Otto Heller," an excerpt from an unknown newspaper, PHFA.

Bibliography

Primary Sources

ARCHIVAL SOURCES

AdK = Akademie der Künste, Berlin:
  Otto Heller, "Der Jude wird verbrannt" [Typoskript], 1939 (Signature: Schlenstedt 94.1)
  Otto Heller an das Internationale Büro der V.R.S. zu Moskau [Johannes Becher], November 27, 1933 (Signature: Becher-Johannes-R-Korrespondenz S1272)
APMAB = Auschwitz-Birkenau State Museum, Oświęcim (Poland):
  Collection of Testimonies
  Resistance Movement Materials (RMM)
  Studies Collection
Archives nationales de France, Paris:
  Heller Otto (Signature: AN-19940451-102, dossier no. 8796)
Bundesarchiv, Berlin:
  Ableben Fritz Heckerts, 1936 (Signature: NY4007/12)
  Aufstellung der Internierten und Deportierten des Lagers Le Vernet, 1940–1943 (Signature: SgY9/64)
  Deutsche antifaschistische Schriftsteller in den Emigrationsländern, 1934 (Signature: RY1/674)
  "Freies Deutschland," Verhaftung deutscher Antifaschisten durch Gestapo in Frankreich 1943/1944 (Signature: RY61/11)
  Konzentrationslager Mauthausen, 1940–1945 (Signature: DO1/32543)
  KPD, "Welt am Abend," 1924–1928 (Signature: RY1/1388)
  KPD, Widerstandskampf in Konzentrationslagern und Haftanstalten, 1945–1946 (Signature: RY1/468)
  Reichssicherheitshauptamt, deutsche Staatsangehörige im Ausland, 1931–1936 (Signature: R58/3414)

Teilnahme deutscher Antifaschisten an der französischen Résistance (Signature: SgY30/1082)
DAVCC = Division Archives des Victimes des Conflict Contemporains, Ministère des Armees, Paris:
Dossier d'Otto Heller (Signature: AC-21P-462307)
DÖW = Dokumentationsarchiv des österreichischen Widerstandes, Vienna:
Otto Heller (Signature: 3834)
Otto Heller, "Der Jude wird verbrannt" [Typoskript], 1939 (Signature: 45920/7)
Robert Neumann, Briefe (Signature: 11548/12)
GRAF = State Archive of the Russian Federation, Moscow:
Ozet (Signature: 9498/1/425)
IKGW = Israelitische Kulturgemeinde Wien, Vienna:
Geburtsbuch der Israelitische Kulturgemeinde Wien
Liberec Archive (Czech Republic):
Meldungen: Otto Heller
Mémorial de la Shoah, Paris:
Cahiers de mutation de Drancy (Signature: FRAN107/F/9/5788/0053/L)
Moreshet Archive, Givat Haviva (Israel):
Interview with Yeḥi'el Harari, Kibbutz Eyn-Shemer, Israel, 1964 [Hebrew] (Signature: 6-1-62/1/13)
Mordekhai Hileli, "Ha-Maḥteret ha-Ṣiyonit be-Oshviṣ" [Hebrew] (Signature: 9-1-3/45/1400)
PHFA = Papineau-Heller Family Archive, Paris
RGASPI = Russian State Archive of Socio-Political History, Moscow:
Otto Heller (Signature: 495-187-2896)
Tolna County Archives, Szekszárd (Hungary):
Állami anyakönyvek, 1895–1975: Őriszentpéter (Vas county) Registry Office
University of Vienna:
Phil. Nationale, SS 1918—WS 1919/20: Otto Heller
Yad Vashem, Jerusalem:
Card file of Jews who perished in the Ebensee camp hospital, 1944–1945 (Signature: O.41-139)
Zeitgeschichte Museum Ebensee (Austria):
Lists of prisoners (Signatures: AMM Y 36, AMM Y 43)

NEWSPAPERS AND PERIODICALS

Abwehr-Blätter
Aufbruch. Kampfblatt im Sinne des Leutnants a.D. Richard Scheringer
Ba-Sha'ar [Hebrew]
Bayerische Israelitische Gemeindezeitung
Berlin am Morgen

Bildungsarbeit: Blätter für das Bildungswesen der deutschösterreichischen
    Sozialdemokratie
C. V.-Zeitung
Der drohende Krieg
Der Hamer [Yiddish]
Der Jude
Der Jüdische Arbeiter
Der Morgen
Der Orden Bne Briss. Mitteilungen d. Großloge für Deutschland VIII. U.O.B.B
Der rote Soldat
Der rote Student
Der sozialistische Kampf
Deutsche Volkszeitung
Die Front
Die Gesellschaft
Die Kommunistische Internationale
Die Linkskurve
Die neue Welt
Die rote Fahne [Berlin]
Die rote Fahne [Vienna]
Die Stimme
Die Welt am Abend
Die Weltbühne
Die Wende
DZZ = Deutsch Zentralzeitung
Geserd = Mittelungensblatt der Gesellschaft zur Förderung des Jüdischen
    Siedlungswerkes in der UdSSR
Grazer Tagblat
Grazer Volkszeitung
Inprekor = Internationale Pressekorrespondenz
Israelitisches Familienblatt
Internationale Literatur
Jüdische Rundschau
Karlsbader Tagblatt
Korunk [Hungarian]
Monatshefte für deutschen Unterricht, deutsche Sprache und Literatur
Neue Deutsche Blätter
Neue Freie Presse
Neues Deutschland
Nieuwsblad voor den Boekhandel [Dutch]
Oesterreichische Buchhändler-Correspondenz
Prager Tagblatt
Südwestliche Rundfunk Zeitung

Tshernovitser Bleter [Yiddish]
Vorwärts [Reichenberg/Liberec, Czechoslovakia]
Weg und Ziel
Wienerwald-Bote
YIVO Bleter [Yiddish]
Yunger Historiker [Yiddish]
Zeitschrift für Sozialforschung Leipzig

OTTO HELLER: BOOKS AND BOOKLETS

(THESE ENTRIES APPEAR IN FOOTNOTES WITHOUT THE AUTHOR'S NAME.)

Die Aufgaben der proletarischen Jugendorganisation im Kampfe um die Diktatur des Proletariats: Eine Erwiderung an die sozialdemokratischen Jugendführer. Teplitz-Schönau: Junge Welt, 1920.
Sibirien: Ein anderes Amerika. Berlin: Universum-Bucherei für Alle, 1930.
Der Untergang des Judentums: Die Judenfrage, ihre Kritik, ihre Lösung durch den Sozialismus. Vienna/Berlin: Verlag für Literatur und Politik, 1931.
2nd ed., revised and extended, 1933.

Translations of Der Untergang des Judentums:

French—*La Fin Du Judaïsme.* Translated by Marcel Ollivier, Vendôme. Paris: Impr. des Presses universitaires de France, 1933.
Polish—*Zmierzch Żydostwa.* Translated by Tadeusz Zabłudowski. Warsaw: M. Fruchtman, 1934.
Turkish—*Yahudiligin Cokusu: Yahudi Sorunu, Yahudi Sorununun Elestiri, Sosyalizm'le Cozumu.* Translated by Suheyla-Saliha N. Kaya. Istanbul: Inter Yayinlari, 1992.

Das Geheimnis der Mandschurei. Hamburg, Berlin: Hoym, 1932.
Wladiwostok! der Kampf um den Fernen Osten. Berlin: Neuer Deutscher Verlag, 1932.
Auf zum Baikal! Der sozialistische Aufbau in Ostsibirien und die Fantasien des Herrn Kamaitzi. Moscow: Verlagsgenossenschaft Ausländischer Arbeiter in der UdSSR, 1933.
Die rote Fahne am Pazifik: Zehn Jahre Sowjetmacht im Fernen Osten. Moscow: Verlagsgenossenschaft Ausländischer Arbeiter in der UdSSR, 1933.

OTTO HELLER: BOOK CHAPTERS AND JOURNAL ARTICLES

(THESE ENTRIES APPEAR IN FOOTNOTES WITH THE AUTHOR'S NAME.)

[O.H.] "Ein Jahr Republik: Eine Vortragsdisposition." *Bildungsarbeit: Blätter für das Bildungswesen der deutschösterreichischen Sozialdemokratie*, 5–6 (December 1919): 1.

[O.H.] "Klassenkampf, Kulturkampf, Wahlkampf: Eine Rededisposition." *Bildungsarbeit: Blätter für das Bildungswesen der deutschösterreichischen Sozialdemokratie*, 1 (January 1920): 27.
"Mit Eisbrecher Krassin nach Sibirien." *Der drohende Krieg* 2, no. 12 (December 1, 1929): 412–14.
"Grundsätzliches zur Judenfrage." *Die Front*, 1/2, 1931, 12–16.
"Beim Grossrabbiner von Buchara." *Die Linkskurve* 3, no. 4 (April 1931): 15–17 (reprinted in *Der Untergang des Judentums*, 325–29).
"Grundsätzliches zum Antisemitismus." *Geserd* III, no. 8 (August 1931) (reprinted in *Der Untergang des Judentums*, 126–28).
"Der Jud' ist schuld!" *Der rote Student* 2, no. 7 (November–December 1931): 144–46.
"Kommunismus und Judenfrage." In E. Johannsen et al. *Klärung: 12 Autoren Politiker über die Judenfrage*. Berlin: W. Kolk, 1932, 80–96.
"Theater in Biro-bidjan." *Geserd* IV, no. 7 (October 1932) (reprinted in *Wladi wostok*, 205–6).
"Schriftsteller über Karl Marx." *Internationale Literatur* 2, no. 2 (1933/1934): 182.
"Das dritte Reich Israel: zur Literatur über die Judenfrage." *Neue Deutsche Blätter* 1, no. 5 (January 1934): 304–13.
"Was ist Rasse?" *Weg und Ziel* 10 (1947): 729ff (a chapter from "Der Jude wird verbrannt," 177–96).

OTTO HELLER: PUBLISHED LETTERS

An Prof. Max Griebsch, *Monatshefte für deutschen Unterricht, deutsche Sprache und Literatur* 26, no. 6 (October 1934): 178–79.
"Aus Brief an E. E. Kisch." *Neue Deutsche Blätter* 2, 5 (June 1935): 281–82.
"Für Egon Erwin Kisch zum 50. Geburtstag." *Internationale Literatur* 5, no. 4 (1935): 15–16.
To Elisabeth Freundlich, May 15, 1941, cited in Freundlich, *The Traveling Years*, 71–73.

OTTO HELLER: SELECTED NEWSPAPER ARTICLES

(THESE ENTRIES APPEAR IN FOOTNOTES WITH THE AUTHOR'S NAME.)

[–r.] "Die 'Große Sowjet-Enzyklopädie.'" *Vorwärts* 16, no. 5 (1926): 9.
"Zum Abschied." *Vorwärts*, June 17, 1926, 3.
"Ein 'Raubmörder' ersucht höflichst um seinen Prozess: Offener Brief an die Zentralprokurator der tschechoslowakischen Republik in Brünn." *Vorwärts*, June 23, 1926, 5.
"Zu Besuch bei Nikolaus II: und bei Karl Kramer." *Vorwärts*, June 27, 1926, 4.
"Der deutsche Normalmensch." *Die Rote Fahne* [Vienna], December 9, 1926, 4.

"Geschichte von einem demokratischen Kuvert." *Der rote Soldat* 10, no. 1 (January 1928): 8.
[Unser Sonderberichterstatter an Bord] "Neue Entdeckerfahrt des Eisbrechers 'Krassin.'" *Berlin am Morgen*, July 7, 1929, 1.
"Die Sowjet-Polarexpedition 1929. Gespräch mit Professor Samollowitsch." *Prager Tagblatt*, July 14, 1929, 5.
"Maxim Gorki spricht in Leningrad." *Die Rote Fahne* (Vienna), July 24, 1929, 6.
"Mätresse des Kardinals. Als Mussolini noch Romane schrieb." *Die Rote Fahne* (Vienna), March 23, 1930, 6.
"300 Jahre Zeitung. 1630–31 erschienen in Paris die ersten modernen Zeitungen." *Die Rote Fahne* (Vienna), April 27, 1930, 6.
"Das verwunschene Volk. Die asiatischen Juden—Das Getto von Turkestan." *Die Welt am Abend*, October 15, 1930, 1–2.
"Wladiwostok, das Tor zur Sonne." *Berlin am Morgen*, November 19, 1930, 7 (reprinted in *Die Rote Fahne* [Vienna], November 23, 1930, 7).
"Juden im Urwald." *Berlin am Morgen*, December 3–14, 1930.
"Mit der russischen Tonfilm-Expedition nach Birobidjan." *Südwestliche Rundfunk Zeitung* 7, no. 9 (March 1, 1931), 4.
"Moskauer Wochenende." *Die Rote Fahne* (Vienna), May 7, 193, 7.
"Der Aufmarsch der Milliarden. Brief aus Ostsibirien, dem Lande der unbegrenzten Möglichkeiten." *Inprekor* 12, no. 57 (July 12, 1932), 1799–1800 (reprinted in *Die Rote Fahne* [Vienna], July 24, 1932, 9).
"Die Lösund der Judenfrage in der Sowjetunion." *Inprekor* 11, no. 15 (1931): 407–5; 11, no. 16 (1931): 424–25.
"Zehn Jahre Burjäto-Mongolische Räterepublik. Aus Nomaden werden Kollektivbauern—Wie eine sozialistische Regierung aussieht." *Inprekor* 12, no. 61 (July 26, 1932): 1982–83.
"Aus der Geschichte der Intervention: Ein Fund in der Bibliotek des Amur-Museums in Blagoweschtschensk." *Inprekor* 12, no. 63 (July 29, 1932): 2016.
"Zwischen Sungari und Ussuri. Verbot des Warentransitverkehr. Drohende Hungernot. Die Antijapanische Bewegung." *Inprekor* 12, no. 64 (May 8, 1932): 2065.
"Die kulturellen und wirtschaftlichen Leistungen der Besonderen Fernöstlichen Roten Armee." *Inprekor* 12, no. 66 (August 9, 1932): 2141–42.
"Der Ferne Sowjetunion: Vor der Zehnjahrsfeier der Befreiung des fernöstlichen Gebiets von der japanischen Intervention und den weißen Banditen." *Inprekor* 12, no. 67 (August 12, 1932): 2163–64.
"Die großen Bauwerk des Fünfjahrplans. Sibiriens neuer Ozeanhaften." *Inprekor* 12, no. 98 (December 12, 1932): 2347.
"Der Krieg am Gelben Meer." *Berlin am Morgen*, January 4, 1933, 7.
"Wer oder was ist 'Lokas'?" *Die rote Fahne* (Berlin), January 11, 1933.

[Rudolf Kern.] "Bei den Männern mit den grünen Mützen." *DZZ* 11, no. 37 (February 14, 1936), 4.
[Rudolf Kern.] "Die deutschen Rotarmisten." *DZZ* 11, no. 44 (February 23, 1936), 1.

OTHER PUBLISHED PRIMARY SOURCES

Adolf Lehman's allgemeiner Wohnungs-Anzeiger nebst Handels- und Gewerbe-Adressbuch für die k.k. Reichs-Haupt- und Residenzstadt Wien. Vienna, 1900; 1910.
Alberton, M. *Biro-Bidschan, die Judenrepublik*. Leipzig-Vienna: E. Prager, 1932.
Baum, Bruno, *Widerstand in Auschwitz*. Berlin VVN, 1949.
Bebel, August. *Sozialdemokratie und Antisemitismus*. Berlin: Buchhandlung Vorwärts, (1893) 1906.
Benjamin, Walter. *The Correspondence of Walter Benjamin, 1910–1940*. Chicago, IL: University of Chicago Press, 1994.
Borokhov, Ber. "Le-She'elat Șion ve-Teritorya" [1905], *Ktavim*, vol. 1. Tel Aviv: Ha-Kibbutz ha-Me'uḥad, 1955, 18–153 [Hebrew].
Brandt, Willi. *Berliner Ausgabe*. Bonn: Dietz, 2002.
Coppi, Hans and Susanne Römer, eds. *Aufbruch: Dokumentation einer Zeitschrift zwischen den Fronten*. Koblenz: Verlag Fölbach, 2001.
Crossman, Richard, ed. *The God that Failed*. London: Hamish Hamilton, 1950.
Döblin, Alfred. *Jüdische Erneuerung*. Amsterdam: Querido, 1933.
DÖW, ed., *Für Spaniens Freiheit: Österreicher an der Seite der Spanischen Republik 1936–1939*. Vienna: Österreichischer Bundesverlag, Vienna-Munich, Jugend und Volk, 1986.
Dubnow, Simon. *Die neueste Geschichte des jüdischen Volkes: Das Zeitalter der ersten Emanzipation (1789–1815)*. Berlin: Jüdischer Verlag, 1930.
Engels, Friedrich. "Über den Antisemitismus." *Arbeiterzeitung*, 19 (May 9, 1890).
Eschwege, Helmut. *Fremd unter meinesgleichen: Erinnerungen eines Dresdner Juden*. Berlin: Linke, 1991.
Feuchtwanger, Lion, and Arnold Zweig. *Die Aufgabe des Judentums*. Paris: Verlag des Europäischen Merkur, 1933.
Feuchtwanger, Lion. *The Devil in France: My Encounter with Him in the Summer of 1940*. Los Angeles: University of Southern California, (1941) 2009.
Fischer, Ernst. *Die fascistische Rassentheorie*. Moscow: Verlag für fremdsprachige Literatur, 1941.
Freundlich, Elisabeth. *The Traveling Years*. Translated by Elizabeth Pennebaker. Riverside, California: Ariadne Press, 1999.
Gebirtig, Mordecai. "Our Town Is Burning." *The Holocaust Encyclopedia* (United States Holocaust Memorial Museum), https://encyclopedia.ushmm.org/content/en/song/our-town-is-burning (retrieved on December 12, 2021).

Goldelman, Salomon. *Löst der Kommunismus die Judenfrage? Rote Assimilation und Sowiet-Zionismus.* Vienna: H. Glantz, 1937.

Gordon, Aharon David. *Ha-Uma ve-ha-A'avoda.* Jerusalem: Ha-Sifriya ha-Ṣionit, 1953 [Hebrew].

Gross, Babette. *Willi Münzenberg: Eine politische Biografie.* Stuttgart: Deutsche Verlags-Anstalt, 1967.

Gutman, Israel. *Men and Ashes: The Story of Auschwitz-Birkenau.* Merḥavya: Sifriat Poalim, 1957 [Hebrew].

Haffner, Sebastian. *Defying Hitler: A Memoir.* Translated by Oliver Pretzel. Lexington, MA: Plunkett Lake Press, 2014.

Herzfeld, Levi. *Handelsgeschichte der Juden in Altertum.* Braunschweig: J. H. Meyer, 1879.

Herzl, Theodor. *The Jewish State.* New York: Dover, (1896) 1988.

Horkheimer, Max. "The Jews and Europe" [1939]. In *Critical Theory and Society: A Reader*, edited by Stephen Eric Bronner and Douglas MacKay Kellner. New York, London: Routledge, 1989, 77–94.

Horkheimer, Max, and Theodor W. Adorno. *Dialectic of Enlightenment: Philosophical Fragments.* Translated by Edmund Jephcott. Stanford, CA: Stanford University Press, (1944) 2002.

Humm, R. J. *Bei uns im Rabenhaus: Aus dem literarischen Zürich der Dreissigerjahre.* Zürich/Stuttgart: Fretz and Wasmuth, 1963.

Johannsen, E., et al., *Klärung: 12 Autoren Politiker über die Judenfrage.* Berlin: W. Kolk, 1932.

Kanterowicz, Alfred. "Liquidation der Judenfrage." In E. Johannsen, et al. *Klärung: 12 Autoren Politiker über die Judenfrage.* Berlin: W. Kolk, 1932, 153–68.

Kats, Moyshe. *Moyshe Kats bukh.* New York: Moyshe Kats bukh komitet, 1963 [Yiddish].

Kautsky, Karl. *Nationalität und Internationalität* (Ergänzungshefte zur Neuen Zeit, 1, January 18, 1908).

Kisch, Egon Erwin. *Tales from Seven Ghettos.* Translated by Edith Bone. London: Anscombe, (1934) 1948.

Klahr, Alfred. *Zur österreichischen Nation.* Vienna: Globus, 1994.

Klatzkin, Jacob. *Probleme des Judentums.* Berlin: L. Schneider, 1930.

Koestler, Arthur. In *The God that Failed*, edited by Richard Crossman. London: Hamish Hamilton, 1950, 15–75.

———. *The Invisible Writing: The Second Volume of an Autobiography, 1932–40.* London: Vintage, (1956) 2005.

———. *The Scum of the Earth.* London: Eland, (1941) 2012.

Körber, Lili. *Begegnungen in Fernen Osten.* Budapest: Biblios, 1936.

Langbein, Hermann. *People in Auschwitz.* Translated by Harry Zohn. Chapel Hill: University of North Carolina Press, 2004.

Leftwich, Joseph. *What Will Happen to the Jews?* London: Robert Anscombe, 1936.
Lenin, V. I. "Anti-Jewish Pogroms," *Collected Works*, vol. 29. Moscow: Progress, (1919) 1972), 252–53.
Lenin über die Judenfrage. Moscow: Verlagsgenossenschat ausländischer Arbeiter in der UdSSR, 1932.
Léon, Abraham. *La Conception Materialiste de la Question Juive.* Paris: EDI, (1946) 1968.
Leon, Abram. *The Jewish Question: A Marxist Interpretation.* New York: Pathfinder, (1946) 2020.
Leshchinsky, Yakov. "The Development of the Jewish People over the Last 100 Years." Translated by Robert Brym. *East European Jewish Affairs* 50 ([1928] 2020): 157–242.
Lessing, Gotthold Ephraim. *Nathan der Weise.* Munich: Wilhelm Goldmann, (1779) 1960.
———. *Nathan the Wise.* Translated by Guenther Reinhardt. New York: Barron's Educational Series, (1779) 1950.
Lukács, Georg, Johannes R. Becher, and Friedrich Wolf et al. *Die Säuberung. Moskau 1936, Stenogramm einer geschlossenen* Parteiversammlung, edited by Reinhard Müller. Reinbek: Rowohlt, 1991.
Luxemburg, Rosa. *The Crisis in the German Social-Democracy (The "Junius" Pamphlet).* New York: Socialist Publication Society, 1919.
Marx, Karl. *Capital*, vol. 1. In Karl Marx and Friedrich Engels, *Collected Works*, vol. 35. New York: International Publishers, (1867) 1975.
———. *Capital*, vol. 3. Translated by David Fernbach. London: Penguin, (1894) 1981.
———. *Grundrisse: Foundations of the Critique of Political Economy.* Translated by Martin Nicolaus. Harmondsworth: Penguin, (1857–1858) 1984.
———. "On the Jewish Question." In *The Marx-Engels Reader*, edited by Robert Tucker. New York: Norton, (1844) 1978, 26–52.
Masson, Jeffrey M., ed. *The Complete Letters of Sigmund Freud to Wilhelm Fliess, 1887–1904.* Cambridge, MA: Harvard University Press, 1985.
Medem, Vladimir. "Di sotsialdemokratye un di natsionale frage." *Tsum tsavntsiksten yortsayt.* New York: Amerikaner reprezentants fun Algemeynem Yidishn Arbeter-Bund in Poyln, (1904) 1943, 173–219 [Yiddish].
Musil, Robert. *The Man without Qualities*, vol. 1. Translated by Eithone Wilkins and Ernst Kaiser. London: Secker and Warburg, (1930) 1953.
[Norden, Albert] Hans Behrend. *Die wahren Herren Deutschlands.* Paris: Prométhée, 1939.
———. *The Real Rulers of Germany.* London: Lawrence and Wishart, 1939.
Norden, Albert. *Ereignisse und Erlebtes.* Berlin: Dietz, 1981.
[Norden, Albert]. "Kommunismus und Judenfrage." In *Der Jud' ist schuld . . . ? Diskussionsbuch zur Judenfrage.* Basel/Leipzig/Berlin/Vienna: Zinnen

Verlag, 1932, 272–86.
Paczyńska, Irena. *Grypsy z Konzentrationslager Auschwitz Józefa Cyrankiewicza i Stanisława Kłodzińskiego*. Kraków: Wydawn. Uniw. Jagiellońskiego, 2013.
Pötsch, Walter. *Die Grundlagen des jüdischen Volkes: Eine notwendige Abrechnung*. Breslau: Pötsch, 1938.
Qolton, Ya'akov Ṣvi. *Le-She'elat ha-Yehudim u-Fitrona*. Tel Aviv, 1932 [Hebrew].
Reichmann-Jungmann, Eva. "Der Untergang des Judentums." *Größe und Verhängnis deutsch-jüdischer Existenz: Zeugnisse einer tragischen Begegnung*. Heidelberg: Schneider, 1974, 38–45.
Rennap I. [Israel Panner], *Anti-Semitism and the Jewish Question*. London: Lawrence and Wishart, 1942.
Röhling, August. *Der Talmudjude: Zur Beherzigung für Juden und Christen aller Stände*. Münster: Russell, 1871.
Roth, Joseph. "Preface to the New Edition (1937)." *The Wandering Jews*. Translated by Michael Hofmann. New York and London: Norton, (1927) 2001.
Ruppin, Arthur. *Die Juden der Gegenwart: Eine sozialwissenschaftliche Studie*. Berlin: S. Calvary, 1904.
———. *Die Juden der Gegenwart: Eine sozialwissenschaftliche Studie*. Berlin: Jüdischer Verlag, 1920.
———. *The Jews in the Modern World*. London: Macmillan, 1934.
Scholem, Gershom. *Walter Benjamin: The Story of a Friendship*. New York: New York Review of Books, 2003.
Schütte-Lihotzky, Margarete. *Errinerungen aus dem Widerstand: Das kämpferische Leben eine Architektin von 1938–1945*. Vienna: Pormedia, 2014.
Seghers, Anna. *Transit*. Translated by James A. Galston. Boston: Little, Brown, 1944.
Silone, Ignazio. In *The God that Failed*, edited by Richard Crossman. London: Hamish Hamilton, 1950, 76–114.
Sombart, Werner. *The Jews and Modern Capitalism*. Translated by M. Epstein. Glencoe, IL: Free Press, (1911) 1951.
Stalin, J. V. "Anti-Semitism" (January 12, 1931). *Works*, vol. 13. Moscow: Foreign Languages Publishing House, 1954, 30.
———. "Marxism and the National Question," *Works*, vol. 2. Moscow: Foreign Languages Publishing House, (1913), 1953: 300–81.
Stern, J. (Rabinner). *Lichtstrahlen aus dem Talmud*. Leipzig: Philipp Reclam, 1886.
Stern, Max. *Geschichte wird gemacht: Vom Lehrlingsstreik 1919 zum Freiheitsbataillon 1945*. Vienna: Globus, 1988.
Strauss, Eli. *Geht das Judentum unter?* Vienna: Zionistische Landeskomitee für Österreich, 1933.
Talmi, Me'ir. *Ha-She'ela ha-Le'umit ve-Hameṣi'ut ha-Yehudit be-Yameynu*. Merḥavya: Sifriat Poalim, 1956 [Hebrew].
Theilhaber, Felix. *Der Untergang der deutschen Juden: Eine volkswirtschaftliche Studie*. Munich: Reinhardt, 1911.

Trotzki, Leo. *Die spanische Revolution und ihre drohenden Gefahren*. Berlin: Grylewicz, 1931.
———. *Probleme der Entwicklung der Soviet Union*. Berlin: Bulletin der Russischen Opposition [Bolschewiki-Leninisten], 1931.
Weber, Max. *Ancient Judaism*. Translated by Hans Gerth and Don Martindale. Glencoe, IL: Free Press, (1917–1919) 1952.
———. *General Economic History*. Translated by F. H. Knight. New York: Greenberg, (1923) 1927.
———. *The Protestant Ethic and the Spirit of Capitalism*. Translated by Talcott Parsons. New York: Scribner, (1904–1905) 1958.
Weinzierl, Ulrich, ed. *Österreicher im Exil Frankreich, 1938–1945. Eine Dokumentation*. Vienna: Österreichischer Bundesverlag, 1984.
Vesper, Walter. "Mit Parteiauftrag nach dem Süden." In *Résistance: Erinerungen deutscher Antifaschisten*, edited by Dora Schaul. Berlin: Dietz, 1985, 232–39.
Zola, Émile. *Nouvelle Campagne*. Paris: Bibliothèque Charpentier, 1897.
Zweig, Stefan. *The World of Yesterday*. London: Cassell, 1943.

Secondary Sources

Lexical Entries on Otto Heller

Archiv Bibliographia Judaica. *Lexikon deutsch-jüdischer Autoren*. Band 11. Munich: Saur, 2002, 60–65.
Bolbecher, Siglinde. *Lexikon der österreichischen Exilliteratur*. Vienna: Deuticke, 2000, 296–97.
Diersen, Inge. *Lexikon sozialistischer deutscher Literatur: Von den Anfängen bis 1945*. Halle: VEB Verlag Sprache und Literatur, 1963, 211–12.
Heuer, Renate. *Bibliographia Judaica: Verzeichnis jüdischer Autoren deutscher Sprache*. Bd. 1, A-K. Frankfurt/New York: Campus Verlag, 1981, 153.
Kiehnel, Holger, "Eine Auswahlbibliografie zum Thema: Antisemitismus, Zionismus, Antizionismus." In *Antisemitismus, Zionismus, Antizionismus, 1850–1940*, edited by Renate Heuer and Ralph-Rainer Wuthenow. Frankfurt/New York: Campus, 1997, 270.
Oberschelp, Reinhardt, ed. *Gesamtverzeichnis des deutschsprachigen Schrifttums (GV) 1911–1965*. Bd. 55. Munich: Verlag Dokumentation, 1978, 98 *Österreicher Kultur und Literatur der 20er Jahre*, https://litkult1920er.aau.at/litkult-lexikon/heller-otto/.
Schütz, Edgar. *Österreichische JournalistInnen und PublizistInnen im Spanischen Bürgerkrieg 1936–1939: Medienpolitik und Presse der Internationalen Brigaden*. Vienna: LIT, 2016, 278–82.

Schlenstedt, Silvia. In *Lexikon sozialistischer Literatur: Ihre Geschichte in Deutschland bis 1945*, edited by Simone Barck and Reinhard Hillich. Stuttgart/Weimar: Metzler, 1994, 193–94.

Schmuck, Hilmar. *Jüdischer Biographischer Index*. Vol. 2, Fe-Kl. Munich: K. G. Saur, 2006, 604.

Sternfeld, Wilhelm, and Eva Tiedemann. *Deutsche Exil-Literatur 1933–1945: Eine Bio-Bibliographie*. Heidelberg: Lambert Schneider, 1962, 206.

Tetzlaff, Walter, *2000 Kurzbiographien bedeutender deutscher Juden des 20. Jahrhunderts*. Lindhorst: Askania, 1982, 133–34.

Walk, Joseph. *Kurzbiographien zur Geschichte der Juden 1918–1945*. Munich: K. G. Saur, 1988: 146.

Weiskopf, W. C., *Unter fremden Himmeln: Ein Abriß der deutschen Literatur im Exil 1933–1947*. Berlin: Aufbau Verlag, 1981, 265–66.

Wilhelm, Leonard. "Biography of Otto Heller" (2016–2017). *Convoi 77*, https://en.convoi77.org/deporte_bio/heller-otto/.

Wlaschek, Rudolf M. *Biographia Judaica Bohemiae*. Dortmund: Forschungsstelle Ostmitteleuropa, 1995, 80.

Books and Articles

Abramsky, Chimen. "The Biro-Bidzhan Project, 1927–1959." In *The Jews in Soviet Russia since 1917*, edited by Lionel Kochan. Oxford, UK: Oxford University Press, 1978, 64–77.

Academy of Sciences of the Soviet Union. *International Solidarity with the Spanish Republic 1936–1939*. Moscow: Progress, 1976.

Alexander, Gabriel. "The Jews of Berlin under the Impact of the Economic Crisis." In *Weimar Jewry and the Crisis of Modernization, 1918–1933*, edited by Oded Heilbronner. Jerusalem: Magnes, 1994, 122–51 [Hebrew].

Almog, Shmu'el. "Shlilat ha-Ṣiyonut o 'Shqi'at ha-Yahadut,' " *Le'umiut, Ṣiyonut, Antishemiyut: Masot u-Meḥkarim*. Jerusalem: Ha-Sifriya Ha-Ṣiyonit, 1992, 77–99 [Hebrew].

Améry, Jean. *At the Mind's Limits: Contemplations by a Survivor on Auschwitz and Its Realities*. Translated by Sidney and Stella P. Rosenfeld. Bloomington: Indiana University Press, 1980.

Anderson, Benedict. *Imagined Communities: Reflections on the Origin and Spread of Nationalism*. New York: Verso, 1991.

Avineri, Shlomo. *Karl Marx: Philosophy and Revolution*. New Haven, CT: Yale University Press, 2019.

Baehrens, Konstantin. "Antisemitismus als 'Fetischisierung': Monographien von Otto Heller, Ernst Ottwalt and Hans Günter um 1933." In *Judentum und Arbeiterbewegung: Das Ringen um Emanzipation in der ersten Hälfte*

des 20: Jahrhunderts, edited by Markus Börner, Anja Jungfer, and Jakob Stürmann. Berlin, Boston: De Gruyter, 2018, 319–36.
Baier, Walter. *Das Kurtze Jahrhundert. Kommunismus in Österreich: KPÖ 1918 bis 2008*. Vienna: Steinbauer, 2009.
Bankier, David. "'Ha-Germanim ha-Ḥofshiyim' ve-ha-Qehila ha-Yehudit be-Meqsiqo: le-Reshit ha-Maga'im beyn ha-Qomunizm ve-ha-Ṣiyonut be-Shnot ha-Arba'im." *Hitler, the Holocaust and German Society: Allied and Aware* (Jerusalem: Yad Vashem, 2007), 271–90 [Hebrew].
———. "The German Communist Party and Nazi Antisemitism, 1933–1938." *Leo Baeck Institute Year Book*, 32 (1987), 325–40.
———. *The Germans and the Final Solution: Public Opinion under Nazism*. Oxford, UK, Cambridge, US: Blackwell, 1992.
Barck, Simone. "Eine unbekannte Bibliographie der DZZ: Zur Ambivalenz einer kulturhistorischen Quelle." In *Verratene Ideale: Zur Geschichte deutscher Emigration in der Sowjetunion in den 30er Jahren*, edited by Oleg Dehl, Natalja Mussienko, and Simone Barck. Berlin: Trafo, 2000, 315–23.
Baron, Salo. "Levi Herzfeld: the first Jewish Economic Historian." In *History and Jewish Historians: Essays and Addresses*. Philadelphia, PA: Jewish Publication Society of America, 1964.
Battini, Michele. *Socialism of Fools: Capitalism and Modern Anti-Semitism*. Translated by Noor Mazhar and Isabella Vergnano. New York: Columbia University Press, 2016.
Bauer, Alfredo. *Kritische Geschichte der Juden*. Essen: Neue Impulse, 2005.
Bein, Alex. "Ma'amaro ha-Rishon shel Herṣl be-She'elat ha-Yehudim." *Im Herṣl u-ve-Iqvotav*. Tel Aviv: Masada, 1954, 14–18 [Hebrew].
Bergbauer, Knut. "'Wider die Rote Assimilation': Die Auseinandersetzungen über Sozialismus, Kommunismus und Zionismus in der jüdischen Jugendbewegung Deutschlands." In *Jugend im Kalten Krieg: zwischen Vereinnahmung, Interessenvertretung und Eigensinn*, edited by Meike Sophia Baader and Alfons Kenkmann. Göttingen: V&R Unipress, 2021, 217–33.
Berghahn, Volker R. "Structuralism and Biography: Some Concluding Thoughts on the Uncertainties of a Historiographical Genre." In *Biography between Structure and Agency: Central European Lives in International Historiography*, edited by Volker R. Berghahn and Simone Lässig. New York: Berghahn, 2008, 234–50.
Bergler, Sabine. "Observations and Travel Reports by Austrian Communists on Red Zion." In *Genosse.Jude: Wir wollten nur das Paradies auf Erden/Comrade. Jew: We only Wanted Paradise on Earth*, edited by Gabriele Kohlbauer-Fritz and Sabine Bergler. Vienna: Amalthea, 2017, 122–41.
Blatman, Daniel. *The Death Marches: The Final Phase of Nazi Genocide*. Translated by Chaya Galai. Cambridge, MA: Harvard University Press, 2011.

Börner, Markus, Anja Jungfer, and Jakob Stürmann, eds. *Judentum und Arbeiterbewegung: Das Ringen um Emanzipation in der ersten Hälfte des 20: Jahrhunderts*. Berlin, Boston: De Gruyter, 2018.

Brenner, Michael. *Prophets of the Past: Interpreters of Jewish History*. Translated by Steven Rendall. Princeton, NJ and Oxford, UK: Princeton University Press, 2010.

Brustein, William I., and Louisa Roberts. *The Socialism of Fools? Leftist Origins of Modern Anti-Semitism*. New York: Cambridge University Press, 2015.

Bunzl, John. *Klassenkampf in der Diaspora: Zur Geschichte der jüdischen Arbeiterbewegung*. Vienna: Europa, 1975.

Cabada, Ladislav. *Intellectuals and the Communist Idea: The Search for a New Way in Czech Lands from 1890 to 1938*. Lanham, MD: Lexington Books, 2010.

Carlebach, Julius. *Karl Marx and the Radical Critique of Judaism*. London: Routledge and Kegan Paul, 1978.

Case, Holly. *The Age of Questions*. Princeton, NJ: Princeton University Press, 2018.

Cesarani, David. *The Left and the Jews, the Jews and the Left*. London: Labour friends of Israel, 2004.

Cohen, Percy S. *Jewish Radicals and Radical Jews*. London: Academic Press, 1981.

Cox, John M. *Circles of Resistance: Jewish, Leftist and Youth Dissidence in Nazi Germany*. New York: Lang, 2009.

Czech, Danuta. "Calendar." In *Auschwitz 1940–1945: Central Issues in the History of the Camp. Vol. V: Epilogue*, edited by Wacław Długoborski and Franciszek Piper. Translated by William Brand. Oświęcim: Auschwitz-Birkenau State Museum, 2000, 119–232.

Danzer, Doris. *Zwischen Vertrauen und Verrat: Deutschsprachige kommunistische Intellektuelle und ihre sozialen Beziehungen (1918–1960)*. Göttingen: V&R Unipress, 2012.

Dekel-Chen, Jonathan. *A Common Camp? Jewish Agricultural Cooperativism in Russia and the World, 1890–1941*. Jerusalem: Magnes, Yad Tabenkin, 2008 [Hebrew].

Delacor, Regina M. "From Potential Friends to Potential Enemies: The Internment of 'Hostile Foreigners' in France at the Beginning of the Second World War." *Journal of Contemporary History* 35, no. 3 (July 2000): 361–68.

Deutscher, Isaac. "The Jew in Modern Society: A Conversation with Isaac Deutscher." *Jewish Quarterly* 13, no. 4 (Winter 1966): 7–12.

———. *The Non-Jewish Jew and other Essays*. London: Verso, 2017.

Dietz, Shoshana. "Jewish-Marxist (Re)presentations: A Study of German and Russian Jewish Writers during the Interwar Period." PhD diss., University of Texas at Austin, 1995.

Diner, Dan. "On the Faculty to Differentiate: Auschwitz and Dresden." *Tabur: Yearbook of European History, Society, Culture and Thought*, no. 1 (2008): 64–67 [Hebrew].

———. "The Catastrophe before the Catastrophe." *Beyond the Conceivable: Studies on Germany, Nazism, and the Holocaust*. Berkeley: University of California Press, 2000, 78–94.

———. "The Limits of Reason: Max Horkheimer on Antisemitism and Extermination." *Beyond the Conceivable: Studies on Germany, Nazism, and the Holocaust*. Berkeley: University of California Press, 2000, 97–116.

———. "Zwischenzeit 1945 bis 1949: Über jüdische und andere Konstellationen." *Aus Politik und Zeitgeschichte* 65, no. 16/17 (2015): 16–20.

Dotan, Shmu'el. *Adumim: Ha-Miflaga ha-Qomunistit be-Eereṣ Yisra'el*. kfar Saba: Shavna ha-Sofer, 1991 [Hebrew].

Draper, Hal. *Karl Marx's Theory of Revolution*. New York: Monthly Review, 1977.

Dubnov-Erlich, Sophie. *The Life and Work of S. M. Dubnov: Diaspora Nationalism and Jewish History*. Translated by Judith Vowles. Bloomington: Indiana University Press, 1991.

Duhnke, Horst. *Die KPD von 1933 bis 1945*. Cologne: Kieperheuter and Witsch, 1972.

"Egon Erwin Kisch (1885–1948)." *Frankfurter Rundschau*, April 5, 2005, https://www.fr.de/politik/egon-erwin-kisch-1885-1948-11727841.html.

Encyclopedia of Camps and Ghettos, 1933–1945. Bloomington and Indianapolis: Indiana University Press, 2012.

Endelman, Todd. *Leaving the Jewish Fold: Conversion and Radical Assimilation in Modern Jewish History*. Princeton, NJ: Princeton University Press 2015.

Estraikh, Gennady. "The Life, Death, and Afterlife of the Jewish Anti-Fascist Committee." *East European Jewish Affairs* 48, no. 2 (2018): 139–48.

Fanta, Maria Bianca. "Die Arbeiter der Feder: Journalistinnen und Journalisten der kommunistischen Parteizeitung 'Österreichische Volksstimme' und die Zäsuren ihrer Lebensgeschichten (1945–1956)." Diss. Andrássy Gyula Deutschsprachige Universität Budapest, 2014.

Faulkner, Richard S. *Muese-Argonne 26 September–11 November 1918*. Washington, DC: Center of Military History, United States Army, 2018.

Federman, Kiril. *The Holocaust in the Crimea and the North Caucasus*. Jerusalem: Yad Vashem, 2016.

Fine, Robert, and Philip Spencer, *Antisemitism and the Left: On the Return of the Jewish Question*. Manchester, UK: Manchester University Press, 2017.

Fischer, Conan. *The German Communists and the Rise of Nazism*. London: Macmillan, 1991.

Fischer, Lars. *The Socialist Response to Antisemitism in Imperial Germany*. New York: Cambridge University Press, 2007.

Flechtheim, Ossip K. *Die KPD in der Weimarer Republik*. Hamburg: Junius, 1986.

Fowkes, Ben. "To Make the Nation or to Break It: Communist Dilemmas in Two Interwar Multinational States." In *Bolshevism, Stalinism and the Comintern: Perspectives on Stalinization, 1917–53*, edited by Norman LaPorte,

Kevin Morgan, and Matthew Worley. New York: Palgrave Macmillan, 2008, 206–25.
Frankel, Jonathan, and Dan Diner, eds. *Dark Times, Dire Decisions: Jews and Communism*, Studies in Contemporary Jewry, vol. 20. New York: Oxford University Press, 2004.
Frei, Bruno. "Marxist Interpretations of the Jewish Question." *Wiener Library Bulletin* 35/36, no. 28 (1975): 2–8.
———. *Socialismus und Antisemitismus*. Vienna/Munich/Zürich: Europaverlag, 1978.
Freund, Florian. *Die Toten von Ebensee: Analyse und Dokumentation der im KZ Ebensee umgekommenen Häftlinge 1943–1945*. Vienna: Braintrust, 2010.
Friedländer, Saul. *The Years of Persecution, 1933–1939: Nazi Germany and the Jews*, vol. 1. New York: Harper Collins, 1997.
———. *The Years of Extermination, 1939–1945: Nazi Germany and the Jews*, vol. 2. New York: Harper Collins, 2007.
Friedman, Philip. *Oshvientshim*. Buenos Aires: Tsentral farband fun Poylishe Yidn in Argentine, 1950 [Yiddish].
Friedrich, Klaus-Peter. *Der nationalsozialistische Judenmord und das polnisch-Jüdische Verhältnis im Diskurs der polnischen Untergrundpresse (1942–1944)*. Marburg: Herder, 2006.
Gai, Carmit. *Standing Alone: The Story of the Hebrew Communists, 1943–1949*. Ben Shemen: Keter, 2019 [Hebrew].
Garliński, Józef, *Fighting Auschwitz: The Resistance Movement in the Concentration Camp*. Los Angeles, CA: Aquila Polonica, 2018.
Gechtman, Roni. "National-Cultural Autonomy and 'Neutralism': Vladimir Medem's Marxist Analysis of the National Question, 1903–1920." *Socialist Studies* 3, no. 1 (May 1, 2007): 69–92.
Gedenkbuch Berlins der jüdischen Opfer des Nationalsozialismus. Berlin: Hentrich, 1995.
Geisel, Eike. *Triumph des guten Willen: Gute Nazis und selbsternannte Opfer. Die Nationalisierung der Erinnerung*. Berlin: Tiamat, 1998.
Gellner, Ernst. *Nations and Nationalism*. Ithaca, NY: Cornell University Press, 1983.
Gerber, Jan. *Die große Allianz: Juden, die Arbeiterbewegung und die Linke, 1848–1968* (unpublished manuscript).
———. "Imperial Residuals: A New Perspective on the Slánský Trial" (unpublished manuscript).
———. " 'Rote Assimilation': Judentum und Kommunismus im mittleren und östlichen Europa (1917–1968)." In *Judentum und Arbeiterbewegung: Das Ringen um Emanzipation in der ersten Hälfte des 20: Jahrhunderts*, edited by Markus Börner, Anja Jungfer, and Jakob Stürmann. Berlin, Boston: De Gruyter, 2018, 183–201.

———. "Sieger der Geschichte: Auschwitz im Spiegel der Geschichtswissenschaft und Geschichtspolitik der DDR." In *Trotz und wegen Auschwitz: Antisemitismus und nationale Identität nach 1945*, edited by Christoph Beyer. Münster: Unrast, 2004, 29–48.
Geyer, Michael. "'There Is a Land Where Everything Is Pure: Its Name Is Land of Death.' Some Observation on Catastrophic Nationalism." In *Sacrifice and National Belonging in Twentieth-Century Germany*, edited by Greg Eghigian and Matthew Paul Berg. College Station: Texas A&M University Press, 2002, 118–47.
Gessen, Masha. *Where the Jews Aren't: The Sad and Absurd Story of Birobidzhan, Russia's Jewish Autonomous Region*. New York: Nextbook, Schocken, 2016.
Gitelman, Zvi. *Anti-Semitism in the USSR: Sources, Types, Consequences*. New York: Synagogue Council of America, 1974.
———. *Jewish Nationality and Soviet Politics: The Jewish Sections of the CPSoviet Union, 1917–1930*. Princeton, NJ: Princeton University Press, 1972.
Gleizer, Daniela. *Unwelcome Exiles: Mexico and the Jewish Refugees from Nazism, 1933–1945*. Leiden, Boston: Brill, 2014.
Goldberg, Chad Alan. *Modernity and the Jews in Western Social Thought*. Chicago, IL: University of Chicago Press, 2017.
———. "The Two Marxes: From Jewish Domination to Supersession of the Jews." *Journal of Classical Sociology* 15, no. 4 (2015): 415–34.
Gordon, Sharon, and Rina Peled, eds. *Vienna 1900: Blooming on the Edge of an Abyss*. Jerusalem: Carmel, 2019 [Hebrew].
Graf, Maximilian, Sarah Knoll, Ina Markova, and Karlo Ruzicic-Kessler. *Franz Marek—Ein europäischer Marxist: Die Biographie*. Berlin: Mandelbaum, 2019.
Graf, Phillip. "Twice Exiled: Leo Zuckermann (1908–85) and the Limits of the Communist Promise." *Journal of Contemporary History* 56, no. 3 (2021): 766–88.
Green, John. *Willi Münzenberg: Fighter against Fascism and Stalinism*. London and New York: Routledge, 2020.
Greif, Gideon. *We Wept without Tears: Testimonies of the Jewish Sonderkommando from Auschwitz*. New Haven: Yale University Press, 2005.
Greif, Gideon, and Itamar Levin. *Revolt in Auschwitz: The Uprising of the Sonderkommando in the Gas Chambers, 7.10.1944*. Rishon le-Ṣiyon: Miskal, 2017 [Hebrew].
Gutman, Yisrael, and Michael Berenbaum, eds. *Anatomy of the Auschwitz Death Camp*. Bloomington: Indiana University Press, 1994.
Gutwein, Daniel. "Beyn ha-Yehudim ve-ha-Qapitalizm be-Tfisato shel Marks: me-Zombart le-Veber," *Zion* 55, no. 4 (1990): 419–48 [Hebrew].
Hackl, Erich. "Die Namen der Dinge: Salut für Elisabeth Freundlich." *Kommune* 3 (2001): 61–66.

Hädicke, Karl-Heinz, "Verlag für Literatur und Politik (VLP)." In *Lexikon sozialistischer Literatur. Ihre Geschichte in Deutschland bis 1945*, edited by Simone Barck and Reinhard Hillich. Stuttgart/Weimar: Metzler, 1994: 484–85.

Hager Halivni, Tzipora. "The Birkenau Revolt: Poles Prevent a Timely Insurrection." *Jewish Social Studies* 51, no. 2 (1979): 123–54.

Hamann, Brigitte. *Hitler's Vienna: A Portrait of the Tyrant as a Young Man*. London: Tauris, 2010.

Hamburger, Ernest. "One Hundred Years of Emancipation." *Leo Baeck Institute Year Book*, 14, no. 1 (1969): 3–66.

Hanebrink, Paul. *A Specter Haunting Europe: The Myth of Judeo-Bolshevism*. Cambridge, MA: Harvard University Press, 2018.

Harris, Abram L. "Sombart and German (National) Socialism." *Journal of Political Economy* 50, no. 6 (December 1942): 805–35.

Hastings, Adrian. *The Construction of Nationhood: Ethnicity, Religion, and Nationalism*. Cambridge, UK: Cambridge University Press, 2001.

Haury, Thomas. *Antisemitismus von links: kommunistische Ideologie, Nationalismus und Antizionismus in der frühen DDR*. Hamburg: Hamburg Ed., 2002.

Hautmann, Hans. *Geschichte der Rätebewegung in Österreich 1918–1924*. Vienna, Zürich: Europaverlag, 1987.

Hartewig, Karin. *Zurückgekehrt. Die Geschichte der jüdischen Kommunisten in der DDR*. Cologne/Weimar/Vienna: Böhlau, 2000.

Hayes, Peter. "Big Businesses and 'Aryanization' in Germany 1933–1939." *Jahrbuch für Antisemitismusforschung* 3 (1994): 254–81.

Hecht, Luise, and Dieter. "Between Two Funerals: Viennese Jews between the Liberal Faith and the National Question." In *Vienna 1900: Blooming on the Edge of an Abyss*, edited by Sharon Gordon and Rina Peled. Jerusalem: Carmel, 2019, 173–206 [Hebrew].

Herf, Jeffrey. "German Communism, the Discourse of 'Antifascist Resistance,' and the Jewish Catastrophe." In *Resistance against the Third Reich*, edited by Michael Geyer. Chicago, IL: University of Chicago Press, 1994, 257–94.

———. *Israel's Moment: International Support for and Opposition to Establishing the Jewish State, 1945–1949*. Cambridge, UK: Cambridge University Press, 2022.

Hermand, Jost. *Engagement als Lebensform: Über Arnold Zweig*. Berlin Ed. Sigma, 1992.

———. "Juden in der Kultur der Weimarer Republik." In *Juden in der Weimarer Republik*, Bd. 6, edited by Walter Grab and Julius H. Schoeps. Stuttgart/Bonn: Burg, Studien zur Geistesgeschichte, 1986, 9–37.

Hermsdorf, Klaus. " 'Deutsche-jüdische' Schriftsteller? Anmerkungen zu einer Literaturdebatte des Exils." *Zeitschrift zur Germanistik* 3, no. 3 (August 1982): 278–92.

Hirshhoyt, Yekhiel. "Mahler, Rafael." In *Leksikon far der nayer literatur*, vol. 5, edited by Shmuel Niger and Yankev Shatski. New York: Alveltlekhn yidishn kultur-kongres veraynikt mit Tsika, 1963, 393–97 [Yiddish].
Historische Kommission beim ZK der KPÖ. *Geschichte der Kommunistische Partei Österreichs: 1918–1955. Kurzer Abriss*. Vienna: Globus, 1977.
"History and Make up of the Convoy," *Convoi* 77, https://en.convoi77.org/history-and-make-up-of-the-convoy (last accessed October 8, 2020).
Hobsbawm, Eric J. *Nations and Nationalism since 1780: Programme, Myth, Reality*. Cambridge, UK: Cambridge University Press, 1990.
Hobsbaum, Eric, and Terence Ranger, eds. *The Invention of Traditions*. Cambridge, UK: Cambridge University Press, 1983.
Hoppe, Bert. *In Stalins Gefolgschaft. Moskau und die KPD 1928–1933*. Oldenbourg: Wissenschaftsverlag, 2011.
Huber, Peter, "The Central Bodies of the Comintern: Stalinization and Changing Social Composition." In *Bolshevism, Stalinism and the Comintern: Perspectives on Stalinization, 1917–53*, edited by Norman LaPorte, Kevin Morgan, and Matthew Worley, 66–88. New York: Palgrave Macmillan, 2008.
Iwaszko, Tadeusz, "Reasons for Confinement in the Camp and Categories of Prisoners." In *Auschwitz 1940–1945: Central Issues in the History of the Camp. Vol. II: The Prisoners: Their Life and Work*, edited by Wacław Długoborski and Franciszek Piper. Translated by William Brand. Oświęcim: Auschwitz-Birkenau State Museum, 2000, 11–44.
Jacobs, Jack, ed. *Jews and Leftist Politics: Judaism, Israel, Antisemitism and Gender*. Cambridge, UK: Cambridge University Press, 2017.
———. *On Socialists and "The Jewish Question" after Marx*. New York: New York University Press, 1992.
———. *The Frankfurt Scholl, Jewish Lives, and Antisemitism*. New York: Cambridge University Press, 2015.
János, Botos. "Árpád Haász (1896–1967)." *Pártélet* 31, no. 7 (July 1986): 88–90.
Jarmatz, Klaus and Simone Barck, "Die 'Deutsche Zentralzeitung.'" In *Exil in der UdSSR*. Leipzig: Philipp Reclam, 1989.
Kageda, Allan L. "American Jews and the Soviet Experiment: The Agro-Joint Project, 1924–1937." *Jewish Social Studies* 43, no. 2 (Spring 1981): 153–64.
Karlip, Joshua M. *The Tragedy of a Generation: The Rise and Fall of Jewish Nationalism in Eastern Europe*. Cambridge, MA, and London: Harvard University Press, 2013.
Karp, Jonathan. "Kopf ohne Körper? Wirtschaftsgeschichte jüdischen Lebenswelten." In *Kapitalismusdebatten um 1900: Über antisemitisierende Semantiken des Jüdischen*, edited by Nicolas Berg. Leipzig: Leipziger Universitätsverlag, 2011, 49–69.
Kershaw, Ian. *Hitler, 1889–1936: Hubris*. London, New York: Penguin, 2001.

Kessler, Mario. *Anti-Semitism and Socialism: Selected Essays*. Berlin: Trafo, 2005.
———. *Antisemitismus, Zionismus und Sozialismus: Arbeiterbewegung und jüdische Frage im 20. Jahrhundert*. Mainz: Decaton, 1994.
———. "Der Stalinsche Terror gegen jüdische Kommunisten 1937/1938." In *Kommunisten verfolgen Kommunisten stalinistischer Terror und "Säuberungen" in den kommunistischen Parteien Europas seit den dreißiger Jahren*, edited by Hermann Weber and Dietrich Staritz. Berlin: Akad.-Verl., 1993, 87–102.
———. "Die KPD und der Antisemitismus in der Weimarer Republik." *Utopie Kreativ* 173 (2005): 223–32.
———. *Die SED und die Juden—zwischen Repression und Toleranz: Politische Entwicklungen bis 1967*. Berlin: Akademie, 1995.
———. "Parteiorganisation und nationale Frage: Lenin und der Jüdische Arbeiterbund 1903–1914." In *Lenin Theorie und Praxis in historischer Perspektive*, edited by Theodor Bergmann, Wladislaw Hedeler, Mario Kessler, and Gert Schäfer. Mainz: Decaton, 1994, 219–31.
———. "Sozialismus und Zionismus in Deutschland 1897–1933." In *Juden und deutsche Arbeiterbewegung bis 1933*, edited by Ludger Heid and Arnold Paucker. Tübingen: Mohr, 1992, 91–102.
———. *Westemigranten. Deutsche Kommunisten zwischen USA-Exil und DDR*. Vienna, Cologne, Weimar: Böhlau, 2019.
———. *Zionismus und internationale Arbeiterbewegung*. Berlin: Akademie Verlag, 1994.
Kirschenbaum, Lisa A. *International Communism and the Spanish Civil War: Solidarity and Suspicion*. New York: Cambridge University Press, 2015.
Kistenmacher, Olaf. *Arbeit und "jüdisches Kapital": Antisemitische Aussagen in der KPD-Tagesyeitung* Die Rote Fahne *während der Weimarer Republik*. Bremen: Edition Lumière, 2016.
Klarsfeld, Serge. *Memorial to the Jews Deported from France, 1942–1944: Documentaion of the Deportation of Victims of the Final Solution in France*. New York: Beate Klarsfeld Foundation, 1983.
Koch, Stephen. *Double Lives: Spies and Writers in the Secret Soviet War of Ideas against the West*. New York: Free Press, 1994.
Kochan, Lionel, ed. *The Jews in Soviet Russia since 1917*. Oxford, UK: Oxford University Press, 1978.
Koplenig, Hilde. "Alfred Klahr (1904–1943)." *Zeitgeschichte* 3, no. 4 (1976): 97–111.
Kostyrchenko, Gennadi. *Out of the Red Shadows: Anti-Semitism in Stalin's Russia*. Amherst, NY: Prometheus Books, 1995.
Knellessen, Dagi, and Felix Pankonin. "Einführung" [Schwerpunkt Jüdische Lebenswege im 20. Jahrhundert—Neue Perspektive der Biographieforschung]. *Jahrbuch des Dubnow-Instituts* 16 (2017): 291–302.

Knütter, Hans-Helmuth. *Die Juden und die deutsche Linke in der Weimarer Republik 1918–1933*. Düsseldorf: Dorste, 1971.
Krajewski, Stanisław. "Jews, Communism, and the Jewish Communists." In *Jewish Studies at the CEU: I. Yearbook 1996–1999*, edited by András Kovács. Budapest: Central European University, 2000, 115–30.
Krenn, Martin, and Michael Tatzber-Schebach. "Alfred Klahr (1904–1944): Neue Forschungen zu seiner Biographie." *Alfred Klahr Gesellschaft Mitteilungen* 19, no. 2 (June 2012): 1–10.
Kuchenbecker, Antje. *Zionismus ohne Zion: Idee und Geschichte eines jüdischen Staates in Sowjet-Fernost* (Dokumente, Texte, Materialien: Zentrum für Antisemitismusforschung der Technischen Universität Berlin, vol. 32). Berlin: Metropol, 2000.
Kwiet, Konrad. "Historians of the GDR on Antisemitism." *Leo Baeck Institute Year Book*, 21 (1976), 173–98.
Kwiet, Konrad and Helmut Eschwege. *Selbstbehauptung and Widerstand: Deutsche Juden in Kampf um Existenz und Menschenwürde 1933–1945*. Hamburg: Christians, 1984.
Lange, Thomas. "Emigration nach China: Wie aus Klara Blum Dshu Bailan wurde." *Exilforschung* 3 (1985): 339–48.
LaPorte, Norman, Kevin Morgan, and Matthew Worley, eds. *Bolshevism, Stalinism and the Comintern: Perspectives on Stalinization, 1917–53*. New York: Palgrave Macmillan, 2008.
Laqueur, Walter. *A History of Zionism*. New York: Schocken, 1989.
———. "Zionism, the Marxist Critique and the Left." In *Israel, the Arabs and the Middle East*, edited by Irving Howe and Carl Gershman. New York: Quadrangle, 1972, 16–44.
Lerner, Michael. *The Socialism of Fools: Anti-Semitism on the Left*. Oakland, CA: Tikkun Books, 1992.
Levin, Nora. *The Jews in the Soviet Union since 1917: Paradox of Survival*. New York: New York University Press, 1988.
———. *While Messiah Tarried: Jewish Socialist Movements, 1871–1917*. New York: Schocken Books, 1977.
Lichtbau, Albert. "Ambivalent Modernity: The Jewish Population of Vienna." *Quest. Issues in Contemporary Jewish History*, 2 (October 2011): 172–87.
Liebman, Arthur. *Jews and the Left*, New York: J. Wiley, 1979.
Linfield, Susie. *The Lion's Den: Zionism and the Left from Hannah Arendt to Noam Chomsky*. New Haven, CT and London: Yale University Press, 2019.
Lohse, Peggy. "Deutsche in Sibirien (1): Wie Otto Heller die Neue Welt im Osten entdeckte." *Russia Beyond* 18, no. 6 (2016), https://de.rbth.com/deutschland_und_russland/menschen/2016/06/18/deutsche-in-sibirien-1-wie-otto-heller-die-neue-welt-im-osten-entdeckte_603967 (retrieved on April 19, 2021).

Low, Alfred D. *Soviet Jewry and Soviet Policy*. New York: Columbia University Press, 1980.

Lustiger, Arno. "German and Austrian Jews in the International Brigade." *Leo Baeck Institute Yearbook* 35 (1990): 297–320.

———. *Stalin and the Jews: The Red Book: The Tragedy of the Jewish Anti-Fascist Committee and the Soviet Jews*. New York: Enigma, 2003.

Lvavi (Babitzky), Jacob. *The Jewish Colonization in Birobijan*. Jerusalem: The Historical Society of Israel, 1965 [Hebrew].

Mallmann, Klaus-Michael. *Kommunisten in der Weimarer Republik: Sozialgeschichte einer revolutionären Bewegung*. Darmstadt: Wissenschaftliche Buchgesellschaft, 1996.

Marcus, Marcel R. *A Critique of Marxist Analysis of Jewish History*. MA thesis, University of Newcastle upon Tyne, 1984.

Marcus, Nathan. "Address Book: Vienna through the Eyes of the Viennese." In *Vienna 1900: Blooming on the Edge of an Abyss*, edited by Sharon Gordon and Rina Peled. Jerusalem: Carmel, 2019, 37–64 [Hebrew].

Margalit, Elkana. *"Hashomer Hatsair": From a Youth Community to Revolutionary Marxism, 1919–1936*. Tel Aviv: University of Tel Aviv, 1971 [Hebrew].

Mark, Ber. *Megiles Oyshvits*: Tel Aviv: Yisroel-bukh, 1977 [Yiddish].

———. *The Scrolls of Auschwitz*. Translated by Sharon Neemani. Tel Aviv: Am Oved, 1985.

Martin, Terry. *The Affirmative Action Empire: Nations and Nationalism in the Soviet Union, 1923–1939*. Ithaca, NY: Cornell University Press, 2001.

McMeekin, Sean. *The Red Millionaire: A Political Biography of Willi Münzenberg, Moscow's Secret Propaganda Tsar in the West*. New Haven, CT: Yale University Press, 2005.

Mendelsohn, Ezra. *On Modern Jewish Politics*. New York, Oxford, UK: Oxford University Press, 1993.

Mendes, Philip. *Jews and the Left: The Rise and Fall of a Political Alliance*. New York: Palgrave Macmillan, 2014.

Michman, Dan. "Particularist and Universalist Interpretations of the Holocaust." In *Beyond "Ordinary Men": Christopher R. Browning and the Holocaust Historiography*, edited by Thomas Pegelow-Kaplan, Jörgen Matthäus, and Mark W. Hornburg. Paderborn: Ferdinand Schöningh, 2019: 269–86.

Miller, Jacob. "Soviet Theory on the Jews." In *The Jews in Soviet Russia since 1917*, edited by Lionel Kochan. Oxford, UK: Oxford University Press, 1978, 46–63.

Muller, Jerry. *Capitalism and the Jews*. Princeton, NJ: Princeton University Press, 2010.

Müller-Salget, Klaus. "Alfred Döblin und das Judentum: Aus Anlass seines 125. Geburtstages." *Literaturkritik.de*, https://literaturkritik.de/id/6305 (retrieved on May 18, 2021).

Myers, David N. *Re-Inventing the Jewish Past: European Jewish Intellectuals and the Zionist Return to History*. New York: Oxford University Press, 1995.
Mishkinsky, Moshe. "Vladimir Medem: ha-Ish be-Tnu'ato." In *Yehudim be-Tnu'ot Mahapkhaniot*, edited by Eli She'alti'el. Jerusalem: Zalman Shazar Center, 1983, 67–74 [Hebrew].
Morgan, Kevin. "Parts of People and Communist Lives." In *Party People, Communist Lives: Explorations in Biography*, edited by Kevin Morgan. London: Lawrence and Wishart, 2001.
Mosse, George L. "German Socialists and the Jewish Question in the Weimar Republic." *Leo Baeck Institute Yearbook* 16 (1971): 123–51.
Na'aman, Shlomo. *Marxismus und Zionismus*. Gerlingen: Bleicher, 1997.
———. "Reshit ha-Yerivut beyn ha-Marqsizm la-Ṣiyonut ha-Soṣyalistit." *Iyunim Bitqumat Yisra'el*, 2 (1992): 28–55 [Hebrew].
Navon, Tom. "At the Crossroad between Communism and Jewish Nationalism: Ber Mark as a Historian of Premodern Jewish Society." *East European Jewish Affairs* 52, no. 2/3 (forthcoming).
———. "*Handelsvolk*: Marx's Definition of the Jews as a Trading-People and Its Implications," *Critique: Journal of Socialist Theory* 96 (forthcoming).
———. "Marxism and Zionism." in *Routledge Handbook on Zionism*, edited by Colin Shindler. London: Routledge (forthcoming).
———. *Marxist Interpretations of Jewish History*. Jerusalem: Zalman Shazar Center, 2023 [Hebrew].
———. "News from Auschwitz: The International Underground's Secret Reports and the Jewish Holocaust." *Yad Vashem Studies* 51, no. 1 (2023): 53–87.
———. "'The Jew Is to Be Burned': A Turning Point in the Communist Approach to the Jewish Question on the Eve of Catastrophe." *Jewish History* 34 (2021): 331–59.
Nedava, Joseph. *Trotsky and the Jews*. Philadelphia, PA: Jewish Publication Society of America, 1971.
Niemann, Mario, and Andreas Herbst, eds. *SED-Kader: die mittlere Ebene: biographisches Lexikon*. Paderborn/Munich/Vienna/Zürich: Schöningh, 2010.
Orbach, William. "A Periodization of Soviet Policy towards the Jews." *Soviet Jewish Affairs* 12, no. 3 (1982): 45–62.
Patka, Marcus G. *Egon Erwin Kisch. Stationen im Leben eines streitbaren Autors*. Vienna: Böhlau, 1997.
Peglau, Andreas. "Die Marxistische Arbeiterschule MASCH." *Anregungen zum (selbst)bewussten Leben*, https://andreas-peglau-psychoanalyse.de/die-marxistische-arbeiterschule-masch/ (retrieved on April 19, 2021).
Peled, Yoav. *Class and Ethnicity in the Pale*. London: Palgrave Macmillan, 1989.
Penslar, Derek J. *Shylock's Children: Economics and Jewish Identity in Modern Europe*. Berkeley, Los Angeles, London: University of California Press, 2001.

Pickhan, Gertrud. *"Gegen den Strom": Der Allgemeine Jüdische Arbeiterbund "Bund" in Polen 1918–1939* (Schriften des Simon-Dubnow-Instituts Leipzig, 1). Stuttgart, Munich: Deutsche Verlags-Anstalt, 2001.
Pinkus, Benjamin. *The Jews of the Soviet Union: The History of a National Minority.* Cambridge, UK: Cambridge University Press, 1988.
Podewin, Norbert. *Der Rabbinersohn im Politbüro: Albert Norden—Stationen eines ungewöhnlichen Lebens.* Berlin: Edition Ost, 2001.
Pohl, Dieter, and Frank Bajohr. *Der Holocaust als offenes Geheimnis: Die Deutschen, die NS-Führung und die Alliierten.* Munich: C. H. Beck, 2006.
Poznanski, Renée. "Jewish Communists in France During World War II: Resistance and Identity." In *Jewish Histories of the Holocaust: New Transnational Approaches*, edited by Omer Bartov and Norman J. W. Goda. New York, Oxford, UK: Berghahn Books, 2014, 209–23.
———. "On Jews, Frenchmen, Communists, and the Second World War." In *Dark Times, Dire Decisions: Jews and Communism*, edited by Jonathan Frankel and Dan Diner. Studies in Contemporary Jewry, vol. 20. New York: Oxford University Press, 2004, 168–98.
Rapoport, Louis. *Stalin's War against the Jews: The Doctors' Plot and the Soviet Solution.* New York: Free Press, 1990.
Redlich, Shimon. *Propaganda and Nationalism in Wartime Russia: The Jewish Antifascist Committee in the USSR, 1941–1948.* Boulder, CO: East European Quarterly, 1982.
Reitter, Paul. *The Anti-Journalist: Karl Kraus and Jewish Self-Fashioning in Fin-de-siècle Europe.* Chicago, IL: University of Chicago Press, 2008.
Rovner, Adam. "Promised Lands: Alfred Döblin as a Territorialist Ideologue." *Maarav*, spring 2012, http://maarav.org.il/english/2012/04/29/promised-lands-alfred-doblin-as-a-territorialist-ideologue-adam-rovner/.
Rozenblit, Marsha. *Reconstructing a National Identity: The Jews of Habsburg Austria during World War I.* Oxford, UK: Oxford University Press, 2001.
———. *The Jews of Vienna, 1867–1914: Assimilation and Identity.* Albany: SUNY Press, 1983.
Rubinstein, W. D. *The Left, the Right, and the Jews.* New York: Universe Books, 1982.
Rubovitch, Yuval. "Austro-Marxism: Socialism Discovers Nationalism." In *Vienna 1900: Blooming on the Edge of an Abyss*, edited by Sharon Gordon and Rina Peled. Jerusalem: Carmel, 2019, 65–100 [Hebrew].
Rürup, Reinhard. *Emanzipation und Antisemitismus: Studien zur "Judenfrage" der bürgerlichen Gesellschaft.* Frankfurt am Main Fischer Taschenbuch, 1975.
Ryan, James G. *Earl Browder: The Failure of American Communism.* Tuscaloosa and London: University of Alabama Press, 1997.
Rybak, Jan. "Marxismus, jüdischer Nationalismus und Zionismus: Historische Analyse eines angespannten Verhältnisses." *Chilufim* 20 (2016): 3–32.

Sagi, Avi. *To Be a Jew: Joseph Chayim Brenner as a Jewish Existentialist*. Translated by Batya Stein. London and New York: Continuum, 2011.
Sartre, JeanPaul. *Anti-Semite and Jew*. Translated by George J. Becker. New York: Schocken, (1944) 1976.
Schatz, Jaff. *The Generation: The Rise and Fall of the Jewish Communists of Poland*. Berkeley: University of California Press, 1991.
Schlenstedt, Dietrich. "Auf der Suche nach den Gründen der Barbarei: Wolfgang Heise auf der Berliner Historiker-Konferenz 1961." In *Nachkriegsliteratur als öffentliche Erinnerung: Deutsche Vergangenheit im europäischen Kontext*, edited by Helmut Peitsch. Berlin/Boston: De Gruyter, 2018: 170–98.
Schlenstedt, Silvia. "Versteckte Unglücke und Freisetzten von Erinnerung Zeichen des Selbstverstädnisses sozialistischer Autoren jüdischer Herkunft in der deutschen Literatur nach 1945." In *The Jewish Self-portrait in European and American Literature*, edited by Hans-Jürgen Schrader, Elliott M. Simon, and Charlotte Wardi. Berlin: De Gruyter, 1996, 171–86.
Schiller, Dieter, Karlheinz Pech, Regine Herrmann, and Manfred Hahn. *Exil in Frankreich* (Kunst und Literatur im antifaschistischen Exil 1933–1945, in Sieben Bände, vol. 7). Leipzig: Reclam, 1981.
Schorske, Carl E. *Fin-de-Siècle Vienna: Politics and Culture*. New York: Alfred A. Knopf: 1979.
Schulz, Susanne. "Malik-Verlag." In *Lexikon sozialistischer Literatur: Ihre Geschichte in Deutschland bis 1945*, edited by Simone Barck and Reinhard Hillich. Stuttgart/Weimar: Metzler, 1994, 311–14.
Schwager, Ernst. *Die österreichische Emigration in Frankreich 1938–1945*. Vienna, Cologne, Graz: Böhlaus, 1984.
———."Österreichische Wissenschaftler in Frankreich." In *Vertriebene Vernunft II: Emigration und Exil österreichischer Wissenschaft 1930–1940*, vol. 2, edited by Friedrich Stadler. Münster: LIT, 2004, 946–51.
Segel, Harold B. "Introduction." In *Egon Erwin Kisch, the Raging Reporter: A Bio-Anthology*. West Lafayette, IN: Purdue University Press, 1997.
Semlitsch, Katharina. *"Mais combien sont restés en route . . ." / "Doch wie viele sind auf der Strecke geblieben . . .": Österreichische Schriftstellerinnen und Schriftsteller im französischen Exil (1933–1945), rezipiert in der Zeitschrift Austriaca*. Universität Wien, MA thesis, 2009.
Shindler, Colin. *Israel and the European Left: Between Solidarity and Delegitimization*. New York: Continuum, 2012.
Silberner, Edmund. *Kommunisten zur Judenfrage: Zur Geschichte von Theorie und Praxis des Kommunismus*. Opladen: Westdeutscher Verlag, 1983.
———. *The Anti-Semitic Tradition in Modern Socialism*. Jerusalem: Hebrew University, 1953.
Şirolnikov, Shlomo. *Ha-Dialeqtiqa shel Mahapekhat Yisra'el*. Tel Aviv: Cheriqover, 1982 [Hebrew].

Slezkine, Yuri. *The Jewish Century*. Princeton, NJ: Princeton University Press, 2019².
Smith, Anthony D. *The Nation in History: Historiographical Debates about Ethnicity and Nationalism*. Cambridge, UK: Polity Press, 2000.
Spiegel, Tilly. *Österreicher in der belgischen und französischen Resistance*. Vienna: Europa Verlag, 1969.
Stadler, Franz, ed. *Robert Neumann: Mit eigener Feder. Aufsätze. Briefe. Nachlassmaterialien*. Innsbruck, Vienna, Bozen: Studien Verlag, 2013.
Staudacher, Anna L. *". . . meldet den Austritt aus dem mosaischen Glauben." 18000 Austritte aus dem Judentum in Wien, 1868–1914: Namen—Quellen—Daten*. Vienna: Lang, 2009.
Stein, Harry. "Buchenwald—Stammlager." In *Der Ort des Terrors, Bd. 3: Sachsenhausen, Buchenwald*. Munich: C. H. Beck, 2006.
Suda, Zdenek. *Zealots and Rebels: A History of the Ruling Communist Party of Czechoslovakia*. Stanford, CA: Hoover, 1980.
Sugarman, Martin. *Against Fascism: Jews who Served in the International Brigade in the Spanish Civil War*, https://www.jewishvirtuallibrary.org/jews-who-served-in-the-international-brigade-in-the-spanish-civil-war.
Surmann, Rolf. *Die Münzenberg-Legende: Zur Publizistik der Revolutionären Arbeiterbewegung 1921–33*. Cologne: Prometh, 1983.
Sutcliffe, Adam. *What Are Jews For? History, Peoplehood, and Purpose*. Princeton, NJ: Princeton University Press, 2020.
Świebocki, Henryk. *Auschwitz 1940–1945: Central Issues in the History of the Camp. Vol. IV: The Resistance Movement*, edited by Wacław Długoborski and Franciszek Piper. Translated by William Brand. Oświęcim: Auschwitz-Birkenau State Museum, 2000.
———. *London Has Been Informed . . . : Reports by Auschwitz Escapees*. Translated by Michael Jacobs and Laurence Weinbaum. Oświęcim: Auschwitz-Birkenau State Museum, 1997.
Tarquini, Alessandra, ed. *The European Left and the Jewish Question, 1848–1992: Between Zionism and Antisemitism*. Cham: Palgrave Macmillan, 2021.
Tischler, Carola. *Flucht in die Verfolgung: Deutsche Emigranten im sowjetischen Exil—1933 bis 1945*. Münster: LIT, 1996.
Toury, Jacob. "The Jewish Question: A Semantic Approach." *Leo Baeck Institute Yearbook* 11 (1966): 85–106.
Traverso, Enzo. *The Jewish Question: History of a Marxist Debate*. Translated by Bernard Gibbons. Leiden: Brill, 2018.
———. *The Marxists and the Jewish Question: The History of a Debate, 1843–1943*. Translated by Bernard Gibbons. Atlantic Highlands, NJ: Humanities Press, 1994.
Tobias, Henry. "The Reassessment of the National Question." In *Essential Papers on Jews and the Left*, edited by Ezra Mendelsohn. New York: New York University Press, 1997, 101–21.

Vaksberg, Arkady. *Stalin against the Jews.* Translated by Antonina W. Bouis. New York: Alfred A. Knopf, 1994.
Volkov, Shulamit. *Germans, Jews, and Antisemites: Trials in Emancipation.* Cambridge, UK: Cambridge University Press, 2006.
Wachsmann, Nikolaus. *KL: Die Geschichte der nationalsozialistischen Konzentrationslager.* Munich: Siedler, 2016.
Walden, Günter. *Ignoranten und Rassisten: Die Bedeutung des Antisemitismus für den Aufstieg der NSDAP in der Weimarer Republik.* Norderstedt: Books on Demand, 2020.
Waltzer, Michael. "The Strangeness of Jewish Leftism." In *Jews and Leftist Politics*, edited by Jack Jacobs. Cambridge, UK: Cambridge University Press, 2017, 29–39.
Weber, Hermann. *Die Wandlung des deutschen Kommunismus: Die Stalinisierung der KPD in der Weimarer Republik.* Frankfurt a.M.: Europäische Verlagsanst, 1971.
———. "The Stalinization of the KPD: Old and New Views." In *Bolshevism, Stalinism and the Comintern: Perspectives on Stalinization, 1917–53*, edited by Norman LaPorte, Kevin Morgan, and Matthew Worley. New York: Palgrave Macmillan, 2008, 22–44.
Weinberg, David H. *A Community on Trial: The Jews of Paris in the 1930s.* Chicago, IL: University of Chicago Press, 1977.
Weinberg, Robert. *Stalin's Forgotten Zion: Birobidzhan and the Making of a Soviet Jewish Homeland.* Berkeley: University of California Press, 1998.
Weinert, Willi. "1938–1945." In *Die Kommunistische Partei Österreich: Beiträge zu ihrer Geschichte und Politik.* Vienna: Globus, 1987, 267–327.
———. "Aus dem Archiv: Otto Heller." *Alfred Klahr Gesellschaft Mitteilungen* 1 (March 1998): 7–8.
Weinstock, Nathan. "Introduction." In Abram Leon, *The Jewish Question: A Marxist Interpretation*, New York: Pathfinder, 1970, 27–63.
Weisberger, Adam M. *The Jewish Ethic and the Spirit of Socialism.* New York: Peter Lang, 1997.
Weiss, Johannes. *Weber and the Marxist World.* Translated by Elizabeth King-Utz and Michael J. King. London and New York: Routledge and Kegan Paul, 1986.
Whiteside, Andrew G. *The Socialism of Fools: Georg Ritter von Schoenerer and Austrian Pan-Germanism.* Berkeley: University of California Press, 1975.
Wilde, Florian. "Ernst Meyer (1887–1930)—vergessene Führungsfigur des deutschen Kommunismus: Eine politische Biographie." Diss., University of Hamburg, 2013.
Wistrich, Robert S. *From Ambivalence to Betrayal: The Left, the Jews, and Israel.* Lincoln: University of Nebraska Press, 2012.
———. *Revolutionary Jews from Marx to Trotsky.* London: Harrap, 1976.
———. *Socialism and the Jews: The Dilemmas of Assimilation in Germany and Austria-Hungary.* Rutherford, NJ: Fairleigh Dickinson University Press, 1982.

Zaagsma, Gerben. *Jewish Volunteers, the International Brigades and the Spanish Civil War*. London: Bloomsbury, 2017.
Zeltser, Arkadi. "Dimanshtein, Semen Markovich." *The YIVO Encyclopedia for Jews in Eastern Europe*, https://yivoencyclopedia.org/article.aspx/Dimanshtein_Semen_Markovich (accessed on June 15, 2021).
Zimmermann, Moshe. "Juden jugendbewegt." In *Aufbruch der Jugend: Deutsche Jugendbewegung zwischen Selbstbestimmung und Verführung*. Nuremberg: Germanischen Nationalmuseums, 2013, 107–12.
Zinner, Paul E. *Communist Strategy and Tactics in Czechoslovakia, 1918–1948*. London and Dunmow: Pall Mall, 1963.

Index

acculturation, 10, 28–29, 67, 189
Adler, Friedrich (Fritz), 35
Adler, Max, 36, 75
Adler, Victor, 30, 32, 35
Aid to Concentration Camp Prisoners (Pomoc Więźniów Obozów Koncentracyjnych [PWOK]), 171, 175, 248n120
All-Soviet Communist Party, *see under* Bolshevism
Almog, Shmu'el, 4, 92–94, 193
Alpári, Gyula (Julius), 43, 114
America, 14, 165
Améry, Jean, 13–14
Amsterdam, 99–102, 106, 108, 152
anarchism, 52, 151
Annenkova, Julia, 110, 113–115
Anschluss, 122, 157, 172
antifascism, 109, 117
antiquity, 86–90, 93, 122, 132–136
antisemitism, 12, 15–16, 18, 24, 71, 111, 131–132, 135, 137–141, 147–150, 168, 190, 193, 195; fascist, 104, 122; in Austria-Hungary, 29–34; in Eastern Europe, 122, 131, 172, 190; in France, 140, 144, 151, 167; in (pre-Nazi) Germany, 8, 75, 131, 134, 139; in the Soviet Union, 6, 62, 116, 189–190, 194; KPD and, 54–55, 81–82; leftist, 7, 9, 18, 202n71; Nazi, 76, 83–84, 103, 108, 126–129, 134, 139–141, 146; "socialism of the fools," 31–32; socialist attitudes toward, 17–19, 57, 76, 83, 126, 129, 138, 140, 143, 167, 169, 192, 239n115, 239n123; Zionist conceptions of, 140, 147, 239n117. *See also* capitalism; racism
Arabs, 80, 85, 142, 190, 193
army: Austrian, 37–38; Austro-Hungarian, 34, 37, 207n63; Red Army, 38, 154, 173, 178; Wehrmacht, 158, 165–166
Aronstein, Fritz, 75
Askonas (née Heller), Joanna Hanni (sister), 29, 161
Askonas, Rudi (brother in-low), 138, 154, 158
assimilation, 2–3, 6–7, 12, 17, 29, 32, 36, 44, 64, 72–73, 90–91, 94, 101, 104–105, 151, 190; complete, 1, 4, 18, 30, 72, 75, 146–147; paradigm of, 57–58, 76; radical, 1–2, 9–10, 22, 97, 189, 196; red, 75, 140–143
Association of friends of the Soviet Union (Bund der Freunde der Sowjetunion), 98
Auschwitz, xi–xii, 1–2, 5, 11, 22, 24, 89, 118, 156, 162, 165, 167–186,

Auschwitz *(continued)*
  195, 198n11, 248n113, 250n138,
  251n163. *See also* Birkenau
Auschwitz Fighting Group
  (Kampfengruppe Auschwitz
  [KGA]), 169–173, 177, 184, 248n115
Aussig (Ústí nad Labem), 41
Austria, xv, 1–2, 25, 27, 37–42, 46,
  54–55, 75–78, 98, 101, 109–110,
  114, 118, 122, 125, 137, 156–165,
  170, 172, 174, 176, 185–186, 192,
  195, 207n63, 226n2; Austrian
  Freedom Front (Österreichische
  Freiheitsfront), 164; Austrian
  National Front (Front National
  Autriche), 164; Austrian workers-
  councils movement, 37
Austria-Hungary, 30–37, 67
autonomism, 16–17, 33, 148. *See also*
  national autonomy

B'nai B'rith, 76
Baeck, Leo, 104
Balfour Declaration, 35
Balkan Korrespondenz, 118–122
Bankier, David, 127–128
Baruch, Joseph, 102
Bauer, Alfredo, 8
Bauer, Otto, 32, 76
Baum, Bruno, 25, 171–177, 183,
  249n122, 251n163
Baum, Herbert, 5
BBC, 177–178, 249n138
Bebel, August, 19, 31, 239n115
Becher, Johaness, 108–109, 115
Beer-Hofmann, Richard, 104
Belguim, 89, 98, 135, 143, 165, 176, 180
Benjamin, Walter, 77, 94
Berghahn, Volker, 24
Berlin, xii, xiv, 2–3, 21, 26, 47–54,
  65–67, 78, 80, 98–99, 102–103, 106,
  117, 139, 152, 157, 167, 173, 178

Berlin am Morgen (Berlin in the
  Morning), 54, 215n226
Birefeld, 64
Birkenau (Brzerzinka), 168, 170,
  179–180
Birobidzhan, 2, 4, 7, 17, 21, 55–56,
  59–60, 63–67, 72–75, 88, 90, 93,
  95, 98, 100–102, 105, 116, 142–143,
  151, 158, 190, 216n237, 226n163
Blum, Klara, 147–148
Blum, Léon, 151
Bohemia, 28, 30, 39–43, 66, 97,
  204n6
Bolshevism, 12, 18–19, 33,
  35, 38, 47–49, 57, 113; All-
  Soviet Communist Party
  (Bolsheviks) (Vsesoyuznaya
  kommunisticheskaya partiya
  [bol'shevikov], [VKP(b)]), 58, 112,
  114–115. *See also* revolution
Bonn, 70
Borokhov, Ber, 74, 140
Bosques, Gilberto, 159
bourgeoisie, 19, 29, 34, 47, 72,
  103–105, 121, 137, 146, 225n160;
  bourgeois habits, 52, 65, 111, 118;
  bourgeois origins, 31, 36, 39, 55,
  97, 116; haute, 28, 79, 127, 138;
  Jewish, 7, 29, 42, 66, 82, 101, 104,
  148, 189, 191; Jews and, 18, 81,
  133–135; nationalism and, 32, 40,
  42; petite, 30, 61, 79, 84, 126, 138,
  157; Zionism and, 64, 142. *See also*
  middle-class
Brandenburg, 48, 50, 109
Brandler, Heinrich, 49, 51
Bratislava, 69
Braun, Leybek, 1–2
Braunthal, Julius, 38
Brebant, 163
Breitscheid, Rudolf, 177–178
Brenner, Yosef Chayim, 13

Britain, 10, 35, 72, 115, 142, 153, 156, 173, 177–178, 192
Brunet, Raymond (Pseudonym of Otto Heller), 165
Brussels, 89
Buber, Martin, 32, 104
Bubnik, Joseph, 44
Buchara, 62
Buchenwald, 177–180
Bulgaria, 176
Bund, 33, 59, 91–92, 142, 148, 150–151
Bunzl, John, 8, 83

capitalism, 129, 132, 154; antisemitism and, 31, 82, 84, 104, 126; Jews and, 18, 24, 72, 90, 111, 128, 132–138, 148, 190, 192; pre-, 71, 87, 133; Zionism and, 142
Cárdenes, Lázaro, 159
Carlebach, Julius, 7
Case, Holly, 15
caste, 18, 62, 71, 76, 84, 87, 89, 93, 128, 133, 135–136, 173
Caucasus, 60
Central Asia, 60–63
Central Association of German Citizens of Jewish Faith (Centralverein deutscher Staatsbürger jüdischen Glaubens [CV]), 74–81, 85, 128
Cercle Culturel Autrichien (Austrian Cultural Circle), 118
Chernivtsi, 76
Chmelnicky, Bogdan, 60, 214n192
Choritza, 61
Christianity, 10, 14, 29, 131, 140, 146–147; Catholicism, 30, 32, 67; Protestantism, 132
Cold War, 15, 17, 195
Collonges au Mont d'Or, 165–166
colonialism, 64

Comintern (Communist International), 19, 23, 31, 39, 42–44, 46, 48–49, 51, 56, 65, 80, 94, 106–107, 109–110, 113, 116–117, 119, 147, 150, 154, 157, 202n79; Executive Committee of the Communist International (ECCI), 46, 56–57, 80
Communist Party of Austria (Kommunistische Partei Österreichs [KPÖ]), 38, 115–118, 120, 122, 125, 128, 163, 165, 172
Communist Party of Czechoslovakia (Komunistická Strana Československa [KSČ]), 42–44, 50, 115, 120, 128, 168, 211n146; German section, 42–44
Communist Party of France (Parti Communiste Français [PCF]), xiii, 150, 161
Communist Party of Germany (Kommunistische Partei Deutschlands [KPD]), 7–8, 25, 48–50, 54–56, 65, 67, 77–84, 94, 97, 107–110, 114–116, 120, 124–127, 148, 153, 171–172, 178, 190, 192–193; Central Committee (Zentralkomitee [ZK]) of, 51, 82–85
Communist Party of Italy, 107
Communist Party of Palestine, 193
Communist Party of Switzerland, 102
Communist Party of the United States, 193
communist university for national minorities (KUNMS), 112
Communist Youth International, 43, 47
Communist Youth Union (in Czechoslovakia), 43

conciliators (Versöhnler), 49–51, 106–108, 113–115, 120, 163, 211n145
conversion, 10, 30–31, 147
crematorium, 149, 168, 170, 178, 180, 184, 186
Crimea, 58–61
Crossman, Richard, 153
Cyrankiewicz, Józef, 170–178, 183, 185
Czech (people/language), 30, 35, 40–43, 46, 97, 122, 168, 170, 203n1, 204n6, 211n146
Czechoslovakia, 2, 21, 39–47, 49, 66, 69, 97–99, 110, 114, 117, 157

Dachau, 162–163
Danzig (Gdańsk), 147
Decline of Judaism (*Der Untergang des Judentums*), xi, 1–2, 21, 27, 97–99, 104, 150–152, 156, 167–169, 190–195; contemporary reception of, 69–71, 74–92, 101, 126, 128; content of, 4, 19, 59–62, 71–72, 79, 86–87, 93, 101, 105, 116, 125, 127, 129–143; scholarly reception of, 4–9, 70, 92–94, 237n73; title of, 4–5, 15, 27, 72–74, 146–147, 198n11, 218n15; translations of, 70, 102–104, 111–112, 122; writing and publication of, 19, 55–56, 65, 67, 80–81. *See also* "Jew Is to Be Burned"
Death March, 1–2, 5, 9, 22, 155, 185, 195
decolonization, 57
de-Judaization, 45–55, 65, 67, 190
Delft, 102
democracy, 31, 38, 48, 79, 89, 117, 135, 161, 183
Denikin, Anton, 60, 214n192
Der Soldat am Mittelmeer (The Soldier in the Mediterranean), 164

Der Soldat am Westen (The Soldier in the West), 164–165
Deuteronomy, 136
Deutsch, Julius, 37
Deutsche Zentral Zeitung ([DZZ], Central German Newspaper), 110–115, 147
Deutschen Ausrüstungswerke (DAW), 172, 248n113
Deutscher, Isaac, 10–13, 191
Diaspora, 89, 136, 140
Diaspora Nationalism, *see under* nationalism
"dictatorship of the proletariat," 41, 53, 152
Die rote Fahne (The Red Flags [Berlin]), 78, 80, 84
Die rote Fahne (The Red Flags [Vienna]), 51
Die Welt am Abend (The World in the Evening), 47, 50–51, 54, 211n145
Dimanshtein, Shimon, 101, 116
Diner, Dan, 180, 253n22
Döblin, Alfred, 25, 105–108, 229n63
Documentation Centre of Austrian Resistance (Dokumentationsarchiv des österreichischen Widerstandes, [DÖW]), 22, 125
dogmatism, 8–9, 70, 77, 92, 144, 150, 153
Dolfuss, Engelbert, 109
Drancy, 165, 167
Dubnov, Simon, 148, 150, 158–159

Ebensee, 185–186, 198n11, 252n180
Eisler, Gerhart, 49, 54
emancipation, 15–16, 31, 53, 91, 140, 146, 239n117
Endelman, Todd, 10
Engels, Friedrich, 18–19, 41, 75, 79, 225n160, 236n34

English (language), 16, 92, 158, 160
ethnicity, 15, 43–44, 57, 71, 87
Europäische Stimme (European Voice), 118
Europe, 1, 3, 6, 11–13, 15–16, 21–22, 29, 53–54, 65, 69–70, 89, 98, 103, 122, 124, 127–128, 140, 148, 160, 168, 175, 179, 189, 192, 195; Central, 14, 16, 24, 27, 33, 101, 111, 131, 150, 155, 189–190; East-Central 40, 42; Eastern, 7, 13–16, 33, 52, 72, 79, 84, 93–94, 122, 131, 137, 144, 148, 150, 190; northwestern, 132; Southern, 84; Western, 7, 13–14, 32, 57, 64, 72, 88, 100, 133, 146
Evsektsiia, 58–60, 94, 101
Ewert, Arther, 49
Executive Committee of the Communist International (ECCI), *see under* Comintern
existentialism, 12–13, 191, 195

federalism, 30, 40
Feuchtwanger, Lion, 25, 99, 104–105, 163
feudalism, 72, 89, 138
"Final Solution," 16, 24, 148, 167, 179
First World War, 29, 34, 36, 39, 66, 114, 122, 129
Fischer, Ernst, 192
Fischer, Ruth, 48, 51, 54
fractions politics (Fraktionspolitik), 48–50, 84, 113, 118, 190
France, xii, 2, 9, 23, 36, 97–98, 102, 110, 115, 117, 119–120, 125, 135, 140, 150–151, 156–167, 169–170, 172, 176, 180, 186, 193
Franco, Francisco, 117
Frankfurt School, 73, 76, 99
Franz Josef, 30

Frei, Bruno, 25, 54, 76, 78, 99, 159, 164, 189
French, 36, 64, 69, 102–103, 111, 118, 122, 135, 143, 161, 164–165, 172
French Resistance, xii, 22
French Revolution, *see under* revolution
Frenzel, Max, 50
Fresnes, 165–166
Freud, Sigmund, 11, 30, 34
Freundlich, Elisabeth, 25, 118–119, 152, 156, 158–161
Frey, Josef, 38
Friedland (Frýdlant), 44
Friedländer, Paul, 51
Friedländer, Saul, 156, 191
Fromm, Erich, 73, 77, 85
Frost, Robert, 194
Fürnberg, Siegfried (Friedel), 25, 43, 120, 128, 137

Galicia, 28, 31, 36
Gallacher, William, 192
Gdud ha-Avoda, 61
Gebirtig, Mordechai, 148
Geisel, Eike, 5
Gelsenkirchen, 99
Georgia, 61–62
German (language), xi, 1, 4, 15, 18, 25, 36, 40, 42, 48, 52–53, 59, 61, 64–65, 69–70, 73, 76, 92, 94, 99, 103, 107–110, 112, 117–120, 126, 128, 135, 147, 159, 168, 192, 204n6, 211n146, 249n122, 249n125
German Democratic Republic (GDR or East Germany), 46, 81, 194
German Jews, 31, 73–75, 84, 94, 97, 100–105, 122, 141, 147–148, 185, 189, 191
German nationalism, *see under* nationalism

German People's Broadcast (Deutscher Volksender), 164
German Socialist Workers Party of Czechoslovakia (Deutsche sozialdemokratische Arbeiterpartei der Tschechoslowakei), 40–42
German-Soviet pact, 139, 153–156, 191
Germanic tribes, 89, 136
Germany, xii, 2, 5–8, 21, 24, 47–56, 75–76, 79, 83–89, 97–105, 109–110, 112, 114, 116, 122, 126–129, 131–132, 137–139, 146–147, 151, 156–159, 162, 164, 167, 170–171, 174, 176–178, 186, 191; Wiemar Republic, 8, 21, 47–48, 66, 83, 126. *See also* Nazi Germany; Third Reich
Geserd (Gesellschaft zur Förderung des jüdischen Siedlungswerkes in der UdSSR, Association for Supporting the Jewish Settlements in the Soviet Union), 65, 78, 85, 100–102, 105, 112, 221n72
Gessen, Masha, 63
Gestapo, 51, 89, 102, 116, 165–167, 186
Gif sur Yvette, xii–xiii
Goldelman, Shalom, 74, 219n44
Gordon, Aharon David, 8
Gottwald, Klement, 114
GPU (Soviet secret police), 52
Great Purge, *see under* purges
Great Terror, *see under* purges
Greeks, 87, 176
Gromyko, Andrei, 194
Gross, Babette, 25, 51
Grynszpan, Herschel, 122
Gutman, Yisra'el, 1–2, 5, 9, 20, 156, 184, 195
gymnasium, 29, 33–34

Haász, Árpád (Albert Haas), 25, 118, 158, 161, 169, 171–175, 183

Habsburg, 29, 33, 40, 47
Haffner, Sebastian, 114
Hais, Josef, 44, 209n110
Hannover, 122
Harari, Yeḥi'el, 69
Hashomer Hatzair, 1, 69, 89
Haury, Thomas, 7, 84
Hebrew, 13, 61, 70, 92, 169
Hebrew Communists, 92, 193
Heine, Heinrich, 11
Hellenism, 89
Heller (née Krause), Emma (wife), xii–xiii, 22–23, 25, 35, 39, 44–48, 98–99, 109, 112, 115, 117–119, 124–125, 156, 158–159, 161, 165–167, 185–186
Heller (née Löwy), Marie (mother), 28, 37, 42, 54, 165
Heller, Lily (daughter), *see* Papineau, Lily
Heller, Ernst (brother), xiv, 28–29
Heller, Franz (father), 28, 31–32, 34, 39, 42, 66
Heller, Karl (brother), 29, 161
Heartfeild, John, 115
Herf, Jeffrey, 127, 193
Herzfelde, Wiland, 115, 124–125
Herzl, Theodor, 16, 30–31, 67, 140–141, 147–148
Hess, Moses, 4, 191
Hileli, Mordekhai, 186, 252n180
historiography, 5, 12, 20, 125; Jewish, 7, 74, 91, 134, 218n19, 236n42
Hitler, Adolf, 6, 16, 20, 33, 49, 74, 99, 103, 116, 139, 146–147, 153–157, 168, 173, 176, 178, 180, 190
Hitler-Stalin pact, *see* German-Soviet pact
Holocaust, 1–3, 5–6, 11–12, 22, 135, 169, 175, 183–184, 193, 195–196
Hołuj, Tadeusz, 174

Home Army (Armia Krajowa), 171
Horkheimer, Max, 76, 239n123
Höss, Rudolf, 179–180
Humbert-Droz, Jules, 107, 115
Humm, Rudolf, 107
Hungary, xi, 40, 43, 70, 114, 118, 122, 137, 172, 176, 179–180

ideology, 6, 32, 48, 58–59, 61, 74–75, 77, 91, 93, 100, 120, 127, 148
I. G. Farben, 174
imperialism, 44, 59, 72, 142
India, 71, 133
industry, 13, 30, 41–42, 54, 61, 88, 138–139, 179, 248n113
Information, 106, 108
integration, 1, 10, 28–29, 53, 133, 147
intellectuals, xi, 1, 3, 5, 8, 10, 12, 24, 47, 64, 67, 76–77, 89–91, 98, 101, 108, 111, 113, 117, 124, 134, 153, 155, 158, 165, 189; anti-intellectualism, 41, 55, 67, 157, 208n91
International Brigades, 117–118, 151, 159, 161, 165
International Workers Aid (Internationale Arbeiterhilfe, IAH), 47, 99
Internationale Pressekorrespondenz (International Press Correspondence, Inprekor), 48, 54
Internationale Rote Hilfe (International Red Aid [formerly IAH]), 99, 110, 118
internationalism, 33, 41–42, 57
Irkutsk, 66
Isonzo, 35
Israel, xi, 1, 4–7, 13–15, 17, 26, 69–70, 74, 92–93, 104–105, 194–195; Land of, 17, 193. *See also* Palestine
Israelites, 87, 133, 136
Italy, 34, 37, 99, 105, 107, 122, 176

Jaurès, Jean, 137
Jergitsch, Lily, 25, 112–113, 116, 119, 152
Jerusalem, 4, 59, 88–89, 146, 191
"Jew Is to Be Burned" ("Der Jude wird verbrannt"), xii, 9, 21, 115, 123–154, 194–195; and *The Decline of Judaism*, 131–144, 146–147, 150, 156, 167, 190–191, 218n15; content of, 103–104, 108, 111, 116, 129–151, 192; scholarly reception of, xii, 125; title of, 15, 123, 125, 130, 144–148; writing of, 98, 122–123, 153
Jewish Anti-Fascist Committee, 193
Jewishness, 4, 10, 16, 21, 55, 67, 75, 162, 169, 172, 184, 190
Judaism, 10, 15, 27, 32, 44, 71–76, 78–79, 83, 89, 93–95, 131, 133, 136–137, 147, 195
Jüdische Rundschau, 79, 148
Jungbunzlau (Mladá Boleslav), 28

Kalinin, Michail, 61; Kalinindorf, 61
Kantorowicz, Alfred, 82, 117
Karlsbad (Karlovy Vary), 98
Kats, Moyshe, 25, 88–91, 93, 135, 143
Kautsky, Karl, 7, 18, 71, 76, 236n34
Kern, Rudolf (pseudonym of Otto Heller), 112
Kersten, Kurt, 47
Kessler, Mario, 8, 83–84
KGA, *see* Auschwitz Fighting Group
Kiev, 52
Kirov, Sergei, 113
Kisch, Egon Erwin, 25, 47, 60, 97, 99, 117, 120, 159, 226n2
Kistenmacher, Olaf, 7, 82, 84, 93
Klahr, Alfred, 171–173, 175, 179, 183–184
Klatzkin, Jakob, 73

Koestler, Arthur, 25, 27, 33, 53, 55, 57, 61, 115, 117, 120, 152–153, 155, 162
Koplenig, Johann, 114
KPD, see Communist Party of Germany
KPÖ, see Communist Party of Austria
Kraków, 171, 173, 178
Kraus, Karl, 119, 233n148
Kreibich, Karl, 43, 46
Kristallnacht, see under pogroms
Kronawetter, Ferdinand, 31
Krosno, 180
Kun, Béla, 43, 114

La Vernet, 162–163
Langbein, Hermann, 170
Langlade, 158
Laqueur, Walter, 6
Lederer, Viktor, 168–169, 174–175, 249n122
Leftwich, Joseph, 151
Lenin, Vladimir, 7, 19, 26, 33, 41, 43, 48, 58–60, 76, 79, 90, 101, 113, 168
Leon, Abram, 16, 25, 89–93, 135, 143
Leopoldstadt, 28, 31
Les Milles, 163–164
Leshchinsky, Yakov, 89, 224n139
Lessing, Gotthold Ephraim, 146–148
liberalism, 14, 17, 20, 29–31, 34–36, 39, 66–67, 70, 74, 76, 137, 162, 217n6
Lille, 165
Linfield, Susie, 6
Lithuania, 33, 137
Lueger, Karl, 29–33, 67
Luxemburg, Rosa, 11, 129, 236n34
Lyon, 165

Madrid, 116–117; Radio, 117
Mahler, Raphael, 25, 36, 88–93

Malik Verlag, 123–124
Manchuria, 66
Mann, Heinrich, 159
Marchwitza, Hans, 99, 159
Marek, Franz, 165
Mark, Ber, 169, 172, 195
Marseille, 159, 163–164
Martin, Terry, 57
Marx, Karl, 11, 13–14, 17–18, 35, 41, 75, 79, 86–90, 133–135, 137, 200n48, 202n71, 225n160, 237n62
Marxism, 8, 10, 13, 18, 24, 26, 36–37, 65, 70–71, 75–77, 79, 105, 122, 126, 192; and Jews, 3–4, 9, 18–20, 31, 57–58, 74, 83, 86–93, 126, 128–134, 138–141, 167, 193; Austro-, 30, 32–33, 40; heterodox, 140, 143, 153; orthodox, 18–19, 70, 77, 90–91, 94, 138, 140, 194
materialism, 16, 30, 36, 71, 74–75, 77, 87–89, 138, 147
Matzot, 65
Medem, Vladimir, 91
Mensheviks, 33, 49
Merker, Paul, 25, 193–194
Meslay-du-Maine, 156
Mexico, 159–160, 165, 193
Meyer, Ernst, 49, 211n145
Middle Ages, 19, 86, 88, 90, 131–133, 137–140, 146–147, 167
Middle East, 17, 70, 194
middle-class, 111, 140. See also petite bourgeoisie
minority, 15, 40, 42, 57, 60
Mishna, 136
modernism (theory of nationalism), 90, 224n142
modernity, 90, 131, 134
modernization, 15–16, 140
Moll, Otto, 178, 184
Montauban, 161
Moravia, 30

Moscow, 21, 23, 25, 42, 46, 48, 63, 94, 100, 102, 108, 110–120, 147, 152–153, 157, 163–164, 192; Radio, 178
Mosse, George, 6
Münzenberg, Willi, 25, 43, 47–48, 51–54, 65, 80, 114, 117, 120, 153, 210n127, 211n145, 215n226
Musil, Robert, 27
Muslims, 146

Na'aman, Shlomo, 5, 198n11
National-Socialist German Workers Party (Nationalsozialistische Deutsche Arbeiterpartei [NSDAP]), 54, 84, 127, 141. *See also* Nazi
national autonomy, 2, 4, 30, 40, 58, 66, 72, 88, 91, 151, 190. *See also* autonomism
nationalism, 30–35, 40, 46, 122, 142, 171–172, 183; Diasporic, 58, 64, 90–91, 104; German, 30–31, 41–42, 54–55, 66, 69, 98, 190; in the Soviet Union, 57–60, 94; Jewish, 2–3, 10, 14–19, 32, 58–61, 70–72, 74, 79, 83, 88–94, 105–106, 111, 135, 148, 169, 189, 191, 193–195; nationalization, 89, 150; patriotism, 34, 38, 41. *See also* autonomism; bourgeoisie; modernism; primordialism; territorialism; Zionism
Nazi: anti-, 158, 165; camps, xii, 1, 4, 6, 24, 100, 125, 149, 155, 162, 165, 167–186, 195; Germany, 2, 5, 21, 33, 97–98, 108, 114, 116, 120, 122, 134, 138–141, 146, 156, 164, 177; National-socialism (Nazism), 9, 55, 65, 76, 105, 109, 126, 130–131, 134, 169, 194, 196; Nazis, 8, 54, 81–82, 99, 109, 125–126, 139, 148, 157, 167, 173, 176, 178, 180, 192–193; rise to power, 15, 98, 100, 102, 104, 126, 141–142, 146, 190. *See also* Third Reich
Nazi antisemitism, *see under* antisemitism
Nazi Party, *see* National-Socialist German Workers Party
Netherlands, 98, 102, 108, 110, 176, 180
Neuilly sur Seine, 118
Neumann, Heinz, 115
Neumann, Robert, 55
neutralism, 91, 142–143
New York, 88, 124–125, 143, 161
Night of the Long Knives, 116
Nîmes, 158
non-Jewish Jew, 9–14, 22, 24–25, 27, 92, 94, 155, 172, 183, 189–191, 196
Norden, Albert, 25, 78–85, 127, 135, 138–140, 189, 239n110
Norwegians, 134, 176
Nouvelles d'Autriche (Austrian News), 118, 156
Nova Vojo, 61
November Pogrom, *see under* pogroms
Novosibirsk, 63

Oedipus complex, 30, 34, 36, 66
Ofner, Julius, 31
Ostjuden, 52, 100, 144
Oświęcim, 168
Ozet, 65, 100–102, 152

pacifism, 34
Palestine, 14, 17, 35, 59–61, 65, 70, 74, 76, 80, 87–90, 92, 100, 104–105, 111, 134, 141–142, 190, 193–194. *See also* Israel
Panner, Israel (I. Rennap), 192
Papineau (née Heller), Lily (daughter), xii–xiv, 25, 44, 99, 110, 117, 125, 156, 158–161, 165–168, 185

pariah, 132–135
Paris, xii–xiv, 21, 25, 101, 109, 116–127, 137, 147, 150, 152, 156–158, 164–165, 172, 185, 193; Commune, 137
Pasicznyk, Myron, 118
patriotism, *see under* nationalism
Periodical Reports, 24, 154, 171–185, 195–196, 248n120
Pernerstorfer, Engelbert, 31–32, 39
Petliura, Symon, 60, 214n192
philosemitism, 17, 30
philosophy, 12–13, 36, 158; of history, 7, 146
Pieck, Wilhelm, 114
plebian, 134–136
pogroms, 58, 60, 64, 80, 85, 103, 108; November Pogrom (*Kristallnacht*), 122, 127–128, 131, 146–147
Poland, 10, 33, 40, 86, 88–89, 122, 137, 148, 150, 153–154, 156, 169–180, 190
Polish (language), 24, 69, 111, 122, 175
Polish Socialist Party (Polska Partia Socjalistyczna [PPS]), 170–171
Popular Front, 109, 116–117, 150–151, 202n79
Portugal, 160
Pötsch, Walter, 128
Prague, 39–41, 44, 110
primordialism (theory of nationalism), 90, 224n142
productivization, 8, 58–59
progress, 62, 90, 116, 135, 137, 140, 174, 176
proletariat, 28, 38, 41–44, 50, 53, 55, 62, 70–71, 102, 127, 141, 190; Jewish, 7, 70, 75–77, 79, 82, 90, 111, 137–138, 148, 150, 190. *See also* "dictatorship of the proletariat"; revolution; working class

proletarianization, 75, 105, 137; de-, 15
proselytization, 89
Protection Association of German Writers (Schützverband deutscher Schriftsteller [SDS]), 99, 120
Protocols of the Elders of Zion, 131
Przytyk, 148
Psychoanalysis, 30, 34, 73
purges, 48, 50, 54, 80, 120, 151–152; Great Purge/Terror, 98, 113–116, 153, 190
PWOK, *see* Aid to Concentration Camp Prisoners
Pyrenees, 117, 162

rabbis, 7, 62–63, 65, 81–82, 87, 136
Rabold, Emil, 47, 51
racism, 16, 55, 125, 129, 131, 134, 146, 148, 192
Radio Madrid, *see under* Madrid
Radio Moscow, *see under* Moscow
Rákosi, Mátyás, 43
Rath, Ernst vom, 122
Ravensbrück, xii–xiii, 167, 185
Red Army, *see under* army
Red Trade-unions International (Rote Gewerkschafts-Internationale [RGI]), 49
reformism, 18, 38, 40
Reichenberg (Liberec), 41–47, 99
Reichmann-Jungmann, Eva, 75, 198n22
Reichstag (Austria), 31
Reichstag (Germany), 54, 99, 112
Reis, Sigmund, 76
religion, 7, 10, 12, 16–17, 28, 36, 70–71, 77, 88–89, 93, 140–141, 146, 152, 169, 217n6
Remmele, Hermann, 115
Renner, Karl, 37–38
revolution, 30, 139, 202n79; and Jews, 128, 131, 137; anti-, 167;

Bolshevik (Communist/October/
Russian), 18–19, 35, 42, 47, 57,
63, 153; French, 137; in Austria,
37–39; Industrial, 13; in Hungary,
43, 172; international, 19, 90, 153;
liberal-democrat, 31; proletarian,
71, 121, 152; revolutionary
optimism, 139, 149; revolutionary
socialism, 18, 40, 43, 48, 76
Revolutionary Trade-unions
Opposition (Revolutionäre
Gewerkschafts-Opposition
[RGO]), 49–50
Ribbentrop-Molotov pact, see
German-Soviet pact
Rhineland, 98
Röhling, August, 236n46
Romania, 76, 137, 176
Romans, 88–89
Rosner, Jakob (G. Hausner), 192
Rote Hilfe, see *Internationale Rote Hilfe*
Roth, Joseph, 25, 189
Rundschau, 109
Ruppersdorf (Ruprechtice), 44
Ruppin, Arthuer, 73, 140, 219n37, 239n117
Russia, 2, 23, 33, 35, 37, 46–47,
52–53, 77, 80, 91, 100, 102, 105,
109, 113, 116, 170, 179; Tsarist
Russia, 18, 59, 62. *See also* Soviet
Union
Russian (language), 53, 64–65, 94
Russian State Archive of Socio-
Political History (RGASPI), 23

Sagi, Avi, 13
Saladin, 146
Sartre, Jean-Paul, 12
Schindel, Gerty, 25, 161, 164
Schipper, Ignacy, 74, 87
Schlenstedt, Silvia, xiv, 6, 125
Scholem, Gershom, 48, 77

Scholem, Werner, 48, 54
Schönerer, Georg von, 31–33, 67
Schorske, Carl, 30, 34, 39, 67
Schütte-Lihotzky, Margarete, 186
Schützbund (protection league), 109
Second World War, xii–xiii, 9, 11,
21, 98, 118, 123–125, 129, 154, 156,
167, 180, 193–195
Seghers, Anna, 25, 117, 120–121, 159
Selinger, Josef, 40
Serbs, 122, 176
Seyffardt, 108
Siberia, 52–54, 61, 63, 66
Silberner, Edmund, 4, 7, 82, 219n33
Silesia, 1–2, 168, 195
Silone, Ignazio (Tranquilli), 25, 99,
107, 152
Şirolnikov, Shlomo, 92–93, 193
Skaret, Ferdinand, 39
Slovakia, 40, 69, 122
Šmeral, Bohumír, 43, 46, 114
social-democracy, 7, 18, 70, 46,
116–117, 202n79, 217n8
Social-Democratic Party of
Austria (Sozialdemokratische
Arbeiterpartei Deutschösterreichs
[SDAP; sometimes mentioned in
the sources as SPÖ]), 37–40, 109,
137
Social-Democratic Party of Germany
(Sozialdemokratische Partei
Deutschlands [SPD]), 18–19, 31,
49, 239n115, 240n146
Social-Democratic Party in
Czechoslovakia, 40, 43–44, 46,
209n110
Social-Democratic Party in Russia,
33, 91
Social-Democratic Workers'
Party (Sozialdemokratische
Arbeiterpartei [SDAP]) in Austria-
Hungary, 30–32, 35–36, 39

"social fascism," 49, 51, 116, 202n79
"socialism of the fools," *see under* antisemitism
Socialist International, 18
Socialist Workers' Youth of Austria, 35
socialist-Zionism, *see under* Zionism
sociology, 75, 131–132, 139, 141
Sombart, Werner, 132–135, 137, 237n62
Sonderkommando, 170–171, 184
Soviet Bloc, 189, 194
Soviet Occupation Zone of East Germany, 194
Soviet Union, 2–3, 19, 46, 49, 53, 57, 66, 97–98, 110, 112–117, 120, 152–154, 156, 190–191; and Jews, 5, 15, 17, 56–62, 71–79, 83, 90, 93–94, 100, 105, 116, 132, 141–144, 151, 190, 192–194. *See also* antisemitism; Geserd; nationalism; Russia
Spain, 98, 150; Spanish Civil War, 98–99, 117–118, 151, 161
Spinoza, Benedict, 11
Spring of Nations, 31, 137
Stahlmann, Erna, 25, 234n153
Stahlmann, Richard, 119, 152, 234n153
Stalin, Joseph, 18–19, 21, 33, 46, 49–50, 54, 58–60, 72, 79, 92–93, 107, 112–113, 116, 143, 147, 151, 153–156, 190, 225n241, 240n134; Stalindorf, 60; Stalinism, 6, 58, 80, 89, 98, 132, 135, 143, 151–153; Stalinizaion, 48, 50, 54–55, 67, 148, 190, 211n134. *See also* German-Soviet pact
Stein, Walter, 156
Steinhaus (née Heller), Emma (sister), 28–29, 165
Steinhaus, Oscar (brother in-low), 165

Stern, Josef Luitpold, 34–38
Stern, Max, 165
Strauss Eli (Eliyahu Ashtor), 74
Stürgkh, Kral Graf, 35, 38
Sturmabteilung (Storm Detachment [SA]), 98–99
Sudeten, 40, 192
superstructure, 71, 75
Süßkind, Heinrich, 115
Sweden, 192
Switzerland, 28, 98–99, 102, 107, 109–110, 115
syndicalism, 44
Syrkin, Nachman, 32

Talmi, Meir, 5
Talmud, 611, 131, 136, 236n46
TASS (the Soviet news agency), 112
Tatars, 59–60
Teplitz-Schönau (Teplice-Šanov), 40–41
territorialism, 17, 105, 151
Thalheimer, August, 49, 54
Thälmann, Ernst, 48–51, 54
Theilhaber, Felix, 73, 219n37
Theresienstadt, 180
Third International, *see* Comintern
Third Period, 19, 49, 80, 116, 202n79
Third Reich, 9, 105, 126, 156. *See also* Nazi Germany
Tikhonkaya, 63, 66. *See also* Birobidzhan
Toulouse, 158
trading-people, 84, 86–89, 92, 133–134, 137
Travail Allemand ([TA], German Work), 164–165
Traverso, Enzo, 83, 129, 138, 141
Trotsky, Leon, 11, 19, 33, 90, 119–120; Trotskyism, 19, 89–91, 108, 113, 119–120, 135, 143, 151, 163
Turkish (language), 70

Tyrol, 34, 36

Ukraine, 58, 60–61, 64, 74, 214n192
Ulbricht, Walter, 114
Union, 172, 248n113
Unitarian Service Committee, 185
United Nations, 194
United States, 15, 135, 160, 164, 178, 193–194, 207n63
"Universum-Bucherei für Alle" (Universe-Library for all), 54
Uzbekistan, 63

Valdheym, 64
Verdun, 36, 207n63
Vichy, 158, 161, 163–164
Vienna, xii, 2, 10, 21–22, 27–39, 41, 47, 51, 54, 65–67, 74, 76, 80, 109–110, 125, 138; University of, 36, 39
Vilna, 33
VKP(b), see under Bolshevism
Vladivostok, 65, 99
Volkov, Shulamit, 140
Vorwärts, 44, 46–47

Wall Street, 54
Wandering Bird (Wandervogel), 29
Warsaw, 1, 39, 142, 173, 179
Weber, Hermann, 148
Weber, Max, 71, 132–135, 137, 143, 148, 150, 190, 192, 237n73
Wedding, 99
Weg und Ziel (Way and Goal), 118
Wegener, Georg (Arnold Metzger), 78–79, 100, 112, 115

Wehrmacht, see under army
Weinstock, Nathan, 143
Wellhausen, Julius, 87
Weltsch, Felix, 74
Wiemar Republic, see under Germany
Wistrich, Robert, 7, 67
Wittfogel, Karl, 99
Wittorf, John, 49–51
working class, 14, 20, 30–31, 41, 90, 112, 127, 190, 208n91. See also proletariat

Yiddish, 17, 36, 52, 58, 60, 63–65, 70, 76, 88, 90, 135, 148, 151, 190
Yugoslavia, 35, 40, 170

Zapotocky, Antonin, 114
Zbąszyń, 122
Zhitlovsky, Khayim, 74
Zionism, 2, 5–6, 8, 17, 30–32, 35, 48, 59, 64–65, 67, 70, 72–83, 93, 100, 104–105, 131, 134, 140–143, 148, 150, 190, 194–195; anti-, 70, 80, 189, 191; right-wing-, 70, 217n6; socialist-, 1, 5, 7–8, 36, 61, 69, 74, 79, 87–92, 140, 151, 217n6, 217n8; World Zionist Organization, 142. See also antisemitism; bourgeoisie; capitalism; naitonalism
ZK, see under Communist Party of Germany
Zola, Émile, 144
Zürich, 39, 97–102, 106–112, 115, 117–118, 152, 161, 227n23
Zweig, Stephan, 25, 29, 34

www.ingramcontent.com/pod-product-compliance
Lightning Source LLC
Chambersburg PA
CBHW051602230426
43668CB00013B/1943